NEWT GINGRICH

CONGRESSIONAL LEADERS

Burdett A. Loomis

Founding Editor

NEWT GINGRICH

THE RISE AND FALL OF A PARTY ENTREPRENEUR

Matthew N. Green and Jeffrey Crouch

University Press of Kansas

Published by the University Press of Kansas (Lawrence, Kansas 66045), which was organized by the Kansas Board of Regents and is operated and funded by Emporia State University, Fort Hays State University, Kansas State University, Pittsburg State University, the University of Kansas, and Wichita State University.

Publication made possible, in part, by funding from The Dirksen Congressional Center.

Library of Congress Cataloging-in-Publication Data
Names: Green, Matthew N., 1970– author. | Crouch, Jeffrey, author.
Title: Newt Gingrich : the rise and fall of a party entrepreneur / Matthew N. Green, and Jeffrey Crouch.
Other titles: Rise and fall of a party entrepreneur
Description: Lawrence, Kansas : University Press of Kansas, 2022. | Series: Congressional leaders | Includes bibliographical references and index.
Identifiers: LCCN 2021043874
ISBN 9780700633265 (cloth)
ISBN 9780700633272 (ebook)
Subjects: LCSH: Gingrich, Newt. | United States. Congress. House—Speakers—Biography. | United States. Congress. House—Biography. | United States—Politics and government—1981–1989. | Legislators—United States—Biography.
Classification: LCC E840.8.G5 G74 2022 | DDC 328.73/092 [B]—dc23
LC record available at https://lccn.loc.gov/2021043874.

British Library Cataloguing-in-Publication Data is available.

Printed in the United States of America
10 9 8 7 6 5 4 3 2 1

The paper used in this publication is acid free and meets the minimum requirements of the American National Standard for Permanence of Paper for Printed Library Materials Z39.48–1992.

CONTENTS

BURDETT "BIRD" LOOMIS (1945–2021) CONGRESSIONAL LEADERS, FOUNDING EDITOR

Burdett "Bird" Loomis was a great colleague, scholar, mentor, teacher, community activist, and patron of the arts. He was often interviewed in national and regional newspapers, and on television and the radio for his insights into national and state politics. He will be missed by his family, colleagues, students, and everyone who knew and admired him for his work in the University of Kansas (KU) and Lawrence communities, in Kansas state government, and in the political science discipline.

A few years after completing his PhD in political science at the University of Wisconsin, Madison, Loomis was lured to the University of Kansas in 1979. His work on congresspersons focused more on individual orientations and behaviors than did earlier scholars, whose research tended to emphasize institutions and structures. Long before today's political dysfunction, Loomis began warning about the declining civility in Congress and the drive toward partisan advantage instead of good policy.

Loomis's legacy includes an extensive list of books and articles, including a coauthored book on interest group politics with Allan Cigler and Anthony J. Nownes that is still considered one of the standard texts in the field. Loomis also took on several administrative roles at KU, including chair of the Political Science Department. He spent a good deal of time in both Washington, DC, and in the state capitol in Topeka. As internship director, he placed dozens of students from KU and other Kansas universities in congressional and state legislative internships. Loomis was one of the first recipients of the Kemper Foundation Teaching Award in 1996 for his work in establishing that program. He also served in the administration of Kansas governor Kathleen Sebelius.

Loomis cofounded the Robert J. Dole Institute for Politics at the University of Kansas after befriending Dole while doing research on Congress. He served as the institute's interim director from 1997 to 2001. The institute has a rich collection and a program of guest speakers, media events, teaching, and discussion sessions, many of which featured him as a speaker or contributor.

Loomis was also highly active in the community, including by authoring regular newspaper columns as part of a group called "Insight Kansas." He was considered one of the leading experts on Kansas politics, particularly from the 1960s to today. He and his wife lived in a gorgeous three-story house in Lawrence filled with original art. They often hosted dinners for people at KU and in the community. In his book for the University Press of Kansas, *Time, Politics, and Policies,* published in 1994, Loomis used extensive interviews and participant observation to document the impact of the Kansas legislature's short, rushed sessions on the policy-making process. His final coauthored book, tracing the changes in Kansas politics from 1960 onward, is forthcoming from Kansas.

Bird Loomis had a love of life. He enjoyed his family and the arts as well as public service, teaching, research, and international travel. He is survived by his wife Michel Loomis, son Dakota, daughter-in-law Krystal, granddaughter Georgia, and their newest granddaughter, Merribelle.

Michael Smith, Emporia State University
John Kennedy, University of Kansas

PREFACE

My enemies will write histories that dismiss me and prove I was unimportant. My friends will write histories that glorify me and prove I was more important than I was. And two generations or three from now, some serious, sober historian will write a history that sort of implies I was whoever I was.

—Newt Gingrich, January 1985

When Newton "Newt" Leroy Gingrich made these remarks to a *Washington Post* reporter, he was a minority party backbencher in the US House of Representatives, effective at grabbing attention but excluded from the political power structure of Congress and unpopular with Democratic and Republican legislators alike. Few could have imagined that, a decade later, he would be sworn in as the first Republican Speaker of the House since the mid-1950s. Nor did anyone—except perhaps Gingrich himself—believe that the Georgia congressman would go down in history as one of the most consequential and controversial figures in American politics.

Whether the result of impressive foresight or an outsized ego, Gingrich's prediction about how his time in Congress would be evaluated has so far been accurate. Most biographies of Gingrich are as polarizing as the man himself: either sharply critical of his congressional career or adamant that he dramatically changed the nation for the better. In this book, we take a different approach. Though we are political scientists, not historians,[1] and we write less than two generations after Gingrich spoke the aforementioned words, our goal is to provide a "serious, sober" review and analysis of his time in Congress and his contributions to US politics. By cutting through the partisan rhetoric that surrounds his time in the House, and by drawing upon both older journalistic accounts and new archival and interview data, we endeavor to shed fresh light onto what Gingrich did, why he did it, and how he may have changed Congress, if not the country, in the process.

The story of Gingrich's twenty years as a US Representative can be told in a variety of ways: from the perspective of bold institutional change in the House, which he helped bring about; as a cautionary tale on how to amass but then lose power in a legislature; or as an example of how individual lawmakers may shape, and be shaped by, political polarization. We examine Gingrich from a fresh perspective. Gingrich, we argue, was a case study of party entrepreneurship in Congress, exemplifying how certain lawmakers devote scarce time and resources toward a particular political or policy outcome that benefits their congressional party. Viewing Gingrich as a party entrepreneur underscores his unremitting drive to bring the House Republican Party to power and revolutionize American society, a level of devotion that differentiated him from most of his colleagues. Our approach also allows us to draw parallels between Gingrich and other congressional entrepreneurs in history. In the end, this perspective helps us to better understand the reasons for Gingrich's successes and failures in Congress, both as a minority party rabble-rouser and as Speaker of the House, and reveals the ways that party entrepreneurs like Gingrich have profoundly influenced legislative politics.

Though our names grace the cover of this book, many people helped bring it to fruition. To begin, we would like to acknowledge the late Burdett Loomis, who urged us to pursue this project as a contribution to his Congressional Leaders book series with the University Press of Kansas. Professor Loomis, widely known as "Bird," passed away before this book could be published. Bird was an outstanding scholar, a well-respected teacher, and a popular mentor, and we are eternally grateful for the encouragement and constructive feedback he gave us as we were writing the book. We will miss him.

We are thankful for the assistance provided by our home institutions, The Catholic University of America and American University. Our research was supported by grant funding from the Carl Albert Congressional Research and Studies Center, the Dirksen Congressional Center, the Association of Centers for the Study of Congress, and the Department of Politics at Catholic University. In 2017, American University awarded a Faculty Research Support Grant to Jeff Crouch in part to pursue this project.

Several archivists provided invaluable assistance in navigating their collections, including Janet Dotterer from the McNairy Library at Millersville University, Jeffrey Flannery from the Manuscript Division of the Library of Congress, Nathan Gerth and Rachel Henson of the Carl Albert Center, Frank Mackaman of the Dirksen Center, Leigh Rupinski from the Special Collections & University Archives at Grand Valley State University, and Blynne Olivieri from the Special Collections Division of the Ingram Library at the University of West Georgia. We thank Speaker Newt Gingrich for granting permission to access his archives at the University of West Georgia and acknowledge the late Mel Steely for opening his own archives to us. We also thank archivists at the University of West Georgia, the Joint Archives of Holland at Hope College, the University of Wyoming, the Ronald Reagan Presidential Library, C-SPAN, the George H. W. Bush Presidential Library and Museum, the William J. Clinton Presidential Library, and the Clerk of the House of Representatives for their assistance with securing photos for the book. Two premiere experts in congressional history, House Historian Matthew Wasniewski and Associate House Historian Kenneth Kato, helped us to locate additional archival material and gave us much sage advice.

For their own constructive comments and suggestions, we thank Ralph Albano, Steve Anthony, Jamie Carson, Michael Crespin, James Curry, David Karol, James Grossman, Greg Koger, Kevin Kosar, John Lawrence, Frances Lee, David Mayhew, Bruce Oppenheimer, Dan Palazzolo, Ron Peters, Billy Pitts, Colleen Shogan, Daniel Stid, Michele Swers, Greg Wawro, John White, and Laurel Harbridge-Yong. We appreciate the helpful feedback offered by participants in the June 2017 Congress and History Conference and the September 2017 American Political Science Association Annual Conference, where we presented portions of the manuscript. Audrey Adams-Mejia, Carly Jones, and Aaron Stuvland served as invaluable research assistants. Special thanks go to the former lawmakers and congressional staffers who were willing to be interviewed for the book. We have also benefitted from the wisdom of Charles Myers and David Congdon, the Press editors who helped guide the book to publication (and, in David's case, awaited its completion with extraordinary patience). Jeff Crouch has valued the support of his colleagues in the Center for Congressional and Presidential

Studies (CCPS), especially CCPS Director David Barker and Founding Director Jim Thurber, and he has appreciated the assistance of his program's deans, Carola Weil and Jill Klein.

Finally, we thank our families for their love and support. Matthew is deeply grateful to his wife, Holly, and his children, Olivia and Joshua, for the joy they give him every day. Special thanks go to Olivia for her artistic contribution to the manuscript. Jeff thanks his parents, Paul and Christine Crouch; his wife, Mistique; and their son, Asher, who was born just weeks after we started working on this book.

NEWT GINGRICH

CHAPTER 1

NEWT GINGRICH, PARTY ENTREPRENEUR

Tip O'Neill, the Speaker of the US House of Representatives, was livid. One week earlier, a junior legislator from Georgia named Newt Gingrich had risen on the floor of the House and accused numerous Democrats of being Communist sympathizers. The chamber was virtually empty at the time, but Gingrich implied that the "pro-Communism" Democrats were sitting quietly in the audience, unwilling to rebut his charges. O'Neill called it unfair and deceptive; Gingrich demanded an opportunity to respond. Now, back on the House floor, O'Neill, Gingrich, and other Democrats were exchanging more heated words. Finally, the Speaker had heard enough. His voice rising in anger, he pointed a finger at Gingrich. "My personal opinion," he said, "is this: You deliberately stood in that well before an empty House and challenged these people, and you challenged their Americanism, and it is the lowest thing that I have ever seen in my thirty-two years in Congress."

O'Neill's words, delivered in fury on that May 1984 day, captured how most Democrats felt about Gingrich. But his remarks also violated the rules of the chamber, which prohibit any lawmaker—including the Speaker—from impugning the character or behavior of another representative. As a result, O'Neill was reprimanded by the presiding officer and his words were taken down, an extremely rare punishment for a Speaker of the House.[1]

Although the skirmish had been brief, it generated a slew of news stories, catapulted Gingrich into the national limelight, and epitomized what made him one of the most important political figures of the twentieth century. First elected to the House in 1978, the Georgia congressman quickly stood out as a tireless critic of the chamber's governing Democratic Party, and he led a cadre of younger Republican lawmakers to employ new tactics and attention-getting feats—including partisan floor battles like the one between him and O'Neill—designed to end the GOP's long-running minority status. He is often credited with bringing his party to power in 1994, ending its forty years in the political desert, and he would become one of the most high-profile and assertive Speakers of the House in modern history.

While there may be broad consensus that Gingrich was a particularly prominent politician, how to properly describe and explain his motives, behavior, and influence is another matter. Scholars and observers have varyingly depicted him as an independent-minded actor who single-handedly altered his party and the House, a leader who tried but failed to be transformative, or an agent who acted in accordance with the wishes of fellow partisans. "It's not easy to explain Newt Gingrich," wrote Frank Gregorsky, one of his erstwhile aides. He was "such a complicated individual," recalled a former GOP leader in an interview with the authors, and speakership scholar Ronald Peters described him as "a man of many parts."[2] Further muddling the effort to explain Gingrich and generalize about his two decades in Congress is that he served in both the minority and the majority, moving from powerless backbencher to Speaker of the House, and that some of his most important contributions occurred when he was outside the formal leadership structure of his party.

In this book, we argue that Gingrich exemplified a particular type of elected representative we call a *party entrepreneur*. Unlike the typical member of Congress who fixates primarily on cultivating support within his own district or state to get reelected, party entrepreneurs dedicate their scarce resources to strategically create or exploit opportunities that will assist their political party. By introducing this new conceptual model and applying it to Gingrich, we underscore what made him unusual while also suggesting similarities between him and other legislators who prioritized the political success of their party. Thinking of Gingrich as a party entrepreneur helps explain much of his behavior and political style, including his iconoclasm, attention to strategy, and willingness to take risks and try fresh tactics, like coordinating floor appearances by his GOP allies and delivering provocative statements in the public sphere, to realize his objectives. Together with insights gleaned from military strategy, the model of party entrepreneurship also helps illuminate some reasons for his successes, particularly during his time in the minority party, when he had less power but greater freedom of action. It also explains Gingrich's failures—including his forced resignation from the House after four tumultuous years as Speaker—which coincided with entrepreneurial goals that were either too ambitious for the resources he had at his disposal or crowded out by the responsibilities of governing.

Besides using a novel paradigm to examine his congressional career, our study differs in several ways from past profiles of Gingrich. Most biographers have concentrated on his time as Speaker; by contrast, we survey his sixteen years in Congress before he became Speaker, when he undertook some of his most noteworthy and consequential acts, as well as his speakership. We also draw upon new interviews and archival data to document Gingrich's major contributions, including those that have received little attention. In addition, we show that while Gingrich did less to shape the country's political landscape than some have asserted, his entrepreneurship had two profound consequences. First, it helped him realize his own ambitions for power and become a Speaker with tremendous, if short-lived, political influence. Second, it pushed the House of Representatives to become what it is today: a centralized chamber in which political parties act as loyalty-based teams that devote substantial time and energy to electioneering and partisan messaging.

Prior Studies of Gingrich

Newt Gingrich has been the subject of more books, articles, and essays than just about any other modern Speaker or member of Congress. Despite his colorful and provocative personality, most academic studies of the man minimize his individual contributions and distinctiveness, explaining his leadership as the result of broad causal variables. Political scientist Richard Fenno argued that Gingrich's speakership was molded by the GOP's forty frustrating years in the minority, and if he had not come along, "it would have been another confrontational partisan very much like him" leading the Republican Conference.[3] Another political scientist, Barbara Sinclair, theorized that because leaders in Congress are focused first and foremost on meeting the expectations of fellow partisans, Gingrich was merely one of many Speakers whose leadership style reflected the goals of his party, whether that required being assertive, as in his first term as Speaker, or more compromising, as in his second.[4] Her approach reflects a widely held view among scholars that factors within Congress, most notably a party's ideological homogeneity, direct the behavior of leaders.[5]

There is a second school of thought, promoted by some social scientists as well as most journalists and nonacademics, that emphasizes Gingrich's independence and exceptionality. Political scientists Ronald Peters and Craig Williams, for instance, write that Gingrich was a transformational leader, but a unique one insofar as his efforts as Speaker to reshape the House, and American politics more broadly, largely failed.[6] Analyzing his worldview, another political scientist, John Pitney, describes Gingrich as ideologically idiosyncratic and unusually intellectual for a member of Congress. "Far more than most political leaders," he writes, "Gingrich roots his actions in books and ideas," and he should not be pigeonholed as a conservative, "at least as people ordinarily define the term."[7] Some have highlighted how, unlike other modern Speakers, Gingrich attempted to turn the federal government into a parliamentary system, centralizing power within the speakership and positioning the chamber to be the center of national policy-making.[8] Several journalists and scholars stress his novel use of procedure and media campaigns to heighten differences between the parties, or his pleas that rank and file Republicans should act more aggressively against Democrats.[9] For others, it was elements of Gingrich's personal style that set him apart, such as his endless embrace of new ideas, his energy and perseverance, his frequent use of hyperbolic and oversimplified rhetoric, or his impulsiveness, inconsistency, and lack of follow-through.[10]

Finally, there have been a few attempts to bridge the perspective of Gingrich as a typical party agent and the argument that he was independent and unique. Political scientist Randall Strahan argued that Gingrich was a transformational Speaker, unusual but not alone in that respect; two other Speakers, Henry Clay and Thomas Brackett Reed, also took bold steps to alter the House and their own political party. Dissenting from Sinclair's depiction of Gingrich as following the will of the GOP Conference, Strahan asserted that he was a "conditional agent" who independently brought about considerable political and policy change because he possessed both strongly held objectives and followers who wanted to end the status quo but disagreed over what change would be best.[11] In an earlier work, one of us noted how Gingrich, like other Speakers of the House, was occasionally motivated to exercise legislative leadership on behalf of issues that mattered to him personally, not necessarily to his party.[12] There are also a handful of scholars who have acknowledged that, even if a party's homogeneity and collective preferences matter a great deal in explaining what leaders in Congress do, one should allow for leader autonomy, provided certain conditions are met and leaders are already inclined to act more independently.[13]

The danger of the first perspective is that it overgeneralizes Gingrich, reducing him to a typical congressional leader when he clearly was not. The second conceptualization avoids that trap, but at the same time fails to acknowledge that he was hardly the only lawmaker of his kind to spend ceaseless hours trying to help his party fulfill its collective goals. Instead, like Strahan, we take the middle ground, honing in on what made Gingrich out of the ordinary, but not quite one of a kind. Unlike Strahan, however, we review Gingrich's entire congressional career, not just his speakership, and we focus more broadly on his entrepreneurial politics, something he shared with other distinctive and consequential party leaders and members of Congress.

Party Entrepreneurship in Congress

Elected representatives can bring about change in many ways. Some do so as *entrepreneurs,* driven individuals who identify opportunities to provide a collective good and who expend resources to make it happen, often at some risk, "stamp[ing] change with their own personal visions" in the process.[14] Two recognized types of entrepreneurs in Congress are *procedural* entrepreneurs, who bring about institutional reforms and rule changes, and *legislative* entrepreneurs, who contribute to policy output by introducing bills, building supportive coalitions around them, and guiding them to enactment.[15]

Procedural and legislative entrepreneurs appear regularly in the US House and Senate and help explain much of what Congress does. But a common prerequisite for their success is the ability to transcend party lines and work in a bipartisan fashion. For example, bills are far more likely to become law when supported by cross-party coalitions.[16] Yet political parties have long been the principal organizing structures within Congress, and in recent decades the House and Senate have become more politically polarized, making party organizations increasingly important. There is thus the potential for a third type of entrepreneur: *party* entrepreneurs, or members of Congress (either formal party leaders or members of the rank and file) who work to achieve their party's collective goals. Party entrepreneurs may, for example, recruit new candidates to challenge incumbents of the other party, raise sums for vulnerable same-party incumbents, or employ communication tactics to improve their party's brand and dent the image of the other party.

If one assumes that some members of Congress act as party entrepreneurs, what motivates them to do so? After all, it seems unlikely that aiding one's congressional party will do much to help an individual lawmaker achieve her preeminent objective of getting reelected, except perhaps indirectly by improving the party's reputation.[17] Indeed, one of the major risks of party entrepreneurship is that it directs time and resources away from passing bills or conducting readily observed, district-centered activities that will please constituents. But more than reelection drives legislator behavior. Richard Fenno identified three goals—reelection, policy enactment, and internal influence—that motivate lawmakers.[18] Whereas party entrepreneurship does not lend itself to the pursuit of making policy, it does correspond well with an aspiration for more internal influence, since an ambitious lawmaker ultimately needs the support of fellow partisans to be selected (or reselected) as leader, and a surefire way of gaining that support is to provide party-wide collective benefits.[19] We therefore expect to see evidence of ambition for greater internal power among party entrepreneurs, though they may also value that entrepreneurship in and of itself.

Party entrepreneurs, like entrepreneurs in general, are usually strategic, acting in ways that are reasonably expected to attain their objectives. What are the strategies that party entrepreneurs follow, and what makes those strategies more or less likely to succeed? While the answers to these questions will vary by entrepreneur, by objective, and by circumstances, we can glean some general insights from theories of strategic action. Strategic decision-making by legislators is often excluded from theories of Congress, with the notable exception of game-theoretic models that offer predictions about the behavior of individuals seeking to maximize their own benefits in uncertain environments.[20] But one field that does consider strategy in great depth, and that can shed light on the nature and consequences of strategic behavior by congressional entrepreneurs, is military theory. Political conflict and military combat are not the same, but as Clausewitz famously observed, they are related,[21] and the combative nature of congressional party politics has encouraged some scholars to draw upon military analogies and theories to explain it.[22] Party entrepreneurs in particular share some similarities with military leaders: they are purposive, risk-taking actors, they possess an array of broader objectives that often include helping one's own party (or "army"), and they engage with an opposing group in conflicts that are frequently zero-sum.

One military-related paradigm that can be used to not just conceptualize the behavior of entrepreneurs in Congress but also analyze their effectiveness is Arthur Lykke Jr.'s "three-legged stool" model of military strategy.[23] Drawing from General Maxwell Taylor's description of strategy as a combination of ends, ways, and means, Lykke posited that military strategy comprises three distinct elements: immediate *objectives*, strategic *concepts* (i.e., the tactics used to achieve those objectives), and the *resources* employed to carry them out. Those objectives, concepts, and resources constitute the three legs of a proverbial stool, and just as a three-legged stool must have all three legs of equal size and strength to avoid tipping over, so too must a sound military strategy with minimal risk of failure include objectives, concepts, and resources that are viable and proportionate to one another (figure I.1).[24] When applied to the congressional setting, this model suggests that, like military strategy, the political strategy of party entrepreneurs can be separated into objectives, methods, and resources, and that a party entrepreneur's likelihood of success is contingent upon all three being reasonable and evenly matched. Lykke's model is not predictive—a strategist can succeed or fail for a host of reasons outside of her control—but it does suggest that when a party entrepreneur in Congress is able to increase the congruence of all three "legs," such as by increasing available resources or tempering her objectives, she is more likely to advance her strategic goals. We explore this idea, along with the claim that the pursuit of power motivates party entrepreneurialism in Congress, by reviewing the

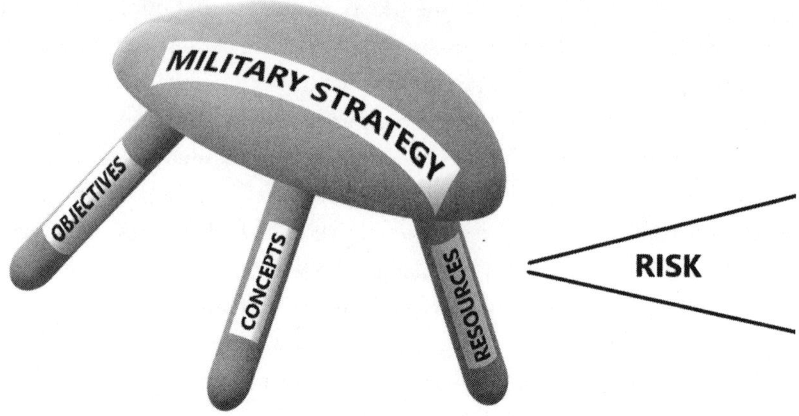

Figure 1.1. Arthur Lykke's Three-Legged Stool Model of Military Strategy. *Source*: Illustration by Olivia Green.

congressional career of Newt Gingrich, whom we posit fits the profile of a party entrepreneur.

Gingrich as a Party Entrepreneur

If Gingrich was an entrepreneur in Congress, he was certainly not a legislative one. Though he did have several policy interests,[25] legislating was never his strong suit. During his first six years in the House, he consistently introduced fewer bills than an average Republican member (see figure 1.2), and when he served as Speaker he generally delegated the task of legislative leadership to others.[26] Another indication that Gingrich was not a legislative entrepreneur is his Legislative Effectiveness Score, a metric developed by Craig Volden and Alan Wiseman that captures how effectively a lawmaker steers bills through the legislative process. Until his last two years in Congress, Gingrich's score was routinely one of the lowest ranked among his GOP peers (see figure 1.3).[27]

Nor was Gingrich principally a procedural entrepreneur. True, he contributed to some important institutional developments in the House, like the formation of the Conservative Opportunity Society caucus in the mid-1980s and the increased centralization of majority party power when he became Speaker.[28] But most of Gingrich's procedural moves were means to greater ends, like helping his political party win and maintain control of the chamber and garnering more power for himself.

When considering Gingrich's most noteworthy endeavors in Congress, it is clear that he was a quintessential party entrepreneur.[29] These endeavors, which we outline in detail throughout the book, included such media and messaging tactics as using floor debate to coordinate verbal attacks on the majority party; operating a one-man press campaign to force the resignation of Speaker Jim Wright (D-TX), which undermined the morale of Democrats and demonstrated that aggressive partisanship could yield political victories for the GOP; and employing creative messaging tactics to improve his party's brand. Other entrepreneurial endeavors included sending inspirational audiotapes to potential congressional candidates, both to convince them to run for office and to persuade them to adopt Gingrich's beliefs of what constituted proper partisan behavior; linking minority party obstruction with electoral success for the party; and pushing an assertive agenda as Speaker to harm the reelection chances of President Bill Clinton and weaken the Democratic Party's electoral base. Entrepreneurs are also usually risk takers, and we show in subsequent chapters that Gingrich risked damaging his reputation, his standing among other Republicans and GOP leaders, and even his own reelection in the name of achieving his entrepreneurial goals.

Applying Lykke's military model to what party entrepreneurs do makes particular sense in Gingrich's case because he was deeply influenced by military history, theory, and strategy. He often drew inspiration and ideas from military theorists like Clausewitz and Sun Tzu. Paraphrasing Mao Tse-Tung, Gingrich told an audience at the Library of Congress that "politics is war without blood."[30] "War is a recurrent theme for this guerrilla captain of the political Right," observed one reporter in 1984, and his one-time confidant Rep. Vin Weber (R-MN) said, "I think that the military analogies are pretty helpful in understanding Newt Gingrich." More generally, he extolled an approach to politics that mirrored strategic thinking. "His greatest asset," a former GOP lawmaker told us, was "his ability to look ahead and then piece together the things needed to move forward."[31] "His thought process is a strategic thought process," noted a Hill staffer who was in Congress with Gingrich, and who explained to us that Gingrich had

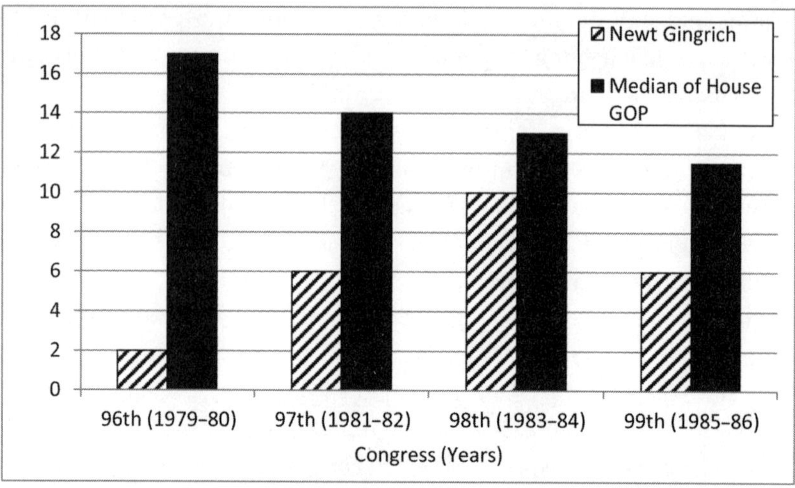

Figure 1.2. Number of Bills Introduced by Gingrich vs. Median Number of Bills Introduced by House Republicans, 1979–1986. *Source*: E. Scott Adler and John Wilkerson, *Congressional Bills Project: 1979–1986* (NSF 00880066 and 00880061).

been influential because "he was very good at taking ideas, tactics, and strategy and winding them into something that made sense."[32] Gingrich often touted "vision, strategy, projects, and tactics," a hierarchical model for achieving one's aims,[33] and he once compared congressional Republicans to "short-order cooks hired to run a gourmet French restaurant," ill-equipped with the skills and long-range thinking required to attain the bigger goal of a GOP-led Congress.[34] Gingrich's emphasis on strategy and willingness to innovate would be critical to his success as a party entrepreneur, especially while serving in the House minority party; as the military scholar Lawrence Freedman wrote, "underdog strategies provide the real tests of creativity."[35]

This is not to say that Gingrich's strategic skills were flawless. In a private memo written in the early 1980s, his aide Frank Gregorsky discussed Gingrich's lack of focus and overly ambitious agenda, and he warned that "the objectives to [achieve] his grander goals change so fast that they amount to sprays of buckshot aimed at the side of a hill."[36] He was prone to writing lengthy treatises for his colleagues calling for revolutionary societal change, particularly during his early years as a congressman, and they were sometimes illustrated with complex geometric diagrams that could

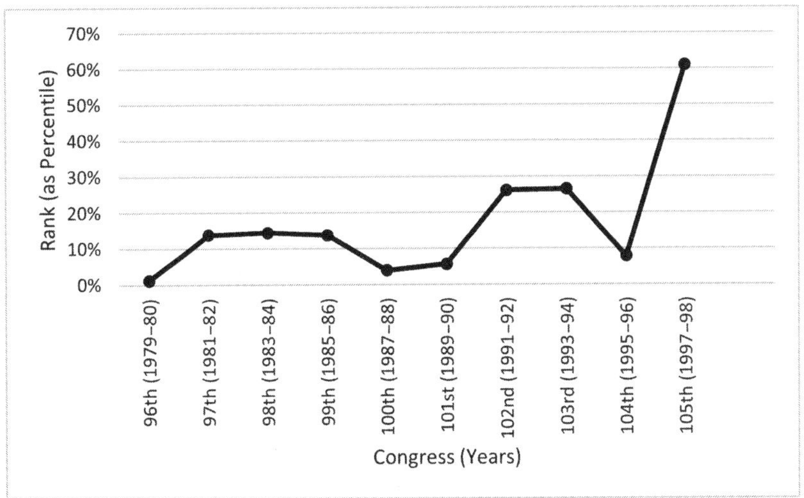

Figure 1.3. Gingrich's Legislative Effectiveness Score, Ranked as a Percentile (among other House Republicans). *Source*: Craig Volden and Alan E. Wiseman, *Legislative Effectiveness in the United States Congress: The Lawmakers* (New York: Cambridge University Press, 2014); the Center for Effective Lawmaking (https://thelawmakers.org/data-download).

be difficult to decipher.[37] One former GOP aide explained that "Newt has a hundred ideas a day, maybe a hundred ideas an hour," and most of them went nowhere. Dennis Hastert (R-IL) recalled that Gingrich was "a great political strategist" but was hard to follow because he "had a good idea every five or six minutes," while a staffer for Minority Leader Robert Michel (R-IL) recalled that in a typical leadership meeting, Gingrich would "pop off with just one idea after another—'we oughta do this, we oughta do that' . . . and he'd be back a week later and have five more ideas, so you kind of had to guestimate how important they were."[38] A common joke was that "Newt's ideas" filled multiple file cabinets, yet just one drawer was enough to hold "Newt's good ideas."[39] His incessant brainstorming, coupled with questionable managerial skills and, after 1994, the challenge of leading a governing party, would eventually create serious problems for him.[40] Nonetheless, he did have goals, albeit grand ones. Gregorksy noted in the same memo describing Gingrich's imperfections that "puny goals are unattractive to Newt," and he could be "aggressive, purposeful, and somewhat Utopian." Gingrich was also unusual in the degree to which he incorporated strategy into his congressional decision-making, and he told his staff, "I dissect myself a great deal analytically at a functional level; does it work? does it not work? what mistakes did I make?"[41]

Gingrich had two party-oriented aims in particular, and he was incentivized to advance them at least partially by his desire for greater influence. His first party-wide goal, and perhaps the most important one while he served in the minority, was to *reverse the GOP's fortunes and make it the governing party of the House of Representatives.*[42] He expressed this objective from the very beginning of his political career. During his successful 1978 campaign for the House, he told the Georgia state chapter of the College Republicans that "the primary purpose of a political leader, above anything else," is "to build a majority capable of sustaining itself." Gregorsky, who first began working for Gingrich in that campaign, recalled that he "started training me as he trains everybody from day one, to think in terms not of ideology . . . but what Republicans needed to do . . . to become a majority."[43] After getting elected to the House, Gingrich immediately sought out Guy Vander Jagt (R-MI), the chairman of the National Republican Congressional Committee (NRCC), even before the new Congress had officially convened. Vander Jagt was impressed with the brash young Georgian's energy and saw him as "the only other member other than myself" who believed the party could rise to power. The following year, Gingrich expressed to one reporter his lack of interest in forming coalitions with majority party Democrats to pass legislation. "I'm willing to be ineffective in the short run," he explained, "if it means that in the long run, we're able to build a majority."[44] To another journalist, he said, "I'm not interested in having an ideological movement. I'm interested in governing the country." During a speech in June 1980 he avowed that "the only real issue for Republicans in the U.S. Congress is, 'How do we win control?,'" and he even proposed letting Democrats win the White House if it meant the GOP could triumph in future congressional elections. In a guide he crafted titled "Cooking Up a Republican Majority for the 1980's," he declared that "the first objective of any political party has to be the creation of an *organized majority* capable of carrying out its principles in the future."[45] Indeed, it is impossible to understand Gingrich without recognizing that he spent most of his time in Congress as a member of a political party that regularly fell short of its increasingly desperate goal to win control of the House of Representatives—and that Gingrich made that goal a top priority.

What became of this objective when Republicans finally did win control of the House in 1994? As might be expected, it shifted to another, but related, goal: sustaining the party's majority. "We badly need to stay in the majority for eight to ten years," he told interviewer Charlie Rose in mid-1995, a goal he believed could be accomplished by showing voters that the GOP would balance the federal budget via lower taxes and a shrunken national government.[46] Gingrich took many steps during his speakership to protect that majority, ranging from making strategic appointments to committees and campaigning on behalf of Republican candidates to reaching a deal with President Clinton on welfare reform.

Gingrich's second collective party goal was to *bring transformational change to society at large*. Though this change included concrete public policy proposals, like decentralizing the country's welfare system, Gingrich saw it as something much bigger: a revolutionary shift in the worldview of American citizens. The desire to "move the country toward a more conservative vision" was, according to his biographer and former aide Mel Steely, one of the main reasons that Gingrich ran for Congress in the first place. Yet Gingrich's vision transcended conservatism, incorporating traditionally liberal ideas as well as the writings of futurologists like Alvin Toffler. GOP activist Paul Weyrich called Gingrich an "experiential" conservative whose views could transcend traditional left-right divisions, and Vin Weber said that he "is more Nixonian than he is Reaganite. Not in the Watergate sense, [but] in the strategic sense. He is not an ideologue." Regardless of how unorthodox his vision might have been, John Pitney wrote at the time of his speakership, Gingrich "wants to influence the entire country."[47] "Anyone who reads Toffler's *Third Wave* will have some notion of the scale of change Newt is talking about," explained one aide in an internal office document written in 1983 to guide Gingrich's staff. "It's the equivalent of the shift from agriculture to industry."[48] While his dream for the future was unconventional and audacious, Gingrich believed that, by replacing the dominant "liberal Democrat world view" with a new one, his party would have built a durable electoral foundation that would allow it to succeed at the ballot box for years to come.[49]

Party entrepreneurs are driven by a desire to increase their personal power and influence, but was this the case for Gingrich? Not all observers believed he was consistently ambitious. One pair of biographers argued that until the late 1980s, "Gingrich had never before shown any interest in being a part of the leadership that he despised," and Gingrich insisted in interviews that his initial goal had never been to become Speaker, only to bring the House GOP into the majority.[50] However, there is compelling evidence that, his denials notwithstanding, Gingrich had wanted more influence from the very beginning. When he set his sights on a congressional seat, he told confidants that he hoped to eventually become Speaker of the House, and people outside of Congress attested to Gingrich's long-standing desire for more political influence.[51] "His level of ambition was clearly known," a former aide to Michel recalled.[52] It thus seems reasonable to suppose that, whether his ambition changed in intensity over time or was initially kept quiet for political purposes,[53] Gingrich acted as a party entrepreneur to some degree, if not completely, in order to *gain power*. A Republican majority would make this possible if Gingrich wanted to become Speaker, though he also tried to expand his formal authority while serving in the minority party. Greater personal power would also make it easier for him to achieve the societal revolution he sought. Gingrich achieved more formal influence when he was elected Speaker in 1995, but his ambition for power remained: he took steps to centralize formal authority in the speakership and even toyed with the idea of running for president against Bill Clinton.[54]

Applying Lykke's three-legged model of strategy, we identify several shorter-term, interrelated strategic objectives that Gingrich pursued in order to reach his party goals of a GOP House and societal change and his individual goal of political power (summarized in table 1.1). For Republicans to retake and retain the House, Gingrich believed that congressional elections needed to become *nationalized*, curtailing the capacity of Democratic incumbents to win conservative districts through constituency service and attention to local issues. He also felt it was imperative to *draw sharp normative policy distinctions* between the parties, denigrating liberal legislative proposals while forcing his own party to be more consistently conservative in word and deed. This would improve the Republican brand, undercut Democrats' reputation with voters, further nationalize elections, and allow his ideas for social change to gain greater traction. He was hardly

Table 1.1. Newt Gingrich's Entrepreneurial Goals and Strategy

Long-Term Goals	* A House Republican majority (party-wide goal) * Conservative social transformation (party-wide goal) * Position of political power (individual goal)
Strategic Objectives	Nationalize elections Draw sharper, more normative policy distinctions between parties Tarnish reputation of (Democratic-led) House Improve electoral competitiveness of GOP Develop, advertise, and (after 1994) enact conservative legislation Heighten personal profile and power
Tactics (Concepts)	Electioneering (recruit strong candidates, provide electoral resources, shape party platform) Messaging (partisan and ideological position-taking) Subverting (criticize, weaken, or eliminate rivals) Legislating (enact or defeat bills or amendments) Power-seeking (run for leadership positions, expand informal influence within the party)
Resources	(News) media/C-SPAN Avenues of communication with (potential) candidates Allies within and outside House Funding and other electoral resources Formal party resources Personal skills (rhetoric, idea generation, energy, and drive)

the first to demand that US elections be nationalized and centered on policy differences. For decades, politicians and political scientists who had advocated for more responsible American party government had also extolled these objectives. Gingrich, however, pursued them not to improve national governance but to accrue more power for his party and for himself.[55] Two other strategic objectives of Gingrich were *tarnishing the reputation of Congress* and thereby that of majority Democrats, at least until the GOP took control of the House,[56] and *improving Republican candidates' electoral competitiveness,* which would not only help the GOP win the House but also bring grateful new Republican legislators to Congress who might serve as a power base for Gingrich. To a lesser degree, he saw the *development and, after 1994, enactment of conservative legislation* as a vital tool for nationalizing elections, distinguishing the two parties, and ultimately transforming

American society along conservative lines. Finally, he sought to *garner more formal influence and heighten his public profile.*

These objectives are not based on conjecture. As we elucidate in later chapters, they were hardly secret, and Gingrich was not shy about sharing them with others. For instance, during a gathering in mid-1979 of select junior congressmen convened by political scientists Thomas Mann and Norman Ornstein, Gingrich argued that to win power, Republicans had to nationalize elections to Congress, stop cooperating with Democrats, and make the national legislature distasteful to voters. In a memo to his GOP colleagues written three years later, he explained that "Governing is the combination of politics and government to ensure that the American people understand it is in their common interest to rally to you and against your opponents."[57]

Gingrich employed multiple, often overlapping tactics ("strategic concepts," in Lykke's nomenclature) to complete these objectives.[58] The first set of tactics, electioneering, focused on winning elections: inspiring quality candidates to run for office in open seat races or against incumbent Democrats; providing those candidates with money, training, and other resources; and shaping the party's election year platform. The second set of tactics, messaging, was geared toward communicating ideas, policy positions, and political themes to the public. For Gingrich, they included making procedural motions and delivering speeches that conveyed electorally salient ideas and scored partisan points against Democrats, conducting provocative interviews with reporters, and introducing "message" bills and amendments that would distinguish Republicans from Democrats. Gingrich was a strong proponent of "crafted talk," branding bills, ideas, individuals, and parties positively or negatively for political gain. He was particularly adroit at aggressive rhetoric that made for good headlines, and early on he bemoaned that within his party "we don't encourage you to be nasty."[59] The third set of tactics, subverting, were Gingrich's (often underhanded) attempts to disempower members of either party who served as roadblocks to his strategic objectives. Pursuing ethical and legal investigations, feeding stories of alleged wrongdoing by other lawmakers to reporters, offering resolutions to expel incumbents on grounds of corruption, and sowing doubts about his party's leaders among the GOP rank and file are examples of Gingrich's subversion.[60] His use of electioneering, partisan messaging, and subversion, often in combination, is why Gingrich was considered an advocate of confrontational political strategies versus cooperative ones.[61]

Gingrich used two other kinds of tactics on behalf of his immediate objectives. Although he was not very active legislatively, he would sometimes employ strategic legislating: in the minority, to differentiate the parties (principally by obstructing Democratic legislation and encouraging voting unity among Republicans), and as Speaker, to both keep the GOP in the majority (by burnishing the GOP's productivity brand and passing widely popular legislation) and help revolutionize American society.[62] Finally, Gingrich pursued power-seeking maneuvers, like running for leadership positions, to gain greater personal influence and make it easier to implement other tactics.

Entrepreneurs need sufficient resources to execute their tactics, and Gingrich cultivated and capitalized on a variety of them. One key resource was the media, including newspapers and television news; cable-televised floor proceedings, inaugurated the year Gingrich was first elected to the House; and conservative talk radio. He also pioneered novel avenues of communication, including newsletters, campaign-related audiotapes, and televised lectures. Following a lesson he had learned from his study of history that "a cohesive group" and a "critical mass" are key to bringing about change, he developed another resource—allies in the House, in conservative think tanks, and in institutions outside of Congress—to construct a loosely organized constellation of supporters.[63] Gradually, Gingrich was able to draw upon additional, election-related assets (money in particular) to give to House candidates, which further expanded as Gingrich's power within the GOP Conference grew.

A final resource was Gingrich himself. He had an unusual aptitude for generating new, sweeping, futuristic ideas and a dogged determination to carry out his objectives despite resistance from his own party and a string of disappointing elections. He also had considerable oratorical acumen—as one journalist put it in 1989, he "is a forceful debater; his sentences pour out rounded, parsed, suitable for framing"—a certain charisma based on his intellectual assuredness, and a knack for charming reporters.[64] His goals could be grandiose, but as one former staffer remembered when Gingrich declared he would "save Western civilization," "Newt has a way of saying things that makes you think. . . . He's really going to try to do that."[65] Gingrich was also adept at using loaded words and phrases, repetition, and other rhetorical devices to shape public impressions and needle his opponents. He once explained that his hope was to make the name of the other party equivalent to "soft on drugs, crime and communism, . . . anti-prayer, . . . and 'not like us,'" while making the GOP represent "calm, problem-solving, traditional values . . . the national party . . . not necessarily 'like us,' but definitely 'for us.'" As historian Julian Zelizer put it, he "had a keen sense of how to take elements of legislative life that most politicians saw as benign and to speak about them in ways that created a media frenzy and tainted the reputation of the person he targeted."[66] "The essence of Newt is that he's a marketing genius," Gregorsky explained.[67] If politics was war, words were Gingrich's weapons, and he was unabashedly willing to malign Democrats, Congress as a whole, and sometimes even other Republicans, earning him a reputation as a bomb-throwing "Neutron Newt."[68]

All of these resources would help Gingrich achieve his purposes as a minority party entrepreneur, but they were poorly matched with the shift in objectives and responsibilities that came with leading a governing party. Furthermore, the need to legislate and manage a lawmaking coalition did not square well with the messaging and oppositional tactics Gingrich had mastered while fighting majority party Democrats. Nor did they fit with the entrepreneurialism that Gingrich gamely tried to continue as Speaker of the House. Together with his own flaws, like the propensity to frequently change his mind and act without consulting with other leaders, these challenges would contribute to his undoing as Speaker.

Outline of the Book

In the rest of this book, we review Gingrich's congressional career as a party entrepreneur, documenting his entrepreneurial tactics, how they connected to his immediate and longer-term goals, and how successful he was at achieving those goals. We divide his service in Congress into five periods. The first three periods cover his time in the minority party. In chapter 2, we discuss Gingrich's labors as an entrepreneurial outsider (1979 through 1984), pursuing a variety of endeavors to aid his party and himself while apart from the formal power structure of the Republican Conference. Though he failed to get Republicans into power or bring about a conservative societal revolution during that period, he did accomplish some immediate objectives and laid the groundwork for completing others, most notably by establishing a small but energetic caucus of GOP rabble-rousers known as the Conservative Opportunity Society. In chapter 3, we review Gingrich's time as an ascendant party warrior (1985 through mid-1989), when he gained more influence within his party, established an important organizational base of electoral power, and was backed by a growing segment of the Conference convinced that partisan confrontation was an effective strategy. We discuss Gingrich's years as an entrepreneurial insider in chapter 4 (mid-1989 through 1994), his last years in the minority, when he spearheaded an important break with his own party's president and used his position as minority whip to expand his control over collective party decision-making and, eventually, attain two of his overarching goals: the speakership and a GOP House.

The next two chapters cover Gingrich's speakership. His first term as Speaker (1995 to 1996), discussed in chapter 5, starts with his heady early months leading a GOP House, which featured bold institutional changes to the party and the chamber and the passage of the Contract with America, and ends with Gingrich attempting to maintain the GOP's control of the House following two unpopular government shutdowns and a decline in public support for the party and himself. In chapter 6, we cover Gingrich's continuing struggles in his second and final term as Speaker (1997 to 1998), including an admitted violation of House ethics rules, a near-coup by restless junior lawmakers and other members of his own leadership team, and an unexpectedly disappointing midterm election that led him to reluctantly depart from both the speakership and Congress. In this period, his flaws as a governing party strategist versus a minority party strategist, and the weaknesses inherent in the party coalition he had helped build, eroded Gingrich's support within the Conference and hampered his ability to keep a GOP majority and enact conservative legislation.

In our final chapter, we discuss how the model of party entrepreneurship may be applied to other lawmakers. We also consider the long-term contributions Newt Gingrich made to American politics. In particular, we argue that he was crucial to several changes that took place within Congress, such as the election of confrontation-minded Republicans to the House in the 1980s and early 1990s, the popularization of public messaging and confrontation by lawmakers and party leaders as tools to defeat the opposing party, and internal rules changes that strengthened the speakership and enforced party discipline as a norm of behavior. However, those changes followed a piecemeal progression that many moderate Republicans in Congress resisted, and they depended upon not only Gingrich's ceaseless efforts, but also like-minded lawmakers lending valuable assistance, GOP revulsion at the abuses of congressional Democrats, and some lucky breaks. Moreover, we find much less evidence that Gingrich was responsible for the larger political developments that are often attributed to his leadership, like the nationalization of elections, greater voter polarization, and the growth of coarse partisan rhetoric in the public sphere. Even the GOP takeover of the House in 1994 was due in no small part to grassroots disillusionment with the Democratic Party and Bill Clinton, a partisan realignment of the South that had been decades in the making, and years of work by campaign professionals both within and outside Congress. Thus, even though Gingrich was without a doubt an influential figure, one can easily overstate his impact on American politics.

CHAPTER 2

ENTREPRENEURIAL OUTSIDER (1979–1984)

During his first three terms in Congress, Newt Gingrich tried a variety of tactics to achieve short-term objectives that he hoped would eventually yield a Republican House, a conservative shift in American society, and more power for himself. He was not very successful at first. In the 95th and 96th Congresses (1979–1982), he was hampered by unsympathetic Republicans in Congress, a lack of organizational support, a party culture that prized legislative output over confrontation, and an electorally disadvantageous environment. Only in the 98th Congress (1983–1984) did his labors begin to bear fruit, though his long-term goals remained distant. Table 2.1 provides a summary of his major activities and strategic objectives over this six-year period.

Gingrich Hits the Ground Running (1979–1980)

Even before he was elected to the US House of Representatives, Gingrich showed a predilection for the aggressive, media-oriented maneuvers that would become his trademark. In his unsuccessful 1974 and 1976 congressional campaigns, he repeatedly attacked the ethical practices of his opponent, incumbent Democrat John Flynt, suggesting that Flynt was unfit to serve in Congress. He attended a hearing of the House Ethics Committee, which Flynt chaired, where committee members deliberated whether to punish reporter Daniel Schorr for receiving classified information from

Table 2.1. Gingrich as Entrepreneurial Outsider (1979–1984)

Congress	Major Activity	Type of Tactic	Primary Strategic Objective(s)
96th (1979–1980)	Forms "Budget of Hope" group	Messaging, Legislating	Draw sharper partisan distinctions
	Keeps tax cut in GOP budget plan	Messaging, Legislating	Draw sharper partisan distinctions
	Organizes Governing Team Day	Electioneering, Legislating	Nationalize elections
	Pushes to expel Democratic MC	Subverting	Tarnish reputation of (Democratic-led) House, heighten personal profile/power
	Undercuts standing of minority leader	Subverting	Heighten personal profile/power
97th (1981–1982)	Forms "Hope and Opportunity" budget group	Messaging, Legislating	Draw sharper partisan distinctions
	Criticizes Reagan WH for poor messaging	Electioneering	Improve electoral competitiveness of GOP
	Opposes Reagan tax and budget bills	Subverting, Legislating	Draw sharper partisan distinctions
98th (1983–1984)	Forms Conservative Opportunity Society	Messaging	Draw sharper partisan distinctions, tarnish reputation of (Democratic-led) House
	Participates in campaign of assertive floor statements, procedural motions	Messaging	Draw sharper partisan distinctions, tarnish reputation of (Democratic-led) House, heighten own profile/power
	Helps revise GOP platform	Electioneering, Messaging	Draw sharper partisan distinctions

someone in Congress and refusing to disclose the name of his source. Gingrich then excoriated Flynt's committee in the press for failing to penalize Schorr and identify the leaker.[1] In a speech in June 1978 to Georgia College Republicans, he urged the audience to be more public and oppositional. "When you see somebody doing something dumb," he advised, "say it. . . . And when you say it, say it in the press, say it out loud, fight, scrap, issue a press release, go make a speech." He warned them that what the GOP needed was not "another generation of cautious, prudent, careful, bland, irrelevant, quasi-leaders" but individuals "willing to take risks, willing to stand up in a slug fest and match it out with their opponent."[2]

The 1978 elections were successful not just for Gingrich but for many Republican congressional candidates. Under the long shadow of Watergate, the GOP had suffered through two punishing election cycles, losing forty-eight seats in 1974 and one additional seat, along with the White House, in 1976. This time, however, the party gained a net fifteen House seats, and thirty-five Republicans, Gingrich among them, joined the ranks of the GOP Conference for the first time.[3] (Gingrich had been aided by Flynt's decision to retire, creating an open congressional seat.) Gingrich's extraordinary ambition to revolutionize society, his unrelenting fixation on attaining a Republican majority in the House, and his belief that publicity and partisan differentiation would make that majority happen were all evident from the start. He told his staff that his purpose was not "to win reelection," "take care of passport problems," or "get a bill through Congress. My job description as I have defined it is to save Western civilization."[4] One House Republican remembered that, while giving him a ride home one evening, Gingrich stated "how determined he was for Republicans to become the majority, . . . that we really ought to be more aggressive about becoming a majority," and that "we were too inclined to go along" with Democrats.[5] Gingrich was elected secretary of his incoming class and, after he met with NRCC chair Guy Vander Jagt and "bombarded Vander Jagt with ideas" of how Republicans could win power, he was named the head of a new group, the Project Majority Task Force, charged with making the GOP a governing party. He proclaimed that his "great fantasy in life" was to unify the Conference and "create a record that allows the 1980 election to bring on a Republican majority in the House."[6]

Gingrich "hit the ground running," one aide to then-Minority Whip Bob Michel (R-IL) recalled, and he demonstrated his aggressive, public, and partisan approach to congressional politics early on.[7] Less than three months into his first term, he exhorted other freshmen to join him in taking on Rep. Charles Diggs, a Michigan Democrat who had been convicted of financial misconduct. Diggs was the subject of Gingrich's very first floor speech in the House and, ignoring the objections of Minority Leader John Rhodes (R-AZ), he introduced a resolution to expel Diggs. When Gingrich then put forth a procedural motion that would bring his resolution to the floor, the resolution was referred to a committee in a lopsided 322–77 vote, effectively killing it. Still, his anti-Diggs campaign had generated a degree of media attention unusual for a new congressman.[8] In mid-1979, one reporter described him as the "most conspicuous member" of the Republican freshman class, and seven months into his first term, the journal *Congressional Quarterly* observed that "his outspoken manner has kept him in the public eye more than most of his freshman GOP colleagues."[9] Diggs was eventually censured by the House, and Gingrich expanded his ethics crusade against the majority party, demanding in a floor speech that all Democratic leaders resign and complaining to constituents that the laws passed by congressional Democrats did not apply to lawmakers themselves.[10]

Besides drawing attention to the questionable practices of Democrats, thereby taking advantage of a new, post-Watergate appetite for rooting out ethical transgressions by politicians,[11] Gingrich initiated or otherwise participated in several efforts during his first two years in Congress to enhance GOP unity and improve his party's national profile and reputation. Under the auspices of the Project Majority Task Force, and with Rhodes's consent, he commissioned an Atlanta consulting firm to conduct interviews with over forty Republicans, hoping to figure out how the GOP Conference could act more cohesively. He also promoted the merits of differentiating Republicans from Democrats via positive, alternative policy proposals, the strategic use of language, and criticism of the majority party. In December 1979, for instance, he wrote a letter to the *Wall Street Journal* emphasizing the need to win "real battles in the struggle," using terms to describe the GOP like "innovation" and "opportunity" that would become common elements of his lexicon.[12]

In the legislative arena, Gingrich's differentiation strategy was best exemplified by his "Budget of Hope" initiative, a budgetary blueprint designed to accentuate differences between the fiscal priorities of Democrats and Republicans. The plan got its start in January 1979, when Gingrich convinced his first-term colleagues to endorse the formation of a freshman-only task force, cochaired by him, that would write a balanced budget proposal. Soon Gingrich was developing the minority party's official alternative to the Democratic budget resolution, an endeavor that became known as the Budget of Hope Project.[13] To put together a budget that the whole party could agree to, Gingrich had to navigate the Conference's internal policy divisions, rivalries between committees, and competition between potential successors to Rhodes. He also had to overcome residual bitterness from a race in June 1979 to fill a vacancy in the position of Conference Chair, in which Gingrich and other Republican freshmen encouraged a failed run by Henry Hyde (R-IL) against Samuel Devine (R-OH).[14] Despite these challenges, Gingrich succeeded in drawing up a budget alternative, and he then crafted a media campaign to garner positive coverage of the proposal and contrast it with what he termed the Democrats' "budget of despair." He worked with Vander Jagt and Bill Brock, chair of the Republican National Committee (RNC), to concoct a messaging strategy and lobby Republicans to support it, and he coordinated with freshman class president Ed Bethune (R-AR) to secure the endorsement of first-term lawmakers.[15]

Unsurprisingly, the alternative budget did not pass the Democratic-led House. But it did preempt an effort by moderate Democrats to coalesce with persuadable Republicans around a budget of their own. Furthermore, Gingrich saw the proposal as a "model" for achieving a Republican majority because, as he wrote to his colleagues, it "unifies our party" on a matter of "real choice" that allowed the GOP to "communicate symbollically [*sic*] and morally dominate" the majority party.[16] In a letter to Dave Hoppe, the executive director of the Republican Research Committee, he explained, "We've shown it's possible for the Republican members to decide on an overall strategy, and then work together to implement one." The following year, Gingrich resumed his role as point person on budget matters, fighting to keep a tax cut in the GOP's budget plan and helping whip conservative Democrats as possible supporters.[17]

Gingrich also advocated for electioneering tactics that could aid Republicans' attempts to win the House in the upcoming election. In a meeting of Republican freshmen in January 1980, he urged attendees to come up with ways to assist endangered incumbents, noting that the defeat of such incumbents in past elections had crippled the party's chances of gaining a majority.[18] The Atlanta consulting firm that Gingrich had hired to guide the Conference toward more unity was also tasked with identifying "long-range plans for generating a Republican majority in the House."[19] The Project Majority Task Force met several times with other lawmakers to brainstorm how the GOP could achieve electoral success. At one meeting, attendees heard from a Republican operative who suggested the party could create a "coherent 'marketing' program" akin to what the British Tories did.[20] At another meeting in June 1979, Republican pollster Robert Teeter suggested using C-SPAN, the then-new cable channel airing the House's floor proceedings, to reach out to voters, and Gingrich followed up with a memo urging that his GOP brethren be single-minded in their pursuit of a majority. During the first gathering of the task force a month earlier, which included several party leaders, Gingrich had complained that House Republicans were insufficiently tough and beseeched them to think more strategically about winning power.[21]

He did more than call for greater attentiveness to winning elections. One former House staffer recalled that Gingrich "essentially had an office in the NRCC," and another GOP lawmaker confirmed that Vander Jagt had "a very close partnership" with Gingrich and gave him "a reach beyond what any regular backbencher would have." With the NRCC's blessing, he met with new congressional candidates about conservative economic policy, surveyed them to identify useful themes that could be used as part of a national election campaign, and penned a fifty-plus-page "economic handbook" for Republican challengers.[22] Gingrich experimented with novel electioneering tactics as well. He reportedly devised a technique of monitoring Democratic incumbents' voting records and providing them to GOP challengers to use as campaign fodder.[23] As the 1980 election neared, he helped craft a pledge for Republican candidates stating that they would vote for conservative policy proposals, and he spearheaded a party-wide event on the steps of the Capitol Building to announce it. He even convinced Ronald Reagan, President Jimmy Carter's Republican challenger, to attend the gathering, though Reagan had been hesitant to do so and, to Gingrich's frustration, his campaign watered down the pledge to a handful of generic promises.[24] Still, "Governing Team Day" was the first time that a minority party in Congress had publicly unveiled an alternative agenda alongside their party's presidential nominee and its congressional hopefuls, and it presaged Gingrich's more famous Contract with America initiative fourteen years later.[25]

These efforts to assist the party did not necessarily extend to its leaders. In a *Washington Post* interview, Gingrich declared that aggressive partisan lawmakers like Bob Bauman (R-MD) and John Rousselot (R-CA) "are the real leaders of the opposition party. . . . They dominate the floor more than the real leadership does and sometimes they do it despite the Republican leadership." It was a brash claim for a novice lawmaker, as was his complaint in another interview that "Republicans have adopted the style in the House of a passive party. The leadership places responsible argument above electoral politics."[26] He also criticized colleagues who crossed party lines to help Democrats win key floor votes, and he scorned their impulse for compromise, especially within committees, as "the whole psychology of master and servant." (It was an accusation he would repeat for years to come. In 1989, he recalled that upon first entering Congress, he had "joined a Republican Party that was used to losing, used to being passive, being browbeaten by the Democrats. They felt morally inferior.")[27] In a more Machiavellian move, Gingrich secretly nudged Minority Leader Rhodes out of power altogether. He encouraged Rhodes to conduct a private survey within the Conference, and the results suggested that lawmakers were unhappy with his leadership. Gingrich "leaked his poll results freely," Rhodes recounted, "and as a result many of our members thought my position was precarious." Though Rhodes was already leaning toward retirement, the event "enhanced" his desire to quit.[28]

Gingrich was, without a doubt, more aggressively and publicly partisan than most House GOP leaders, but he also overstated his differences with them. Far from trying to obstruct the Georgia congressman, Rhodes had consented to the aforementioned survey of GOP rank and file members, had attended all but one of the Project Majority Task Force's meetings through the fall of 1979, had whipped Republicans on behalf of Gingrich's failed scheme to expel Diggs (despite his personal opposition to expulsion), had given Gingrich a leadership role in developing the Budget of Hope, and had asked GOP candidates to attend his Governing Team Day event.[29] Republican leaders were not lackadaisical, nor did they represent "a sleepy family-owned company ripe for a takeover," as one journalist described them. Rather, they had concluded—quite reasonably, given the Democratic Party's strong lock on so many congressional districts—that achieving majority status was unrealistic, so it made more sense for House Republicans to work with the majority party when possible, and not to jeopardize the benefits of bipartisan cooperation by unnecessarily provoking Democrats.[30] As Rhodes put it, "you don't get anywhere by having a reputation as somebody that just blows [hot air]." It was a view shared by the party at large. While Gingrich wrote in a memo in September 1979 that the country's worsening economy meant "it is possible to win a majority in one jump," one reporter noted that "almost no one, except perhaps some of the freshmen themselves, believe this is possible."[31]

It should also be noted that Gingrich's style and strategic outlook were not unique. He was one of several Republican lawmakers pressing for more campaign-oriented, confrontational, or media-friendly partisan tactics in that Congress, and his freshmen class was numerous, organized, active, relatively unified, and willing to challenge authority.[32] For Gingrich, these fellow travelers were not competitors but a potential resource. On more than one occasion, he used the official organization of Republican freshmen to develop original initiatives and recruit legislators to carry them out, and before long he was identified as a representative who held some sway within the class.[33] Certain senior Republicans, such as Vander Jagt, Bauman, Rousselot, and John Ashbrook (R-OH), were also sympathetic supporters and had been waging partisan battles against Democrats for years, while Bud Shuster (R-PA) pursued a similarly assertive strategy as head of the Republican Policy Committee.[34] Gingrich cultivated alliances outside of Congress as well, most notably with Paul Weyrich, the then-director of the Committee for the Survival of a Free Congress and a cofounder of the Heritage Foundation, who would become a valuable mentor. Gingrich's public profile was boosted by another influential figure, Robert Novak, a conservative *Washington Post* essayist whose nationally syndicated columns (coauthored with Rowland Evans) touted Gingrich as an "innovative" and "insightful" political player.[35]

But even with these allies, Gingrich could not overcome major roadblocks to achieving his goals. There was little money available to give to Republican challengers. Meetings of the Project Majority Task Force sometimes suffered from low attendance, and Gingrich ultimately resigned from the group. Although his boundless energy was a useful asset, it was tempered by a chronic inability to stay focused, a trait that unnerved Weyrich and other conservative activists.[36] Not all Republican freshmen were as confrontation minded as Gingrich, and even among those who were, their shared experience as new lawmakers was unlikely to keep the class united past the 1980 elections.[37] There were also other junior stars in the Conference, like Trent Lott (R-MS) and Jack Kemp (R-NY), who were considered more promising leadership material than Gingrich.

In fact, while it is tempting in hindsight to see Gingrich's first term as the triumphant inauguration of a new style of conflictual politics in Congress, an observer at the time could have easily assumed that he and his bellicose colleagues were but the latest examples of junior Republicans unsuccessfully trying to make their party more confrontational and ideologically distinct. At the initial meeting of the Project Majority Task Force, eleven-term Illinois Congressman Ed Derwinski recalled how he had attempted, without luck, to push his party's leaders to be more forceful when he had first joined Congress. In 1965, younger GOP rebels replaced their top leader with Gerald Ford (R-MI), in part because Ford called for developing positive alternatives to Democrats rather than building cross-party coalitions with southern Democrats, but the Conference's strategic focus did not change dramatically.[38] There was little reason to think that Gingrich and his fellow advocates for greater partisan conflict would be any more effective than their rebellious predecessors.

The Mixed Blessing of a Larger Minority (1981–1982)

The 1980 elections gave Gingrich and his fellow Republicans much to celebrate. Reagan was elected president, defeating Carter in an overwhelming Electoral College victory; the GOP won control of the Senate; and House Republicans won 192 seats, matching their previous post-1932 record set in 1956. In addition, many commentators saw the election as a sign that the Republican Party was finally a serious competitor on the electoral battlefield, and some thought that it could win back the House as early as 1982.[39] In a little known and now largely forgotten gambit, Gingrich decided that, rather than wait until then, he would convert his party's near-numerical majority into an actual, cross-party governing majority. Inspired by similar arrangements in state legislatures, and following a suggestion by Weyrich, he instigated a plan to recruit conservative Democrats to vote with the minority party and replace Speaker Tip O'Neill with a right-leaning Democrat. He hoped to win the votes of a "Dirty Thirty" group of Democrats who were the least loyal to their party, and he went so far as to draft a list of Republicans and conservative Democrats who would be appointed committee chairmen if O'Neill were ousted.[40]

The campaign to pick a more conservative Speaker fizzled out, however. Even worse from Gingrich's perspective, the election gave many Republicans a disincentive to adopt strategies of confrontation and differentiation. GOP leaders realized that, if their party stayed unified, they could win votes on the floor with defections by just twenty-six Democrats. The more appealing strategy was therefore to build cross-partisan coalitions with moderate Democrats. The election of Bob Michel over the campaign-centric Vander Jagt to be the party's next minority leader implied that a majority of the Conference shared this sentiment.[41] Michel's "interest was in getting legislation through the House," a one-time aide recalled, and he would write amendments to bills "with the primary purpose of getting something enacted into law," not to force Democrats to cast politically difficult votes.[42] Republicans' inclination toward compromise coincided with their skepticism that the House was imminently gettable. For instance, when Gingrich told a group of conservative activists shortly after the election that the GOP could become the House majority within a decade, he was met with laughter.[43]

Undaunted, Gingrich was determined to find some way to propel the House GOP into power. Though not the most legislatively oriented member of Congress, he initiated bills and participated in the legislative process in ways designed to label his party positively and Democrats negatively—part of his larger view that congressional Republicans, as historian Julian Zelizer put it, should be "more conscious of the electoral implications of the bills they supported (or opposed) and . . . thoroughly politicize every decision."[44] In a replay from the previous Congress, Gingrich recruited a group of lawmakers to formulate a conservative budget proposal, and in early 1981 he was invited by Michel and Lott to lead a task force that would defend Reagan's signature tax cut plan, which was based on a bill first introduced by Representative Kemp and Senator William Roth (R-DE) in the 95th Congress (1977–1978).[45] The following year, Gingrich developed a list of thirty-plus bills that could be introduced to promote the party[46] and advised Michel to treat that year's GOP budget resolution as a messaging opportunity rather than a legislative one. He also asked his colleagues to craft and advertise an alternative budget bill that reflected conservative policy objectives so "we can pit everyone in America who favors our policy directions against the liberal Democrats who are willing to sacrifice everyone's future for the survival of the liberal welfare state."[47] Gingrich told a reporter in August 1981 that if his party continued to vote in unison with the Reagan White House to pass major legislation, a "de facto parliamentary system of government" could take shape, hinting at the kind of governance he would try to implement as Speaker—albeit with himself, not the president, as the leader of the national government.[48]

Gingrich had been disappointed by the diluted message of Governing Team Day in 1980, and the event persuaded him that better candidate recruitment and different, more intensive campaign activities were necessary.[49] Publicity remained Gingrich's special emphasis, however, and as the midterm elections approached, he became increasingly frustrated that, in his opinion, the GOP was not managing public communications well. In February 1982, he lambasted Reagan's chief of staff, James Baker, after Baker suggested in a televised interview that a Republican loss of fewer than thirty-eight seats could be considered a victory. This statement, Gingrich wrote to Baker, threatened to sow "dismay and despair among your own troops," would encourage stronger Democratic candidates to run for office, and would lead to a fresh wave of campaign donations to the Democratic Party.[50] A month later, he penned a seventeen-page memo to his fellow minority party members, detailing ways that Republican officials who appeared on a dozen Sunday morning news programs lacked message discipline and spoke too kindly about Democrats. "As a party," he wrote bluntly, "we have no strategy, no themes, no slogans." Complaining that Republicans "tend to have blurred and unfocused opening statements" on television, he encouraged them to be better prepared before showing up on TV, and he suggested that the themes of their remarks could be amplified by encouraging state and local Republicans to mimic them.[51]

Gingrich also looked for methods to spread his bold, transformative ideas about politics and society more widely. In the fall of 1981, he spoke to a group of several GOP candidates and campaign aides about how to win elections, and he and his wife Marianne wrote up a longer, extended version of his remarks in a twenty-five-page manual titled "Key Steps in Developing a Survivable United States." The document included a twenty-three-step roadmap not just for getting Republicans elected but also for implementing a "conservative opportunity society," a phrase he had coined to describe a positive Republican alternative to the Democratic platform. At various public events he distributed another, similar memo that contrasted the conservative opportunity society with what he argued Democrats advocated for, a "liberal welfare state."[52]

Gingrich was unafraid to challenge President Reagan or House GOP leaders if he felt they were impeding his entrepreneurial endeavors. Privately, the Georgian could be contemptuous of Michel, Reagan, and Reagan's aides. Gingrich's staffer Frank Gregorsky remarked that "he calls them stupid all the time" and has "assumed that he's the whole Republican Party."[53] Though Gingrich's disagreements with his party's leaders were more tempered in public, he did push back against those leaders on occasion. For example, after Michel had reached an agreement with House Democratic leaders to schedule a vote on Reagan's tax cut in June 1981, two GOP freshmen wrote a letter criticizing Michel and Speaker O'Neill for not scheduling the vote earlier. Gingrich did not write the letter, yet he made a point of inserting it into the *Congressional Record* and asking others to sign it. The missive embarrassed Michel and threatened to undo the agreement. Reagan was able to enact the cuts anyway, along with other major legislation, but Gingrich eventually became frustrated that, in his view, the White House did not market its agenda well and yielded more to Democrats than it needed to.[54]

Gingrich's biggest break from the president came in 1982 on spending and tax policy. Reagan, congressional leaders, and many Republicans expressed growing alarm at the country's expanding budget deficit. When over fifty House Republicans voted to defeat a proposal that would have sharply cut domestic nondefense spending as a means of reducing the deficit, GOP spending hawks were dismayed. In protest, Gingrich led a group of "Yellow Jacket" conservatives to target a Democratic amendment to Reagan's budget plan that repealed the plan's reductions to Medicare and instead reduced the level of defense spending. The group unexpectedly refrained from voting on the amendment, and in the ensuing confusion, enough members in both parties voted for the amendment that it passed, delivering an unexpected win to liberal Democrats and dashing Michel's hope to prevent changes to the president's budget.[55] A few months afterward, Gingrich was alarmed when the president stood behind a package of tax increases negotiated with Democratic leaders in Congress to raise much-needed revenue. Convinced the bill would dangerously blur the lines between the parties, and ignoring Reagan's pleas for support, he and other fervent antitax Republicans openly campaigned against it. Gingrich gave numerous interviews berating what he called a "Jimmy Carter tax bill" and wrote a *Washington Post* op-ed titled "The Tax Bill Is a Turkey." The bill passed anyway, 226–207, with slim majorities of both parties voting for it, though the Georgian claimed he had convinced over two hundred lawmakers to reject Reagan's proposal.[56]

Overall, the 97th Congress, particularly its first year, was a relatively successful one for the GOP on the legislative front. Despite leading a minority party, Michel and Lott had persuaded enough conservative Democrats to defect on several key floor votes, winning major policy victories like the passage of Reagan's tax cuts and an increase in defense spending, and inflicting a higher rate of vote losses on Democrats than in the previous Congress.[57] For Gingrich in particular, the 1980 election brought new Republican lawmakers to the House who would serve as key associates, including Vin Weber (R-WI) and Steve Gunderson (R-WI), and he had earned some publicity for his outspoken opposition to Reagan's tax measure in 1982. Viewed through the lens of Gingrich's strategic objectives, however, the past two years were mostly a letdown. Gingrich believed that passing legislation with cross-party coalitions had damaged the GOP's capacity to differentiate itself from Democrats. Compromise "helps you to govern, but it collapses your majority," he lamented, and he would later call the White House's choice to endorse higher taxes in 1982 "the dumbest decision of the Reagan Administration," which "totally blurred all the issues between the parties."[58] GOP leaders had not opposed all of Gingrich's tactics; Vander Jagt and Michel had held a series of breakfast meetings in late 1982 to get GOP candidates to use harmonized positive campaign messages, for example. But neither they nor many rank and file Republicans seemed interested in adopting partisan confrontation as a core strategy when policy wins were well within their grasp.[59] Michel's office was also suspicious of Gingrich's motives. One Michel staffer wrote in an internal memo that Gingrich appeared more intent on attacking the minority leader than working with him, and he recoiled at the notion of giving Gingrich carte blanche to communicate party policy to voters, counseling that "there should be no direct link with the leadership" when "the rhetoric is strictly negative or partisan."[60]

Gingrich Turns to Guerrilla Tactics (1983–1984)

The 1982 elections were discouraging for House Republicans, especially for those anticipating an electoral realignment in which they would finally join their brethren in the US Senate as a governing party.[61] The GOP lost twenty-six House seats, making it much tougher to form coalitions with southern Democrats, let alone seize the chamber in the future. "We're going to be at the mercy of Tip [O'Neill]," lamented Michel, and an internal Gingrich office memo written six months after the elections admitted that "a Republican majority is possible in the 1980s, but it isn't probable."[62]

Gingrich sought counsel from former president Richard Nixon, who had himself spent time in Congress as a member of the minority party. Nixon advised the Georgia congressman that he alone could not build a Republican majority. In his view, "the House Republicans were boring and had always been boring," and he recommended that Gingrich organize a faction of dedicated "noisy" lawmakers who could develop an alternative conservative agenda and inspire voters. The erstwhile president's suggestion coincided with Gingrich's own conclusion that GOP leaders would never adopt the aggressive partisan tactics he believed were essential to win power. Nor could Gingrich count on the party's large and well-established caucus of conservatives, the Republican Study Committee (RSC), a group that he believed had lost its edge. Gingrich realized that he needed to recruit a fresh group of House colleagues who believed in his vision of how to win a Republican House majority.[63]

The result was a new intraparty caucus, the Conservative Opportunity Society (COS), which Gingrich formed in early 1983 with about a dozen or so mostly junior and conservative House Republicans.[64] Its members "look[ed] to make the party more activist," one former COS member recalled. The organization had three objectives in particular: draft a new conservative policy agenda, use the media to spotlight that agenda and tarnish the reputation of the Democratic Party, and convince the Conference to adopt its strategic approach to politics.[65] To do this, the COS would primarily use messaging tactics, particularly on television, highlighting "wedge issues" that divided Democrats and "magnet issues" that could attract conservative-leaning voters like school prayer, anticommunism, and opposition to the Equal Rights Amendment. In effect, the group would try to exercise what is known as the "second face of power," forcing novel issues onto the legislative agenda or, barring that, expanding the scope of conflict by attracting voter attention to their cause.[66] The strategy resembled a battle of attrition in which one side wears out the opposition or compels them to react rashly. Indeed, a political consultant named Bill Lee told Gingrich that the faction should model itself after the Viet Cong. "It can and must be a revolutionary guerrilla movement," he wrote.[67]

The creation of the Conservative Opportunity Society was an important institutional development, but its underlying purpose spoke to Gingrich's role as a party entrepreneur. As a forum for messaging development and a coordinating mechanism to amplify the power of like-minded activists, the COS would be an important resource for him to achieve collective party goals. It could help tarnish the reputation of the Democrats—a frequent theme of COS statements was that the Democratic Caucus was the party of tyranny—while advocating positive conservative policy proposals, thus differentiating the two parties. As Gingrich wrote in the very first sentence of a newspaper column in April 1983 touting the group, "The main reason the Republican Party can't build a lasting national majority is that it offers no alternative vision." In a planning memo penned the following month, he argued that the COS could introduce conservative bills and use national and local media to "win the election by emphasizing the contrasts between our positive and their [liberal Democrats'] negative impact on each person's future." The COS could also, Gingrich believed, encourage "effective" team-oriented thinking in the Conference and implement what an aide called "our strategy of slowly recruiting the GOP towards radical behavior."[68] There were loftier goals as well. At least one lawmaker, Bobbi Fiedler (R-CA), argued that it would usher in a more conservative society, one of Gingrich's main objectives. As an internal Gingrich office document put it, "Saving the West is our purpose. . . . The vehicle for achieving that is the COS."[69]

Gingrich was the group's "intellectual leader," but several COS participants contributed to the development and implementation of strategy and tactics. Vin Weber, recalled a member of the COS, "was very instrumental . . . basically, being the guy who ran the group," and another Republican aide remarked that Weber, who had a knack for organization, kept the group focused amid Gingrich's propensity to generate an endless stream of ideas.[70] (As Gingrich acknowledged in a private memo, "Every time I get involved in daily management, I goof it up.")[71] Hank Brown (R-CO) took charge of its overall legislative agenda and proposed ways to force the House to comply with statutory budget caps. Judd Gregg (R-NH) suggested issues for the group to concentrate on, including ones that would later emerge in the party's Contract with America campaign platform in 1994, like restructuring welfare and adopting a balanced budget amendment to the Constitution. Echoing Robert Teeter's recommendation in 1979, Bob Walker (R-PA) urged fellow COS members to deliver provocative statements that would excite C-SPAN viewers, a tactic that had proven effective for Walker when he discovered that his partisan floor speeches generated phone calls from around the country.[72] Gingrich concurred. The sixteen to seventeen million viewers of the channel, the vast majority of them voters, were, in his words, "not a bad crowd."[73]

The COS had a complex relationship with party leaders. On one hand, Michel acknowledged that the COS reflected junior Republicans' exasperation with the governing party. Taking advantage of the GOP's reduced size, Democrats now paid Republicans less heed than before, enacted rules that gave Republican House members fewer opportunities to revise legislation, and employed procedural tools more boldly to curb the minority party's influence.[74] Accordingly, Michel followed both the COS's lead and the recommendations of his own staff to more assertively denounce Democrats and highlight his party's agenda.[75] Other sympathetic members of leadership included Conference Chair Kemp and NRCC Chair Vander Jagt. In addition, Minority Whip Lott was "making sure he had someone who was his friend at the meetings" and, along with Republican Policy Committee chair Richard Cheney (R-WY), served as a liaison between the COS and GOP leaders. By early 1984, the COS was working with party leaders to develop policy and political strategy. Lott supported Gingrich's suggestion that the Conference should create task forces to examine, among other things, "how all House members can function as a conference team." Michel had endorsed the group's use of C-SPAN coverage to advocate for proposals blocked by House Democrats, and a former Michel staffer recalled that "we made an effort from the outside to keep [the lines of] communication open [with the COS] and make sure that we didn't get crosswise with each other."[76]

On the other hand, the COS was organized independently from the party's official leadership structure, and its more aggressive tactics were frequently frowned upon. When COS member Dan Coats (R-IN) met with Cheney in January 1984, Cheney explained that leaders were "open to the COS idea" of "a majority status in the House via a radical campaign strategy," but added that "we have seen this before" and "we are basically skeptical that such a result can be achieved." Michel "basically just didn't want these guys [in the COS] to be trouble," one GOP aide recounted, and worried that incendiary partisan harangues would damage his professional and personal relationship with Speaker Tip O'Neill. "I think he finds all of us a little bit too pushy, too aggressive, too TV-oriented," Gingrich admitted in an interview in 1984. Michel in particular was already wary of Gingrich, an unabashed critic of his leadership, and Michel and other leaders were unmoved by Gingrich's claims that allowing Republicans to criticize one another would encourage them to do the same against Democrats, build Conference morale, and counter a minority party mentality. One of Michel's aides forewarned him that "I doubt any real working relationship [with Gingrich] is possible." Many, if not most, rank and file Republicans shared Michel's doubts about the effectiveness of the COS's methods. Tom Tauke (R-IA), one of Gingrich's fellow members of the Class of 1978, voiced the fear of many that obstructionism could "stand in the way of my being effective in my committee and subcommittee."[77]

Lott urged Gingrich to emphasize the GOP's positive policy alternatives rather than berate his colleagues for a lack of fighting spirit, and the Georgian initially vowed to his skeptical staff that he would be a better team player. But it was a promise he did not keep. When Gingrich insisted that the House expel a Republican (Daniel Crane of Illinois) as well as a Democrat (Gerry Studds of Massachusetts) for sexual misconduct, Cheney complained that Gingrich was "a pain in the fanny."[78] In mid-1983, Gingrich caught considerable flack when he sent a letter to other Republicans presumptuously suggesting that the GOP whip office should stop deferring to the White House, that the party's Research Committee and Policy Committee should do better long-term planning, and that the Conference should hire a staffer to advertise the party's agenda.[79] Such moves were risky for a backbencher like Gingrich. Nonetheless, from the COS's perspective, cooperation with party leaders was not a high priority anyway: the group would probably never win over leaders who did not already agree with its strategic vision, and it did not want to compromise its vision for the sake of intraparty harmony. As the consultant Bill Lee told Gingrich, the Democrats and the official Republican Party were the COS's "two enemies."[80]

Public communication was a central COS tactic. In its weekly meetings, the group brainstormed topics for daily one-minute statements on the House floor and for longer special-order speeches, which were delivered after the chamber had completed its daily legislative business, and it kept careful track of who would speak on which issues.[81] It also dabbled in parliamentary tactics: shortly after it was formed, several COS members participated in a ploy, spearheaded by Lott, to fatally delay a nuclear freeze bill by offering numerous amendments to the legislation.[82] However, much of the group's work during its first year happened out of the public eye. It spent some time formulating its mission statement,[83] and it conducted a poll of ranking members of committees to learn about their priority projects and ideas ("vision") for the party's agenda.[84] COS member Connie Mack (R-FL) organized a conference in October that drew over fifty Republicans to Baltimore to hone a legislative agenda, discuss how the majority Democrats exercised power unfairly, and "provide a leadership aura for at least one way of thinking about the party."[85] Mack called the well-attended gathering, which Michel ultimately endorsed, "the beginning of the beginning," but its Gingrich-inspired use of buzzwords, metaphors, and ideas from futurist writers John Naisbitt and Alvin Toffler left some attendees "scratching their heads, not quite sure what to do with their heightened collective consciousness or how it could help make the GOP the majority party in the House."[86] Meanwhile, Eddie Mahe Jr., a consultant and former RNC staffer, warned Gingrich that he was shifting his attention to fresh issues too often and proposing schemes "much as dew forms on the grass in the Spring—enough to cover every blade, no matter how big the lawn."[87]

In late 1983, the group began developing a strategic plan that included highlighting key issues in the public sphere. This would be accomplished in part through an escalation of guerrilla floor tactics, starting with a "Showdown on [the] Floor" and subsequently "Dominat[ing the] floor morally and energetically," pursuing what Gingrich dubbed a political form of

"Chinese water torture."[88] One-minute and special-order speeches had been utilized by lawmakers for partisan purposes for several years,[89] but COS members—inspired not only by the recent past but also by the oratory of anti–Vietnam War Democrats in the early 1970s—decided to employ them more aggressively, persistently, and in conjunction with procedural motions. The COS also hoped to join forces with outside advocacy groups like the National Association of Evangelicals, draw the notice of national news outlets, and receive at least tacit backing from party leaders.[90] In the longer term, it anticipated that turning the floor into a partisan battleground would undermine the deference that too many Republicans gave to Democrat-dominated committees, thereby aiding conservatives who were outnumbered on their committees and, as with the nuclear freeze bill, encouraging Republicans to alter or kill legislation when it came to the floor—or, at a minimum, demonstrate differences between the parties.[91] Counting up to fifty Republicans as tactical allies, the COS embraced a suggestion from Mahe to do something on the first day of the second session of the 98th Congress that would bring scrutiny to how Democrats refused to bring popular bills to the floor, and then follow up with "an accelerating and intensifying effort to focus attention on this series of issues."[92] The campaign would highlight "wedge messages" against Democrats and "magnet messages" for Republicans, peaking at both parties' national conventions that summer.[93]

When the second session of the House convened in January, Gingrich, Walker, Ron Packard (R-CA), and COS member Dan Lungren (R-CA) each asked unanimous consent on the floor to consider constitutional amendments allowing for school prayer, mandating a balanced budget, granting a line-item veto to the president, and banning abortion.[94] After Democrats objected, Walker proposed reserving the next ten months of special-order speeches for just four people: himself, Gingrich, Mack, and Weber. Democrats rejected the audacious request, whereupon Walker lamented "the kind of dictatorship that this House has become."[95] A second day of unanimous consent requests by COS members followed, and the NRCC amplified Walker's message of majority party tyranny by issuing press releases pillorying the individual Democrats who had objected to the unanimous consent requests.[96] Annoyed by these tactics, Speaker O'Neill prohibited such requests if they were not approved by both parties' leaders, but COS members were undeterred. They, together with others sympathetic to their cause, continued for months to request consideration of the four constitutional amendments, offering to yield floor time to Democratic leaders to get their approval and then blaming them when no approval was forthcoming.[97] Majority party leaders dismissed these tactics as publicity stunts that made the GOP look petty, but some irritated Democrats suggested striking back by limiting C-SPAN coverage of the floor, not telling Republicans what the future floor schedule would be, or even restricting the GOP's procedural rights.[98]

Meanwhile, the COS expanded its activities into other spheres. By early May, the group had held a twenty-four hour "school prayer vigil" outside the Capitol featuring fifty lawmakers from both parties, and it was managing nearly a dozen different recruitment and communication projects, preparing a second party conference in Baltimore, and trying (unsuccessfully) to coordinate town hall meetings around the country to discuss topics like crime that it felt were advantageous to the GOP.[99] If he and others could create awareness of the GOP's positions on such matters and how they differed from Democrats, Gingrich believed, voters "would choose the Republicans by an overwhelming majority."[100] Gingrich was also pontificating far more often on the House floor than he had in the past, especially during COS-sponsored special orders. As shown in figure 2.1, he was gradually participating in a greater number of general legislative debates, and his special-order speeches and statements more than tripled in number from 1983 to 1984. Gingrich had begun making more parliamentary inquiries as well, often to challenge the Democrats' use of House procedures.

Gingrich and the COS eventually managed to prod the majority party into making an emotionally charged mistake, which was the kind of reaction they had been hoping for. In March 1984, ten House Democrats, including Majority Leader Jim Wright of Texas, wrote a letter to Daniel Ortega, the communist leader of Nicaragua, complimenting his decision to hold elections and condemning US support for the Contra rebels fighting his regime. Gingrich and other conservatives condemned the letter writers for expressing sympathy toward Ortega and threatening President Reagan's authority over foreign affairs. At a press conference they accused the signers of being "soft" on communism. Gingrich and Walker then repeated the charge against multiple Democratic lawmakers on the House floor, even though those Democrats were not present to defend themselves, which

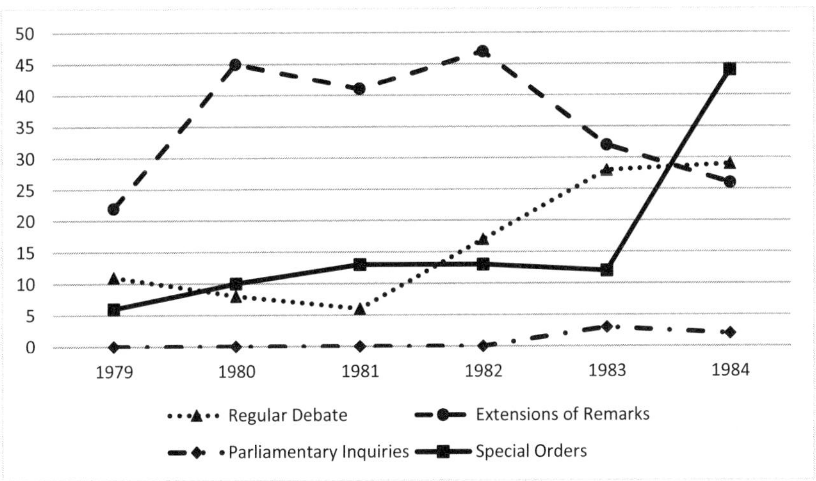

Figure 2.1. Number of Gingrich's House Floor Appearances, by Category (1979–1984). *Source: Congressional Record.*

was a violation of House protocol.[101] In retaliation, and having heard complaints from members of his party that the COS was monopolizing floor time, Speaker O'Neill quietly ordered the House's TV cameras to scan the chamber while Bob Walker gave a special-order speech. COS members had sometimes delivered these speeches as if speaking to a full audience of lawmakers, but now the panning camera revealed what legislators knew, but C-SPAN viewers did not: the orators were addressing a nearly empty chamber.[102]

Republicans were outraged by O'Neill's surprise move, which a reporter dubbed "Camscam." Michel told O'Neill that it was "an act of dictatorial retribution," and COS members redoubled their verbal attacks against Democrats. Matters escalated on May 14, when the Speaker scolded Gingrich on the House floor while standing behind the new camera policy, and the next day Gingrich made a point of personal privilege to respond.[103] In a fateful moment, as Gingrich tried to defend himself, an infuriated O'Neill declared that Gingrich's earlier accusation against absent Democrats was "the lowest thing that I've ever seen in my thirty-two years in Congress." Lott then moved to have O'Neill's words taken down because he had broken House rules by admonishing Gingrich personally. This highly unusual rebuke to a Speaker was covered extensively by the national press for days afterward.[104]

The COS had achieved its goal of dramatic floor action before the party conventions. There were personal payoffs for Gingrich: as one Republican aide said, it "made him a household name," and Gingrich brashly declared that "I am now a famous person." More importantly, the fracas signaled that O'Neill's "all politics is local" style of governing could be countered by a nationalized strategy centered on media coverage of partisan conflict in the chamber. National news stories about O'Neill violating the House's rules gave the COS an audience that went beyond C-SPAN's limited viewership, confirming Gingrich's belief that the media preferred to cover controversy and that a skillful member of Congress could use skirmishes as a means of attracting and educating a wider audience. ("Conflict equals exposure equals power," as one journalist succinctly put it.) The event also pleased many rank and file congressional Republicans who enjoyed needling O'Neill.[105] Republican Leader Michel, who wanted to sustain his good relationship with O'Neill and cultivate an alliance with moderate Democrats to support Reagan's foreign and military policy, was not enamored with the outcome. When Republicans stood and applauded Gingrich following his point of personal privilege, Michel remained in his seat.[106] But Lott, the GOP's next in command, had been the one to demand that O'Neill's words be taken down, which Bob Walker believed "legitimized" the COS. It was the COS's first victorious blow in an "escalatory challenge" to the Democratic Party that featured Gingrich and his allies successfully using conflict and provocation as partisan weapons.[107]

The COS took advantage of the kerfuffle to continue its partisan public campaign. Working at times with the NRCC and the Republican Study Committee, the group scheduled more floor speeches and press events, encouraged other House Republicans to participate in them, and urged the NRCC to run ads disparaging O'Neill. COS member Lungren suggested additional ways that the COS could "cause a possible repeat performance by the Speaker and methods by which we can communicate our message to the American people." [108] The group recruited lawmakers to sign discharge petitions—which brought bills to the floor, circumventing the committees that were supposed to consider them first, provided the petitions were signed by a majority of the House—and it published the names of signatories on an "honor roll." Members of COS also coached congressional candidates and campaign workers, creating a "Big Brother/Little Brother" mentorship training program. COS paid particular attention to promising conservative candidates like Dick Armey, an ambitious economist who would be elected to the House in 1984 and eventually become House majority leader under Speaker Gingrich.[109] Meanwhile, Democrats—in a sign they were taking Gingrich more seriously—began going after him. Pete Stark (D-CA) asked the IRS to review the operations of the American Opportunity Foundation, a nonprofit organization started by Gingrich, while Majority Whip Tony Coelho (D-CA) started amassing negative media stories about the Georgia congressman.[110]

Two months after Camscam, Gingrich contributed to another important but lesser-known step toward differentiating the two parties. The previous November, consultant Eddie Mahe had written to Gingrich and Weber urging that a "special effort should be made to try and get the believers" in the COS's agenda appointed to the committee that was responsible for composing the party's official platform, which would meet in Dallas at the Republican National Convention. After getting himself selected to that committee, Gingrich labored with committee allies at the convention, including Kemp, Lott, Weber, and Tom Loeffler (R-TX), to make the party platform more conservative so that it "reflected a COS agenda."[111] With a goal to "move to have a no-tax pledge written into the platform," one participant later recalled, a single comma was added between the words "taxes" and "which" so that the platform went from being conditionally to unconditionally against tax increases.[112] This clever maneuver, along with other changes to the platform (such as a Gingrich-led venture to more firmly endorse school prayer), garnered attention from reporters and young party activists and "kept the press from writing about [more divisive matters like] abortion," one platform committee participant recalled, while allowing Reagan to attack the Democratic presidential nominee, Walter Mondale, on taxes.

Gingrich and the COS were active at the 1984 convention in other ways. Gingrich passed out copies of his book *Window of Opportunity* to attendees, and he was frequently quoted in the press explaining his bids to pull the platform further to the right and claiming these changes would accelerate the party's antitax movement that had begun in the late 1970s.[113] The COS also hosted a series of briefings at the convention. One of them had to be relocated to a larger room, a COS member recollected, because "we literally had hundreds of people that showed up. . . . It made it really clear to us that the activists in the party saw us as providing real leadership."[114] These efforts to generate broader awareness of the COS were less successful than hoped,[115] but Gingrich was unapologetic about the group's participation at the convention or the conservative changes that had been made to the party's platform. When some worried that the revisions would unnecessarily constrain the president, Gingrich brazenly warned that Reagan and his aides "better be thinking about what we believe, or they'll face a revolution in their own party." And he insisted to one reporter that House Republicans would do much better in the upcoming elections if the president openly embraced conservatism.[116]

More generally, Gingrich did not shy from criticizing White House aides or other high-profile Republicans if they wavered from their allegiance to a conservative platform or failed to embrace an ideological "revolution." He derided Senator Bob Dole (R-KS) as the "tax collector for the welfare state." Shortly before the November elections, he wrote a letter to Reagan's Office of Management and Budget (OMB) Director David Stockman (which was later published in the *Washington Post*) pronouncing that "we [the COS] are revolutionaries" while Stockman was "becoming the greatest obstacle to a successful revolution" because of his attempts to compromise with congressional Democrats, which would "blur the distinction between the revolutionary effort, the creative Opportunity Society and the Liberal Welfare State establishment." In a sign of the COS's growing influence, President Reagan had started using the term "conservative opportunity society" in his speeches.[117]

Gingrich maintained a laser-like focus on winning a majority with electioneering endeavors. He served on the NRCC Executive Committee, counseled the committee to employ "key words and phrases . . . distinguishing us from the liberals" in its mailings, and was invited to party fundraising events around the country. He also pressed the NRCC to expand the electoral playing field by donating more funds to Republicans who were running against incumbent Democrats.[118] Developing popular campaign themes, keeping candidates on script, forcing members of the governing party to side with liberal lobbying groups against the will of voters, creating a coalition of conservative activists that would launch verbal bombs at incumbent Democrats, paying greater heed to rightward voting trends in House districts—all were campaign ideas that Gingrich proposed to party leaders as a way to win seats, if not an outright majority.[119] In the waning months of 1984, Gingrich advocated for a unified electoral message, better communication with same-party candidates, and even another 1980-like rally near the steps of the Capitol building (which did not happen until a decade later).

Gingrich also used tactics intended to sully the reputation of House Democrats. The attempt to expel Representatives Studds and Crane for sexual transgressions with underage House pages—mimicking his previous crusade against Congressman Diggs—fit the narrative of a corrupt Congress and, by extension, the Democratic Party that governed it. (Rather than expel the pair, the House ultimately voted for a Michel-backed proposal to censure them both.) Even when the lines between the parties were blurred, Gingrich tried to spin events as victories exclusively for the House GOP. For example, when some Democrats unexpectedly defected from their own party and helped Republicans pass a major crime bill in the fall of 1984, he resisted sharing credit and instead castigated those Democrats for having previously voted against the measure.[120]

Gingrich's best efforts on all these fronts seemed destined to come up short, at least for the immediately foreseeable future. As one journalist wrote in March 1984, "few GOP leaders or rank-and-file troops expect that the party will soon gain a majority in the House to match its control of the White House and Senate." In private, even Gingrich acknowledged that winning a GOP majority in the chamber would be "the hardest challenge in national politics" and could take up to a decade to achieve.[121]

Conclusion

A review of Gingrich's first three terms in the House reveals that, even in his earliest years as a congressman, he was a tenacious party entrepreneur. Gingrich conducted a variety of electioneering and legislating activities to help his party, like writing alternative budget bills, training candidates and summoning them to the Capitol to tout the benefits of a GOP House, and nudging the party's platform further rightward. But messaging was his forte, whether it meant advertising those budget bills, inspiring conservative C-SPAN watchers with floor speeches, or provoking the Speaker into violating the rules of the House during debate. He was also not above rebuking members of his own party, whether for messaging purposes or to heighten his own influence and profile.

By late 1984, Gingrich was a better-known backbencher and had shown other Republicans that public confrontation could generate headlines. Yet despite his entrepreneurial ventures, he had made little headway toward achieving his core goals. The election results that year were another disappointment for Republicans. Although Reagan was reelected in a landslide, House Democrats' incumbency advantage remained a powerful barrier, and the GOP gained just fifteen seats—far fewer than what some prognosticators had predicted, not enough to retake the House and certainly not enough to form viable cross-party coalitions as the party had been able to do in 1981 and 1982.[122] Gingrich was far from having "save[d] Western civilization," the goal he had set for himself at the start of his congressional career, and there was little evidence that the public's attitudes toward politics and society had been even remotely transformed. In fact, whereas some surveys suggested that the percentage of Americans self-identifying as conservative had risen slightly since the mid-1970s, others showed no such trend, and political scientist James Stimson's "mood" index of voter sentiment indicates that there was a liberal, not conservative, shift in public opinion over the course of Reagan's presidency.[123] In terms of influence, Gingrich had helped push Minority Leader Rhodes out of office, but he was regarded with suspicion by Michel, Rhodes's successor, and he had little sway with his colleagues outside of the COS. The ranking member on the powerful Ways and Means Committee, Barber Conable (R-NY), reflected the view of many House Republicans when he said that "the Conservative Opportunity Society does a lot of posturing but they have no sense of responsibility" and speculated that its members would lose interest in confrontational tactics as they inculcated norms of cooperative behavior.[124]

Gingrich also had mixed success in achieving his more immediate strategic objectives. On the positive side, federal elections were starting to become more nationalized. The percentage of voters who split their tickets between presidential and congressional candidates had declined in 1984 from its all-time high four years before, and in 1982, the percentage of voters whose approval of the president matched that of their incumbent lawmaker jumped by over ten points from the previous election (though that percentage would drop and not rise again for another decade). In addition, the

1984 elections offered one indication of greater competitiveness between the parties: the number of self-described Republicans increased noticeably that year, the beginning of a gradual upward trend in Republican Party identification.[125] The GOP platform from that year was also more clearly antitax and therefore more distinct from the Democratic Party platform. On the negative side of the ledger, Gingrich had contributed little to his party's legislative victories, and those that did occur happened because of support from conservative Democrats, which presumably watered down the differences between the two parties. Furthermore, surveys suggested that by the mid-1980s the public was no more negative toward, or distrustful of, Congress than they had been in the late 1970s.[126] In terms of political power, Gingrich had acquired leadership positions in the NRCC, as well as the Republican Research Committee and the Committee on Committees (which made the party's committee assignments),[127] but he was not an elected Conference leader, nor was he a ranking member of any standing committee.

It seems unlikely that any single backbencher, even one as ambitious as Gingrich, could singlehandedly shift the sentiment of the country's voters or improve the competitiveness of a national political party. In addition, just as a military strategy cannot succeed if its objectives and tactics are more ambitious than what the available resources will allow, Gingrich at this stage of his career lacked enough assets for what he hoped to accomplish. The GOP had insufficient funds to compete against entrenched Democratic incumbents, and the party was far from being unified or electorally aggressive. In late 1984, Gingrich lamented to Vin Weber that "we're still essentially an old style, passive, traditional Republican Party."[128] The 1978 freshman class was a valuable organization during Gingrich's first term, but it did not last beyond the 1980 elections; his influence as a member of the party's platform-writing committee ceased when the convention was over; and outside groups that favored his style of politics were often dubious about Gingrich's leadership abilities.

It was not until Gingrich created the Conservative Opportunity Society caucus in 1983—perhaps his most consequential entrepreneurial move to date—that the Georgian had a durable organizational base with the motivation and shared talent required to make his tactics successful. The COS was a useful platform for mounting various campaign and unity-building pursuits, and its sustained, strategically planned and coordinated floor protests and speeches, coupled with Gingrich's unique rhetorical style, played well on television and reached millions of viewers via C-SPAN. COS was also a regular irritant to Democrats, whose responses to the group were a boon to Gingrich. Gingrich's tactics culminated in Speaker O'Neill's rash reaction on the House floor in 1984, an outburst covered by all the major television networks that propelled the young Georgia congressman and his conservative compatriots into the spotlight. "You and Gingrich owe me," O'Neill later told a member of COS. "Until I took you on, you were backbenchers nobody knew. I made you and Newt into national figures."[129] If House Democrats continued to focus their attention on Gingrich and the COS—or retaliated in ways that alienated non-COS Republicans—they might inadvertently convince more members of the minority to be a part of the radicalized, activist, and unified Conference that Gingrich sought.

CHAPTER 3

ASCENDANT PARTY WARRIOR (1985–1989)

By the end of 1984, Newt Gingrich had achieved a new level of public notoriety and organizational authority. But he also had several reasons to be glum. For starters, his party was still in the minority in the House. Many GOP leaders—and probably a majority of the Republican Conference—rejected his emphasis on confrontation and sharp partisan rhetoric over legislating. In addition, shortly before the November elections, he was subject to the first of what would be many attacks on his personal character: a scathing article in *Mother Jones* magazine that revealed sordid details of his private life. He reportedly fell into a period of depression and even considered leaving Congress altogether.[1]

Over the next four-plus years, Gingrich overcame these setbacks, expanded his strategic resources, and exploited opportunities in pursuit of a Republican majority in the House, a conservative transformation of society, and greater personal influence (see table 3.1). Before the end of the decade, the man once seen by skeptics as little more than an annoyance would be credited with the resignation of a House Speaker and awarded the second-highest leadership post in the GOP Conference.

The GOP Moves toward Confrontation (1985–1986)

Gingrich soon got past his bout of dejection and, with his customary self-confidence, expressed a renewed devotion to his long-term goals. "I

Table 3.1. Gingrich as Ascendant Party Warrior (1985–1989)

Congress	Major Activity	Type of Tactic	Primary Strategic Objective(s)
99th (1985–1986)	Ousts fellow Republican as ranking committee member	Power-Seeking	Heighten personal profile/ power
	Contributes to fight over contested Indiana election	Messaging	Draw sharper partisan distinctions, tarnish reputation of (Democratic-led) House
	Lobbies against Reagan tax bill	Messaging, Legislating	Draw sharper partisan distinctions
	Becomes director of GOPAC	Electioneering	Improve electoral competitiveness of GOP
100th (1987–1988)	Campaigns against ethics of House Democrats	Messaging	Tarnish reputation of (Democratic-led) House
	Mounts effort to remove Speaker Jim Wright	Subverting	Tarnish reputation of (Democratic-led) House
	Helps GOP candidates, develops a nationalized strategy for GOPAC	Electioneering	Nationalize elections, improve electoral competitiveness of GOP
	Provides messaging ideas to House GOP and President Bush	Messaging	Improve electoral competitiveness of GOP
101st (January–May 1989)	Continues campaign against Speaker Wright	Subverting	Tarnish reputation of (Democratic-led) House
	Runs for GOP whip	Power-Seeking	Heighten personal profile/ power
	Helps revise GOP platform	Electioneering, Messaging	Draw sharper partisan distinctions

want to shift the entire planet. And I'm doing it," he boasted to one reporter in early January, and an internal memo from March 1985, almost certainly written by Gingrich, envisioned worldwide movements on behalf of a conservative opportunity society.[2] He also maintained some influence within the party by serving as treasurer of the Republican Study Committee (RSC).[3]

The Georgia congressman still believed that messaging was central to winning a GOP majority and instigating societal change. "We are engaged in reshaping a whole nation through the news media," he announced in early 1985.[4] Much of that messaging was hyperbolic and highly critical of the other party. Shortly after the 1984 elections, he forwarded a letter to his Republican colleagues from the RSC that accused the Democratic Party of being "an elite, Northeastern and welfare statist collection of interest groups" that exercised power through "corrupt bargains" and unfair electoral procedures and congressional rules. He also encouraged members of the COS to dismiss Democrats' election victories as "essentially illegitimate" because they had benefited from federal funding projects in swing districts and ran misleading campaigns.[5]

Gingrich was willing to target both Democrats and Republicans when it came to gaining more power or improving his reelection chances, and in doing so, he sometimes went beyond mere words to more concrete acts of subversion. In the previous Congress, Gingrich had accrued enough seniority to become the ranking member of a subcommittee of the House Public Works and Transportation Committee, but he had given that ranking position to a more junior committee member, Guy Molinari (R-NY). Gingrich now broke a pledge he had made to Molinari to let him keep the post following the 1984 elections, forcing the New York congressman to relinquish the slot. Even worse, Gingrich's gambit came too late for Molinari to become the ranking member of a different subcommittee without bumping someone else from their ranking position. (Perhaps not coincidentally, Molinari had used the ranking committee position to draw attention to the safety practices of airlines, including the Atlanta based Delta Airlines, an important Gingrich constituency.)[6]

Molinari was furious with Gingrich about the betrayal. And he was hardly the only Republican who viewed Gingrich with suspicion and resentment. Gingrich's disparagement of fellow partisans and his transparent desire for more influence rubbed many of his colleagues the wrong way. His claims that he could single-handedly alter the globe, and statements like "the system is now geared to carry me" and "I represent real power," did little to dispel the image of him as an egoist who openly craved the spotlight. Lawmakers dismissed him as "ruthlessly ambitious" and a "charlatan."[7] "It was pitiful," one former House GOP member remarked, "how he had no respect for people who had been around the horn a few times and knew how to pass legislation."[8] A month after the elections, outgoing Conference

Chair Mickey Edwards (R-OK) wrote to fellow Republicans warning them not to adopt Gingrich's tactics or follow him like a "lemming." He also penned a thinly veiled criticism of Gingrich in the *Washington Post*, assailing those who were "attempting to burn down the Capitol" and blame Democrats for it, and who insisted his party could seize control of Congress through "highly publicized confrontations with the Democratic leadership and denunciations of all Republicans who are not part of the 'revolution.'" In Edwards's view, the party needed to focus on legislative victories, working with Democrats if need be, and follow a localized approach to winning elections—the opposite strategy of Gingrich.[9]

The COS faced blowback as well. When the group had promised to hold press events at the previous year's Democratic National Convention, over two dozen House Republicans sought assurances from Minority Leader Bob Michel that the Conference was not sponsoring its attendance and thereby giving its stamp of approval to the COS's confrontational tactics.[10] GOP leaders cautioned freshmen first elected in 1984 to stay away from the COS, and when Hank Brown (R-CO) was denied a seat on the Ways and Means Committee, some interpreted it as retribution for his COS membership.[11] Detractors dismissed the organization as the "conservative opportun*istic* society," a self-serving means through which Gingrich could pursue greater personal power. As the COS began a protracted internal debate over its mission, a rival organization emerged: the '92 Group, a collection of some thirty lawmakers who advocated for ideological moderation rather than conservative orthodoxy as the electoral strategy that would, as their name anticipated, culminate in GOP control of the House in 1992.[12]

Following the advice of friends who worried about his standing in the Conference and how it would affect his political influence, Gingrich vowed to be less abrasive and to limit his media appearances.[13] The COS also assumed a lower public profile. But far from being moribund, the organization established its own political action committee, allowing it to raise and donate campaign funds, and it made plans to form an "ally group" of sympathetic representatives who, in the words of an internal planning document, lacked "the time, energy, or resources to be a full-time COS Member."[14] Gingrich recognized that the shared goal of the '92 Group and the COS could be the basis for fruitful cooperation, and in a key move, he persuaded one of the members of the '92 Group, self-described "militant moderate" Steve Gunderson of Wisconsin, to establish an informal partnership between the two caucuses.[15] The COS's membership grew to about two dozen Republicans, including more activist, confrontationally inclined freshmen like Dick Armey (R-TX), who spearheaded a group of "budget commandos" in his first term to monitor Democratic appropriations bills and offer floor amendments that would curtail spending.[16] Gingrich also maintained the loyalty of some conservative leaders outside of Congress. After Edwards published his scathing *Washington Post* editorial, an angry Paul Weyrich pulled his organization's sponsorship of the annual Conservative Political Action Conference, which Edwards chaired.[17]

The influence and reputation of Gingrich and the COS among their fellow House partisans were ultimately boosted less by these endeavors than by congressional Democrats flexing their muscles. The majority party Democrats had started putting the squeeze on Republicans in the late 1970s, when they gradually brought more bills to the House floor under restrictive rules that limited opportunities to debate and amend them. Though initially justified as a means of curtailing an unruly number of floor amendments, restrictive rules increasingly became a tool that the Democratic Party used to prevent minority party Republicans from offering legislative proposals that might pass or otherwise force marginal Democrats to cast politically difficult votes. Democrats felt especially besieged after the 1980 elections, when Reagan was elected, Republicans took over the Senate, and the House GOP expanded to its largest size in years. As noted in the previous chapter, this growth in the GOP Conference allowed bipartisan coalitions of Republicans and right-leaning Democrats to pass conservative legislation and caused the majority party to lose a larger-than-usual percentage of floor votes. The Democratic Party was emboldened following seat gains in the 1982 midterm elections, however, and it started using restrictive rules more often in the years that followed.[18] After 1984, majority party leaders floated the idea of limiting the amount of floor time dedicated to special-order speeches—a blatant effort to rein in the COS's rhetoric excoriating Democrats—but backed off in the face of anticipated protests by the GOP.[19] Still, congressional Republicans groused about their diminishing influence at the hands of House Democrats.

A controversial event in the opening months of the new Congress would sow deep doubts among Republicans that cooperation and compromise with the majority party were possible. When the November elections were over, the Democratic incumbent in Indiana's 8th congressional district, Frank McCloskey, appeared to have won by just seventy-two votes. Following the discovery of some double counting of ballots, a revised count put his GOP challenger, Richard McIntyre, in the lead by thirty-four votes, and McIntyre was certified the winner by the Indiana Secretary of State. McCloskey demanded a recount, and House Democrats voted on the opening day of Congress not to seat either candidate while the recount was underway. Gingrich immediately advocated for an assertive messaging campaign on behalf of McIntyre, whom the COS had targeted for mentorship as part of their "Big Brother/Little Brother" training program for novice candidates in 1984, but GOP leaders urged restraint. Their strategy seemed warranted when the completed recount gave McIntyre an even bigger, 418-vote margin of victory. However, House Democrats contended that the recount had been handled inconsistently across the state's counties and, ignoring the protestations of Republicans, they formed a special task force of two Democrats and one Republican to decide the outcome of the election.[20]

Suspicious of the majority party's intentions, Bob Michel and other GOP leaders adopted Gingrich's idea and organized a media and lobbying initiative to make the case for seating McIntyre. Minority Whip Trent Lott recruited Gingrich to help generate favorable press coverage, under the condition he would not try to dominate the spotlight. Gingrich went to work, recruiting Republicans to keep the contested election in the headlines of local newspapers, arranging floor time for lawmakers to speak out against seating McCloskey, and even coordinating with the NRCC in anticipation of a special election to fill the Indiana seat.[21] When the task force voted along strict party lines that McCloskey had won the seat by only four votes, Michel, Lott, and other leaders met with O'Neill and warned him that Republican lawmakers were spoiling for a fight.[22] Outraged Republicans kept the House in session overnight with floor speeches blasting Democrats, and they halted chamber business with a "sample Thursday" of endless parliamentary motions. Ignoring their protests, Democrats voted to give the seat to McCloskey, and the entire Republican Conference walked out of the chamber.[23]

In their futile efforts to seat McIntyre, Republican leaders had employed many of the same tactics used in the past by Gingrich and the COS:

press conferences, synchronized floor speeches, and even procedural tricks (such as making an unexpected floor motion to declare McIntyre the winner, which nearly passed because many Democrats were absent).[24] To what extent could Gingrich be given credit for this? He did funnel tactical ideas to Republican leaders through Lynn Martin (R-IL), an intermediary who was leading the Conference fight to seat McIntyre.[25] Yet many Republicans besides Gingrich had pushed for a unified, aggressive, and sustained fight, and they were not necessarily doing so because of Gingrich. They included relatively staid lawmakers like Bill Frenzel (R-MN), who complained that Democrats "think they were born to be kings, and that there's a servant class, and that's the Republicans," and insisted that GOP leaders must speak out on the floor against McCloskey's seating and would "really have to be nasty," even if it meant breaking House rules.[26] And although Gingrich publicly praised Michel for employing bolder techniques than in the past, he did not always seem satisfied with Michel's leadership, and Gingrich and other COS members privately grumbled that GOP leaders were often too tepid or indecisive in the campaign to give McIntyre the seat.[27]

More important than the question of how much credit should be awarded to Gingrich for his party's response to the contested election is whether the operation had convinced Gingrich's colleagues that confrontational tactics held long-term strategic worth. On one hand, an aggressive approach had failed to secure a House seat for McIntyre, and many Conference leaders and senior legislators continued to believe in bipartisan cooperation as the way to achieve valuable legislative successes, especially with a Republican White House and Senate—a fact that Gingrich himself acknowledged. Michel especially did not want the McCloskey-McIntyre dispute to poison the bipartisan well; tellingly, after Republicans had stormed off the floor in protest against seating McCloskey, the minority leader returned to personally congratulate the belatedly elected congressman.[28] On the other hand, there were signs that the Democrats' power play, even if it had been successful in seating McCloskey, had gained Gingrich additional acolytes and would eventually, as Gingrich predicted, help forge "a greatly tougher and more combative Republican Party."[29] In a mid-April meeting of the Conference, attendees were asked their opinion of various tactics that could be used on behalf of McIntyre. The least popular options were the confrontational ones, such as walking out of the chamber or using parliamentary motions to gum up the works, yet they each still received the votes of over two-thirds of survey takers.[30] GOP freshmen were perhaps the most likely converts, having been introduced to the House of Representatives as a place where the governing party played hardball and Gingrich was the most outspoken advocate of fighting back.[31] Recalled one minority party member, "when they stole the Indiana 8 . . . that radicalized a number of Republicans."[32] Interparty tensions also ran high in the months that followed. Verbal tussles broke out, Republicans accused Democrats of more abuses of power, and GOP unity increased on such issues as funding for the Nicaraguan Contras in their guerrilla war against the ruling communist Sandinista regime.[33]

Another important rift in 1985—this time within the Republican Party, not between the two parties—briefly aligned Gingrich and Michel against President Reagan and gave Gingrich a fresh opportunity to underscore the value of party differentiation. The White House had endorsed a major rewrite of the federal tax code, but when faced with a Reagan-endorsed bill crafted principally by House Democrats that eliminated many prized exemptions, congressional Republicans revolted. Most of them, including leaders like Michel, Lott, and Conference Chair Jack Kemp, had wanted a bill that contained larger tax cuts and were frustrated that they had been ignored or contradicted by the president and Democrats throughout the bill drafting process. Gingrich was included in leadership discussions about how to block the bill. In mid-December, shortly before the measure was due to be voted on, he and GOP leaders noticed that, during floor debate about the rule for considering the legislation, some Democrats were griping that the rule denied them the right to amend the bill and protect certain tax benefits for government employees. The Republicans quickly concocted a scheme to stop tax reform by rallying their colleagues to vote against the rule. All but fourteen did so (with Michel and Gingrich among those voting to reject it) and they were joined by enough Democrats to defeat the rule.[34] It was a major embarrassment to the president, and Gingrich was tasked by Michel to prepare congressional Republicans on how to respond to criticism that they had betrayed Reagan.[35]

The defiance of the House GOP leadership swiftly evaporated. Michel did not want to further humiliate the president, who appeared before a meeting of the Conference to ask that lawmakers reconsider their opposition to the tax bill, and White House staff lobbied Republicans to vote with Reagan. Many party leaders ultimately agreed to change their vote on the rule, even if they were unwilling to support the bill itself, but it was the switch of Kemp in particular that drew the ire of Gingrich and other party conservatives. Kemp was the intellectual leader of antitax conservatives in the House, and if he endorsed Reagan's bill, it would mean not only reversing his prior position but also going against the will of the Conference he chaired. However, Kemp worried that opposing tax reform could damage his own plans to run for president. He eventually decided to back the measure, and he announced his decision to the Conference, creating a major intraparty backlash.[36] The breach this created between Gingrich and Kemp was eventually repaired, but Kemp's about-face led to broad demands for greater enforcement of internal party discipline, via changes to party rules if necessary.[37]

Gingrich continued to develop and pursue electioneering tactics in the 99th Congress. He served as a member at large of the NRCC and maintained an alliance with its chair, Guy Vander Jagt. The NRCC also circulated a videotape to Republican candidates that featured Gingrich offering advice on how to rebut Democratic campaign attacks.[38] Per the request of Tennessee Governor Lamar Alexander, Gingrich attended a small gathering of party leaders in mid-1985 to encourage the development of positive themes that might help elect Republicans at the state and local level, and he wrote a lengthy guide for candidates that contained examples of his forward-thinking partisan messaging, including a plea to "listen, learn, and lead" and to think like an "ascending majority party."[39]

Of greater long-term consequence was Gingrich's inheritance of a new external organization with which he could expand his entrepreneurial activities. In the late 1970s, Delaware Governor Pete DuPont had founded GOPAC, a political recruitment and training entity that assisted GOP candidates in state and local races. When DuPont left GOPAC to run for president in the 1988 election, he anointed Gingrich as his successor.[40] Gingrich had already been exploring ways to build an organizational base outside of Congress, having previously created his own political action committee (Conservatives for Hope and Opportunity) and his nonprofit group American Opportunity Foundation, which had worked with the RNC to sponsor student rallies on the one-year anniversary of the military invasion of

Grenada.[41] He envisioned GOPAC as a means to recruit candidates for the US Congress but, more importantly, to teach those candidates how to run on a unified and distinctive conservative message and ultimately, as two journalists put it, to "transform their thinking about what it means to be a Republican."[42] Five years earlier, Gingrich had proposed the creation of party task forces that would inculcate among first-term members his view of effective legislator habits until that behavior "would become the norm for Republican House members." Now GOPAC could fulfill that task. A new nationalized role for GOPAC dovetailed with Gingrich's other electioneering activities, and since the organization was independent, it had more flexibility than the NRCC in how it raised and contributed campaign funds, though it was prohibited from donating directly to congressional campaigns.[43]

As the 99th Congress wound down, Gingrich remained in many ways a gadfly outsider. For example, Michel and Lott were reluctant to let Gingrich lead GOP strategy on Central American policy, a major issue for the party at the time.[44] But Gingrich had been a part of strategic decision-making on the contested Indiana election and the tax bill reform, he was actively involved in the NRCC, and he enjoyed a widening array of institutional resources thanks to a steadily growing COS and his acquisition of GOPAC. Also, a sizeable number of House Republicans had shown that they were not opposed to using bellicose partisan messaging and forceful tactics to take on Democrats. Even presumably institutionalist members like Republican Policy Committee Chair Dick Cheney were echoing Gingrich's call for greater party differentiation and conflict in order to win power in the House. "If there are no real issues dividing us from Democrats," Cheney asked, "why should the country change and make us the majority?" A Cheney-led task force suggested procedural reforms that reflected Gingrich's desire for greater internal harmony. Inspired by rules already adopted by Democrats to promote party unity, the Conference agreed to its own new rules after the 1986 elections. One allowed Michel to identify "leadership issues" that committee Republicans and GOP leaders must cooperate on, and another stated that when a bill came to the floor, the Republican managing the legislation should follow whatever position was taken by the party as a whole. The Conference also adopted a resolution stating that party leaders should follow the dictates of the rank and file, a direct response to Kemp's reversal on tax reform. Taken together, these new Republican Party rules opened the door to greater enforcement of the kind of party cohesion that Gingrich had sought for years.

Conference rules aside, by several measures the House was becoming a place with stronger and more differentiated political parties.[45] Nonetheless, the Republican dream of a GOP House still seemed distant to most. Texas Republican Tom DeLay, who was then finishing his first term in Congress, later recalled his ambition to become his party's whip. But "at that time," he acknowledged, "I thought I'd always be the Minority Whip for . . . my entire career."[46]

Speaker Wright Becomes a Target (1987–1988)

The next Congress got off to an inauspicious start for Gingrich. He was reelected handily despite being targeted for defeat by the Democratic Congressional Campaign Committee (DCCC), but the Republican Party fared poorly in the 1986 midterm elections, losing five seats in the House and their majority in the Senate. Outgoing Speaker Tip O'Neill, a valuable foil for the GOP, would be replaced by Majority Leader Jim Wright of Texas, and while some cautioned that Wright was an aggressive partisan, Gingrich and others wondered if he might be more conciliatory than O'Neill, given Wright's track record of working with Republicans on issues like antidrug policy. If true, the new Speaker would incentivize congressional Republicans to seek compromise rather than confrontation, undermining Gingrich's ongoing efforts to distinguish the two parties.[47]

Undaunted, Gingrich looked for ways he could magnify his influence and that of his allies. The COS, now headed by Bob Walker, had grown to some three dozen members by January 1987.[48] Gingrich remained an active member of the group, chairing its executive committee, giving speeches on its behalf, urging regular attendance at meetings, finding and recruiting outside supporters, developing COS's electoral and messaging strategy, and plugging his "vision, projects, strategies, and tactics" approach to achieving party goals.[49] The COS was also continuing to build its organizational ties within the Conference. Steve Gunderson of the '92 Group had joined the COS's executive committee and became an official COS member in early 1987, and the two organizations worked together on various projects, such as lobbying on a tax and entitlement spending bill in the fall of 1987 and writing position papers for Republican candidates in 1988.[50] Gingrich was named manager of the Conservative Action Team, a group spearheaded by Walker that identified one Republican from each standing committee to be responsible for ensuring that conservative viewpoints were considered by committees and represented on the House floor—a process that could help turn the GOP into what COS member Dick Armey dubbed a "legislative cartel."[51] Another chance for Gingrich to expand his network emerged when notable COS critic Mickey Edwards, the newly elected Republican Research Committee chair, proposed creating an executive committee consisting of the heads of the COS, the '92 Group, and the moderate Wednesday Group to facilitate communication between various wings of the party.[52] Thanks to Gingrich's heightened public profile and years of cultivating the news media, reporters were describing him as a "leader" of his party and of assertive House conservatives in particular.[53]

Gingrich kept composing Manichean messages designed to portray House Democrats as the evil counterparts of a noble Republican Party. At one meeting of the COS in April 1987, he suggested that the declining economy should be coined the "Democrat Recession of 1987–88." He recommended at another meeting that his colleagues should compare Democrats with defeated left-wing parties in Europe, and he declared that "the Republicans are the party to renew the American dream; the Democrats believe the dream is dead."[54] Gingrich highlighted several popular initiatives that could distinguish the two parties, such as stricter drug enforcement and fighting communism, and he promoted a broad agenda of positive, solution-oriented "humanitarian Republicanism" that reflected a party that "thinks and acts like a majority." Democrats' poor fiscal policies and mismanagement of the House were common themes, and Gingrich and other COS members wrote chapters on the subject in a book titled *House of Ill Repute*, which they paid to publish and distribute.[55]

Ethics became the issue that would quickly subsume all others. When the new Congress opened, the House Ethics Committee was in the middle of a probe into the potentially illegal activities of two Democratic incumbents, Bill Boner (TN) and Banking Committee Chairman Fernand St Germain (RI). In February 1987, two other congressional Democrats were linked to a defense firm that admitted paying bribes to elected officials.[56]

By emphasizing corruption within the Democratic Party—as he had done previously against Democrats like Charles Diggs and Gerry Studds—Gingrich could construct a novel line of attack against the majority while simultaneously distracting voters from the burgeoning Iran-Contra White House scandal and ethics accusations against Attorney General Edwin Meese.[57] Yet Gingrich insisted to his COS collaborators that congressional ethics was "a real and institutional fight, not a right-wing political vendetta."[58]

St Germain was the most prominent initial target of Gingrich and the COS. When the Ethics Committee cleared him in mid-April 1987, Gingrich wrote letters to the chair of the committee questioning its rationale for exonerating St Germain, and he brought a privileged resolution to the House floor that would start a fresh investigation into the chairman.[59] Gingrich wanted to go even further and make the case for widespread Democratic corruption within the entire House. The COS concurred with Gingrich that the group should establish its own ethics task force to investigate unethical lawmakers. In addition, Gingrich and three other COS members offered an amendment to the legislative appropriations bill in June that would create an independent commission in the House to investigate ethical violations by lawmakers and propose ways the chamber could better police itself. Gingrich and his likeminded colleagues repeated the theme of ethical misconduct by Democrats in speeches delivered around the country, and they eagerly spoke to reporters about the ethics of the governing party, hoping to drum up national, state, and even local news coverage. For instance, the morning before they offered their amendment, Gingrich and fellow amendment sponsors released a list of ten House Democrats suspected of legal or ethical wrongdoing. By the end of 1987, Gingrich was decrying the House as "an essentially corrupt left-wing machine whose ethics committee's job is to run a sequence of whitewashes."[60]

Meanwhile, House Republicans grew increasingly distressed about Speaker Jim Wright. Those who had warned he would be an assertive and impetuous party loyalist had been proven correct. Wright believed the speakership should be the center of policy-making leadership for the nation as well as the House, and unlike his predecessor, he involved himself deeply in crafting bills and sought unilateral authority to appoint Democrats to key decision-making committees. He pushed for quick action on an ambitious legislative agenda that included trade, welfare reform, aid for the homeless, and funding for water projects. Republicans were offended by Wright's efforts to end the Nicaraguan civil war through personal diplomacy, which undercut the pro-Contra stance of the White House and threatened President Reagan's ability to set American foreign policy.[61] Even worse from their perspective, many bills brought to the floor in the first few months of 1987 were considered under restrictive rules that prevented minority party members from offering amendments.[62] Wright was threatening to make the House GOP entirely irrelevant.

Republican leaders responded by spotlighting the Speaker's centralization of power and pressing for more opportunities for the minority party and individual lawmakers to legislate. Gingrich feared that Wright would amass more power if left unchecked, so he treated the Speaker as a strategic "center of gravity" who, if damaged politically, could weaken the entire majority party.[63] Specifically, he made investigating Wright a key part of his campaign against what he and his allies described as an unethical Democratic Party. They began searching for evidence of possible malfeasance, feeding those bits of evidence to reporters along with accusatory quotes from Gingrich, and then circulating the news stories they wrote as mounting proof of corruption. Gingrich included Wright on his June 1987 list of ten corrupt Democrats, and shortly thereafter, he put the COS on notice that he would file ethics charges against both the Speaker and his second in command, Majority Whip Tony Coelho (D-CA).[64] He was encouraged to keep digging for dirt when the *Washington Post* revealed in September that lobbyists had bought large numbers of Wright's book *Reflections of a Public Man*, and that the Speaker had received royalties of over half the revenue, an unusually generous amount.[65]

GOP leaders stood behind many of Gingrich's efforts to draw attention to ethical misconduct in Congress. Michel said he was open to forming some sort of ethics investigatory group in the Conference; he established a task force led by Dick Cheney to examine the way the House was run, including how it policed the behavior of its members; and he joined all but two members of Conference leadership in voting for Gingrich's June ethics amendment.[66] Charging the Speaker himself with breaking House rules was another matter, however. Even some of Gingrich's closest associates doubted his claims and worried about the potential blowback from accusing Wright directly. When Gingrich suggested at a COS meeting in September

1987 that Wright was so tainted that a cross-party coalition could be persuaded to replace him as Speaker with a moderate Democrat (a repeat of his idea from seven years earlier to remove Tip O'Neill as Speaker via a cross-party coalition), others dismissed the idea as unrealistic.[67]

The Speaker was in little danger so long as enough Republicans did not become exasperated with him to the point that they joined Gingrich's crusade. But Wright did himself no favors. In late October 1987, he made a controversial last-minute decision to allow welfare reform legislation to be added to an unrelated, must-pass budget reconciliation bill (so called because it "reconciled" spending and taxes with what Congress had agreed to in a budget resolution passed earlier that year). When the rule for considering the ungainly bill was defeated, Democrats adjourned the House and, minutes later, reconvened to create a new "legislative day," thereby permitting the chamber to vote on a second, modified rule. After that rule passed, the reconciliation bill, now without the welfare reform language, passed—but only after the voting clock was held open long enough for one Democrat to switch his vote. Gingrich jumped to his feet and made a series of parliamentary inquiries to delay the final vote, but his efforts were in vain.[68]

Michel appointed Gingrich to lead their party's messaging in response to the Democrats' procedural stunts, and COS members swore to fight back hard against future shenanigans. One COS member, Joe Barton (R-TX), wondered whether it would be possible to impeach Wright.[69] Outrage over how the governing party had passed reconciliation, which had robbed the GOP of two floor victories in one day, went well beyond the COS, though. Michel was irate, and Conference Chair Dick Cheney, normally measured in tone, called the Speaker "a heavy-handed son of a bitch." Lott, who had broken his lectern in anger when the bill passed, declared that he was "so mad at Jim Wright and [Majority Leader] Tom Foley I don't want to talk to them."[70] Moderate rank and file Republicans expressed fury too—members like Bill Gradison (R-OH), who announced, "I'm partisan as hell now." Even some Democrats were alarmed that legislative trickery had been required to overcome poor decision-making by their leaders that had nearly killed a major bill.[71]

Though incensed with Wright, this incident alone was not enough to convince Michel or other Republicans that the Speaker had broken the chamber's ethics rules, as Gingrich charged, let alone had committed a crime. Skeptical colleagues rolled their eyes at Gingrich's shotgun approach to attacking the Speaker, making allegations against Wright that were taken out of context or had little evidentiary support, and at his harsh language peppered with exaggerations and insinuations. He frequently called Wright the "most corrupt" or "least ethical" Speaker of the century. At one time, Gingrich compared Wright to Mussolini; at another, he suggested that the Speaker had browbeat a magazine into not publishing a negative story about him; and on yet another occasion, by mentioning that a former election challenger to Wright had later been murdered, he implied that perhaps the Speaker was not above assassinating his opponents.[72] Michel admitted to a reporter that "I from time to time have problems with his [Gingrich's] methodology," and that questioning Wright's ethics "certainly is not my agenda," which prompted an aggrieved written retort from Gingrich to the minority leader.[73] As Democrats began demanding scrutiny into Gingrich's own campaign activities,[74] members of the '92 Group warned him of the risks associated with targeting the Speaker, and they advised him to consult legal experts about his accusations against Wright and to ask party leaders for help.[75] When Michel told Gingrich that his evidence of Wright's supposed wrongdoings needed to be reviewed privately by lawmakers with legal training, he relented, and the results were discouraging: after examining the materials, Bob Livingston (R-LA) and Jim Sensenbrenner (R-WI) concluded that Gingrich had a very weak case. "I tried to restrain him," Livingston subsequently recalled. "I was trying to advise him to do it right, without getting too inflammatory in the friggin' press."[76]

Wright burned another bridge with the GOP in late February 1988. Each party had offered a bill to fund the Nicaraguan Contras, differing in both the amounts provided and the proportion of funds given for humanitarian purposes. Michel believed he had Wright's word that the Republicans' funding measure would get an up-or-down vote. Instead, both bills were brought to the floor in such a way that the first vote cast by lawmakers would be to amend the Republican bill with language from the Democratic bill; only in the unlikely event that that amendment failed would lawmakers be able to vote on the minority party's proposal directly. Republicans were mad all over again. Even Michel, who once confessed his discomfort at being a "perpetual antagonist," was livid, and he complained that Wright could not be trusted.[77]

Republican leaders countered these intemperate abuses of power by Democrats, as well as other grievances, such as the steady rise in the number of restrictive rules, by continuing to publicize them in the media and on the House floor. In May 1988, for example, they sponsored a day of press releases and floor speeches to educate voters about Democratic mismanagement and explain how, in Lott's words, "the Speaker is destroying the comity and uniformity" of the chamber.[78] Other Republicans reacted differently. For some, including Gingrich, it justified new Conference rules and practices to enforce stronger party discipline, thus denying Democrats the luxury of passing legislation and restrictive rules with help from members of the minority party.[79] At a COS meeting held in July 1987, Gingrich stipulated that ranking committee members who lobbied Republicans to vote against the party ought to be demoted.[80] Seven months later, when a dozen defecting GOPers helped defeat Reagan's Contra aid package in February 1988, they did so hours after Henry Hyde (R-IL) had suggested at a COS meeting that Republicans who cost their party a win on Contra funding should lose their committee assignments.[81] For other members of the minority, the partisan abuse was reason enough to exit the House altogether. Lott called 1987 "a totally useless year" and, seeing no hope that Republicans would retake the chamber any time soon, opted to run for the Senate—a decision that would begin a chain of events resulting in even more influence for Gingrich and his colleagues who relished political confrontation.[82] Finally, there was a growing segment of the Conference who, like Gingrich, shared the sentiment of Dick Cheney toward Wright: "We want his head."[83]

While all this was going on, Gingrich had enlisted the help of attorneys to strengthen his ethics case versus the Speaker while redoubling efforts to build a self-reinforcing media loop of negative stories about Wright. More reporters were taking the bait, writing articles that often contained more innuendo than fact but that nonetheless painted a portrait of unseemly behavior by the Speaker. A particularly damaging story published in the DC magazine *Regardie's* revealed that before becoming Speaker, Wright had intervened with federal overseers of the banking system to prevent excessive scrutiny of financially unstable banks in his home state of Texas—including banks that, it later turned out, had mismanaged their funds.[84]

May 1988 was a critical turning point. Gingrich's calls for an investigation of Wright had been echoed by over forty newspapers by then, and on May 10 the *Wall Street Journal* joined the chorus, the most prominent media outlet to do so at that point.[85] Gingrich earned another valuable endorsement eight days afterward, when the good-government group Common Cause, whose president he had been courting assiduously for nearly a year, requested that the House Ethics Committee investigate Wright. The request was covered by the country's top newspapers and television networks, and one congressional Democrat feared that Common Cause was lending "greater credibility to what has been a partisan effort."[86] The Speaker was irritated by what he saw as a smear campaign based on unfounded allegations, but he begrudgingly agreed to cooperate with a probe by the House Ethics Committee. On May 26, Gingrich finally submitted a formal complaint against the Speaker to the committee. By now, Gingrich was far from alone in believing that Wright had broken House rules: he released a letter supporting an investigation into the complaint that was signed by seventy-two other Republicans—over 40 percent of the Conference, including every elected GOP leader but Michel.[87] Two weeks later, the Ethics Committee began an inquiry into six different accusations lodged against Wright, and in July the committee agreed to hire a special prosecutor to lead it.[88]

What had been a quixotic one-man operation to dig up dirt on the most powerful person in the House had blossomed into a serious investigation with potentially dire consequences for Speaker Wright. Both Vice President George H. W. Bush, who was running for his party's nomination to succeed President Reagan, and Reagan himself publicly called for a formal inquiry into Wright.[89] That Gingrich had managed to convince a House committee to look into the Speaker's ethics was seen by many Republicans, especially those who detested how the Speaker ran the chamber, as a major victory. As Gingrich dined in a nearby restaurant while the Ethics Committee voted to look into Wright, several of his fellow minority party members came by to congratulate him, and an exultant Carl Pursell (R-MI) called out, "Way to go, Newt!"[90]

Gingrich did not suspend his anticorruption campaign while the Ethics

Committee's investigatory process was underway. He warned of protests at the 1988 Democratic National Convention if Wright remained its chair, though the protests never materialized.[91] In September, he and Bob Walker wrote to fellow Republicans identifying seventeen Democrats who, they argued, also deserved close examination by the Ethics Committee, and they tossed in new allegations against the Speaker for good measure.[92] In a private memo he wrote to other GOP House members that same month, Gingrich admitted that his broadsides on Democrats' ethics might undermine interparty relations in the chamber, but "Republicans can never accept collegiality at the price of corruption or rigged elections."[93] Even Michel eventually joined in, demanding an ethics investigation into Wright after the Speaker appeared to reveal classified CIA information on US covert activities in Central America.[94]

While his crusade against Democratic ethics garnered him the most headlines, Gingrich also spent much of the 100th Congress engaged in party-wide electioneering. He traveled around the country to recruit candidates, distributed funds from his Friends of Newt Gingrich political action committee, and worked with party leaders to develop election-year narratives.[95] Gingrich maintained GOPAC's involvement in state legislative elections,[96] helping Republicans like Robert Wicker, who was elected to a formerly Democratic state senate seat in Mississippi and who would later join the House of Representatives in 1994.[97] Gingrich also began formulating plans to increase GOPAC's membership and finances and use it to produce messages that all Republicans running for office would echo.[98] For the 1988 election, he came up with three themes: the un-American, "left-wing value system" of "Dukakis Democrats" (referring to the Democratic presidential nominee, Massachusetts Governor Michael Dukakis); a GOP agenda of "choice and empowerment"; and expanding the Republican Party's "center-right, anti-left" coalition by following one of his favorite models for action, "listen, learn, help, lead." Gingrich touted other ideas and tactics in audio and video recordings for congressional candidates[99]—recordings like "We Are a Majority," in which he urged Republicans to conceptualize politics as a dichotomy between the good "center-right" majority and bad liberals. Gingrich's objective was transformational as well as electoral. One memo crafted by his office proclaimed that "the goal is not just to elect candidates to office, but to create a political environment nationwide in which Republican philosophy dominates political thought, with the main beneficiary being Republicans in the House of Representatives."[100]

The presidential election absorbed much of Gingrich's attention. He initially supported the candidacy of his longtime House colleague Jack Kemp, offering feedback on Kemp's media appearances and stumping in Iowa on his behalf.[101] For Gingrich, however, the election was less about the fate of any particular Republican presidential candidate than it was about creating coattails for a GOP takeover of the House and shifting the country in a conservative direction. The COS posed questions to the party's nominees for the presidency, looking to decide which one best matched its strategic perspective and policy agenda, and Gingrich told the group that all the nominees should echo the organization's rhetoric so that the COS "defines the fight."[102] During his speech at the Republican National Convention in August, Gingrich wore a button that read "no more 98.4%," referring to the high reelection rate of House incumbents that helped keep Democrats in power.[103]

When Kemp's campaign faltered in early 1988, Gingrich shifted his allegiance to Vice President Bush. Doing so angered other Georgia Republicans who had been supporting Pat Robertson's candidacy, and in retaliation they blocked Gingrich from winning a seat at the Republican National Convention. But Gingrich had made a prescient maneuver: when Bush won the nomination, he had an inside track to help shape Bush's general election campaign, and he sent the campaign a variety of themes and tactics to try, such as using carefully written rhetoric to "define Daffy Dukakis and the Loony Left."[104] Gingrich was joined in the effort by the COS. In conjunction with members of the '92 Group, the COS wrote up a list of needed reforms to Congress, to be submitted to Bush "to run against the House with," and Gingrich recruited COS member Bob Smith (R-NH) to write a Dear Colleague letter to lawmakers highlighting Governor Dukakis's controversial prisoner furlough program.[105]

For all of Gingrich's attempts to push his party to victory, the results of the 1988 elections were dispiriting. Bush's decisive triumph over Dukakis was tempered by the failure of the GOP to gain control of either chamber of Congress, and the House Democratic majority grew slightly, a historically unusual event for the party that had lost the presidential election.

Gingrich's other entrepreneurial activities, however, had paid off in the 100th Congress. His tireless focus on Wright's ethics, his manipulation of the news media, and post-Watergate reporters' innate interest in political scandal had resulted in an unprecedented ethics probe of the Speaker. By the end of that year, Gingrich had received more mentions in the country's top newspapers than either of his party's top two House leaders (see chapter 7). The confrontational strategy of Gingrich and the COS was also gaining adherents, and even Michel's tone had become more partisan and barbed. "The record of [ethics] enforcement in this House is a national disgrace," Michel told the Conference in December 1988, adding that the GOP would stand behind another Democrat challenging Wright for the speakership, the same scheme Gingrich had briefly contemplated against Wright a year earlier, and more seriously against Tip O'Neill in 1980.

In addition, Gingrich's organizational sources of power were expanding in size and reach. The Conference—frustrated by majority party violations of regular order and by the defections of GOP leaders and committee ranking members on floor votes, and building upon the rules it had adopted two years before—was now marching toward a greater embrace of partisan activism and empowerment of its leaders to enforce internal unity. The party restructured its committee assignment process to give leadership more say in those assignments and, following Gingrich's suggestion, allowed Michel to pick new minority party members of the powerful Rules Committee, which drafted the procedures for considering individual bills.[106] Continuing the informal partnership that had begun the previous year, the COS and the '92 Group held a joint meeting after the election to formulate strategy for the next Congress. The unexpected resignation of the House GOP's minority counsel, an institutionally minded Michel staffer named Hyde Murray, was taken as a sign of the ascendancy of conservative Conference activists who had criticized Murray in the past. The party also elected several COS members to leadership positions in December 1988: Bill McCollum (R-FL), who beat outgoing Conference Secretary Robert Lagomarsino (R-CA) in the race for Conference Vice Chair; Vin Weber, who defeated Joe McDade (R-PA) in a bid to replace Lagomarsino as Conference Secretary; and Duncan Hunter (R-CA), a failed candidate for the chairmanship of the Republican Policy Committee the year before, who was elected to head the GOP Research Committee over Steve Bartlett (R-TX).[107]

Yet Michel and other senior lawmakers were still wary of Gingrich, and while "there was a lot less animosity between Newt and Bob than historians have concluded," a Michel staffer later told the authors, there remained important differences between them.[108] The minority leader was still not convinced that nationalizing congressional elections was wise, believing that elections were won at the district level, a view endorsed by a task force he had formed after the 1986 elections.[109] Even more distasteful to Michel was Gingrich's willingness to publicly assail Republicans who, he claimed, were insufficiently conservative, had failed to campaign aggressively to win control of Congress, or had blurred the differences between the parties. For example, when White House Office of Management and Budget (OMB) Director James Miller defended a budget agreement with congressional Democrats before a group of COS members in December 1987, Gingrich retorted that the White House was helping "those who are trying to ruin Republicans" with a budget that "sells out Republican values."[110] "Republicans are stupid" for failing to reach out to urban voters, Gingrich told an audience of party members at the 1988 Republican National Convention; "No other word is strong enough." He also complained to the journalist Hedrick Smith that "the House Republican party, as a culture, has a defeatist, minority mentality" with "no internal habits of inventing a coherent strategy or following it through for any length of time." Gingrich bemoaned the fact that the GOP lacked a strong leader in Congress. Reagan, he told Smith, was "this tremendously nice, likeable King Victoria. Everybody likes him but where the hell's Disraeli? Or Gladstone?"[111]

Gingrich Rises, Wright Falls (January–May 1989)

Gingrich did not let the disappointing 1988 elections keep him from continuing his entrepreneurial efforts. At an office meeting in December, Gingrich announced that he had formulated new plans to "help design a majority-empowering, community-growing, vision oriented, humanitarian GOP system." Accordingly, he kept up efforts during the first five months of 1989 to sharpen the differences between both parties, tarnish the image of Democrats, and eventually bring about an electoral and policy realignment.[112] These months were also marked by a pair of critical events that heightened Gingrich's formal power and further burnished his reputation as a formidable antagonist to the majority party. To many lawmakers and outside observers, these two events seemed to confirm that relying on harsh partisan rhetoric and confrontation was an effective and profitable strategy for those who instigated it.

The first event was Gingrich's election as whip in March 1989. Gingrich and the COS had long seen their party's leadership as an obstacle to achieving their strategic goals, and COS members occasionally debated how to oust Conference leaders if they could not be persuaded to change their strategies and tactics. An aide to Bob Walker advised the congressman in 1984 that many COS lawmakers needed to visit the districts of freshmen Republican candidates because, if those candidates were elected, "you won't have an incoming class owing their loyalty to just three or four of you. You'll have an incoming class owing their loyalty to 15 or 20. Your bloc becomes that much more effective *come leadership election time* [emphasis added]." In mid-1987, COS member Buz Lukens (R-OH) adamantly insisted that removing even one "squishy leader" of the party would be a success, and the following February the group despaired over the "incompetence" of GOP leaders who had, among other things, failed to pass Reagan's Contra funding bill that month.[113] Talk turned into action after the 1988 elections, when several members of the COS were elected to Conference leadership positions. Yet Gingrich opted not to seek a formal leadership post, apart from becoming the ranking member of the House Administration Committee, and many still shared the sentiments expressed by a Republican leader four years before: "He's a very creative guy, but he couldn't get elected dogcatcher on our side of the aisle."[114]

A fortuitous series of developments soon provided Gingrich with the potential to not only dispel that impression, but also outrank all of his COS brethren. When Trent Lott was elected to the US Senate, Dick Cheney was chosen by the Conference to succeed him as GOP whip. Not long afterward, the Senate rejected President Bush's first choice for Secretary of Defense, Sen. John Tower (R-TX), due to allegations of womanizing and excessive drinking. Bush then nominated Cheney to the post instead.[115] This move left the Republican whip position vacant, and Gingrich decided to grab the opportunity, throwing his hat into the ring along with Chief Deputy Whip Ed Madigan (R-IL), a Michel ally and a more establishment-minded Republican. Vin Weber warned Gingrich that "this is a concrete job, not a visionary job. It's not what you're good at."[116] But other COS Republicans applauded the chance to embed the intellectual leader of their group within party leadership. Shortly after Gingrich announced his candidacy, COS aide Tracy Updegraff wrote to the organization that "we now have the opportunity to put Newt into the official leadership as House Republican Whip where his vision can turn the minority mentality into a governing, majority, House Republican Party."[117]

Gingrich and his campaign team, led by the organizationally adept Weber, worked diligently ahead of the election on March 22 to round up votes, solicit lobbying assistance from outside interest groups, and claim enough commitments of support to convince undecided Republicans that Gingrich would win. Other COS members also helped. Joe Barton, for example, called over thirty Republicans within days of Gingrich's announcement to urge them to vote for him.[118] Gingrich's friends also promoted the idea that he, unlike Madigan, would eschew pointless bipartisan compromises and fight hard for GOP control of Congress, while Gingrich downplayed ideology with his less conservative colleagues to overcome their doubts about making him whip. For his part, Michel took some early steps to keep Gingrich from winning: not only did he lobby Madigan to run in the first place, but he also convinced Conference Chair Jerry Lewis (R-CA) to withdraw from the race, lest he and Madigan divide the anti-Gingrich vote. Michel moved to the sidelines, however, following a surprise visit to his office by Gingrich's closest moderate and conservative allies, who demanded that the minority leader not intervene directly in the election.[119]

Gingrich's victory in that election—by the narrowest of margins, 87 to 85—was a watershed moment. Now, Gingrich was near the very top of the Republican leadership ladder. As one GOP leadership aide later put it, "In January 1989, who would have imagined that Newt would be whip and Dick Cheney would be Secretary of Defense? That was just impossible."[120] The Georgia congressman would have a say in committee assignments, thanks to the rules adopted by his party the previous December that granted leaders more influence in assigning lawmakers to committees, and going forward, he could take advantage of his formal authority and the resources of the whip's office to bring the Conference closer to embracing his strategic objectives and tactics.

How did Gingrich manage to pull off his narrow win? Though he drew obvious support from the party's younger members and its growing Southern contingent, a number of his votes came from moderate Republicans. Gingrich had astutely cultivated them as partners over the years, and he may have promised to give them more influence in exchange for their support. Steve Gunderson, a member of Gingrich's campaign team, later explained that many of his fellow moderates did not think Gingrich was a threatening vanguard of extreme conservatism but "saw him as embodying a kind of activism that . . . concentrated instead on an agenda that promised to unite Republicans."[121] Meanwhile, Republicans who preferred a regionally diverse leadership team were hesitant to select another party leader from the same state as Michel. Madigan "may have lost some votes simply because some people didn't want to put all their eggs in the Illinois basket," one of Madigan's committee colleagues recalled.[122] Frustration with Speaker Wright and congressional Democrats aided Gingrich as well. Indeed, those who signed the letter in May 1988 supporting Gingrich's ethics charges against Wright were more likely to vote for Gingrich than those who did not, controlling for other factors.[123] Perhaps most important of all, Gingrich's election was seen by both his fans and his detractors as validation of the confrontational and message-oriented partisan tactics he touted. He was "the Great Divider," wrote the columnist Thomas Edsall, who "was perhaps the most aggressive proponent of using divisive strategies" on behalf of his party.[124] Gingrich described his election victory in a *Washington Post* article as an endorsement of "greater activism, new ideas and energy and an aggressive effort to build a GOP majority in the House." He pledged to "fight when the Democrats try to cheat and use the rules and other devices to avoid giving Republicans a fair break," and he announced that voters wanted to "overhaul the political corruption which has become endemic to the liberal welfare state." Gingrich's spin aside, Michel conceded that the election of the new whip "says to me . . . that they [House Republicans] want us to be more activated and more visible and more aggressive and that we can't be content with business as usual."[125]

The second major event in 1989 that further strengthened Gingrich's position in the Conference was sudden turnover in the leadership of both the House and the Democratic Caucus. Expecting that the Ethics

Committee would find abundant proof of Speaker Wright's misconduct, Gingrich pressed the committee to open its findings to the public. He and other Republicans also continued to hammer away at Wright's reputation, especially after the Senate rejected John Tower as Defense Secretary, which angered Republicans who either thought Wright's offenses had been more severe than Tower's or, as one told Wright privately, simply "want[ed] a Texan for a Texan" in retaliation.[126]

In mid-April, the Ethics Committee, led by its hard-hitting special counsel, Richard Phelan, accused the Speaker of having broken nearly seventy rules of the House. Many of the charges were redundant, were predicated on weak evidence, or used questionable interpretations of chamber rules, and Wright promised to fight them.[127] But the Speaker would need support from his Caucus to win— support that had been weakened by deep disgruntlement over his micro-managerial, standoffish leadership style, which included not only pushing bills through the House but unilaterally appointing certain Democrats to leadership posts without consultation. Wright "talks to people about doing something they already had planned to do and they end up feeling that their arm is broken," one Democratic staffer complained. Dan Rostenkowski, chair of the powerful Ways and Means Committee, warned that "Jim's concern is to make the trains run on time, but he doesn't know that the trains are loaded with dynamite." Democrats were especially angry at Wright after he botched a salary increase for lawmakers in early 1989. Wright had revealed the results of a private poll that embarrassed legislators by showing that they wanted a pay raise without having to vote for one.[128]

As the days passed, the news media piled on, digging up more negative stories about the Speaker—including a damning discovery that his top aide, John Mack, had committed aggravated assault as a young man—while columnists predicted that his days were numbered. The investigatory media atmosphere encouraged by Gingrich prompted journalists to scrutinize other congressmen too. Smelling blood, reporters began to pry into the financial dealings of the Democratic whip, Tony Coelho (D-CA), prompting Coelho's sudden resignation from Congress, which put even more pressure on Wright to do the same and which seemed to vindicate Gingrich's anticorruption crusade. Finally, on May 31, Wright addressed the House and announced he would step down from the speakership in early June and leave the House later that month. He would be the first Speaker in history to quit office mid-term following charges of ethical violations. Democrats were stunned and demoralized.[129]

In many ways, Wright had himself to blame for his ignominious departure from the House. His forceful partisanship, distant personal relationships with the Democratic rank and file, shabby treatment of the minority party, and poor financial choices and political decisions had left him vulnerable. But to Gingrich goes the credit for being the first and most vocal House Republican to claim that Wright was unethical and then pursue that claim unrelentingly with reporters and other members of his party. By bringing down the Speaker, the Georgian had established a reputation as a giant-killer, demonstrating how partisan messaging designed to be repeated by reporters and influential outside groups could raise an entrepreneur's public profile and stain the image of Congress and its governing party. At a Conference meeting held the day after Wright's resignation, Gingrich's GOP colleagues stood and applauded him.[130]

Conclusion

It is hard to overstate the change in Gingrich's fortunes from early 1985 to mid-1989. In just over four years, he had evolved from a backbencher known for his arrogance and ineffective confrontational tactics into the second-highest leader in his party. By claiming Speaker Jim Wright's head for a trophy (as Dick Cheney had demanded), Gingrich had finally convinced a majority of the Conference that he—not Minority Leader Michel—could fight back effectively against Democrats, if not end the GOP's decades-long stint as the House minority party. No longer an outsider, Gingrich was now a rising star.

As a party entrepreneur, Gingrich had employed a variety of strategic means to achieve his objectives. Messaging may have been his most noteworthy tactic during this time. By relentlessly bombarding reporters, editorial writers, and good government advocates with allegations of Jim Wright's improprieties, he was able to create a degree of reasonable doubt about the Speaker's ethics and compel an internal investigation that yielded enough damning accusations to pressure Wright to go. Gingrich also composed provocative missives to attack the ethics of other congressional

Democrats and aid the campaigns of GOP candidates. Messaging was not the only kind of tactic that Gingrich used effectively, however. He had also run a successful campaign for whip and had been involved in a panoply of campaign activities on behalf of his party. In addition, he was able to draw upon the support of his allies in the COS and bring moderates into the group's orbit, building an organizational base broad enough to support his messaging campaigns and, eventually, his election as party whip. He had also started expanding the role of GOPAC as an electioneering tool.

However, for all of Gingrich's entrepreneurial endeavors, he had not dramatically altered voters' behavior or moved the needle of public opinion very far. One poll conducted in March 1989 found that 63 percent of Americans believed that members of Congress were "living up to the ethical standards of their office" fairly or very well, and after the Ethics Committee issued its damning report on Wright, a *Washington Post* survey found that only 35 percent of respondents were following the news about the Speaker's ethics fairly or very closely.[131] In another survey taken in early May 1989, 70 percent said that Wright's ethics would not impact their vote for Congress, and while three times as many respondents believed the Speaker was guilty than not, nearly half (45 percent) were unsure. Although House Republicans might have complained loudly about how Democrats ran the chamber, Michel admitted that, for most citizens, such griping results only in "'MEGO'—my eyes glaze over."[132]

Gingrich's entrepreneurialism was more successful at altering the internal dynamics of Congress than it was at influencing public perceptions of the majority party or the institution. His unswerving eagerness to fight Democrats and gain a GOP majority in the House; his foundation, acquisition, and expansion of organizations to carry out his entrepreneurial tactics; his strategic partnership with GOP moderates; his campaign assistance to Republican candidates, especially new ones—all helped extend Gingrich's reach within the Conference, as did his party's reaction to the oppressive rule of House Democrats. For Gingrich, the three legs of the Lykke stool of military strategy were becoming more equal in length. It would take additional hard work, aid from others, and good fortune if Gingrich wanted to gain more power and bring a GOP majority and a more conservative American society to fruition.

CHAPTER 4

ENTREPRENEURIAL INSIDER (1989–1994)

Newt Gingrich's election as Republican whip inaugurated a new stage in his congressional career. No longer a party outsider, Gingrich was now second in command, responsible for counting votes and helping craft party strategy. In this chapter, we outline his major entrepreneurial activities from the beginning of his term as minority whip through the end of the 103rd Congress (1993–1994) and explain how they stemmed from his partisan and personal goals (see table 4.1). Although this period ended with Gingrich's two greatest triumphs—a Republican majority in the House of Representatives, and his own election as House Speaker—it also foreshadowed problems he would face in the years that followed.

Fresh Challenges and Opportunities (1989–1990)

Gingrich faced several potential hurdles as a newly minted whip. First, he had become a major target for Democrats, who were fed up with his incendiary politics and vowed to take revenge on him for driving Jim Wright out of the speakership. The new majority whip, Bill Alexander (D-AR), led the way, denouncing Gingrich as a "neo-McCarthyite" and formally charging him with both misusing campaign contributions and securing a shady deal to publicize his 1984 book *Window of Opportunity* (an obvious parallel to what Gingrich had accused Wright of doing). In response, Gingrich asked his staff to flag any potential ethical problems in his own background.

Table 4.1. Gingrich as Entrepreneurial Insider (1989–1994)

Congress	Major Activity	Type of Tactic	Primary Strategic Objective(s)
101st (1989–1990)	Expands messaging operations of whip	Messaging	Draw sharper partisan distinctions
	Opposes Bush-endorsed budget and tax plan	Subverting, Legislating	Draw sharper partisan distinctions
	Expands GOPAC electioneering activities	Electioneering	Nationalize elections, improve electoral competitiveness of GOP
102nd (1991–1992)	Criticizes Democrats on ethics	Messaging	Tarnish reputation of (Democratic-led) House
	Develops and advertises broad "transformative" policy proposals	Electioneering, Messaging	Nationalize elections, heighten personal profile/power
	Expands GOPAC electioneering activities	Electioneering	Nationalize elections, improve electoral competitiveness of GOP
	Seeks replacement of party leaders	Power-Seeking	Heighten personal profile/ power
103rd (1993–1994)	Whips opposition against Democratic bills	Legislating	Draw sharper partisan distinctions, improve electoral competitiveness of GOP
	Works to pass NAFTA	Legislating	Develop/enact conservative legislation
	Threatens to challenge Michel, announces his candidacy	Subverting, Power-Seeking	Heighten personal profile/ power
	GOPAC training, recruitment, mailings	Electioneering	Nationalize elections, improve electoral competitiveness of GOP
	Urges colleagues to contribute to GOP campaigns	Electioneering	Improve electoral competitiveness of GOP
	Teaches and disseminates college course	Messaging	Nationalize elections, draw sharper partisan distinctions
	Initiates, helps write and advertise Contract with America	Messaging	Nationalize elections, develop/enact conservative legislation

Alexander's charges were eventually dismissed or settled, but lingering Democratic anger would fuel future attacks.[1]

Democrats were not the only ones unhappy with Gingrich's political ascendancy. A second obstacle for Gingrich was that many Republicans remained distrustful of his confrontational approach to politics. Vin Weber divulged that Gingrich did "not have a lot of personal friends." The leader of the party, Bob Michel, was especially suspicious. He acknowledged privately that he would have to "make do with Newt as my whip," but he disliked Gingrich's tactics and was irritated by the Georgian's accusations that he and other senior Republicans were ideological moderates who had settled for minority status.[2] One of Gingrich's colleagues later insisted that the Georgian "saw Bob as being a very honest guy who was really attempting to do the best for the country," yet Gingrich did not shy away from exceeding his own authority and being surreptitiously dismissive of Michel.[3] In mid-1989, when Gingrich proposed tackling campaign finance and ethics issues in a partisan way that contradicted Michel's strategy, the minority leader shot it down and scolded Gingrich in front of other House Republicans. Gingrich recalled it as the start of a "very rocky period when I didn't understand the responsibilities of whip and he [Michel] clubbed me around the head and shoulders occasionally."[4] The whip tried to improve his relationship with the minority leader, but tensions between the pair would last for as long as Michel served in Congress.[5]

A third potential hindrance to Gingrich was the loss of both Wright and Democratic whip Tony Coelho as foils. The new Speaker, Tom Foley (D-WA), had a more sedate and genial temperament than Wright, and when one of Gingrich's aides circulated a rumor that Foley was gay, the GOP whip was forced to distance himself from the widely condemned insinuation.[6] But the change in leadership proved to be less of a problem for Gingrich because House Democrats were still clamping down on the procedural rights of minority party Republicans—for the first time, the majority of the rules for considering bills were restrictive, limiting debate time and amendments—which eroded bipartisan comity and gave Gingrich greater license to use confrontational tactics against the party in power.[7] Subdued at first, by the spring of 1990 Gingrich was back to his old self, calling the majority party a collection of "cultural masochists" who used "Jim Wright–style machine politics" and supported a "bureaucratic welfare state" that "cripples children," and he took the lead in a campaign to oust Barney Frank (D-MA) from his subcommittee chairmanship for ethics violations.[8] "If you're the minority party," Gingrich said in May 1989, "you better be able to generate attention."[9]

Fourth, it was far from clear that Gingrich would be a successful whip, for he was a novice at vote counting and his organizational skills were questionable at best. To address these weaknesses, Weber hired several expert staff to manage the whip's office, while Gingrich appointed Bob Walker, a skillful vote counter, as his deputy whip in charge of tallying votes. Gingrich also turned the whip office into an opportunity for party entrepreneurialism. He anointed Steve Gunderson to be a second deputy whip in charge of a newly formed "Strategy Whip Organization," consisting of five additional whips responsible for crafting political and communication strategies, identifying supporters outside of the House, and fostering future "stars" in the Republican Conference.[10] This combination of delegation and innovation ensured that votes were counted accurately while giving Gingrich a platform to circulate his strategic plans, shape party messaging, and expand his network.[11] He made sure to appoint an ideologically diverse collection of whips, starting with Gunderson, who could build his cross-party appeal and win votes from competing GOP factions. "Where there was a moderate member that was recalcitrant," one member of the whip team later explained, "Steve [Gunderson] could go talk to them."[12] The revamped whip organization did create some turmoil, as the strategy whips had overlapping duties with Michel and Conference Chair Jerry Lewis (R-CA).[13] Discord aside, Gingrich's whip operation was fairly successful at a variety of tasks, including polling members on bills, recruiting cosponsors for legislation, identifying issues where the party enjoyed an advantage over Democrats, and developing rhetorical themes that contrasted Republicans—the "Party of the Future" and of "Economic Growth"—with Democrats, the "Party of the Past" and of "Government Growth."[14] By October 1990, the Strategy Whip Organization had nearly doubled the number of invitees to its weekly meetings, adding party leaders and rising stars from both the COS and the moderate wing of the party.[15]

The final challenge was how Gingrich would square the expectation that leaders work as a team with his proclivity to disparage fellow Republicans. In the beginning, it seemed possible that Gingrich had abandoned the latter path, such as when he abided by Michel's decision to support a bipartisan congressional pay increase in 1989 and lobbied other Republicans to vote for it.[16] This led to grumbling by right-wing activists, however, and Gingrich worried that he could lose their loyalty if he stopped challenging more moderate-minded GOP leaders. Those leaders included the new Republican president, George H. W. Bush. Many conservatives were guarded toward Bush, who was from an older generation of Republicans that emphasized policy moderation, balanced budgets, and cross-party deal making over confrontation. Furthermore, Gingrich was disappointed that Bush had not run his campaign on a platform of conservative principles that were clearly distinguishable from the Democratic Party platform and that could be turned into legislation.[17] He and the COS did initially voice support for the president and suggest bills for his agenda, and COS member Christopher Cox (R-CA) even wrote a pledge for fellow Republicans to sign that committed them to sustain any Bush veto.[18] But Bush often ignored Gingrich's advice that he emphasize partisan differences over legislating, and by the end of his first two years in office, he had signed into law several measures supported by Democrats that expanded the regulatory authority of the federal government, such as new clean air enforcement measures and the Americans with Disabilities Act. At a lunch meeting in November 1989 with *Washington Post* reporters, Gingrich warned that Bush risked becoming a nonreformist president who did nothing to help his party win power in Congress. Unsurprisingly, White House officials were upset when the interview was published.[19]

In what became a defining moment in the Bush-Gingrich relationship, the minority whip cast his lot with discontented partisans by defying the president on a major budget bill. "Read my lips: no new taxes," Bush had declared during the 1988 Republican National Convention, but growing budget imbalances, along with the threat of automatic across-the-board spending cuts that would be imposed by statute in the event of excessive deficit spending, put pressure on the president to compromise with Democrats on budget policy. Following a series of bipartisan meetings between Bush aides and congressional leaders, including Gingrich, the White House signaled in June 1990 that tax increases were on the table. At the outset, Gingrich hinted that he could support a tax hike, provided it was coupled with GOP policy priorities like cuts to entitlement programs. Yet taxation was a major issue on which Gingrich had long sought to distinguish the two parties, and in the face of sharp criticism from conservatives, he reversed course.[20] When Bush and other negotiators held a Rose Garden news conference to announce their final deficit reduction plan, which included new tax revenues, Gingrich, who was noticeably absent from the press conference, came out against the plan soon thereafter.[21]

Recognizing the risks, Gingrich initially tried to minimize his rupture with Bush. "My intention is not to embarrass the president," he insisted, and he spun his rebellion as a form of loyalty to the GOP by calling the deal a job-killing "Democratic budget package."[22] Other party leaders nonetheless felt caught off guard, noting that Gingrich had been conspicuously silent during the budget negotiations, "read[ing] novels and [writing] notes to colleagues and advisors," and the whip was faulted for fomenting a major intraparty split. Michel implored his colleagues to vote for the budget bill, but to no avail: when it came to the House floor in early October, it was rejected by majorities of both parties, including 105 out of 176 voting Republicans. One reporter called it "the worst domestic policy defeat of the Bush Presidency," and another described it as a "disaster" that left Bush "nothing but humiliation to show for abandoning his no-new-taxes pledge." The president was forced to reach a second budget agreement with Democrats that was even less favorable to his party's budgetary priorities.[23] White House Budget Director Richard Darman complained bitterly about Gingrich's betrayal, accusing him of making Bush appear weak to satisfy his own political ambitions. A small group of disgruntled House Republicans even tried persuading Jerry Lewis to run against Gingrich for whip, though Lewis did not, preferring to bide his time and run for minority leader when Michel retired.[24]

How responsible was Gingrich for Bush's high-profile failure? He did strategize with Walker and Weber to defeat the measure, and some complained that by breaking with the president, which drew the attention of the Washington press corps, he gave warrant to other members of the Conference to reject the bill. Yet there was plenty of blame to go around. Both Democrats and Republicans in Congress felt excluded from the negotiations over the budget, and the White House had alienated legislators with its belligerent lobbying tactics, particularly those of Bush's chief of staff, John Sununu. Many Democrats were unhappy with the measure's cuts to social welfare programs, while right-leaning writers and commentators had trashed the deal, the Republican Study Committee came out against it before it was defeated, and the NRCC's cochair, Ed Rollins, advised lawmakers to vote no.[25] Few members of Congress wanted to go on the record supporting an increase in taxes just weeks before Election Day. Furthermore, scores of Republicans had committed themselves to oppose tax increases well before the plan was announced at the White House. Over one hundred GOP lawmakers had put their names on a "no tax" pledge circulated by Grover Norquist, head of the antitax group Americans for Tax Reform, and in April 1990 more than eighty Republicans had signed a letter committing to sustain any veto by Bush of tax-raising legislation. Mere hours after the White House's June announcement on taxes, ninety Republicans had added their signatures to a letter from COS cofounder Bob Walker opposing tax increases, and the next month the Conference approved a resolution, introduced by COS member Dick Armey, objecting to higher taxes.[26]

Though Gingrich had attempted to soften his defection from Bush and Michel, when conservative legislators and interest groups rose to his defense, he embraced his heterodoxy. His opposition to Bush's budget, he declared, was "a major turning point for the whole society," and he identified himself as "the leader, the insider-revolutionary in this country." After the defeat of the budget bill, he continued denouncing the White House's domestic agenda, and when Darman gave a speech criticizing the policy proposals of Gingrich, he demanded Darman's resignation.[27] While open conflict with Bush seemingly violated his vision of a party working as a unit, Gingrich and Republican ideologues believed their rebellion was justified because, from their perspective, GOP moderates, the president, and other leaders had been straying from the party's core tenets. Bush's "tendency is to see himself as the NFL commissioner," Gingrich explained, "when I see him as the head of one of two teams."[28]

Within the House, the perceived apostasy of the president and less ideologically absolutist Republicans spurred conservative lawmakers to adopt additional Conference rules and practices (and better enforce existing ones) to encourage unity around policy proposals they desired. Gingrich suggested that the party should take unified positions on legislative issues that were clearly different from what liberals advocated for, and then use those positions as a template for public appearances by GOP incumbents.

He also prodded Michel into using his recently granted power over Rules Committee assignments to name Gerald Solomon (R-NY), a fiery partisan, as the committee's ranking member.[29]

The participation of COS members like Walker and Armey in the fight over Bush's budget bill underscored the continuing role of the organization—now boasting nearly forty members, including a majority of the GOP leadership, and chaired by cofounder Jon Kyl (R-AZ)—in pushing the Conference further toward partisan activism and unity. Several COS members were appointed to Gingrich's whip operation, and the group remained a useful conduit through which he could funnel his seemingly never-ending strategic plans and messaging ideas.[30] At the same time, Gingrich was dedicating more time and attention to his responsibilities as general chairman of GOPAC.[31] In February 1989, GOPAC sponsored a two-day conference featuring Grover Norquist, Paul Weyrich, and other notable Republican consultants and journalists, centered on a Gingrich proposal to realign the country electorally by increasing voter turnout, "creating a positive organizing vision," and instigating "a civil war within the opposition."[32] Gingrich held a retreat in Colorado later that summer with GOPAC contributors and advisors to discuss how Republicans could win seats in the 1990 elections if they espoused a constructive policy platform (another early manifestation of the Contract with America in 1994). During a subsequent GOPAC meeting, participants identified 1992 as the target year for the GOP to win control of the House, and GOPAC officials proposed recruiting candidates from among the six thousand Republicans that were already part of the organization's "farm team." At these meetings, Gingrich often tied electoral success to broader societal transformation. "I am interested in causing change," he announced at one gathering in 1989, "as a consequence of which we will win control of the House and of the country."[33]

GOPAC did a considerable amount of messaging. It recruited focus groups to hone language that would motivate voters and, hoping to inspire a grassroots movement, helped design the *American Opportunities Workshop*, a televised program that extolled conservative policy ideas and was broadcast to hundreds of locations around the country.[34] It also circulated Gingrich-written material, such as a pamphlet touting "The America That Can Be," which compared the challenge of reforming the nation's "decaying bureaucratic welfare state" to a geometrical puzzle that could only be solved with unconventional thinking.[35] In addition, it mailed thirty-six thousand copies of audiotapes featuring Gingrich to state politicians and party activists. New York state lawmakers who received the tapes "were fired up by them," one former assemblyman recalled, and the tapes would be credited with encouraging many Republicans to run for office, including future Speaker John Boehner (R-OH). Nearly three decades afterward, one colleague remarked, "I still run into state legislators who say their earliest recollection of getting excited about politics was listening to those tapes."[36]

GOPAC activities could be controversial. One Gingrich audio recording was accompanied by a memo titled "Language: A Key Mechanism of Control," which urged candidates to draw from a list of over 130 words and phrases in their public communications so they could "speak like Newt." Roughly half were "Optimistic Positive Governing words," while the rest were "Contrasting words" to describe Democrats, ranging from the predictable ("liberal," "red tape," "welfare") to the polemical ("corrupt," "traitors," "greed," and "sick"). Though both GOPAC and Gingrich attempted to distance themselves from the memo's incendiary contents, it reinforced the impression that Gingrich was unscrupulous and aggressively partisan.[37] Also problematic was the extent to which GOPAC aided Gingrich with a possible presidential run and reimbursed his consultants for various expenses.[38]

Other legally questionable GOPAC activities during this period would come back to haunt Gingrich. For example, by distributing Gingrich's writings and recordings to political candidates and soliciting contributions to elect a Republican House, the organization risked violating a federal prohibition against groups like GOPAC contributing directly to congressional campaigns. And some GOPAC donors received assistance from Gingrich in their dealings with the federal government, creating the appearance of a quid pro quo. When the operations of the *American Opportunities Workshop* (renamed *American Citizens' Television*) were shifted to a tax-exempt nonprofit located in GOPAC headquarters that employed GOPAC staff, it looked like the organization was trying to circumvent laws against using tax-deductible donations for political activities.[39] Gingrich's proclivity for taking unorthodox positions could also turn off the activists whose support for GOPAC he needed to cultivate.[40]

There were some indications that Gingrich's belief in the power of a unified message was gaining greater traction within the Conference. Under the leadership of Mickey Edwards, the Republican Policy Committee was selecting weekly themes related to Democratic abuses of House rules and recruiting rank and file lawmakers to echo them in their public comments. Both parties were also starting to coordinate the content of, and participation of lawmakers in, the House's daily morning speeches.[41] Gingrich's other strategies and tactics were less universally accepted, however. For instance, while Edwards concurred that "we must arouse and mobilize the public," he advised Gingrich that "congressional races are primarily local races," that a campaign message "must be strong . . . but it must also remain within the bounds of credibility," and that demands for reforms that were intended to rob Democratic incumbents of electoral advantages would endanger incumbent Republicans, too. Edwards went further at a NRCC candidate forum in December 1989, warning that "if you attempt to convince the public at large that Democrats as a group are nothing but a bunch of corrupt thugs, you will have gone so far over the line of believability that you will be laughed at." Another skeptic, NRCC cochair Ed Rollins, dismissed "whip-driven" political realignments and insisted that only a district-by-district campaign strategy would work, leading Gingrich to call for Rollins to be fired.[42]

The November 1990 elections were a letdown for the House Republican Party, which lost eight seats, shrinking the Conference to its smallest size since 1980. Gingrich himself barely eked out a win, defeating his Democratic opponent by less than a thousand votes. Many of his constituents had become disillusioned by his limited attentiveness to local issues, and striking Eastern Airlines workers in his district were mad that Gingrich had refused to facilitate negotiations between them and the airline's management.[43] Furthermore, Gingrich's ploy to add another ally to the GOP leadership team failed when his candidate of choice, Carl Pursell (R-MI), lost decisively in a bid to oust incumbent Conference Chair Jerry Lewis, 98 to 64.[44] Moderates had abandoned their plan to challenge Gingrich for whip, however—an early indication that they were losing whatever influence they once had over the direction of the Conference.[45] Gingrich had also donated campaign money from his Friends of Newt political action committee to more than half of the incoming class, and many had received training tapes and other instructional materials from GOPAC. Freshmen members of the GOPAC farm team would include surprise victors like Rick Santorum (R-PA) and Frank Riggs (R-CA), both of whom, Gingrich noted acidly, had been given up as lost causes by the NRCC.[46] Thus, the next Congress would feature more Republicans who owed Gingrich at least in part for their electoral success, thereby bringing the Conference another step closer to his vision of a unified, communication-oriented party that was loyal to him.

Gingrich Takes Advantage of More Scandals (1991–1992)

In the aftermath of yet another discouraging election, Michel and others expressed fresh doubt that nationalizing elections, a central strategic objective for Gingrich, was the wisest plan for winning power. Mickey Edwards circulated a memo in February 1991 to the GOP leadership calling for a localized approach to elections, challenging Gingrich on several fronts. "Voters think what they think, not what we want them to think," he wrote. Complaining that "we continually sit around in small groups deciding what we are going to put forth as the next big 'wedge' issue," he argued that nothing could replace "more basic and fundamental campaign activities" at the local level. In response, Gingrich conceded that localized campaigns were to some degree necessary. Nonetheless, he refused to abandon the idea that the nationalization of elections was an essential element of what he described to fellow leaders as a "moral obligation" to pursue "an ongoing, permanent effort to compete permanently for control of the House."[47]

Meanwhile, the House became engulfed in several ethics controversies. The first, the so-called House bank scandal, involved lawmakers who had overdrawn funds from their House-managed personal financial accounts without penalty. Improprieties in the bank—which was technically not a bank, but rather a clearinghouse that dispensed paychecks—had initially been reported by the General Accounting Office (GAO) in early 1990. The story did not gain traction until September 1991, when the GAO documented over eight thousand bounced checks from the prior Congress. Speaker Foley declared an end to the practice of covering overdrafts and publicly admonished legislators for overdrawing their accounts.[48]

With that, it seemed as if the matter would fade away, especially when Michel backed Foley and even GOP firebrands like Bob Dornan called it "a very small issue." Gingrich stayed largely mum about the bank at first. But a group of freshmen Republicans, dubbed the "Gang of Seven," emerged as outspoken and persistent bank critics. They held a news conference to demand disclosure of the names of the check bouncers, arguing that the offenders had benefited from a privilege denied to ordinary citizens. One member of the Gang of Seven, Jim Nussle (R-IA), said he was embarrassed enough to hide his face in a paper bag, and then did precisely that on the House floor.[49] Pressure was building to take sterner steps, and in October the House voted overwhelmingly to close the bank and authorize an Ethics Committee investigation. By early March 1992, Gingrich was pushing for full disclosure of all check bouncers, a move approved unanimously by the chamber later that month after weeks of unrelenting criticism from the Gang of Seven, the media, and good government advocates.[50]

The Gang of Seven's effective crusade revealed both novel opportunities and fresh perils for Gingrich. On one hand, he clearly had a new, if small, set of acolytes eager to adopt his partisan tactics. This was no coincidence: Gingrich and GOPAC had supported several of the group's members in their initial election campaigns, and Gingrich had advised them behind the scenes on strategy regarding the bank.[51] Furthermore, by letting freshmen serve as the advance guard of reform, Gingrich could avoid publicly dissenting from Michel, who preferred a bipartisan resolution to the bank scandal. And the group's success in compelling Democrats to release the names of all the bank's abusers suggested that highlighting ethics could yield wins for the minority party.

On the other hand, the bank scandal showed that Gingrich could be forced to act by groups like the Gang of Seven, possibly creating more problems for him and the party. Indeed, when Gingrich finally joined the call to publicize the names of the House's bank abusers, he created another awkward moment of disagreement between the Conference's two top leaders.[52] More embarrassingly, it became clear that several Republicans had also bounced multiple checks—a group that included Gingrich himself, who had overdrawn twenty-two times, nineteen more than he had originally claimed. ("You'd better be doggone sure you are pure yourself," Michel warned, "before you take on all this aura of purity.") Several of Gingrich's allies and sympathizers, including Vin Weber, faced electoral danger after their own check bouncing was revealed.[53] The scandal thus served as an early warning that reform-minded freshmen House members might not be easily tamed, and it gave credence to the admonitions of Michel and others that attacking the ethics of the House could hurt Republicans as much as it did Democrats.

The House bank scandal prompted journalists to look more closely at the special perks that lawmakers received. Reports swiftly surfaced that some members of Congress had unpaid restaurant and catering bills or had asked the Sergeant-at-Arms to process their parking tickets. More serious legal trouble loomed after a story broke that federal law enforcement officials were looking into allegations of theft, embezzlement, and drug distribution by clerks working in the House Post Office.[54] Gingrich eagerly played up these accusations, which were both more salacious and more easily connectable to Democrats than the bank scandal. Sometimes Gingrich resorted to innuendo and hints at broader conspiracies. In February 1992, during floor debate over a resolution to investigate the Post Office, he proclaimed that majority party leaders were involved in a cover-up. The following month, he implied that the new Democratic appointee for Sergeant-at-Arms might have prevented an internal probe into drug dealing in the Post Office—a claim so brazen that the usually sedate Foley angrily decried Gingrich's "despicable act" on the floor of the House.[55]

Reacting to these and other allegations of wrongdoing,[56] House Democrats created a new nonpartisan administrative position responsible for overseeing the chamber's operations. To Republicans, though, this response missed their larger point: the governing party chronically abused its power. Democrats had brought a higher percentage of bills to the floor under restrictive procedures than ever before, for instance, and in December 1992 they even tried to cap the amount of floor time dedicated to special-order speeches, backing off only after Gingrich and other Republicans vigorously complained. ("You'll see open warfare," vowed GOP moderate Chris Shays of Connecticut.) These ongoing abuses by the majority party threatened to convert more Republicans to Gingrich's militant view of politics. Indeed, Gang of Seven member Frank Riggs (R-CA) made ethics his central focus after realizing he had little say over legislation.[57]

Meanwhile, Gingrich's whip duties kept him busy counting votes, composing partisan messages, and developing alternative policy proposals.[58] In September 1991, as the nation's economy was emerging from a recession, he tried unsuccessfully to add tax cuts to a bill extending unemployment benefits, using the attempt to juxtapose the GOP's support for tax reduction with Democrats' emphasis on spending. The COS, its membership having grown to around fifty lawmakers, also served as a useful venue for Gingrich's ideas and strategies.[59] In one meeting, members were encouraged to practice "confrontational politics" that put Democrats on the defensive, and in another they were urged to frame Congress' scandals as entirely the fault of the majority party. GOP leaders viewed COS members as valuable assets and recruited them to participate in coordinated floor speeches,[60] and Gingrich kept lobbing verbal barbs at Democrats and criticizing their agenda both on and off the House floor.[61]

Gingrich also embraced aspirational agendas, designed not to enact bills under a Democratic majority but to promise them under a future Republican one. For example, he contributed to a series of speeches by GOP leaders in January 1992, promising floor votes on ten policy items, including a balanced budget constitutional amendment, federal tax reductions, and welfare reform, if the GOP took control of the House.[62] As was typical for Gingrich, his agendas were framed as part of a transformational change to American society and frequently coupled with harsh condemnation of Democrats. GOP control of Congress was what he termed the "Necessary Revolution" to pass good public policy, especially a reform of the liberal welfare state, which he blamed for incentivizing ignorance and promiscuity. In a February 1992 memo he proclaimed that "we are becoming a revolutionary movement," and by educating Republicans in elected office about the movement, "the revolutionary energy [generated] can become the decisive moral force recruiting volunteers and raising money for our congressional candidates this fall."[63] A proposal for restructuring the federal welfare system was unveiled in April and, in an impressive display of coordination, embraced by nearly one hundred GOP House challengers. That summer, Gingrich told a group of college-age party volunteers that "I am essentially a revolutionary."[64]

Relations between Gingrich and President Bush appeared to be improving somewhat at the start of the 102nd Congress. Conservatives were pleased with Bush's hawkish opposition to Iraq's invasion of Kuwait, and when US troops won an easy victory over Iraqi forces, Gingrich demanded that Democrats who opposed the authorization of force confess their error.

He also praised Bush's 1991 State of the Union speech and told participants at the Conservative Political Action Conference in February that it is a "huge disservice to America when we spend 60 to 80 percent of our time beating up on the president."[65] Yet these moments of agreement papered over deeper fissures between the pair, and the White House—worried by the prospect of a Gingrich-led GOP Conference—pleaded with Michel not to retire from Congress.[66] Bush opted not to participate in a 1980-style campaign event that would feature a pledge to vote on legislative proposals within one hundred days of his next term, should he and a GOP-majority Congress be elected. The White House paid little mind to Gingrich's multiple missives laden with strategic political advice, dismissing them as "Newtgrams." As Bush press secretary Marlin Fitzwater sarcastically told reporters, Gingrich was "kind of a modern Plato," and "the man is brilliant. . . . Everybody just reads Newt's memos."[67]

Bush was not the only Republican leader suspicious of Gingrich's intentions. Rumors circulated that Gingrich would challenge Michel if Bush lost his reelection bid. Michel eventually announced he would run for reelection in 1992, and no challenge to his leadership position materialized. Still, it was unclear how long Michel would want to head a COS-dominated leadership team or a party increasingly made up of outspoken younger lawmakers spoiling for fights with House Democrats—in short, a party less oriented toward legislating and more toward messaging.[68]

Gingrich continued to channel many of his entrepreneurial electioneering activities through GOPAC, which had expanded its fundraising and campaign operations to the point that it resembled a shadow NRCC. It conducted a host of campaign activities, dubbed "Change Congress NOW!," with the goal of winning control of the House in 1992. Moreover, it urged strong potential candidates to run for office; directed contributors to those candidates; offered coaching from eager freshmen like Santorum and Scott Klug (R-WI), who provided phone-based training programs to over five hundred Republicans running for office; and established weekly conference calls between Gingrich and dozens of GOP candidates to discuss campaign strategy. GOPAC also distributed literature that reflected Gingrich's propensity for thinking in terms of broad societal change. One memo contained an illustrated "Circle of American Success," divided into four quarters that were labeled "American Culture," "Technology," "Quality," and

"Economic and Management Principles."[69] As in past election cycles, GOPAC sent audio recordings of Gingrich to potential candidates, particularly more conservative ones in districts that they were likely to win. Although ethics was a centerpiece of Gingrich's campaign-oriented strategy, some were doubtful that it could be converted into a plea for a Republican House or would be as effective as a policy- or district-oriented approach. Indeed, surveys showed that sizeable majorities of Americans blamed both parties for the House bank scandal and considered the ethics and truthfulness of their own representative in Congress to be good or excellent.[70]

Ironically, GOPAC continued to face ethical and legal challenges of its own. Democrats were upset by GOPAC's mailings on behalf of GOP candidates and accused the organization, whose mission was presumably to help Republican candidates for state office, of illegally meddling in federal elections. In May 1991, the FEC announced that the accusation had merit, whereupon GOPAC immediately registered as a federal political action committee.[71] GOPAC also conducted dubious financial practices behind the scenes. In mid-1992, the *Wall Street Journal* reported that the organization spent the bulk of its revenue on consultants, on Gingrich's travel, and on staff salaries rather than on actual campaigns. Those who wished to contribute more to the group than allowed by law were directed to give money to a nonprofit group run by GOPAC supporter Bo Callaway; the funds were then used to pay off debts to GOPAC—a legally suspect maneuver.[72]

Even though many Republicans had believed the 1992 elections were their best chance to finally wrest control of Congress from Democrats, Gingrich came to the reluctant conclusion that the chances of this happening were low—one in seven at best—especially since the Democratic Party continued to draw from a large pool of state and local officials to run for open seats. Sure enough, Democrats not only kept control of the House but also defeated Bush in his reelection bid.[73] The bank scandal, along with other factors (like the 1990 round of congressional redistricting, which put numerous lawmakers in less friendly House districts), led to the defeat or retirement of an unusually large number of Republicans as well as Democrats.[74] This included not only Vin Weber, who chose not to run for reelection, but also Gingrich's longtime rival Mickey Edwards, who lost his primary.[75] Gingrich himself narrowly survived his second close election in a row. Forced to jump to a new congressional district when his old one was split up by Georgia state Democrats, he won his primary race by the slim margin of less than one thousand votes. In the general election, he was attacked so relentlessly for his own House bank overdrafts and for divorcing his first wife while she recovered from cancer surgery that he contemplated abandoning the race, but he ultimately fought his way to victory, receiving 58 percent of the vote.[76]

However, the election results also intimated that the GOP was getting closer to winning the House. The party gained seats in the chamber for the first time in eight years, a sign that incoming president Bill Clinton had very short coattails on which his fellow Democrats could ride in the future. In addition, a sizeable percentage of the majority party would be the most vulnerable type of incumbent—first termers—and the South, a bastion of the Democratic Party for generations, was continuing to trend Republican.[77] The elections also offered Gingrich fresh opportunities to accumulate more influence. The death in 1991 of Silvio Conte (R-MA), the compromise-minded and influential ranking member of the Appropriations Committee, had already "greatly weakened the small liberal bloc in the House GOP" that had considered fielding a candidate for whip to challenge Gingrich in 1990.[78] GOPAC took credit for contributing to the victories of "at least two dozen, and perhaps as many as 40, of the 47 members of the 1992 freshman class," and roughly half of the Conference had either supported Gingrich as a candidate for whip in 1989 or received GOPAC recordings prior to their first election to Congress.[79]

Gingrich and his allies moved rapidly to take advantage of this promising political environment. The minority whip believed that Congressman Bill Thomas (R-CA) was too accommodating to Democrats, so he pressed for Thomas's removal as ranking member of the House Administration Committee. Thomas ultimately stayed in place, but Gingrich had reinforced the notion that party loyalty was a prerequisite for being entrusted with a position of power.[80] More successful was COS member Dick Armey's challenge against Conference Chair Jerry Lewis. Armey ousted Lewis, 88 to 84, with the support of many incoming freshmen and, Lewis suspected, behind-the-scenes help from Gingrich. This leadership election was nearly as consequential as the one that made Gingrich whip: Armey would become a critical Gingrich ally in the next Congress, and Michel was now the sole remaining member of leadership from the shrinking wing of the party that favored legislating and bipartisan compromise over messaging and sharp partisan opposition.[81]

Gingrich drafted a campaign plan to run for Michel's post and reportedly started asking newly elected Republicans for their vote for minority leader after the 1994 elections. It was unclear, however, whether Michel would retire in the next Congress, or if Gingrich would actually risk challenging Michel if he didn't. Nor would Gingrich's election to GOP leader be a fait accompli, since, as Vin Weber had noted, Gingrich lacked many close friends in Congress. He also might not be able to rely on the loyalty of his more ambitious supporters, including Armey. When Armey beat Lewis, Karl Rove, a Texas political operative and future advisor to President George W. Bush, warned, "if I were Newt, I wouldn't look over my shoulder and say, 'That's my guy.'"[82]

Newfound Unity and Reaching the Promised Land (1993–1994)

On the eve of the new Congress, Democrats had good reason to be optimistic. With unified control of the national government, they would have their best opportunity in a dozen years to enact a liberal legislative agenda, and some congressional Republicans—Gingrich himself among them—suggested they were willing to work with President-Elect Bill Clinton.[83] However, Clinton would face a very different Congress than the one encountered by Jimmy Carter, his most recent Democratic predecessor, in the late 1970s. Not only was the level of partisan voting substantially higher, but Congress was dominated by a different breed of lawmaker—one that was more media-savvy, confrontational, and election-oriented. This was especially the case among House Republicans, particularly the forty-plus GOP freshmen, who appeared more interested in partisan conflict than in policymaking.[84] Many Republicans in the House interpreted President Bush's defeat not as a rejection of their party but instead as the consequence of his wobbly commitment to conservatism and the sense that he was too willing to compromise with Democrats.[85] Conference rules adopted over the past decade made intraparty dissent less likely, and after the 1992 elections, the GOP approved a requirement that certain floor motions "shall be used, to the extent possible, to support the positions of the Conference and the

Leadership." It also imposed a three-term limit on all ranking committee members, limiting their ability to establish independent committee fiefdoms.[86] Gingrich urged ranking members to work with leaders on action plans for bills considered by their committees and to otherwise contribute to electing a Republican majority.[87]

Gingrich had considerable political resources at his disposal going into the 103rd Congress. His forty-five-member whip team could lean on any colleague who might be inclined to cooperate with Democrats, and he planned to expand its portfolio to include helping "renew American civilization by replacing the welfare state" and convincing the party to back him as Michel's successor.[88] As a sign that the whip team was transforming into a Gingrich-centered and less ideologically diverse operation, two independent-minded moderates, Steve Gunderson and Fred Upton (R-MI), quit. ("The whip organization doesn't necessarily encourage individual thinking," one Upton staffer later confided.)[89]

The Republican Conference's phalanx of activist leaders, though eyed warily by Gingrich as possible rivals, could further contribute to his strategic objectives. Incoming NRCC Chair Bill Paxon (R-NY) spearheaded a major restructuring of the campaign committee, which was only months from bankruptcy—"the place was on life support," Paxon recalled—and he ended Vander Jagt's guarantee of financial support to all incumbents regardless of need. Echoing Gingrich, Armey said that "the politics of confrontation works and the politics of appeasement fails," and he formed a "rapid response team" to rebut statements by the White House.[90] Gingrich created an informal leadership council that included Armey, Paxon, Bob Walker, and Conference Secretary Tom DeLay.[91] The whip also had the support of an array of interest groups on the Right who were hungry for a GOP-led House, and new right-wing media outlets that could amplify the message of partisan differentiation, including a nationally syndicated radio program hosted by a rising star named Rush Limbaugh.[92]

Decisions made by the White House and by House Republican leaders in the early days of the Clinton presidency extinguished any hope of bipartisan détente. The president, seeking to avoid the debilitating fights that Carter had endured with congressional Democrats, and expecting mostly opposition from the GOP, cultivated closer ties with Democratic leaders than with Republicans in Congress. Clinton also committed some early unforced errors. He proposed a nominee for attorney general, Zoë Baird, who had employed undocumented workers, and he tried to overturn the widely accepted military ban on gay service members. Though Gingrich was impressed by Clinton's charisma and intelligence, these mistakes buttressed Gingrich's belief that the president "was superficial and lacking both discipline and backbone." Allegations of questionable real estate dealings involving the Clintons and a failed business venture in Arkansas known as the Whitewater Development Corporation led Gingrich to conclude that Clinton was electorally vulnerable.[93]

Gingrich, the COS, and like-minded Republicans soon made clear that they would aggressively defend their political and policy interests. They accused House Democrats of trying to pad their majority by giving voting rights to the chamber's nonvoting delegates, all but one of whom were members of the majority party; after GOP pushback, the delegates were only granted limited voting power.[94] Gingrich was among the first Republicans to speak out against Baird's nomination, which was soon withdrawn.[95] When Clinton laid out his economic agenda to Congress during an address to Congress in February 1993, COS Chairman John Boehner urged fellow members to brainstorm ways to convince voters that "Clinton and his plan represent nothing short of the failed, old, liberal Democrat ideology of tax and spend."[96] GOP opposition hardened as Democrats, striving to keep themselves united and compensating for having fewer Republicans they could rely upon to cross party lines, deployed restrictive rules on bills and sometimes even procedural gimmicks, such as keeping the voting clock open past the customary deadline so they could round up votes—all of which reinforced Gingrich's narrative that Democrats played dirty.[97] Michel, Gingrich, and other GOP leaders pleaded in vain for more open floor rules and endeavored to bring their plight to the attention of the public.[98]

A major battle erupted in the spring of 1993 over a Democratic budget reconciliation bill that included tax increases. Republican leaders, including Gingrich, marshaled outside groups to gin up resistance to the reconciliation bill, Armey encouraged his colleagues to broadcast their party's opposition widely, and the minority whip appeared on Rush Limbaugh's radio show to speak out against the measure. With Democrats getting nervous about raising people's taxes, and unable to count on Republican votes, Clinton, Foley, and other leaders in the Democratic Caucus worked overtime to persuade just enough members of their party to pass it by a narrow six-vote margin.[99] But their victory was costly. Several Democrats in swing districts had been forced to align themselves with a hike in taxes, and as political scientists Thomas Mann and Norman Ornstein observed, "it took humiliating efforts for a president to bring around individual lawmakers from his own party."[100]

Though oppositional politics was coming to define the Conference, Gingrich was not entirely against cooperating with the governing party.[101] This proved true for one major measure, the North American Free Trade Agreement (NAFTA) between the United States, Canada, and Mexico. Many congressional Democrats believed that the agreement would eliminate American jobs and incentivize companies to relocate to Mexico to skirt environmental regulations. Yet Gingrich saw the agreement as good public policy, and he and Michel offered to round up at least 110 Republican votes for it, provided the majority party could get a minimum of 100 more from their own ranks.[102] The two GOP leaders gathered information on member preferences, circulated endorsements of NAFTA, and strategized over how best to win over undecided or skeptical Republicans. Offended by the pro-NAFTA business community's poor organizing, Gingrich lashed out at NAFTA's lead lobbyist, and then gave him a tutorial on how to amass grassroots support. The hard work paid off: when the measure came to the floor in November 1993, it was approved with the votes of 132 Republicans and 102 Democrats.[103]

As the 103rd Congress unfolded, a major leadership question loomed over the GOP Conference: Would Bob Michel retire? Although he remained a highly active leader—speaking to the press, arranging floor speeches, and forming task forces[104]—in private, he had been tiring of the job. As early as 1987, Michel had openly speculated about stepping down if a Democrat were to become president.[105] In the years since, his party had been steadily voting more conservatively than him, and it had a less-bounded view of what constituted appropriate partisan conduct. Michel questioned whether it was worth staying "when there would be those continuing to harp at your brand of leadership."[106] A pair of events in early 1993 generated more friction between Michel and members of his party. In February, House Republicans had unexpectedly managed to defeat a resolution on the floor that reauthorized the Select Committee on Narcotics, a committee that Republicans (and many Democrats) complained was not worth the cost, especially since it did not have the power to pass legislation. But Michel undid their victory by forging a tentative agreement with Democratic leaders to keep the committee in place. They were upset again the following month when Michel said that the GOP had acted recklessly by opposing Clinton's reconciliation bill.[107] Speculation spread that the minority leader would soon face a revolt within his ranks.

Gingrich's denials notwithstanding, it was an open secret inside the Beltway that any rebellion against Michel would be led by Gingrich, and he and his allies may have even explicitly warned the minority leader that one was brewing. Michel believed he could win reelection as GOP leader, but at the cost of dividing his party and putting himself at risk of future challenges.[108] Finally, in October 1993, Michel announced that he would not run for reelection. Though Gingrich was not the only lawmaker seeking to replace him—Gerald Solomon of New York had his eye on the job as well—Gingrich declared within days that he had already collected enough votes to be elected minority leader and was ready to "build a team that can fulfill our rendezvous with destiny."[109] Many of his fellow partisans, especially the newer ones, were thrilled. Ernest Istook (R-OK), the freshman who had defeated Mickey Edwards in his 1992 primary, predicted that the Conference's new leadership would ensure that "lines of distinction [are] more clearly drawn between us and the Democrats in Congress."[110]

Gingrich had spent years trying to turn the Conference into a unified team, and he continued these efforts as Michel's heir apparent. In early 1994, he held a party-wide retreat in Salisbury, Maryland, to construct a possible policy agenda and draft a strategic plan for the GOP. Pollster Frank Luntz offered suggestions for how Republicans could triumph in November, such as developing an alternative legislative agenda, and advised them that they would need to "start acting like a majority before voters will consider making you a majority." Paxon offered some encouraging news—lots of GOP candidates were running, and the NRCC was nearly free of debt—but he warned that incumbents needed to ensure they got themselves reelected if their party was to have any chance at winning control of the chamber. The meeting was attended by over half of the Conference, and Gingrich came away convinced that more House Republicans than ever before supported his push for greater party differentiation and coordinated communication.[111] Dick Armey followed up by publishing a new intraparty journal, *Catalyst*, containing ideas for how Republicans could be, as he put it, "more effective individually and as a team."[112]

While congressional Republicans had helped the White House pass NAFTA, it hardly guaranteed that bipartisan cooperation would be forthcoming on another major Clinton initiative: health care reform. Increasing health care costs and rising numbers of uninsured Americans encouraged Democrats to pursue their long-sought goal of a nationalized health care system, and many Republicans assumed that reform was inevitable. Gingrich and fellow Conference leaders wrote to the president in early October 1993 offering to work with him on a bill.[113] Privately, however, the GOP whip feared that a fix to the country's health care system spearheaded by Clinton would create a generation of voters loyal to Democrats. For its part, the White House, distrustful of Republicans, decided not to pursue a modest legislative solution that might have earned GOP votes. Instead, in November 1993 it introduced a more progressive bill that made bold, if somewhat convoluted, changes to the American medical system, mandating that employers provide insurance coverage for all citizens and expanding the regulatory authority of the federal government over the nature of that coverage. Many Republicans were dismayed by the possibility that a huge new bureaucracy would be created to regulate a major sector of the economy. Internal GOP polling also suggested that killing the measure could bring them control of the House, and the steady trickle of negative stories about Whitewater further discouraged Republicans from doing anything that might help Clinton politically.[114]

Gingrich was not initially involved in GOP strategizing on health care. Michel had given fellow Illinoisan Dennis Hastert the job of leading the minority party's campaign on the issue (infuriating Gingrich, who had cochaired a task force on health care policy in the previous Congress).[115] Armey circulated a flowchart full of boxes and arrows that vividly depicted the plan's complexity. Lamar Smith ran a communication operation to oppose a "government-run health plan," and conservatives in the Senate sought to dissuade compromise-oriented colleagues from working with Democrats. Antireform interest groups, encouraged by Armey, rushed in to condemn Clinton's proposal—one ran a series of famous ads featuring two actors playing "Harry and Louise," a married couple expressing doubts about the bill—while skeptical newspaper editorials and Limbaugh's regular broadsides further eroded public support.[116] Bill Kristol, a GOP activist, fervently decried the Clinton plan and implored Republicans to stop it, to the point that Gingrich grew concerned that Kristol might be overdoing it.[117]

Within months, however, Gingrich had moved to the forefront of a quiet crusade to kill health care reform. He lobbied Republican lawmakers against the measure, warning that their ability to get plum committee assignments in the next Congress would be at stake. Together with COS members and other party leaders, he convinced the US Chamber of Commerce not to endorse the bill's employer insurance mandates, told corporate leaders that supporting reform would endanger their long-term interests, coordinated with an outside advocacy group to have protestors shadow the traveling caravan that had been commissioned to sell Clinton's bill, and interceded to prevent GOP moderate Fred Grandy (R-IA) from offering an amendment that might improve the measure's chances of passage.[118] Ultimately, however, it was Gingrich's decision to target another White House bill, anticrime legislation, that delivered the coup-de-grace to health care reform. He and Armey relentlessly attacked the bill for being too liberal—paying for youth to play "midnight basketball," for instance—and they complained that the minority party in the House had been given no opportunity to amend it. Because the two kept the Conference largely united against the crime bill, Democratic leaders could not give a pass to doubters within their own ranks who wanted to vote no. Democrats plowed ahead anyway, and when the rule for considering the crime bill came to the floor in August 1994, it unexpectedly lost, 210 to 225. Gingrich subsequently gave the green light to GOP moderates to negotiate a compromise crime bill, but the damage had been done: Democrats looked like a party in disarray, and with little time left to legislate before Election Day, they decided to postpone health care legislation indefinitely.[119]

Gingrich had vividly demonstrated the political value of unremitting and unified minority party opposition. By the summer of 1994, he "had united Republicans in the House to an extent no party in Congress has been unified in the last half-century," one journalist opined. GOP opposition had slowed the Democrats' legislative progress and had made the majority look divided and ineffectual. Gingrich argued that Democrats could not plausibly respond by blaming their problems on Republicans while simultaneously insisting that they were legislatively effective and deserved the right to govern. As Bill Richardson (D-NM) had warned in January 1994, if his party could not pass health care and crime legislation, "we're history."[120] Successful obstruction improved the Conference's morale as well, and GOP House candidates were rewarded with a wave of campaign contributions from energized supporters. The minority whip continued this strategy when he put the brakes on a Democratic lobbying disclosure bill in September with a last-minute campaign against it. Gingrich, whom one reporter called "the dominant figure of the turbulent final days of this year's House session," warned Democrats that if they didn't work with the GOP, "every chance I get to wreck the train I'm going to wreck it."[121]

Legislative obstruction was not Gingrich's only means of achieving a Republican majority. GOPAC spent an impressive $2 million to accomplish what it called in an internal document its "most fundamental goal—winning Republican control of the U.S. House."[122] Much of that money went to candidate recruitment, training, advertising, and the continued distribution of Gingrich's audiotapes to potential election candidates. Millions of dollars flowed to GOPAC from wealthy business owners who could stay anonymous because, Gingrich maintained, the organization was not a federal election entity that required the disclosure of donors. GOPAC also connected candidates with wealthy individuals who then gave money directly to their campaigns.[123]

After some initial friction between Paxon and Gingrich—Paxon pushed back when Gingrich "tried to inject himself into" the NRCC's business by suggesting whom to hire as executive director—the pair developed a strong working partnership. The GOP whip personally visited over 120 congressional districts around the country and raised some $3 million for the party's coffers, and Paxon described him as the party's "chief cheerleader, chief fund-raiser, chief recruiter and chief message developer." In a crucial move that would become the norm for both congressional parties, he and Paxon indicated to their more ambitious brethren that the assignment of future committee leadership posts would be contingent on lawmakers' fundraising prowess. This helped increase donations by incumbent Republicans to the NRCC a hundredfold, from $50,000 two years before to $5 million in the 1994 election cycle. Lobbying groups were also warned that their influence in Washington could wane if they failed to contribute to Republicans who were challenging Democratic incumbents.[124]

By late 1993, the electoral environment was noticeably shifting in the GOP's favor. Tellingly, Democratic Caucus Chairman Steny Hoyer (D-MD) tried to lower the bar for evaluating that year's elections. "If we perform and if the economy remains strong," he told one reporter in January 1994, "we've got a good chance at losing a minimal number of seats." Four months later, Oklahoma Republican Frank Lucas won a special election to a seat previously held by a Democrat; two weeks after that, following the decision by Gingrich and Paxon to pour resources into a special election in Kentucky, the GOP candidate, Ron Lewis, won in an upset. The outlook for Republicans continued to brighten: the reelection bids of a growing number of Democratic incumbents were rated too close to call, internal surveys indicated a possible Republican electoral wave in November, and generic congressional ballot polls showed that, for the first time since the early 1950s, voters leaned more toward the GOP.[125] Gingrich publicly predicted a thirty-four-seat pickup by his party, which would move it close to majority status, and Dick Armey entertained the notion of running for *majority* leader after the November elections.[126] One House Republican aide told a Senate colleague, "We're having daily meetings planning what we're going to do when we take over the House. This is not a joke. They have it all planned out."[127]

Much of the electoral communication by GOPAC, Gingrich, and Gingrich's peers was inflammatory and highly partisan. Shortly before the 1994 elections, the whip cited the recent murder of two children by their mother Susan Smith as a reason to vote for the GOP (to "change" the country's "sick society"), and *Time* magazine wrote that Gingrich "has perfected the politics of anger."[128] But the Georgia congressman also hoped to capture the House with a positive alternative program. As in the past, much of his agenda-related rhetoric, at least in the early months of the 103rd Congress, reflected an enduring desire for transformational change via an election-driven, Gingrich-led "revolution." At a GOPAC meeting held shortly after the 1992 elections, he explained that everything they did had to be aimed at building a new opportunity society, and he identified his "primary mission" as being the "advocate of civilization," "definer of civilization," and the "leader (possibly) of the civilizing forces."[129] He tried to communicate his transformational vision with a two-hour, ten-week university course, Renewing American Civilization, taught at Kennesaw State College in 1993 and made available to a wider audience by satellite and videotape.[130] Gingrich contended that the class was purely educational, but its title mirrored language he used to frame the midterm elections for House Republicans, and it plugged companies that had provided tax-deductible donations to develop the course. The nonprofit think tank responsible for its production, the Progress and Freedom Foundation, was headed by a past executive director of GOPAC, suggesting close ties between the course and Gingrich's campaign operations. Ben Jones, a former Democratic congressman and television star who was running against Gingrich in 1994, filed a formal complaint about the class with the House Ethics Committee, which would later cause trouble for Gingrich.[131]

A top priority for Gingrich was to put together a constructive election-year platform that would be endorsed by the entire Conference and sufficiently concrete in its particulars to justify reversing four decades of one-party control in the House. Crafting a promissory agenda to improve the minority party's brand was hardly unprecedented, having been tried in Congress as far back as the 1940s, and Gingrich had developed contract-like treatises for voters multiple times before.[132] Unlike his previous attempts, however, this time Gingrich had the backing of party leaders and junior Republicans, an opportunity to contrast the agenda with a Democratic White House, and a real possibility that it would be a roadmap for governing.[133] Not even the ethical problems of President Clinton—a tempting topic for Gingrich, given his history of disparaging the behavior of partisan opponents—were to distract from this agenda. He advised Republicans in an internal memo that "our theme must be [that] 'White water [*sic*] . . . will not save a single family, educate a single child, help cure a disease or create job[s]—Republican initiatives will—let's talk about these.'"[134]

Initial proposals for an election manifesto centered on a "pro-active 'replace the welfare state' legislative agenda" that would borrow ideas from Gingrich's Renewing American Civilization courses.[135] Following the Salisbury gathering, Gingrich tasked Armey with drafting a "contract with the American people" that would be considered by a GOP House within its first one hundred days.[136] With input from Republican incumbents and challengers, Armey identified agenda items that could garner broad support within the party and among voters and allied interest groups.[137] Some of the items had been advocated by Republicans for years, such as federal tax cuts, a balanced budget constitutional amendment, and welfare reform. Others were new. Rep. Chris Shays, for instance, proposed a rule that members of Congress must be subject to the laws they pass.[138] After the list was narrowed down to ten policy items, working groups hashed out the details and put them in the form of actual bills, and focus groups and polls were solicited to assess how best to frame them.[139]

The job of selling the document to the outside world was delegated to a "planning and learning team" of lawmakers and staff, and Gingrich marketed it as well.[140] When the Contract with America was revealed at the GOP's Capitol Hill Club, Frank Luntz assured the audience that, "if you phrase your support for each Contract item the way it is written, you will find that at least 60% of your constituents will support you." Gingrich mollified prochoice Republicans who were unhappy with language (slyly added by Armey) that would bar counseling on abortion for welfare recipients. Efforts to get buy-in from the Senate proved less successful. One GOP aide recollected that "[Trent] Lott was sympathetic," but Minority Leader Robert Dole "hated the idea" and decided that his party should not sign on.[141] Still, Gingrich managed to secure signatures from most House Republican incumbents and many GOP challengers. He wanted to release the Contract with maximum fanfare, and on September 27 he unveiled the document before the Capitol building, joined by over 350 Republican candidates. The event was followed up with ads touting the Contract in widely read magazines like *Reader's Digest* and *TV Guide*, and Gingrich encouraged talk radio personalities to publicize it on their shows.[142]

It was not immediately clear that the Contract would actually help Republicans get elected. Gunderson recalled that many of his colleagues "didn't take it seriously," and polling showed that few voters were aware of the document.[143] Even worse, Democrats started using the Contract as a partisan weapon. They attacked their GOP challengers as "clones of Newt Gingrich who had signed away their independence." President Clinton dismissed what he called the "Contract *on* America" as a collection of unrealistic promises, and Democratic leaders circulated talking points against the document and criticisms of it by Fred Grandy and other Republicans.[144] Gingrich insisted that these critiques only served to give the document more publicity, but he nonetheless did not let the attacks go undefended. His aide Joe Gaylord counseled GOP campaign managers on ways to respond, and the RNC put together a "Red Book" of talking points to rebut arguments against the Contract. Gingrich, Armey, and Paxon offered tips to besieged candidates, such as accusing their opponents of harboring a "secret plan" to increase taxes and cut social welfare programs.[145]

Even before the Contract with America had been made public, the conventional wisdom was that 1994 would be a bad election year for the Democratic Party. Clinton was unpopular in many states and congressional districts, and multiple polls showed deep voter dissatisfaction with Democratic incumbents. Gephardt encouraged fellow partisans to "expose the rust on the Republicans' armor," and the White House gathered opposition research on Gingrich, but the DCCC had waged what the columnist E. J. Dionne called "a largely defensive campaign," and the White House had put electioneering on the backburner while trying to pass the health care and anticrime measures.[146] Political observers expected the GOP to retake the Senate, though few predicted a Republican House of Representatives. As one journalist wrote in October, "a Republican takeover of the House is still a longshot."[147] "Not a lot of us believed that we would gain the majority" that year, remembered DeLay, and as Ray LaHood, Michel's chief of staff who was running for Michel's seat, recounted, "I had listened to Gingrich predict victory so many times that I ignored his predictions in 1994."[148]

On Election Day, House Democrats nervously awaited the verdict of voters, and Republicans prayed that they would finally be victorious. GOP hopes grew when the initial election returns came in. Republicans were winning one open seat after another, while Democratic incumbents fell like dominos. It soon became clear that the election would be a major Republican wave. Indeed, not only were rank and file Democrats losing their seats, but so too were some of the majority party's most powerful and entrenched senior lawmakers. The latter included Judiciary Committee Chairman Jack Brooks (D-TX), who had served in Congress since 1953, and Ways and Means Chairman Dan Rostenkowski (D-IL), who lost to a political newcomer despite representing a heavily Democratic district, in part because he had been indicted for criminal activity uncovered during investigations of the House Post Office. Even Tom Foley was defeated—the first time a Speaker of the House had lost a reelection bid in over a century.

At long last, Gingrich's party had broken its unprecedented losing streak. For the first time since 1954, Republicans would have a majority in the US House of Representatives. They ultimately won an astonishing fifty-two seats, flipping Democratic districts across the country, especially in the once-impenetrable South, and not one GOP House incumbent lost reelection. Astounded DC insiders and reporters drew comparisons to powerful forces of nature, describing it as a "sea change," a "tsunami," a "tidal wave," and an "earthquake." The cover illustration of *Time* magazine depicted a massive elephant squashing a donkey, its eyes bulging from its head because of the weight.[149] Come January 1995, Gingrich would finally achieve two of his biggest goals: a Republican House and the speakership.

Conclusion

Gingrich spent his last six years in the minority doggedly engaged in entrepreneurial efforts to assist both his party and himself. By expanding the candidate outreach of GOPAC, raising massive amounts of campaign cash, recruiting more allies, encouraging House members to adopt his strategic vision, formulating a party agenda, and maneuvering to be Bob Michel's successor, Gingrich had positioned himself to become the first Republican Speaker of the House in forty years and to take credit for the seemingly impossible GOP takeover of the House of Representatives.

During this period, the ambitious party entrepreneur had righted his strategic stool, in part by accumulating more resources and deemphasizing (though not abandoning) his audacious goal to transform society. But was Gingrich truly the "modern-day Moses" who had single-handedly brought Republicans to the promised land, as many claimed?[150] Whether he really was or not—a point we return to in our concluding chapter—what mattered more, at least for the internal politics of Congress, is that lawmakers *believed* Gingrich was responsible. As evidence, they could point to his unceasing efforts to create a GOP majority and his investment of incalculable hours toward that goal. To them, the message of 1994 was clear: voters preferred a Republican-led House over a Democratic one because of Gingrich's oppositional strategies, nationalized partisan messaging, and aggressive campaign tactics.[151] This belief would allow Gingrich to begin his speakership with a rare degree of intraparty goodwill and deference.

However, even as House Republicans were still flush with victory, those who looked carefully could spot potential dangers that, if unheeded, could cause them trouble, including the fact that the Republican majority would be highly inexperienced at the art of governance. A half-dozen years earlier, Gingrich had lamented that his party lost opportunities to do more during Reagan's presidency because "we had grown up in opposition. We weren't prepared for governing."[152] Would the new Speaker-to-be recall his own cautionary words?

Having come up short in his efforts to win a congressional seat in 1974 and 1976, Gingrich was finally elected to the House for the first time in 1978. *Source*: Mel Steely papers, University of West Georgia Special Collections.

Congressman Guy Vander Jagt was the NRCC chair who named Gingrich to head the new Project Majority Task Force early in the Georgian's congressional career. *Source*: The Joint Archives of Holland at Hope College.

Paul Weyrich, cofounder of the Heritage Foundation, was one of Gingrich's allies and informal advisers during his first years in Congress. *Source*: Paul Weyrich Collection, American Heritage Center, University of Wyoming.

Gingrich with President Ronald Reagan in 1983. While President Reagan helped shift the Republican Party in the conservative direction that Gingrich wanted, the Georgian did not hesitate to challenge Reagan when he thought the president stood in the way of electing a GOP House majority. *Source*: The Ronald Reagan Presidential Library.

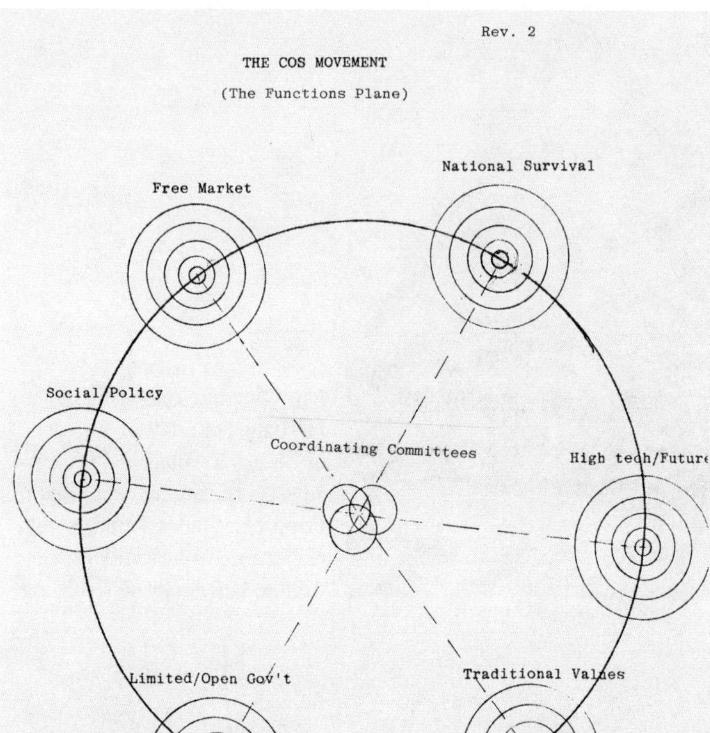

Gingrich tried to meld political tactics with broader theories of revolutionary change, and he sometimes illustrated his ideas with images like this one, taken from an early Gingrich memo. *Source*: Gingrich Papers, University of West Georgia Special Collections.

This button was one of many ways that Gingrich and GOPAC tried to bring attention to the high incumbency rate of Democrats and the need for a GOP House majority. *Source*: Matthew N. Green's private collection.

A furious Speaker Tip O'Neill admonishes Gingrich on the House floor on May 15, 1984. His outburst, which violated the rules of the chamber, raised Gingrich's public profile dramatically. *Source*: C-SPAN.

Gingrich meeting with President George H. W. Bush, Minority Leader Bob Michel, and others at the White House. Gingrich's relationships with Michel and Bush were often strained, and his successful campaign to defeat Bush's budget agreement in 1990 was a serious blow to the Bush presidency. *Source*: George H. W. Bush Presidential Library and Museum.

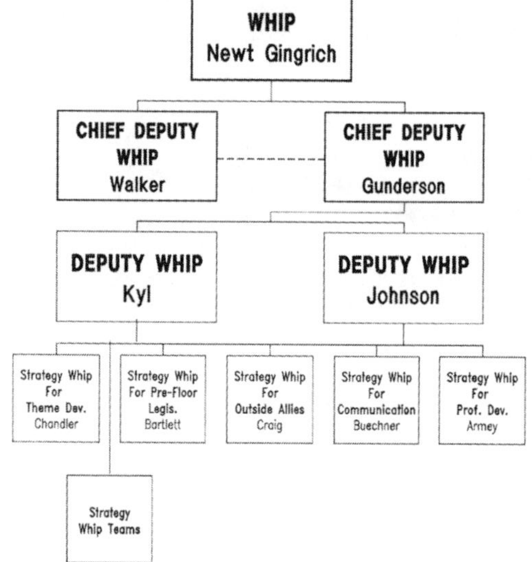

As minority whip, Gingrich changed the structure of the whip's office to add communication operations and include both moderates and conservative allies. *Source*: Gingrich Papers, University of West Georgia Special Collections.

Gingrich touts the Contract with America, which was credited by many with giving Republicans control of the House for the first time in forty years. It also served as a valuable roadmap for legislative action in the first few months of the 104th Congress. *Source*: C-SPAN.

Many of the ad-hoc management practices of the House were streamlined, professionalized, or eliminated under the Gingrich speakership. *Source*: Clerk of the House of Representatives.

Speaker Gingrich often drew fierce opposition from Democrats and progressives. *Source*: Matthew N. Green's private collection.

Gingrich and President Bill Clinton negotiating in December 1995. Conflicts between President Clinton and congressional Republicans were a major theme of Gingrich's speakership. Though some negotiations proved fruitful for the Speaker, others led to stalemate and, in late 1995 and early 1996, two politically damaging government shutdowns. *Source*: William J. Clinton Presidential Library.

Serving as Speaker of the House is an exhausting, high-pressure job. It was especially so for Gingrich. *Source*: Mel Steely papers, University of West Georgia Special Collections.

CHAPTER 5

PROMISE AND PITFALLS (1995–1996)

On January 4, 1995, the House voted along almost perfect party lines to elect Newt Gingrich as their next Speaker. Sworn in by John Dingell (D-MI), the most senior member of the chamber, Gingrich became the first Republican Speaker since Joseph W. Martin some forty years earlier. It was a truly remarkable achievement for the longtime minority party backbencher.[1]

Gingrich began his speakership in a position of strength, centralizing power in his new office with a sizeable, highly energized, and seemingly cohesive House majority behind him. But power was not all that mattered to Gingrich. As journalist Elizabeth Drew observed, "he was out to destroy the entire force behind the idea of an activist federal government."[2] Doing so would require effective legislative leadership, keeping a GOP majority in Congress, and, if President Clinton did not cooperate, electing a Republican to the White House who would sign their bills into law.[3]

In this chapter, we look at Gingrich's speakership in the 104th Congress (1995–1996). We begin with an overview of his goals, which shifted somewhat after the 1994 elections, and his resources and liabilities in pursuing those goals. Then we look at the major institutional changes initiated by Gingrich, along with his role as a public leader. Finally, we examine Gingrich's legislative record in the 104th Congress, which included both impressive policy wins and some prominent failures.

Gingrich's Goals, Assets, and Liabilities

Even though he had become Speaker of the House, Gingrich still saw himself as a party entrepreneur. Instead of focusing on winning a GOP majority, he now shifted his goal to protecting that majority. His other party-wide objective, social transformation, remained unchanged. Indeed, Gingrich believed this latter goal was closer at hand and could be accomplished by making the House the center of national policy making while repositioning the speakership as a vanguard for citizen mobilization. Unlike past Speakers, Gingrich saw himself as "essentially a political leader of a grassroots movement seeking to do nothing less than reshape the federal government along with the political culture of the nation," as he himself put it.[4] Finally, with respect to his interest in personal power, Gingrich wanted not only to protect his newfound influence but to enhance it—perhaps by running for president.

For Gingrich to achieve these objectives, he and his fellow House Republicans would need to demonstrate to voters that ending Democrats' four-decade reign in the majority had not been for naught.[5] This would require Gingrich to be a responsible, effective leader who could help bring about substantive legislative victories. Was this possible? In the plus column, Gingrich was poised to benefit from his own assets and skills as well as significant resources and a favorable political environment. As the tireless cheerleader for a GOP takeover of the House, he had earned a warrant to exercise substantial influence.[6] Nearly three-fifths of the Conference was starting their third term or less, and many of them were grateful to Gingrich for campaigning on their behalf, including the estimated 45 percent of freshmen Republicans who had received audiotapes of Gingrich or other support from GOPAC in their election bids.[7] The party was more ideologically cohesive, or at least more unified in their voting behavior,[8] and most of its members shared his belief in parties-as-teams with the Speaker as head coach.[9] The bulk of his skeptics had left Congress, and those that remained put their concerns about Gingrich on the backburner. Gingrich further benefited from an inner circle of talented leaders, including Majority Leader Dick Armey, Bob Walker, Bill Paxon (NRCC chair), and John Kasich of Ohio, the incoming chairman of the Budget Committee.[10] Gingrich institutionalized their collaboration by forming a Speaker Advisory Group, led by Walker, which included the Speaker, Armey, Paxon, Majority Whip Tom DeLay, Deputy Whip Dennis Hastert, and Conference Chair John Boehner. He would also retain GOPAC as an external instrument of electioneering, along with his Renewing American Civilization class and other institutional bases of support that made him the first Speaker with a "far-flung political empire," described by two journalists as "Newt Inc."[11]

In addition, as a "conservative futurist" who kept one eye on the twenty-first century and the other on the conservatism of the past,[12] Gingrich's penchant for strategic thinking and his broad intellectual vision could channel the ambitions of newer members while offering a set of ideas for the entire party to rally around. Within weeks of the 1994 elections, he introduced the incoming freshmen to his "vision, strategies, projects, and tactics" model, declared that "our current problems are largely intellectual and that we need new ideas," and unabashedly described "five great truths of our generation."[13] "We have to accelerate the transition from a second-wave mechanical, bureaucratic society to a third-wave information society," he said in a speech in November 1994, and "replace the welfare state with an opportunity society." Such language might further inspire his junior colleagues going forward, as would Gingrich's penchant for evoking the historic nature of the election, and lessen the threat any potentially wayward Republicans could pose to "making history."[14]

The new Speaker's rhetorical abilities and emphasis on generating sympathetic press coverage were also resources that could help him and his party compete against resentful congressional Democrats and persuade voters to keep Republicans in power. Gingrich especially believed that communication would be vital to his speakership, and his press team was designed to mimic the White House's own operation in its speed and coordination. In one memo from 1996, he encouraged his colleagues to demonstrate empathy and relate to their audience through family and children, and, in an allusion to the Clinton campaign mantra "it's the economy, stupid," he suggested the alternative phrase "it's Washington, stupid!"[15]

Lastly, the 1994 elections created an amenable political climate for legislatively minded Republicans. The GOP controlled the Senate, and while Clinton remained president, he was clearly taken aback by having, as he later put it, "the living daylights beat out of us." House Democrats were stunned by their 1994 defeat and ill prepared for political battle, for unlike their colleagues in the Senate, virtually none of them had ever served in the minority before.[16] Moreover, several of their more conservative brethren, including Nathan Deal (D-GA), Greg Laughlin (D-TX), and Billy Tauzin (D-LA), would switch to the Republican Party the following year, further demoralizing the Democratic rank and file.[17]

On the minus side of the ledger, Gingrich would have to navigate the shifting winds of the political environment while overcoming his own flaws. He could be intellectually unfocused, with a mind that, as Drew wrote, "hopped and skipped about, from idea to idea, snippet to snippet," and he could be similarly undisciplined in his public rhetoric.[18] Shortly before the new Congress met, outgoing Republican leader Bob Michel warned in a speech to the Cosmetic, Toiletry, and Fragrance Association that although Gingrich was intelligent and verbally gifted, he "fires off far too many memos" and suffers from a "failure to follow up."[19] The new Speaker's questionable organizational skills would be put to the test like never before, yet he lacked allies who could help him focus and stay on task, such as Vin Weber, who had retired after the check-bouncing scandal in 1992, and Bob Walker, who, while personally close to Gingrich, had lost the race for GOP whip to Tom DeLay.

Gingrich also faced nagging questions about his own ethics. The charges filed by Ben Jones against Gingrich in September 1994 over his Renewing American Civilization course remained unresolved. Two weeks before the new Congress would convene, the *Washington Post* reported that Gingrich had struck a $4.5 million deal to write two books for a publisher owned by the wealthy media magnate Rupert Murdoch. Though Gingrich said that he would surrender the generous advance, it raised uncomfortable comparisons with former Speaker Jim Wright, whom Gingrich had attacked for his own questionable book deal. Gingrich's book contract, along with the Jones complaint, threatened to distract the Conference.[20] Jones added the book deal to his ethics complaint, and when Republicans objected on the House floor to accusations by Carrie Meek (D-FL) about the Speaker's contract, the resulting fracas was widely covered in the press.[21]

Another potential hindrance was Gingrich's inexperience as a legislative leader. He had introduced fewer bills than the average member of Congress (see chapter 1) and, unlike his immediate predecessors as Speaker, lacked extensive committee knowhow. This was a problem insofar as his entire party was similarly green: very few of its members had ever served in a legislative majority, and the skill set required to govern was markedly different from the one Republicans had developed as a minority party. That Gingrich and his colleagues were inexperienced at being in the majority brought both possibilities and perils. On one hand, their new ability to set the House agenda might make the GOP rank and file more open to Gingrich's bold reforms and policy proposals. On the other hand, House Republicans would not have the luxury of time to learn how to be effective: the countdown to the 1996 elections started the moment Gingrich's hand grasped the Speaker's gavel.

Even more troubling than his lack of leadership experience was how Gingrich did not seem especially concerned about the legislative side of the job. He told Elizabeth Drew that "a whole new debate, with new terms" was "more important than legislative achievements. . . . We'll be building a bow-wave of change."[22] While perhaps inspiring to conservative true believers, such grand rhetoric and lofty transformational goals could not substitute for the nitty-gritty, coalition-building duties of the speakership. Gingrich risked undercutting his own effectiveness if he refused to compromise his grand ideological visions in order to achieve smaller, more practical victories.

The political context also posed several obstacles to swiftly enacting a conservative legislative agenda—obstacles that Gingrich and his compatriots, flush with their electoral victory, would either minimize or ignore. The Speaker-elect insisted that the GOP "clearly had a mandate," and as far back as the early 1980s, he had advocated for the House of Representatives to lead the national government. But the House alone could not make law. The president was highly unlikely to agree with Republicans' overall agenda, even if he did support a few elements of the Contract with America. The Senate traditionally acted more slowly than the House, had internal rules that empowered minorities and encouraged compromise over ideological purity, and would be led by longtime Gingrich rival Bob Dole (R-KS).[23]

Dangers lurked within the House as well. The GOP held 230 seats and a relatively small majority that gave Gingrich little room to maneuver.[24] The rebelliousness of the Gang of Seven in the 102nd Congress suggested that Republican freshmen, who would dominate the 104th Congress, could go rogue, and the newest class was unusually young and lacking in prior governmental experience.[25] Though Gingrich hoped to cement their loyalty by appointing them to choice committees, the new lawmakers began to organize on their own and planned to move fast. As journalist Linda Killian wrote, "the mood of the freshmen was, 'Let's do it all right now.'" Nor could the loyalty of Gingrich's fellow leaders be assured. Particularly concerning were Dick Armey, the ambitious new majority leader, and Tom DeLay. DeLay had managed the 1989 whip campaign of Gingrich's opponent, Ed Madigan, had beaten longtime Gingrich ally Bob Walker in the election for majority whip, and was disliked by Gingrich for his merciless approach to politics.[26]

Finally, although Democrats were shell-shocked by the election results, their leaders soon regrouped. "Our focus, our obsession," recalled one former aide to Minority Leader Richard Gephardt, "was trying to get back the majority."[27] Many Democrats wanted to take on Gingrich specifically—either because they were still bitter about how he had helped bring down Speaker Wright in 1987, because he had headed "a project specifically designed to beat the other party," or because, as one Republican put it, "the Democrats could not believe they had lost, therefore by definition we had cheated." Regardless, the Democratic Congressional Campaign Committee had been amassing material to use against Gingrich in the event he became Speaker, and in December 1994 the Democratic National Committee developed a plan of opposition that proposed attacking him on multiple fronts, from his questionable ethics to being "mean-spirited" and "really weird." Gingrich naively believed that Democrats would shift to the right, rather than employ the same aggressive tactics he had used against them. But Democrats began criticizing Gingrich almost immediately, not only about his questionable book deal but also for his decision to hire as the House's first official historian a former academic colleague who once criticized a Holocaust class for giving insufficient attention to the Nazi perspective.[28]

In short, Gingrich remained a party entrepreneur after the 1994 elections, focusing on how to help his party keep (rather than win) control of the House, instigate a conservative revolution of society, and gain more influence for himself. But even with the many advantages he had in the 104th Congress—a grateful and united Republican Conference, other talented leaders, the organizational reach of GOPAC, his rhetorical and media skills, and the ability to set the legislative agenda—he and his party had several liabilities that could hamper his entrepreneurial objectives.

Institutional Changes in the House

Though primarily a party entrepreneur, Gingrich had also demonstrated procedural entrepreneurship while serving in the minority by creating the Conservative Opportunity Society and expanding the size and responsibilities of the GOP whip's office. He used this entrepreneurial skill again shortly after the 1994 elections. Taking advantage of his party's gratitude and lack of experience in the majority, he worked with Rules Committee member David Dreier (R-CA) and other GOP leaders to institute several bold changes to House and Conference rules.[29] These changes empowered Gingrich and weakened Democrats in the short run, and in the long run, they accelerated a decades-long shift in power from congressional committees and individual legislators to parties and party leaders.[30]

The first target for reform was the operations of the House. The Contract with America promised an audit of the chamber, and the audit's final report, revealed in July, documented shoddy bookkeeping, wasteful spending, and redundant administrative tasks, prompting a variety of internal reforms. To make lawmakers' activities more open to the public, Gingrich led an initiative that created a public Internet database of bills and roll call votes. Other operational changes were more about power than transparency or cost efficiency. Republicans put an end to the House's internal printing and mailing operations, practices that had given incumbents a natural advantage over challengers by effectively subsidizing their constituent mailings. Gingrich also eliminated legislative service organizations—member-funded groups like the Democratic Study Group (DSG) and the Republican Study Committee (RSC)—which could serve as rival power bases, as well as the House's Office of Technology Assessment, which had helped inform lawmakers on technology policy but which conservatives dismissed as an ideologically biased boondoggle.[31]

The House's committee system was a second focus for institutional restructuring. Some changes that were implemented strengthened committee chairs: for example, chairs were permitted to appoint both the leaders and members of subcommittees, hire their committee's majority party staff, and manage their committee's budget. But far more important were reforms that weakened committees and those who would lead them. For instance, following promises made in the preamble of the Contract with America, Republicans kept their existing six-year term limit on committee chairs and made it part of the chamber's rules (extending the limit to subcommittee chairs as well), banned the practice of "proxy voting" (whereby the chair could cast votes on behalf of missing committee members), and eliminated one-third of committee staff. Dreier also oversaw the dismantling of three minor committees deemed unnecessary or too beholden to liberal constituencies. Although a bolder restructuring of the committee system was abandoned for fear of alienating Republicans who would benefit from the status quo, the changes that were adopted were still substantial. Among other things, they weakened institutional rivals to party leaders and, it was hoped, they would "break the links between the Democratic power structure and the organized interests that support it."[32]

The third major area of reform involved leadership. The party and chamber rules adopted by Republicans clearly redistributed much of the influence lost by committees to party leaders, and to the new Speaker above all. The right to end floor debate over amendments that cut spending was moved from committee chairs to the majority leader. The Speaker of the House was granted primary authority over the administrative offices of the chamber. The whip organization was expanded, while the Republican Party's Research Committee, created thirty years earlier to give reformers more say in party decision-making, was abolished. Gingrich and his aides spearheaded a rule change giving the Speaker a larger percentage of the votes cast in the party's steering committee, the body responsible for determining the committee assignments of Republican lawmakers. Pressure from GOP freshmen led Gingrich to accept a term limit for the speakership, but it would be for eight years, two years longer than the term limit for chairs of committees, thereby ensuring that the Speaker could pick the next round of committee chairs after their six-year terms had expired.[33]

Even more important than his formal powers was how Gingrich exercised them during his first few months as Speaker. Gingrich formed task forces and working groups to craft legislation, as past Speakers had done, but expanded their number and jurisdiction markedly—creating at least fifteen in the early months of the 104th Congress—which allowed him to circumvent the committee system and move legislation more quickly. Unlike committees, noted two political scientists at the time, the task forces "have no budgets and no staff . . . and perhaps most important, no Democrats." He also made strategic use of committee assignments, even acting in ways that violated the spirit, if not the letter, of party rules. Deciding that the lawmakers first in line to chair the powerful Appropriations, Commerce, and Judiciary committees were too compromise-oriented and insufficiently activist, he unilaterally skipped them in favor of more junior lawmakers who fit his ideal profile, acting without the prior approval of the Conference. He also disregarded seniority by allowing some freshmen to receive sought-after committee assignments ahead of longer-serving Republicans. Enid Waldholtz (R-UT) became the first freshman in eight decades to join the Rules Committee; over a dozen first-time Republicans were given positions on Appropriations and Commerce; three more were named to Ways and Means; and three new House members were made subcommittee chairs.[34]

A Public Speaker of the House

Gingrich wanted to modify not only the formal powers of the speakership but its public profile as well. The public role of the office had been expanded well before Gingrich, with prior Speakers like Carl Albert (D-OK), Tip O'Neill, and others experimenting with new ways to reach the public directly.[35] But Gingrich, the keen student of communications who had spent years employing speeches, public events, and media interviews to tarnish the reputation of Democrats, was prepared to dramatically widen that role. He welcomed television and radio reporters to join newspaper journalists at his daily press conference and did not hesitate to defend his party's legislative agenda while attacking congressional Democrats and President Clinton. He wanted other legislators to be similarly communicative, and Conference Chair Boehner generated "a constant stream of bulletins" to other Republicans with suggested talking points. The Speaker also opened committee hearings to television cameras and directed floor cameras to show lawmakers responding to speeches and employ wide images of the full House chamber while it was in session. In one memo, he identified seven principles that should guide a politician's interactions with the press, including practicing how to use a teleprompter without sounding rehearsed, carefully controlling the circumstances of interviews, and limiting appearances on public talk shows to "very brief call-ins." Reagan, he wrote, was a model of effective communication; "neither lucky nor a genius," the former president was "an attractive, pleasant disciplined student of the art of communicating in the electronic age."[36] Gingrich surely saw himself as the same.

Some of the Speaker's early efforts to expand coverage of himself and the House backfired. C-SPAN coverage of the full House chamber revealed lawmakers paying little attention to the proceedings. Gingrich's televised press conferences sometimes became unruly or brought scrutiny to his occasional misstatements, and some Republicans resented his disproportionate media coverage. Though Gingrich soon abandoned the press conferences, he still saw the normal legislative management responsibilities of the speakership as less important than its public role. He eventually entrusted most day-to-day legislative and scheduling tasks to Majority Leader Dick Armey to have, as political scientist Paul Herrnson observed, "more time to make speeches, lecture in college classrooms, and appear on television and radio talk shows."[37]

Passing the Contract with America

The marathon first day of the 104th Congress, which lasted until well past two in the morning, included Gingrich's selection as Speaker, the adoption of new House rules, and the passage of a measure requiring that federal laws apply to members of Congress and the public alike. The next order of business was to pass all ten legislative items in the Contract with America within one hundred days.[38] Though GOP leaders had shrewdly kept divisive social issues out of the Contract,[39] and the document pledged only an up-or-down vote on its ten items rather than their actual passage, let alone enactment into law, it was "a more ambitious 'hundred days' agenda than any president has offered since FDR," noted political scientist Norman Ornstein at the time.[40] Republicans had an incredibly short window to work with and needed to strike while the iron was hot.[41] Unsurprisingly, it became a leadership-driven enterprise, with Gingrich and Armey serving as "guardians of the party manifesto," directing the process by which the Contract would pass.[42]

The first items in the Contract, known jointly as the Fiscal Responsibility Act, consisted of two separate measures: a balanced budget constitutional amendment to prohibit deficit spending, and the power for presidents to strike specific items from legislation, known as a line-item veto.[43] Since it was an amendment to the Constitution, the balanced budget proposal needed a supermajority vote to pass, a threshold that would be hard for House Republicans to meet—especially since Democrats and balanced budget–minded Republicans were unhappy that the amendment required a three-fifths vote in Congress to increase taxes. After negotiations with different factions in the Conference, including a last-minute meeting with disgruntled GOP freshmen, Gingrich successfully managed in late January to secure the votes needed to approve it, albeit without the more controversial supermajority tax provision. It was a major early victory, but the need for lengthy negotiations to build a coalition also revealed the potential for dangerous intraparty divisions, even regarding proposals upon which the entire party had presumably agreed. In addition, while the line-item veto passed easily two weeks later, 294 to 134 (with 71 Democrats joining all but four Republicans in favor), the ultimate fate of both the budget amendment and the line-item veto underscored the difficulty of turning Contract items into actual law. In the "biggest single blow dealt to the contract by the Senate," the amendment narrowly failed to receive the necessary two-thirds vote in that chamber, while the line-item veto, though signed into law by Clinton, was struck down by the Supreme Court in June 1998.[44]

Passing the Contract's bills absorbed most of the energy and attention of House Republicans, and the Speaker played a major role in the process, meeting regularly with party factions to build consensus and even threatening to remove a chairman who insisted that his committee could not finish a bill on time. "We are exactly on schedule with not much room for slippage," Gingrich reported in mid-February. "We are learning by doing."[45] The need for speed meant lawmakers were not always familiar with the bills they were passing, and leaders relied on interest groups to an unusual degree for help with lobbying legislators to vote for key bills. The grueling schedule took its toll: in late February, Frank Wolf (R-VA) privately warned Dick Armey that "schedules, nerves and tempers are beginning to fray." Republican Vice Chair Susan Molinari (R-NY) recalled in her memoir, "We had revved the engine of the train up to such a high speed that we had no time to consider, to rethink, even to go grocery shopping and remember how real people live."[46] Nonetheless, the Contract provided Republicans with "collective momentum," kept the party largely unified, and helped them overcome, in Armey's words, "contract compliance fatigue."[47] Other Contract proposals readily passed the House: crime control, welfare reform, limits on UN supervision over the US military, changes to Social Security benefits, a ban on unfunded mandates for states and localities, and limits on shareholder lawsuits. Only one item, a constitutional amendment imposing term limits on members of Congress, failed to get the necessary two-thirds vote in the chamber, a loss that zealous GOP freshmen blamed on "halfhearted" leadership by Gingrich and others.[48]

Gingrich's role in securing majorities for these bills varied, but he did contribute significantly to the successful passage of one major Contract proposal in particular: a cut in federal income taxes. Though the Conference broadly agreed about cutting taxes, dissent on tax cuts began to percolate among different segments of the party. Some were worried about its likely impact on the federal debt, while others were upset that the bill's child tax credit would disproportionately benefit wealthier Americans. Gingrich made some concessions—agreeing, for instance, to delay implementing the bill until Congress had agreed to balance the budget within seven years—but otherwise stayed firm on keeping the bill as it was, and he effectively dared his colleagues to oppose it on the floor. Though resistance continued until the very end, his gambit worked. The Contract's "crowning jewel," as Gingrich put it, passed in early April, the final Contract item to do so.[49]

The Speaker and his fellow House Republicans could rightly take pride that they had met their ambitious objective. It was the first time that a congressional party had campaigned on, and then pledged to pass, so many major bills in so short a timeline without direction from the White House.[50] Gingrich led a "promises made, promises kept"–themed pep rally for his colleagues,[51] and then commemorated the event with a more statesmanlike (and, for a Speaker, unprecedented) nationally televised speech touting the House's success and laying out the Republican agenda going forward, prompting several journalists to ask Gingrich whether he planned to run for president.[52]

The ultimate fate of the Contract bills lay out of Gingrich's hands, and as with the line-item veto and balanced budget amendment, many were buried in the cemetery of the Senate or were vetoed by the White House.[53] Nonetheless, several elements of the Contract were eventually signed into law, often as parts of other bills. These included antiterrorism and death penalty proposals,[54] child-related tax credits,[55] a measure increasing punishment for crimes involving children,[56] language that increased seniors' earning limits and their ability to pay for long-term care insurance,[57] a capital gains tax cut,[58] the ban on unfunded mandates,[59] a reduction in government paperwork,[60] and a limit on shareholder lawsuits (by veto override).[61] And Gingrich did indeed entertain the notion of riding that tide of legislative success into the White House. He visited the early primary state of New Hampshire with Clinton in June 1995, and that same month the Speaker told Bob Dole, another presidential aspirant, that he would not run "short of you ending up in a hospital *or some unforeseen reason*" (emphasis added). When Dole tied for first in the Iowa Republican straw poll in August, Gingrich told reporters that the results suggested "a remarkably open race" that "did nothing to discourage me from running." Not until November 27 did Gingrich definitively announce he would not seek his party's nomination to challenge Clinton.[62]

Conflicts with Clinton and within the GOP

Passage of the Contract was part of a bigger story in the early months of the 104th Congress: the House GOP was now able to successfully challenge congressional Democrats while also putting the White House on the defensive. Political scientist Charles O. Jones argued that "the period following the State of the Union Address [January 24, 1995] until April was essentially given over to the Republicans. . . . Those who did not know better might have thought that the House of Representatives was the government for the first hundred days of the 104th Congress." Gingrich and his fellow Republicans soaked up media attention for weeks in the postelection afterglow, while the president was relegated to the back pages. Clinton may have shied from the spotlight intentionally, hoping Gingrich would falter and the public would hold the Speaker and House Republicans responsible for unpopular legislative or political outcomes. Explained one official in the

White House after the election, "Part of the strategy, to the extent that there is a strategy, is to wait and see what Gingrich and company do."[63] But White House staff also feared that power had shifted to the legislative branch, and in a sign that Clinton was worried about what the GOP's triumphs augured for his own reelection, he tacked to the right, at least rhetorically, in the wake of the GOP wave. In his State of the Union Address in January 1995, he resurrected his "New Covenant" campaign theme from 1992, which rejected centralized governmental decision-making over empowering communities, and he sounded a conservative note on such Republican policy priorities as welfare reform, crime reduction, and illegal immigration. By April, an overshadowed Clinton gamely insisted that "the president is relevant here."[64]

Clinton's move away from the Left notwithstanding, his veto pen and bully pulpit were powerful tools that could thwart Gingrich, and conflicts between the president and congressional Republicans continued after completion of the Contract in April 1995. Clinton frequently complained about the GOP's domestic policy initiatives, and even foreign affairs, an area that once garnered bipartisan support in Washington, was not immune from an occasional disagreement between the branches. Amid seemingly unending ethnic violence in the former Eastern European country of Yugoslavia, Clinton looked for congressional support for deploying twenty thousand US military personnel as part of a NATO peacekeeping operation. Gingrich felt "ambivalence," however, lacking confidence in Clinton's military leadership and unconvinced that deploying American troops was necessary, yet also seeing merit in bringing peace to the region. Eventually, the House voted to support American military forces in the region while Republicans maintained their disagreement with the president's policy choice, a stance that had the benefit of allowing the GOP to keep up its criticism of the president without taking blame for torpedoing the peace effort.[65]

Figuring out how to circumvent an uncooperative executive branch was not the only trial facing Gingrich as the 104th Congress progressed. The Contract had given House Republicans a preset agenda that helped keep them mostly united,[66] and it also followed logically from Gingrich's novel vision of a House-led national government, "transform[ing] a weak, discredited institution [the House] into a humming legislative engine that could tow the Senate and White House behind it," as two reporters put it.[67] But to keep that legislative engine from stalling after the first hundred days, Gingrich would need new bills and issues to hold his party together and bridge the gap between more senior and moderate lawmakers on the one side and the party's conservatives and freshmen on the other. He would also have to deal with the fatigue that had set in after the House had been in session for nearly 530 hours, over double the time spent in session during the previous Congress. Gingrich "began to get overextended," he later recalled, trying to juggle a panoply of personal and legislative initiatives.[68]

The January intraparty fight over the balanced budget amendment was one of the first fractures that appeared between Gingrich and party conservatives. Around the same time, disagreements also emerged over a Clinton proposal to offer loan guarantees to Mexico to keep that country solvent without first having to get congressional approval. Though the Speaker supported the president, many Democrats were unhappy with the idea, as were GOP conservatives who detested the idea of using US dollars to bail out another country. A group containing some freshmen Republicans endorsed a bill sponsored by one of their own, Steve Stockman of Texas, which would have forbidden any American aid to Mexico unless Congress approved it first. Gingrich resolved the matter by allowing the Conference to vote on whether to bring Stockman's bill to the floor; when Republicans voted 105–59 against doing so, the measure was effectively dead.[69]

As the House shifted its attention to passing appropriations bills to fund the government, more disputes bubbled up between Gingrich on the one hand and restless committees or groups of rank and file Republicans on the other. Gingrich had to press moderates to go along with a government spending measure that included antiabortion provisions and reductions in social services. When Gingrich took a laissez-faire attitude toward another appropriations bill, moderate Republican Sherwood Boehlert (NY) successfully derailed it, objecting to its antienvironmental proposals. Appropriations Chairman Bob Livingston grew increasingly irritated that the Speaker, who had insisted that appropriation subcommittee chairs pledge to follow the directives of party leaders, "played the role of appropriations overseer" and insisted over Livingston's objections that contentious policy riders be inserted into spending bills.[70]

Intraparty conflicts popped up on other issues as well. In a further sign that Gingrich's sway over his party had its limits, the Agriculture

Committee rejected a leadership-backed bill to reorganize federal agricultural programs, ignoring a threat from Gingrich and other leaders to cut or derail farm programs if their measure was not adopted. On another occasion, freshmen Republicans forced GOP leaders to hold a vote earlier than they had planned on a bill imposing stricter registration rules on lobbyists; they did so by credibly threatening to help Democrats add those rules to a different bill. Republican defectors joined the minority party to kill two major spending bills that year, and in October, Gingrich was forced by GOP freshmen to give a second coveted committee assignment to one of their own, Mark Neumann (R-WI), after the Speaker had backed Neumann's removal from an Appropriations subcommittee for his uncompromising approach to budget cutting. The Conference's first-term lawmakers, Gingrich jokingly remarked, were like a third party, but their ability to cause Gingrich headaches was no laughing matter.[71]

The Government Shutdowns

A key turning point that shifted the narrative of Gingrich and House Republicans from popular drivers of national policy to extremist, uncaring ideologues was the high-stakes battle with President Clinton over tax and budget policy. Though Republicans had endorsed a balanced budget in principle, the Speaker wanted to enact actual budget cuts that would eliminate the federal deficit within seven years. Budget Committee Chairman Kasich warned that doing so was unrealistic, but Gingrich and other leaders outvoted Kasich. "It was Newt way out there on his own," a staffer later recalled.[72]

Some Republicans were alarmed when Gingrich informed them about his plans for huge budget cuts. Nonetheless, following weeks of internal negotiations with various factions in the party, often mediated by Gingrich himself, the House enacted a budget resolution in May that spelled out the spending reductions necessary to create a balanced budget, and Gingrich headed a new task force to write the particulars. Anticipating criticism from Democrats, an internal Conference memo outlined several themes that could be used to defend the plan, such as promises to "balance the budget by cutting spending first" but also "protecting Social Security" and standing behind a commitment to "preserve, protect and improve Medicare."[73]

Republicans seemed to have momentum behind them. Clinton ceded considerable ground by proposing his own budget-balancing plan, albeit over ten years, rather than seven—a move that infuriated Democrats, especially when the president suggested cutting Medicare and Medicaid spending to do it. But Gingrich and other Republicans believed they could get Clinton to go further and accept their own budget-cutting bill. Internal party surveys from August indicated that the GOP agenda was popular with voters and that Republicans were more trusted on Medicare than Democrats. After the Speaker helped resolve disagreements within his party over the details of the massive reconciliation measure, it passed the House and Senate in late October. The bill reduced federal spending, including funding for Medicaid and Medicare, by nearly $900 billion over a seven-year time span, while also offering a substantial $245 billion tax cut. The Speaker was prepared to confront the president directly on the issue. "I will not blink," he insisted, bolstered by House freshmen and other congressional conservatives who balked at any sign of compromise.[74]

Congress had fallen behind schedule in passing appropriations for the coming fiscal year, but the Speaker believed the delay could be advantageous. Starting in the spring, he had been suggesting that the threat of a government shutdown, caused by the failure to enact appropriations bills, could compel the president to approve Republican budget cuts,[75] and the backlog of appropriations legislation made that threat seem more credible. Gingrich figured that the White House would want to avoid being blamed for a shutdown, and he was further encouraged by Clinton's reversal on cutting Medicare spending as well as rumors that the president was inclined to make additional compromises.[76] This would prove to be a costly miscalculation. Gingrich had not adequately considered that the size of many of the cuts included in their reconciliation bill would be unpopular with the general public and especially with Democratic voters, and that the months of attention focused on House Republicans as the drivers of legislation meant they would likely be held accountable for any negative policy outcomes.[77] He also badly discounted the ability of Democrats and Clinton to move public opinion in their direction and seriously overestimated his own skills at doing the same.

In private, Gingrich gave White House staff the impression that he wanted to reach an agreement with Clinton to avoid shutting down the government, and the Speaker and the president held regular talks about a possible deal on reconciliation. But distrust between the pair, coupled with Gingrich's belief that he held the upper hand and pressure from the flanks of both parties not to compromise, hindered an agreement. After Gingrich hinted in September that some funding cuts could be restored if Clinton agreed to other legislative priorities, such as welfare reform, "the [GOP] freshmen went ballistic," and he backed away from the idea. Meanwhile, Democrats were waging a full-court public relations campaign against Republicans, accusing them of slashing the social safety net in the reconciliation measure to provide tax breaks for the rich. When Gingrich suggested in an October speech that he wanted Medicare to "wither on the vine," Democrats pounced, pointing to the statement as proof that the GOP secretly wanted to eliminate the program. At a meeting with Clinton and other congressional leaders on November 1, Gingrich slammed the president and vice president for running unfair attack ads against Republicans, while Clinton said that if they wanted their budget approved, "you're going to have to get yourself another president."[78]

These disputes culminated in a dramatic budget showdown in November. To keep government operations funded while negotiations continued, Congress had approved a spending bill that would fund the government through midnight on November 13. As that date approached, and without any breakthrough in the negotiations, congressional Republicans passed another short-term appropriations bill, but this time they included structural changes to Medicare, figuring Clinton would not risk shutting down the government by vetoing the bill. The president, calling their bluff, swiftly vetoed the bill, and a last-minute White House meeting between Clinton, Gingrich, Armey, and Dole was unsuccessful. Lacking funds, several federal agencies closed the next day, and some eight hundred thousand nonessential government employees were unable to report for work. Parks were shuttered, passports could not be processed, and checks to veterans were suspended.[79]

Clinton initially feared that the Republicans would successfully blame him for the unpopular shutdown. But then the Speaker made a major public relations error. The previous week, on an Air Force One flight with the president and other dignitaries to the funeral of Israel's assassinated prime minister Yitzhak Rabin, Gingrich had been given little face time with Clinton and had to leave from the rear of the aircraft rather than with the president. Gingrich felt frustrated and slighted. Against the advice of his press secretary, he complained about his treatment at a breakfast press event and suggested it had contributed to his decision to pass the short-term funding bill containing the Medicare language that Clinton had opposed.[80] Democrats leapt at the chance to exploit the impression that the Speaker of the House would make American citizens suffer over a petty personal slight. With false sincerity, Clinton told the press, "If it would get the government open, I'd be glad to tell him I'm sorry." The cover of the *New York Daily News* featured an illustration of an infantilized Gingrich under the heading "Crybaby," which House Democrats enlarged and attempted to show on the floor. Gingrich had become the face of GOP intransigence and wanton cruelty. "One of the dumbest things I've done," he later admitted.[81]

Over the next several days, interparty negotiations continued, as did heated debates on the House floor—including an impromptu sit-in on the floor by angry Democrats—and new polls that showed voters believed Republicans were to blame for the shutdown.[82] Finally, Senate Majority Leader Dole told his GOP colleagues that the shutdown needed to end, and Clinton relented to Republicans' insistence that the deficit should be eliminated in seven years rather than ten. It was enough to get the government reopened, at least temporarily, and on November 19, Congress passed a bill restoring government funds for another month.[83]

The two sides continued to discuss the details of reconciliation. Gingrich was irritated that the White House had been backing away from the seven-year balanced budget commitment, and he felt pressure from House Republicans not to give in to the president. The Speaker still insisted that Clinton should accept Congress' reconciliation bill and, to prevent any chicanery by the White House, measure its impact on the deficit with numbers from the Congressional Budget Office (CBO) rather than the White House's Office of Management and Budget (OMB). Clinton, widely seen as the winner of the first shutdown battle, refused to budge, deeming the bill's tax cuts to be fiscally irresponsible and characterizing its spending reductions as too damaging to social welfare programs. Republicans sent him their bill anyway, and he vetoed it on December 6, closing the government for a second time. Though fewer federal workers were affected than during the first shutdown because Clinton had since signed several individual appropriations bills into law, the news was again dominated by negative stories of taxpayers inconvenienced by suspended services while federal employees were forced to stay at home without pay just before the Christmas holidays. Meanwhile, the White House had been employing an aggressive media campaign since November that labeled Republicans as extremists, and congressional Democrats and liberal interest groups started running attack ads against first-term House Republicans for the shutdown. A *New York Times*/CBS News poll undertaken in early December showed that Clinton's job approval ratings had climbed to over 50 percent, while Gingrich and Republicans were losing public support.[84]

The standoff also exposed a rift within the GOP. Some senior and moderate congressional Republicans, particularly in the Senate, worried that the shutdown was hurting their party's electoral chances. Senate Majority Whip Trent Lott recalled that he had told Gingrich that "we're overplaying our hand" and "pleaded with him not to do it," while Majority Leader Dole, who had also been skeptical of the strategy, wanted the standoff to end so he could focus on his presidential campaign. But more hardline Republicans and some party leaders believed in the efficacy of the approach, including Armey, DeLay, Boehner, and Appropriations Chairman Livingston. Indeed, Livingston insisted that the shutdown gave them leverage, while Boehner argued that the bad publicity that they had been enduring would reverse course if they could show real progress in balancing the budget.[85]

Gingrich initially stood with his hardline colleagues, but as negative headlines and poor polling numbers accumulated, he gradually moved toward Dole's position. When Clinton agreed to Republican demands that the budget be based on CBO projections, the Speaker tried to reopen negotiations with the White House but met with stiff resistance from within his own party. Finally, after nearly three weeks, Gingrich had had enough: he declared to the Conference that the shutdown would end, and he dared those who disagreed to "run against me" for Speaker. Republicans had brought Clinton along to the idea of balancing the budget in seven years, a not-insignificant concession by the White House, but politically it was a Pyrrhic victory.[86] Democrats had won the public relations battle, portraying the GOP as the party that wanted to cut popular government programs and that was willing to hold the federal government hostage to do so.

The bloom was off the rose for both Republicans in general and

Gingrich in particular. While 52 percent of Americans had approved of the GOP agenda in December 1994, by January 1996 that number had dropped below 30 percent.[87] The Speaker had been named *Time* magazine's "Man of the Year" in December 1995, but his approval ratings were underwater by early September, and by January 1996 they were close to Richard Nixon's numbers during Watergate, making him the nation's least-liked national political figure.[88] Freshman David Weldon (R-FL) observed that "to a certain extent our fate lives or dies on the things [Gingrich] says and does, and that's not a perfect situation." Another freshman, Mark Souder (R-IN), warned that Gingrich has "been weakened in his ability to convince us that his political judgment is always wise."[89]

Even more problematic for Gingrich and his strategic objectives, Clinton had reestablished the presidency as the focal point of American governance[90] and effectively pitted Republicans against one another while offering himself as the more reasonable, left-center leader of the country. Gingrich had, ironically, mimicked the aggressive, partisan, House-centered approach to leadership taken by his one-time nemesis, Speaker Jim Wright—and, like Wright, he had encountered strong partisan push-back that weakened his ability to govern.[91]

The Second Session of the 104th Congress

With less than a year to go before the November elections, Gingrich and fellow party leaders decided that the Conference should focus on five issues in the second session of the 104th Congress: drug enforcement, illegal immigration, the economy, welfare reform, and presidential ethics. The hope was not only to enact conservative legislation and protect their party's House majority but to achieve more lofty electoral goals, including winning the presidency, increasing their majority to hedge against future seat losses, helping increase the party's majority in the Senate, and winning more state and local races. Gingrich continued to see himself as the Republican Party's primary planner and the national leader of American conservatism; an internal leadership presentation from mid-1996 boasted that "Newt is the leader of a movement" and "should speak as the leader of the movement, not as the Speaker of the House."[92] Yet initially, at least, Gingrich opted for a less prominent profile and tried to emphasize a "kinder and gentler image," hoping to resuscitate his dismal poll numbers. He also planned to defer more to Armey on legislative strategy and focus instead on the 1996 elections, a move endorsed by many of his GOP colleagues who were unhappy about how Gingrich had managed the budget impasses with Clinton. Even some of the party's freshmen felt chastened by the government shutdowns and expressed an openness to shifting from an all-or-nothing approach to prudent compromise in order to pass legislation.[93]

Gingrich proved key to guiding his party's most dramatic and far-reaching legislative achievement in the second session of the 104th Congress: reforming the federal welfare system. There was some reason to believe that bipartisan compromise on welfare reform was possible. Clinton had promised during his 1992 presidential campaign to "end welfare as we know it," and after putting the issue aside to focus on his failed health care proposal, he offered a reform plan that provided job training, required welfare recipients to work, and limited the amount of time a welfare recipient would be eligible to receive benefits. The House GOP picked up Clinton's general ideas and carried them further. Welfare reform was a major promise in the Contract, and after the 1994 elections, Gingrich followed the lead of Republican governors and conservative activists by endorsing an overhaul of the entire welfare system from a federally run entitlement program into one in which block grants would be given to states to devise and administer their own welfare assistance programs.[94] It was a dramatic move that would implement the Speaker's long-touted desire to replace the "liberal welfare state" and undo one of the biggest legislative accomplishments of President Franklin Delano Roosevelt.

There was, however, a notable absence of consensus among Republicans over the best way to reform welfare. Social conservatives wanted stricter limits on eligibility and feared the House GOP's measure failed to discourage abortions, while party moderates were apprehensive about the effect of cutting benefits to citizens in need. But Gingrich and other leaders managed to hold the Conference together long enough to pass a more conservative welfare reform bill in March 1995, and moderates held their noses in the hope that the Senate would enact a less draconian version, which it did in September.[95]

Democrats complained loudly that even the Senate-modified bill was too harsh, as it would still cut off aid to millions of needy Americans, force millions more to comply with what they saw as unnecessarily punitive restrictions on receiving much-needed assistance, and create inequalities across the country by giving states the power to determine qualifications for receiving welfare. Clinton vetoed the measure in early January 1996, having already vetoed the budget reconciliation measure the previous month that included elements of welfare reform.[96] Republicans sought to frame the issue as a choice between opting for welfare (the Democrats' preference) or for work (the Republican goal), but Gingrich's inflammatory rhetoric did not help. For example, he generated considerable controversy by blaming the existing welfare system for the high-profile murders of a pregnant woman, Debra Evans, and her young daughter and son.[97]

After the two government shutdowns, the stalemate on welfare reform between Clinton and Congress became entangled with the politics of the 1996 presidential election. Dole, the likely GOP nominee to challenge Clinton, saw welfare reform as a useful vehicle to differentiate himself from the president. He pressed for linking Medicaid cuts to welfare reform, knowing it would prompt presidential vetoes that Dole could exploit in his campaign. However, House Republicans, eager to notch a significant legislative win, pushed to bring the bill closer to the president's preferences so Clinton would sign it. Lobbied heavily by the Dole campaign, Gingrich initially took the Kansan's side, believing only a Dole victory could keep the House in GOP hands come November. But Dick Armey and others strenuously disagreed, and amid signs that Dole's presidential campaign was faltering, the Speaker decided that the opportunity to enact welfare reform was too good to pass up. To Dole's chagrin, in July the Speaker publicly endorsed dropping cuts to Medicaid from welfare reform. When a bipartisan alternative bill with more limited restrictions on welfare recipients began gaining momentum, Gingrich lobbied lawmakers on the floor to oppose it, and the alternative bill was easily rejected. The revised, GOP-endorsed bill passed both chambers (with no resistance from Dole, who had resigned from the Senate for the presidential campaign), and in August, Clinton signed it into law. With a stroke of his pen, the president had turned a major federal entitlement into a state-led block grant program that put time limits on welfare eligibility. The new law gave congressional Republicans a huge win and inoculated Clinton from criticism by Dole, though dispirited liberals saw it as "the largest blot on his Presidency thus far."[98]

The Speaker contributed to other legislative achievements as well. One was the Telecommunications Act of 1996, signed into law on February 8, which made fundamental changes to a six-decade-old regulatory regime, introducing more competition into the telephone industry and encouraging the development of new communication technologies. Though many legislators were involved in its passage, Gingrich crucially helped facilitate a compromise between Senator Trent Lott, who sought a less expansive bill to avoid a filibuster in his chamber, and House Republicans, who preferred the law to have a more right-leaning, deregulatory focus. Political scientists C. Lawrence Evans and Walter J. Oleszek observed that Gingrich "basically brought the group together; he facilitated the bargaining process," and one staffer told them that "Gingrich was a lot different than he appears to be in public. He was quiet, just sitting there listening. Then out of the blue he came up with the solution. Gingrich totally commanded the room."[99]

Gingrich was less successful on the federal minimum wage, another issue that faced the House in 1996. Conservatives generally opposed raising it, arguing that doing so would impose undue burdens on businesses, but House Democrats achieved one of their key legislative priorities with passage of the Small Business Job Protection Act of 1996, which increased the federal hourly minimum wage from $4.25 to $4.75 before topping out at $5.15. Although the Speaker later conceded that the bill "was clearly the American people's will," the GOP did not come away empty-handed: Gingrich secured in the bill new tax cuts targeted at small businesses.[100]

The Republican Congress enacted several other major laws in the second session of the 104th Congress. They included the Helms-Burton Act, which established a statutory embargo against Cuba and the Castro government and which Gingrich touted on the floor as a "freedom contract" with the Cuban people;[101] an antiterrorism bill, passed in the wake of the Oklahoma City bombings over the objections of some House freshmen that it infringed on citizens' constitutional rights;[102] the Taxpayer Bill of Rights II, giving taxpayers a stronger bargaining position vis-à-vis the Internal Revenue Service;[103] food safety and clean water bills;[104] the Health Insurance Portability and Accountability Act of 1996 (also known as the Kennedy-Kassebaum Act, after its two cosponsors), which allowed those with health insurance keep their coverage intact even if their employment or health situations changed;[105] and the Defense of Marriage Act, which both allowed states to ignore same-sex unions and codified a legal definition of marriage that excluded gay couples.[106] Gingrich was not always central to the enactment of these measures, but he could at least take credit for their passage in the House under his watch.

The 1996 Elections

Legislative successes notwithstanding, by the fall of 1996 Gingrich and House Republicans appeared politically bruised. The twin government shutdowns had hurt their reputation. The Speaker was dogged by a continuing ethics probe into his book deal, and the Ethics Committee had appointed an independent counsel to examine his use of GOPAC and other organizations for electioneering purposes. He and other GOP leaders were criticized for an aggressive fundraising campaign that included pushing interest groups to give only to their party's candidates.[107] Democrats attacked Gingrich in thousands of negative ads and tried to tie Republican incumbents to the unpopular Speaker and the government shutdowns whenever they could. One survey suggested that voters would be less inclined to punch their ballots for a congressional candidate who supported the Speaker.[108] Gingrich repeatedly touted his success at banning ice bucket deliveries in the House, hoping to remind voters that the GOP had eliminated many of Congress's antiquated and wasteful practices, but as Elizabeth Drew put it, "the story trivialize[d] his own efforts to cut the budget and transform government."[109]

All of this did not mean that the Republican Party was destined to lose control of the House in 1996, though. The GOP had notched many remarkable policy achievements, negating any possible claim that they had led a "do-nothing" Congress. Though their aggressive fundraising raised the ire of some, including several reform-minded GOP freshmen, Gingrich, Paxon, and Tom DeLay did generate millions of needed dollars for Republican candidates,[110] and Paxon's NRCC was able to buy $8 million worth of TV campaign ads.[111] Republicans hurried to finish legislating by September so they could get back to their districts to campaign, and the GOP Conference distributed an "adjournment packet" that reiterated the passage of Contract items, offered talking points for incumbents, and suggested ways of "getting your message across through earned media." Gingrich himself campaigned in some 130 congressional districts to help Republican House candidates, and as he had for previous GOP presidential nominees, he offered to help Dole craft an agenda and strategic plan to win the November election, an offer Dole politely declined.[112]

Ultimately, the 1996 elections were a mixed bag for the GOP. Republicans maintained their majorities in Congress, allowing Gingrich to again run for Speaker, although the party lost nine seats in the House, slightly more than Republican strategists had expected. The defeat of Dole, though perhaps unsurprising given his less-than-inspiring campaign, the country's healthy economic growth, and Clinton's strong poll numbers, was nonetheless a disappointment to congressional Republicans, including Gingrich. To the extent it contributed to his victory, Clinton had demonstrated the effectiveness of advisor Dick Morris's "triangulation" strategy, working with either party when it served him best.[113]

Conclusion

The 104th Congress was historic, and not only because it was the first one since 1954 led by Republicans. The GOP sweep of Congress in 1994 presaged some of the most significant procedural reforms and policy enactments in decades. The management of the House was professionalized and power was centralized to a degree not seen for nearly a century. The national welfare system was transformed from a federal entitlement program to one in which states had considerable leeway in who received benefits and under what conditions. Greater competition was introduced into the nation's telecommunications system. Unfunded federal mandates were sharply curtailed, and the nation's budget was put on a path toward balance. By one estimate, 1996 had been the "third most productive year for major legislation" since World War II. Journalists Dan Balz and Ronald Brownstein observed that the Republican House majority meant the "policy debate [was] shifting inexorably to the right."[114] Gingrich, progenitor of the Contract with America, key negotiator on several major bills, and chief visionary of the party, could justifiably take much of the credit for this productivity.[115]

Many of the GOP's accomplishments, however, came after a difficult first year in power. The party had asserted the legislature's role vis-à-vis the president and refocused the public's attention on GOP policy priorities, but not all the items in the Contract with America became law, and the government shutdowns allowed Clinton to reassert presidential power vis-à-vis Congress. Though Republicans reformed the House in many ways, they had abandoned the more sweeping changes to the committee system hoped for by some reformers. By the end of 1995, Gingrich's hope for more transformational changes to what Republicans viewed as a bloated federal bureaucracy had not been realized.[116]

Some of these setbacks were the inevitable consequence of divided party government and unrealistic expectations shared by zealous House Republicans (particularly freshmen) and their supporters. But Gingrich also shouldered considerable blame. He overestimated his party agenda's popularity with voters and discounted the independent role of the Senate and the president in the legislative process. His grand rhetoric often failed to sway practical-minded lawmakers who dismissed it as "gobbledygook" or "psychobabble." His tendency toward gaffes at critical moments damaged his approval ratings, undermined his authority as a negotiator with the president, and hurt his standing in the Conference—a remarkable irony for someone who prized communication as a key to power. And he failed to provide a clear, realistic plan for governing after the first hundred days of the 104th Congress. In a scathing pair of memos sent to Gingrich shortly after the 1996 elections, Peter Hoekstra (R-MI) observed that "we talk vision, strategy, projects and tactics, and our performance is good at the vision level. But at the strategy and tactical levels, we are mediocre to poor." Democrats, he warned, "are better prepared to win the political battles of 1997 because they seem to have a plan and we don't."[117]

More generally, Gingrich was unable to square his role as party entrepreneur with his job as Speaker. He no longer enjoyed the luxury of being a provocative backbencher or a philosophical visionary with the flexibility to move from one big idea to the next without producing any real change. The time-consuming institutional responsibilities of the speakership not only kept Gingrich from devoting much attention to his broader entrepreneurial goals, but they also required a set of skills—coalition management, legislative leadership, and rhetorical statesmanship—that were not among his strengths.[118]

While he and his party had survived the 1996 elections, Gingrich was showing signs of losing his grip on the Conference. Other leaders had begun to tire of being subjected to long lectures about history and needlessly antagonized by his intemperate remarks, such as when he dismissed Dick Armey's plan to impose a national flat tax as "nonsense." One Republican told a reporter that "the willingness in the Republican Conference to protect him is pretty well exhausted." Ominous rumors began circulating in mid-1996 that Gingrich might be replaced. Particular danger lurked with the freshmen, who were disappointed that the Speaker had failed to extract enough concessions from the White House with the government shutdowns and were increasingly exasperated by his lack of communication about strategy and tactics. Gingrich later admitted that the new members, along with himself, "were in what turned out to be too big a hurry."[119]

CHAPTER 6

A FAILING SPEAKERSHIP (1997–1998)

The 104th Congress had produced many notable accomplishments, but by the end of 1996, the consensus was that Gingrich was a less effective Speaker than he could had been. His reputation had been tarnished by two largely fruitless government shutdowns and many verbal missteps, and he was dogged by an investigation into his past campaign practices. The 1996 elections made matters even worse for Gingrich: voters had elected Bill Clinton to a second term, and the Republican Party's majority in the House had shrunk. Going forward, the GOP lacked a Contract-like document to direct its agenda, and both leaders and rank and file members of the House Republican Party were disillusioned and uncertain about Gingrich's ability to lead the Conference.

In this chapter, we consider the second and final term of the Gingrich speakership in the 105th Congress (1997–1998), a period that was largely characterized by Gingrich's continuing inability to govern effectively and his plummeting popularity both within and outside the House. The term started badly for Gingrich, with a critical finding by the House Ethics Committee that seriously threatened his reelection as Speaker. More high-profile and avoidable mistakes led to an embarrassing coup attempt by disgruntled Republicans in July 1997. The final blow came the following November, with unanticipated seat losses by his own party, prompting Gingrich's decision to resign from Congress.

Ethics Charges and a Narrow Election for Speaker

Gingrich's road to reelection as Speaker in 1997 would not be as smooth as it had been two years before. The poor showing of House Republicans in the elections, and enduring worries about Gingrich's leadership skills and ethics problems, had cultivated doubts about whether he should remain in charge. One influential conservative, Steve Largent (R-OK), openly endorsed the idea of Gingrich stepping down during the Ethics Committee's investigation into his campaign practices, and there was speculation that other GOP lawmakers shared that sentiment.[1] There was a real possibility, then, that Gingrich might not even be renominated by his party to be a candidate for Speaker. Accordingly, he worked the phones in the days after the election, calling over fifty of his colleagues to ask for both their vote and their help with lobbying others in the Conference. He appealed to fellow party leaders for help, and he targeted members who had influence over moderates and junior lawmakers, the two groups whose support for Gingrich was especially soft. Gingrich even invited several rank and file Republicans to play a larger role in decision-making, presumably to alleviate concerns that the party had become too centralized under his leadership.[2] His campaign did the trick, and the Conference met and, without dissent, endorsed a motion to nominate him as Speaker. Gingrich struck a conciliatory tone with the press, admitted "a few big errors" in his previous term, and promised a more productive and less confrontational Congress.[3]

There was still the matter of his election for Speaker on the floor, which would require almost perfect party unity, since no Democrat was likely to vote for him and the margin between the two parties was small. Gingrich nearly derailed his own campaign when he made a startling confession in late December. After two years of having denied doing anything inappropriate, Gingrich quietly made a deal with the House Ethics Committee in which he acknowledged giving false information to the committee and failing to follow federal tax law in the operation of both his Renewing American Civilization course and a GOPAC-led televised town hall meeting. Gingrich made the bargain, as he put it, to "bring the process to an end as quickly as possible" and address the concerns of Largent and others that he could not serve as Speaker while the ethics charges remained unresolved.[4]

But his colleagues were stunned by Gingrich's unexpected admission of guilt, which created fresh misgivings about his judgment, not to mention fear that negative public reaction could hurt them all.

Gingrich did not sit idly by to see how this new development might affect the election for Speaker. The same day that he made his deal with the Ethics Committee, and in apparent violation of a pledge not to fight the committee's verdict, he held a conference call with fellow GOP leaders to develop a strategy to minimize the fallout.[5] Party leaders in turn released a letter endorsing Gingrich and began lobbying other lawmakers on his behalf. NRCC Chair Bill Paxon and Conference Vice Chair Susan Molinari (R-NY)—Paxon's spouse and daughter of Guy Molinari, whom Gingrich had blocked from becoming a subcommittee ranking member a decade earlier—held a joint news conference to emphasize that Gingrich had not broken any federal laws, and other leaders appeared on television to defend the Speaker.[6] A pair of GOP members of the Ethics Committee, Porter Goss (R-FL) and Steve Schiff (R-NM), wrote to Majority Whip Tom DeLay to announce that they would be voting for Gingrich, an endorsement that alleviated many Republicans' concern that Gingrich's ethical violations hindered his ability to serve as Speaker.[7]

Gingrich also reached out to dozens of his colleagues in late December and early January. The vast majority expressed support for his speakership; some offered strategic advice for his campaign, and at least two recounted how they had been inspired by his lectures or helped by GOPAC when they had first run for Congress.[8] But a handful conveyed qualms about reelecting him to another term. Virginia Congressman Frank Wolf refused to commit, telling Gingrich that he was thinking the matter over, and Bob Inglis (R-SC) "worried about [Gingrich's] forthrightness." John Hostettler (R-IN) expressed fear that Gingrich would remain "the center of controversy for six months," while Jon Fox (R-PA) noted that his own narrow reelection to the House made it perilous for him to support the Speaker. Two GOP lawmakers, Connie Morella of Maryland and Matt Salmon of Arizona, floated the idea of an interim or pro-tem Speaker to temporarily take the reins. Others told the Speaker they would support him "unless something terrible" or "very big breaks,"[9] though fortunately for Gingrich, the floor vote for Speaker was scheduled to occur in early January, before the Ethics

Committee issued its official report and made any recommendations for disciplinary action.[10]

The behind-the-scenes lobbying failed to stop some Republicans from openly breaking ranks. Michael Forbes (R-NY) announced in late December that he would oppose Gingrich, followed a week later by Jim Leach of Iowa.[11] But there was no concerted effort within the Conference to replace Gingrich with an alternative candidate. DeLay cautioned rank and file members who might hope to stay neutral in the Speaker election by voting "present" that, if too many of them did so, Gingrich would not have enough votes to win, and the Democratic nominee, Richard Gephardt, could be elected instead. Leaders combatted the impression of widespread doubt within the Conference by convincing a dozen Republicans who had been identified by reporters as undecided to announce their support for Gingrich.[12] The Speaker also made one final peacemaking effort, summoning the Conference to an emotional gathering at which he fielded angry complaints from several fellow partisans and promised his colleagues that he would step down if he remained a liability to the party.[13]

Given the balance of power between the two parties, as few as twenty Republicans could deny Gingrich the speakership if they voted present or chose to cast their ballots for other candidates. (Technically, fewer Republicans could frustrate Gingrich's bid if they voted for Gephardt, though none indicated they would). For a time, it seemed that as many as twenty-seven of his fellow Republicans might not support another term for the Georgian.[14] "None of us were sure he had the votes," one Gingrich aide later recalled. However, the incumbent ultimately triumphed, winning in a close election against Gephardt, who received 205 votes to Gingrich's 216.[15] Despite his victory, Gingrich had received the bare minimum of votes he needed to win, and he had lost the votes of nine Republicans—four who cast ballots for other individuals and five who voted "present"—the most defections from the majority party in a Speaker vote in seven decades.[16] And while Gingrich and his allies had successfully quelled a potential rebellion within the party ranks, a nontrivial number of Republicans probably voted for the Georgian "with serious reservations."[17]

The election was followed by another reminder of Gingrich's ethical transgressions later that month. Special Counsel James M. Cole told the

Ethics Committee that he had evidence that Gingrich had intentionally broken tax laws and then tried to cover it up. After digesting Cole's findings, the House Ethics Committee voted 7–1 to recommend a reprimand of the Speaker, along with a staggering $300,000 penalty. The full House voted 395–28 to endorse the Committee's recommendation.[18] It was one of the lowest moments in Gingrich's career: he would enter the history books as the first Speaker of the House to be officially reprimanded by the chamber. If there was a silver lining for Republicans, it was that the vote had been overshadowed in the press by Clinton's swearing-in as president and inaugural celebrations around Washington, DC.[19] Nonetheless, one aide strongly cautioned the Speaker that "the members don't like you and don't support you," and Gingrich later conceded that "some of the Republican members had grown uneasy about my leadership." As their patience with the Speaker wore thin, his margin for error rapidly diminished.[20] A journalist had prophetically cautioned the previous December that "the Gingrich galaxy has broken apart and even if he salvages his speakership . . . he may never succeed in restoring his political dominance within the country." One GOP strategist even predicted that an effort to overthrow Gingrich "could happen any minute."[21]

Attempts at Image Rehabilitation

Bob Dole's failed presidential bid and subsequent retirement from public service left Gingrich and Trent Lott, Dole's replacement as Senate Majority Leader, as the GOP's leading nationally elected officials.[22] Unlike Lott, a popular figure with a well-established reputation as a strong party leader, Gingrich had to improve his standing both among his congressional colleagues and in the eyes of the public. This proved difficult. At first, he tempered his often-polarizing appearances in the national press. Gingrich still did interviews with local media, however, and when he told Georgia reporters that a biased media and bad lawyers were to blame for his reprimand by the House, annoyed members of the idealistic Class of 1994 "saw this as just another example of his refusing to tell the truth and to take responsibility for his actions," according to journalist Linda Killian.[23]

The Speaker also pledged to be more bipartisan and focus on substance over conflict, and he made public overtures to Democrats and liberal activists, even appearing on a television program hosted by civil rights activist Jesse Jackson. Unfortunately, this alienated Republican stalwarts, and he soon abandoned that path and returned to the national spotlight as a conservative activist ideologue.[24] In March 1997, Gingrich gave "his most partisan blast since he was reprimanded by the House in January" by comparing Bill Clinton's fundraising practices to Watergate. Later that month he waded into international affairs, telling China to dial back its aggressive stance toward Taiwan or the United States would use troops to force them to do so. He also made an appeal for the passage of tax cuts and attacked government funding for the National Endowment for the Arts. As the *Washington Post* noted in mid-April, "Gingrich's full schedule of appearances this week marked the end of a period of largely shunning the spotlight." After months of avoiding nationally televised interview programs, the Speaker, who had lost fourteen pounds, sought out the media spotlight by going on the widely watched CNN interview show *Larry King Live*.[25]

Gingrich's public reemergence allowed him to resume leadership in the manner he was most comfortable with. As political scientist John Pitney had pointed out months earlier, "The essence of Gingrich's leadership style is high profile. . . . He came to power precisely through the use of the media and his public leadership style."[26] He also strategically used the press as a scapegoat, condemning reporters for not understanding what Republicans were trying to accomplish or what the public wanted. Unfortunately for Gingrich, there was little sign that his return to the public eye was improving his public approval ratings. He privately fumed that the news media were not giving him a fair shake, writing to his staff that "if a Republican cashes [a] check and a Democrat robs a bank the story begins 'the two parties withdrew money from a bank today.'" Yet Gingrich himself later admitted that "sometimes my discipline broke down and . . . I would respond with hostility to the unfavorable things that were being said about me" in the press, which in turn generated more negative stories about him.[27]

Gingrich Gaffes and Growing Disgruntlement

Gingrich was trying to improve his public reputation, but he would also need to manage his status within the Conference. At first, he and fellow leaders tried to convey a sense of forward momentum. Shortly after the elections, Conference Chair John Boehner urged his fellow House Republicans to follow Gingrich's vision of "a common purpose, a common language, and a common model for action," noting that "the Speaker has tasked the House Republican Conference with developing a framework that would articulate our fundamental operating principles." The House met only a handful of times during the entire month of January, however, and the GOP leadership offered far less legislative direction than it had in early 1995. Gingrich biographer and former aide Mel Steely later wrote that "it was evident that Newt was more focused on self-renewal than on leading the majority in the House."[28] Committees reasserted their role as agenda-setters, which made for a slower pace than in the 104th Congress, disappointing ardent party members.[29]

The fractures that had emerged within the Conference in the last Congress further complicated Gingrich's ability to lead. Moderates pushed back against what they saw as an overly zealous conservative wing that had endangered the GOP's ability to retain control of the House. One of them, Nancy Johnson (R-CT), warned in a private memo to Sue Myrick (R-NC) that "we have organized ourselves to fight, not to win," because certain "ideological organizations" were insisting on purity within the party, which made Gingrich's job extremely difficult.[30] To conservatives, meanwhile, the Speaker appeared adrift, and many of them, including members of an informal caucus called the Conservative Action Team (CAT), openly questioned his judgment.[31] In response to complaints that leadership decisions had been too centralized in the previous Congress, Gingrich eliminated the Speaker Advisory Group and replaced it with a twenty-three-member committee that included representatives from various factions within the Conference. But the new system soon proved unwieldy, and as one member grumbled, "Newt never asks us to make decisions."[32] Others complained that Joe Gaylord, the Speaker's chief of staff, was shutting out valuable advisors and allies, including Frank Luntz and Vin Weber.[33]

Easily avoidable mistakes made things worse. Amid budget negotiations between House Republicans and the president, Gingrich suggested at a press conference on March 18 that cutting taxes—a core Republican principle, and one that Gingrich himself had helped cement in the party platform in 1984—was less important than keeping the federal budget balanced. "So let's take tax cuts away for a moment," he said. "Let's just talk about balancing the budget."[34] One aide tried to rationalize the Speaker's statement, explaining that "removing tax cuts from the table temporarily will require that the liberals and the administration bring a real plan to the table that cuts spending,"[35] but conservatives weren't buying it. David McIntosh (R-IN) circulated a statement signed by over twenty fellow Republicans pledging to oppose any budget proposal unless it also contained tax cuts—enough signatories to defeat such legislation, assuming no Democrats voted for it. The Speaker retreated, and just before the House recessed for the spring, a chastened Gingrich took to the well of the House to publicly reaffirm his devotion to tax cuts. But his earlier misstatement was only one of the many ways that the Speaker had slipped back into his bad habit of following an unpredictable operating style and failing to inform other House Republicans of his plans before announcing them. Dissatisfaction in the Conference continued to fester, particularly among the party's younger conservative members, who decided to express their unhappiness more concretely. Several of them began meeting privately to air their grievances and entertain the possibility of replacing Gingrich.[36]

Two days after the Speaker's press conference snafu, the chamber considered a congressional spending bill that would increase funds for the operation of House committees. Though the increase was relatively small, eleven Republicans, including nine who had been first elected in 1994, were bothered by what they saw as a profligate use of taxpayer dollars. Looking for an opportunity to openly defy Gingrich and "forc[e] the Republican leadership to take note that many junior members were determined that the party maintain the original mission associated with the Contract with America," they joined with enough Democrats to defeat the rule for considering the bill, forcing Republican leaders to temporarily pull the spending measure from the floor.[37] This humiliating and unexpected loss was just the second occasion since the 1994 elections in which the GOP leadership had been defeated on a vote for a rule. Furious, Gingrich called for a meeting of the full Conference, at which he forced the defectors to explain the reason for their defiance and warned them that their committee assignments were in jeopardy. But some of the dissenters were unrepentant and angry that, as one of them put it, they were made to feel "like little children." Gingrich's scolding, which never translated into more serious punishment, had the unintended effect of pushing the dissenters closer to mutiny.[38]

Displeasure with Gingrich was not limited to these eleven malcontents. The Speaker's public "rehabilitation tour" had done him little good, and a poll from early April revealed that 51 percent of respondents felt unfavorably about Gingrich, compared to just 14 percent with favorable views, making him what one journalist called "by far the least popular national political figure in the country." Though he may have been "the man Democrats most love to hate," dislike for Gingrich was spreading among congressional Republicans too. "He still suffers from hubris," according to one anonymous party member. "He still thinks that whatever he says, people are going to do."[39] In a short editorial that garnered widespread attention within the House, Peter King (R-NY) described Gingrich as "roadkill on the highway of American politics" who was shifting the party too far to the left.[40]

Granted, Gingrich's job appeared to be safe despite the turmoil: he was still supported by most of his colleagues, and no other House Republican had expressed an interest in challenging him for the speakership. But a journalist presciently forewarned in late March that, if enough Republicans were sufficiently dissatisfied to seek an alternative Speaker, it could "force into the open what has been a quiet and subtle competition among prospective successors," including Armey, Boehner, and DeLay.[41]

Gingrich soon suffered yet another avoidable legislative defeat, this time at the hands of both the president and factions within his own party. Republican leaders attempted to add two controversial provisions to a bill that provided billions in emergency flood relief to the upper Midwest and reimbursed money spent on peacekeeping efforts in Bosnia. The first new provision kept the Commerce Department from using sampling in the 2000 census, a technique designed to help count Latinos and African Americans, both traditional Democratic constituencies who were often undercounted by more traditional census methods. The second new provision prevented government agencies from shutting down, thus allowing Congress to recover some negotiating strength it had lost in its 1995–1996 budget confrontations with Clinton.[42] Republicans hoped that President Clinton, eager to fund the peacekeeping operations and fearing the political consequences of vetoing flood relief, would sign the loaded-down measure. This tactic worked about as effectively as it did before—which is to say, not well at all. Clinton promptly vetoed the legislation, and the public sided with the president as news reports highlighted the abysmal conditions faced by those in flooded areas who were still waiting for federal relief.[43]

Inexplicably, Gingrich and his colleagues had failed to consider the possibility of a Clinton veto, and the GOP was again blamed for exploiting human suffering for narrow partisan purposes. Groups within the Conference began to squabble over what to do next. On June 11, twenty moderates wrote to Gingrich and asked him to heed Clinton's demands and send the president a second, "clean" bill without the two legislative riders. Recognizing that twenty votes was the difference between victory and defeat, and wanting to extricate the party from a losing battle, Gingrich granted their wish. He presented his decision to the Conference as a fait accompli and steered the measure through the House the next day; it was quickly signed into law by the president.[44] But conservatives fumed that, once again, Gingrich had lost a public relations battle with Clinton, abandoned his own "listen, learn, help, and lead" model by making a tactical decision without consulting others, and demonstrated a lack of fidelity to the party's core ideological mission. GOP leaders were also upset, for the Speaker had decided to pass the shorter bill without informing them first. In an alarming sign for Gingrich, several party leaders, including his next in command, Dick Armey (who had pushed hard for the anti-shutdown language), voted against the revised bill. One news story reported that as many as fifty members of his party were ready to push for a change at the top. Yet Gingrich was not taking seriously the dangerous undercurrents of rebellion.[45]

The Attempted Coup and Its Aftermath

Frustrations within the Conference finally boiled over in July. A group of eleven sophomore Republicans who had been meeting periodically since the defeat of the committee-funding measure began talking earnestly about Gingrich's future. They eventually formulated a secret plan to replace him as Speaker by making a privileged motion on the House floor to vacate the chair. If it passed, Gingrich would have to step down, and the House could then vote for another lawmaker to take his place.[46] Armey, DeLay, Boehner, and NRCC chair Bill Paxon, who had all become fed up with Gingrich's erratic and unilateral style of leadership, became entwined in the plot. There were tensions among them; DeLay resented Gingrich and Armey for cutting funds for the whip's office after the 1994 elections, Boehner and DeLay did not get along well, and none of them had a long history of working together. But they bonded over what Armey termed "Newt fatigue."[47] On Wednesday, July 9, the four discussed rumors that had been circulating since mid-June of a possible revolt against Gingrich. The following evening, Armey and Paxon dispatched DeLay to meet with about twenty rank and file rebels who had gathered separately to formulate plans to fix their party's leadership problems, possibly by replacing Gingrich. DeLay suggested to the plotters that other party leaders would stand with them to force Gingrich out of the speakership, but he urged the group to act quickly, warning that news of the coup had started leaking to reporters. DeLay then rejoined Paxon and Armey, and the three of them agreed that, once Gingrich was gone, Paxon would take Armey's job as majority leader while Armey became Speaker.[48]

DeLay was already having doubts about the scheme, however, and Armey had developed cold feet as well, unsure that the Conference would back him as Gingrich's replacement. In fact, it was already too late to carry out a revolt. Moderate Republican Chris Shays (CT), who had complained in March that "I've got 500 constituents angry at me for voting for him [Gingrich] for speaker, and he shouldn't be getting me into this position," was invited by one of the rebels to join them. The plotters had misread Shays, however. The Connecticut congressman had no interest in fomenting a coup, and he quickly told Gingrich about their plans a few hours before the group met on Thursday evening. Armey's chief of staff had also tipped off Gingrich's top aide, and Armey confirmed the news to Gingrich, who was "hurt and angry."[49] Armey and DeLay immediately distanced themselves from the plan, pinning the blame on junior Republicans, who were in turn incensed by their leaders' double-cross, especially since they would not have pushed to remove Gingrich so quickly but for DeLay's encouragement.[50]

The rebels' motivation was obvious: they and other younger conservatives had been complaining for months about Gingrich's erratic and opaque leadership and wavering ideological commitments. The motives and degree of culpability of other party leaders were more difficult to discern, however. Many Republicans pointed fingers at Armey for pushing to remove Gingrich, but he claimed he had nothing to do with the attempted coup and insisted he had urged his colleagues not to participate. Still, he was ambitious (as Karl Rove had warned about five years before), and there had been signs during the prior month that he was disgruntled enough with Gingrich to encourage rebellion by junior members of the party.[51] Armey later wrote a letter to Gingrich that, while regretful, was also pleading ("I just want my good name back") and defensive (noting that he had sent a message via Gingrich's aides that a coup was forthcoming and declaring that "if there was an effort to throw Newt overboard they would have to throw me overboard also").[52] Paxon remained sore over Gingrich's decision earlier in the year to take away some of his leadership responsibilities, while Boehner, who had clashed with Gingrich in the past over communication strategy, had attended some of the rebels' meetings but was excluded from the leadership confab on July 10.[53] DeLay was suspected by many of being a prime instigator of the junior coup plotters—some rebels maintained that he had called for the fateful Thursday evening meeting in the first place—but the GOP whip ultimately remained unpunished. Despite having backed away from the plan, he retained the support of conservatives, who saw him as the only ideological true believer serving in a formal leadership role.[54]

Paxon was the only top lieutenant of Gingrich who incurred a penalty for his role in the coup. After a "stormy" meeting of the Conference on July 16, Paxon—who, unlike Armey, DeLay, and Boehner, was appointed to his post by Gingrich, rather than elected by the full Conference—offered to quit leadership, and Gingrich accepted his resignation.[55] The meeting itself suggested that the Speaker's position in the party was still solid: his colleagues gave him a standing ovation, and Jennifer Dunn (R-WA), the Speaker's choice to replace Susan Molinari as Conference Vice Chair (following Molinari's departure from Congress to serve as a news anchor), was elected over leadership critic Jim Nussle (R-IN). However, Paxon's exit was not enough to mollify Republicans who believed other leaders also shared the blame.[56] A petition calling for another party meeting quickly accumulated signatures from House Republicans, and though the Speaker was warned against convening the Conference again, he felt he had no choice.[57]

In the follow-up gathering on July 23, described as a "revivalist tent meeting" by the *New York Times*, Armey, DeLay, and Boehner each apologized to their colleagues for their roles in the coup. Speaking for the junior members, Lindsey Graham (R-SC) complained that his own reelection was endangered by the Speaker's unpopularity and poor leadership. Gingrich announced that he had no plans to exact retribution from DeLay, Armey, or Boehner, asserted that he planned to keep his role as Speaker until being term limited out of the job in 2002, and declared that the "family discussion" was now over. The meeting helped ease the tensions that had been steadily growing within the party, and the Speaker was able to end any further talk of a revolt. But the botched coup attempt was the most serious sign yet that Gingrich's stature among his fellow Republicans was weak.[58]

Ironically, to the extent that Gingrich was secure in his post, it was due in no small part to the support of the party's more senior, legislative-minded wing, which he had long railed against—lawmakers like Ray LaHood (R-IL), Bob Michel's former chief of staff who now held Michel's seat in Congress, and Jerry Lewis (R-CA), whom Gingrich had worked for years to remove from leadership.[59] His near-death experience seemed to motivate Gingrich to pay closer attention to his responsibilities as Speaker. He concentrated on the daily details of leadership and refrained from unilateral decision-making,[60] and he kept a sharper focus on a conservative policy agenda that his party could run on in the 1998 elections. Gingrich also maintained a positive public profile. He coauthored an op-ed in the *New York Times* critiquing "the education bureaucracy" and affirmative action while praising school vouchers, held a meeting at a Washington, DC, school to talk about vouchers, worked on a Habitat for Humanity house to emphasize volunteering, visited the Florida Everglades to discuss water conservation, and stopped in Miami's Little Havana to meet with Hispanic leaders.[61]

Legislative Successes

Despite the soap opera–like turmoil that had gripped the House GOP, Gingrich and others did manage to get some legislating done, both before and after the attempted coup. Republicans and Clinton had reached a five-year, bipartisan budget deal in the spring of 1997, and the majority party managed to stay sufficiently united to pass a resolution codifying the deal against the strong objections of Democrats. Gingrich and the White House also banded together to stop Bud Shuster (R-PA), chairman of the Transportation Committee, from amending the resolution to add more spending for highway construction. Up against a heavy lobbying campaign by Shuster and support for the amendment from his huge seventy-three-member committee, they successfully won over enough lawmakers to defeat Shuster's proposal in late May by two votes, though Armey and other lawmakers were unhappy that Gingrich had allowed Shuster to bring the amendment to the floor in the first place.[62]

In late July, congressional Republicans and the White House publicly unveiled plans for a balanced budget and tax cuts, and a week later, President Clinton signed both the Balanced Budget Act of 1997 and the Taxpayer Relief Act of 1997 into law. The Balanced Budget Act aimed at ending federal deficit spending by 2002, while the Taxpayer Relief Act cut taxes by nearly $100 billion over that same time frame. Though *Congressional Quarterly Almanac* dubbed it "perhaps Clinton's greatest legislative triumph," Republicans could take credit for persuading Clinton to agree to tax cuts, reduced federal outlays, and a balanced budget. They had showed how both parties could benefit from a strong economy that made more plausible the goal of reaching a balanced budget in five years while still cutting taxes.[63]

These policy wins offered strong examples of successful legislative leadership. Yet some conservatives, whom Gingrich dismissed as "perfectionists," remained dissatisfied with what the Speaker had been able to obtain in talks with the White House. To their mind, the GOP had still not secured many of the big-ticket items that they had ran for public office to achieve, such as elimination of executive departments and major changes to the structure and funding levels of federal entitlements. And while one of the Republican dissidents acknowledged in September that the Speaker "is more popular than he's been all Congress," there remained pockets of resentment within the Conference and the lingering danger that Gingrich would be challenged for his leadership post in the next Congress.[64]

In 1998, Republicans managed to enact several other major laws. The Transportation Equity Act for the 21st Century allotted $218 billion in transportation funding over six years. Though it provided a 40 percent boost in monies spent over its predecessor bill from 1991, the measure gave smaller entities greater leeway in how the money would be spent, epitomizing the Republican philosophy of returning power to state and local governments.[65] Both parties worked together on the Taxpayer Bill of Rights III, a bill designed to make the Internal Revenue Service (IRS) more user-friendly. Republicans saw it as another step toward scrapping the current IRS tax code, which Gingrich called "a monstrosity," and starting over.[66] Another bipartisan measure, transforming roughly sixty worker-training programs into block grants and transferring responsibility for administering them from the federal government to the states, passed both chambers and was signed into law in August.[67] The House passed two bills designed to protect children from harm while online, the Children's Online Privacy Protection Act (COPPA) and the Protection of Children from Sexual Predators Act of 1998, which both became law.[68] In addition, a pair of significant copyright-related bills supported by the Speaker were enacted in the fall: one that extended the length of copyright protections, and another, the Digital Millennium Copyright Act, which one news source described as "the first significant rewrite of the nation's copyright laws in two decades."[69]

These accomplishments helped damper criticism of the Speaker as a poor legislative leader, but Gingrich was not out of the woods. Some Republicans, including members of CAT, continued to have reservations about his leadership, but the Speaker still clung to the entrepreneurial goals that had driven his congressional career despite the possibility that they might distract him from the more mundane but essential duties of the speakership. As he wrote in 1998, "I see my work as Speaker as a form of venture capitalism."[70] Gingrich's transparent drive for greater personal power and his lack of interest in the day-to-day responsibilities of the speakership signaled to potential challengers that the Speaker might be vulnerable. Indeed, widespread rumors that he was again eyeing the presidency, fueled by nonessential trips he made to the early primary states of New Hampshire and Iowa, encouraged the ambitious Appropriations Chairman Bob Livingston to begin preparations to run for Speaker himself.[71] Furthermore, bickering within the Conference between ideological "true believers" and moderate Republicans had delayed the passage of several measures, including a supplemental spending bill and the annual budget resolution.[72] Gingrich was either unwilling or unable to impose his will on the legislative process as firmly as he had in early 1995, and defections by party moderates on floor votes and other matters put pressure on the Speaker to establish stronger party discipline.[73] Moreover, the aborted coup had soured relations between members of the GOP leadership team, pitting Gingrich and Armey against DeLay, damaging Boehner's standing with fellow leaders, and compelling Gingrich to look to an outside, informal "kitchen cabinet" of lawmakers for guidance.[74]

The Clinton Impeachment

The legislative successes of the 105th Congress would be overshadowed by something far more politically consequential: an effort by congressional Republicans to remove the president from office for personal and legal malfeasance. Though the impeachment drive against President Clinton was initially perceived by the GOP as politically advantageous, the fallout would eventually help end Gingrich's career as Speaker.

Bill Clinton had faced rumors of sexually inappropriate behavior in his private life for years. During his 1992 presidential campaign, a former news broadcaster and Arkansas government employee named Gennifer Flowers announced that she had had a twelve-year affair with Clinton, an explosive allegation that was defused when Hillary Clinton sat beside her husband and defended him in a televised interview. Two years later, however, another Arkansas state worker, Paula Jones, accused Clinton of sexual harassment while he was governor of the state and sued him for damages. Clinton's legal strategy was to delay Jones's lawsuit, and the Supreme Court did not rule on the suit until three years later, in May 1997, when it decided unanimously that a Chief Executive cannot be held immune from civil litigation related to nonpresidential activity.[75]

The Paula Jones lawsuit would prove far more harmful to the president than Flowers's allegations. Cleared to pursue their lawsuit by the Supreme Court's decision, Jones's legal team hoped to show that Clinton had propositioned several women in addition to their client. They soon learned from a Department of Defense staffer named Linda Tripp of another possible affair: one with a White House intern named Monica Lewinsky, an acquaintance of Tripp. When Jones's lawyers subpoenaed Lewinsky in December 1997, she denied having had sexual contact with Clinton, but secret recordings that Tripp had made of conversations between her and Lewinsky indicated otherwise.[76]

Kenneth Starr, an independent counsel who had been appointed by the Justice Department to look into the failed Whitewater land deal, received Tripp's recordings and obtained permission from Attorney General Janet Reno to explore the matter. As word leaked of the alleged Clinton-Lewinsky dalliance in January 1998, the president repeatedly denied it, and did so under oath in a deposition with the Jones legal team and in subsequent grand jury testimony. When Lewinsky produced a blue dress with physical evidence that tied her to Clinton, however, the president was forced to do an about-face. On August 17, in a nationally televised address, he confessed that he had been intimate with the intern. Starr's final report, released the next month, made the case for eleven counts of impeachable conduct against Clinton, based on the president's attempts to both hide the affair from White House aides and lie about it to Jones's lawyers and the grand jury.[77]

The president was both politically and legally vulnerable. He had committed adultery with a young intern and violated federal law by perjuring himself, and his behavior implied the veracity of Jones's more serious allegations of sexual harassment. The situation presented congressional Republicans with a golden opportunity to damage Clinton, if not remove him from office altogether. But there were sharp differences of opinion within the GOP over how best to do so. Some believed the president's behavior had been foolish but not necessarily criminal; even if they were personally offended by his behavior and wanted to impose at least some punishment, they did not think it was worthy of impeachment. Others were convinced the president had committed an impeachable crime or otherwise hoped to exploit the situation to remove a longtime political nemesis. The latter group believed that, if they took a hard line against the president, public opinion would follow suit, convincing enough Senate Democrats to join with Republicans and provide the necessary two-thirds vote to convict Clinton.[78]

Gingrich was uncertain about what to do. He wavered between insisting that legislating mattered more than the president's personal conduct and criticizing the president for obstructing justice and lying under oath. His hesitancy may have stemmed from worries that Clinton's public approval ratings showed little sign of sinking, that the Speaker's direct involvement would undermine impeachment by making the process look too partisan, or that he might be accused of hypocrisy, given his own history of marital problems.[79] Impeachment was instead driven primarily by Henry Hyde, chairman of the House Judiciary Committee—the committee that would have jurisdiction over articles of impeachment—and by Tom DeLay. Fervid advocates of impeachment, including Republicans on Hyde's committee (who were also more conservative and ideological than the party's median member), tried to bring Gingrich into their corner. For instance, Judiciary Committee member Bob Barr (R-GA) sent Gingrich preprinted petitions from his constituents calling for impeachment proceedings.[80]

Finally, in mid-October, just weeks before the 1998 midterm elections, Gingrich concluded that pushing for impeachment would be the wisest strategy for the Conference. GOP polling data indicated that voters prioritized moral issues and trusted Republicans more than Democrats to address them, and the Speaker predicted that impeachment would help his party win at least twenty House seats. Nonetheless, Gingrich worried that nationalizing the issue could backfire, so he approved a series of Clinton/Lewinsky-related television ads that would only appear in targeted media markets, hoping to turn out GOP voters in just those regions. Unfortunately for him, the tactic failed: the ads garnered so much national attention that they invoked a backlash, and Democrats lambasted Gingrich, accusing him of pursuing impeachment just to win an election.[81]

The 1998 Elections and Gingrich's Resignation

As the 1998 elections approached, Gingrich tried valiantly to recapture the electoral magic of 1994. He had spent much of the prior two years fundraising and visiting congressional districts to help Republican candidates, even at the risk of neglecting his own duties and relationships in Washington. The Speaker had helped negotiate a budget agreement with the president in October that prevented another government shutdown and allowed the House to adjourn so GOP lawmakers could rush home to campaign. Gingrich also remained optimistic in public, and he and other Republican leaders predicted that the Conference might increase its size in November by between ten and forty seats.[82]

Instead of gaining seats, however, the party lost five, leaving them with just 223 Republican House members—a threadbare majority.[83] For the first time in over six decades, the president's party had expanded its size in the House via a midterm election. In the next Congress, the defection of a mere six Republicans could thwart the wishes of the GOP. Gingrich gamely tried to spin the results, pointing out that Republicans had kept control of Congress for three consecutive election cycles, something that had not happened since the 1920s. But as Mel Steely succinctly put it, "a drop from 228 to 223 seats was not a victory."[84] Rightly or wrongly, the elections were interpreted as a rejection of Clinton's impeachment, a process that Gingrich had eventually embraced. Conservatives claimed that a different event, the October budget agreement, was to blame, because the GOP had surrendered too much to the White House and failed to differentiate itself from Democrats. Some saw Gingrich's chronically abysmal poll ratings as blameworthy as well.[85] Most of this was conjecture; in fact, there had been few swing districts available for Republicans to pick up in the elections, and predictions of sizeable GOP gains that year had always been far-fetched. But perception was what mattered, and the perception was that Gingrich had nearly cost the Conference its majority.[86]

The election capped a difficult and often disappointing Congress for Gingrich. Hoping to turn things around after a challenging first session, his office had developed several goals for 1998, including "maintain highest ethical standards," "communicate clearly who Newt is and what he stands for," and "continue to strengthen member relations to ensure reelection a[s] Speaker."[87] Gingrich had accomplished none of these. Rather, the party felt more electorally vulnerable than ever, led by a directionless Speaker who either would not or could not adjust course. A "somber" Gingrich concluded that he "could never satisfy every ideological instinct and faction," and contemplated how to stay in charge of a party that questioned his conservative credentials and strategic judgment.[88]

It would not be easy. Matt Salmon (R-AZ), a member of the troublesome Class of 1994, suggested publicly that at least seven Republicans would not vote to give Gingrich another term as Speaker, enough to deny him the post. Gingrich also faced a formidable competitor for his leadership job: Bob Livingston, who showed no signs of ending the campaign for Speaker he had been building since the spring. Another lurking danger was that Gingrich had been engaged in an illicit relationship with House staffer Callista Bisek, an affair that, if discovered, could generate fresh charges of hypocrisy for attacking Clinton's infidelity and damage Gingrich's reputation among social conservatives.[89]

Despite the daunting prospects of victory, Gingrich tried to hang on to another term in power. As he had two years before, he dutifully began working the phones to ask fellow lawmakers for their vote. This time, however, they expressed far more unease with the thought of keeping him as their leader. Hoping Gingrich would abandon the campaign, Livingston demanded that he endorse rules changes that would curtail the powers of the speakership. When Gingrich refused and showed no sign of stepping down, Livingston announced that he would challenge the embattled Speaker. It was a bitter turn of events for Gingrich, given that Livingston had considered retiring from the House years earlier before Gingrich had persuaded him to stay.[90]

While the Speaker and his remaining allies in the Conference felt confident that Gingrich could win the party's nomination, a victory on the floor was far less certain, and he reluctantly concluded that it would be nearly impossible for him to lead effectively even if he were reelected. Hours after Livingston's announcement, Gingrich released a statement to the press announcing that he would step down from the speakership. Shortly thereafter, he declared his intention to resign from the House, which he did in early January.[91] Gingrich's speakership and his career in Congress were over.

Conclusion

The 105th Congress had been a difficult one for Newt Gingrich. Facing a newly reelected Democratic president, a smaller majority, and pockets of discontent within the Conference, Gingrich struggled to lead his congressional party. He was further hurt by the absence of a clear policy agenda akin to the Contract with America, by ethics violations that had damaged his reputation, and by his own weaknesses as a legislative leader, which led to a series of avoidable mistakes and an effort by junior lawmakers and party leaders to remove him from the speakership. Though Gingrich survived the attempted coup and could point to numerous legislative achievements during that Congress, his position in the party was highly vulnerable, and the GOP's unexpected loss of House seats in 1998 was enough for the Conference to turn against him.

In the next and final chapter, we discuss what Gingrich's downfall tells us about the perils of party entrepreneurship for those who move from minority party status to majority party leadership, and why it is important for strategic entrepreneurs to keep their objectives, means, and resources balanced. We also review Gingrich's contributions to American politics and explore how the party entrepreneur model of lawmaker behavior sheds light on congressional politics more broadly.

CONCLUSION

Newt Gingrich was the classic example of a congressional party entrepreneur. For over fifteen years, he labored to bring House Republicans to power and organize a conservative transformation of American society with an eye toward increasing his own influence. He assumed considerable risks to do so, alienating other Republicans, incurring the wrath of influential House leaders and Republican presidents, being targeted for ethics investigations by vengeful Democrats, and nearly losing reelection in 1990 and 1992. Two of his goals were finally achieved in November 1994, when Republicans ended their decades-long spell as the minority party and Gingrich became Speaker of the House. He then helped to enact major legislation and pushed through significant institutional changes in the chamber that further strengthened his party and himself. But Gingrich was often outmaneuvered by President Bill Clinton, who dashed his hopes of a House-led transformation of government and society, and the duties of the speakership proved incompatible with his leadership style and entrepreneurial approach. Back-to-back election losses for House Republicans made the job untenable for Gingrich, who ended up leaving Congress altogether.

Considering Gingrich's entrepreneurial efforts through the prism of Arthur Lykke's military model of strategy suggests answers to the key questions of why it took Gingrich more than a decade to achieve any of his goals and why he subsequently struggled as Speaker. Initially, his objectives were far more ambitious than what he could reasonably expect to accomplish with the limited resources available to him. However, Gingrich's "sheer persistence," as one former GOP leader put it, together with his focus on building an organizational base, gradually increased the number of supporters he had in Congress, in the conservative media, and in influential think tanks, and he acquired more and more resources from both within and outside the House. He also adjusted his strategic means: rather than relying solely on "big idea" treatises or chastising fellow Republicans for being too complaisant toward Democrats, he cultivated a following among mainstream reporters, used the Democratic majority's egregious abuses to make the case for a GOP-led House, and found ways to stymie the Democrats' legislative agenda.[1] Lykke's model is not predictive—having objectives, means, and resources that are balanced does not guarantee a successful strategy—but the presence of all three in equal amounts does increase a strategic plan's likelihood of success. And by the time Gingrich reached the 1994 elections, he was the titular leader of the Conference, Republican challengers were awash in campaign funds, a constellation of activists and media figures were supporting the House GOP, and voters were ready to kick out the governing party.

When Gingrich became Speaker in early 1995, his resources expanded geometrically, and he guided his party to several early legislative and procedural wins. Yet a fresh mismatch emerged between his methods—which were frequently inappropriate or ineffectual, such as using a government shutdown to try to coerce the White House into a budget agreement—and his strategic objectives, which were often too lofty for even the Speaker of the House to achieve. No matter how impressive his oratorical talents, or how grateful fellow Republicans might be for how he helped their party win power within the chamber, Gingrich was never going to be able to run the entire federal government from the House of Representatives, let alone shift all of society in a conservative direction. Gingrich's eroding public popularity, coupled with widening divisions within the Conference—caused in part by unhappiness with the Speaker's failure to meet his own unachievable goals, and in part by his inadequate attempts at legislating and coalition maintenance—limited what he could accomplish. Ironically, just as Democrats were an inadvertent asset to Republicans, Gingrich became what journalist David Broder described as "the bogeyman Democrats have used to raise money and roll up the vote."[2] The Speaker saw his own hold on power gradually slip away, and when he finally resigned, it was Democrats who were sad to see him go. Admitted one anonymous Clinton aide, "we are mourning the loss of having Newt to kick around anymore."[3]

Although it is a single case, Gingrich's career suggests some general principles of party entrepreneurialism in Congress. First, party entrepreneurs can be procedural entrepreneurs as well, changing chamber or party rules, altering existing congressional organizations, or founding novel ones to help their party achieve its collective goals. Second, they may be tempted to align themselves with, or even take over, organizations outside of Congress to heighten their influence, as Gingrich did with GOPAC. Third, party entrepreneurs that recruit new candidates to run for Congress as a means of achieving their party-wide goals can also benefit from those candidates serving as a foundation for personal power if they are elected to office, though their continuing fealty may not always be guaranteed.

Finally, and perhaps most centrally, Gingrich's example suggests that it is easier to be a party entrepreneur as a member of the minority party, where expectations are lower and legislative responsibilities are necessarily fewer, than as a member of the governing party. This is especially true for entrepreneurs who have the added responsibility of being a formal leader, which comes with the expectation to meet the party's collective legislative needs while also serving the parochial demands of individual colleagues. The Georgian "was a great guerrilla leader when you're in the mountains trying to take the city," one fellow GOP leader recollected, but less effective "once you take the city."[4] Gingrich would later rue trying to hurdle from the minority whip post to "not just Speaker but leader of a national movement," as he put it, without sufficient preparation.[5] Gingrich's inexperience in governing was not his only problem, however. Speakers "do not change character when they take office," as political scientists Ron Peters and Craig Williams observed, and Gingrich insisted on viewing the speakership as an office through which he could continue to carry out his long-standing entrepreneurialism. This perspective was difficult to square with the multiple and often conflicting goals and duties that traditionally encompass the job.[6] Gingrich recognized that his obsession with high-level strategizing nearly cost him his speakership in mid-1997, because, in his words, he "was thinking about long-range planning" rather than "diving in to deal with immediate problems and to rebond relationships." He also found the responsibilities of being Speaker overwhelming at times and lamented the "flat" hierarchy of congressional leadership (in contrast to the top-down structure of the military) and the lack of organizational resources available to him. Yet Gingrich's disposition was inherently entrepreneurial, and he was enamored with the application of historical lessons and abstract strategic theories to the governance of the House. Even after surviving an attempted coup in 1997, he stubbornly maintained that the GOP needed to be a party of idea generation and "independent thinking," and that its members should act as "entrepreneurs of social policy."[7] His inability to adapt would prove to be his undoing.

In the remainder of this chapter, we first explore Gingrich's long-term contributions to Congress and the country. He influenced Congress in many ways, we argue, but it is less clear whether he substantially changed American politics beyond Capitol Hill. We then make the case that our model of party entrepreneurship has wider applicability within Congress, and we identify several lawmakers who, like Gingrich, sought to aid their congressional parties in the pursuit of collective political objectives. We conclude with a brief review of Gingrich's career after he left the House.

Evaluating Gingrich's Influence and Legacy

By the end of his speakership, Gingrich had achieved a Republican majority in the House and heightened his personal influence, two of his main goals. Were these feats accomplished because of Gingrich's entrepreneurial deeds, or would those outcomes have come about without them? And what about the claims by some that Gingrich's influence was deeper and longer lasting—that he centralized power in the House; popularized election-oriented messaging, obstruction, and "ruthless" political tactics by our political parties; tribalized American politics; made Congress distasteful to the public; or even ruined the ability of the national government to function?[8]

These questions about the lasting impact of the man himself reflect broader, more enduring philosophical debates about the relative contribution of individuals to political outcomes compared with the influence of large societal forces.[9] In Gingrich's case, the evidence presented in prior chapters, together with the research of others, suggests that his entrepreneurial undertakings had a profound impact on his own political standing and the politics of Congress.[10] First, his media-oriented activities as a member of the minority party—wooing reporters, offering quotable quips, issuing provocative attacks on members of both parties, providing an unusual, historically framed take on congressional affairs—along with other initiatives, like the conflicts orchestrated by himself and the Conservative Opportunity Society, heightened his public profile. Figures 7.1 and 7.2 compare the number of mentions received by Gingrich in major newspapers to the level of attention paid by these outlets to other prominent House leaders across time. Note that in 1984, before ever holding a formal leadership post, Gingrich appeared in newspapers at nearly the same rate as the GOP's top two elected leaders.[11] This frequency declined somewhat over the next two years as he backed away from the media spotlight, but in 1989 Gingrich appeared in nearly twice the number of news stories as Minority Leader Bob Michel, even rivaling the number of newspaper references to Speaker Tom Foley. Though correlation is not itself proof of causation, it is hard to imagine that Gingrich would have garnered such attention absent his maneuvers to win and maintain press attention for himself and his like-minded congressional Republicans, or his successful crusade against Speaker Jim Wright and election as GOP whip.

Second, Gingrich encouraged the resignation or retirement of no fewer than three top party leaders in the House. Minority Leader John Rhodes cited Gingrich's internal survey of lawmakers, which suggested deep disgruntlement with his leadership of the Conference, as a factor in his decision to quit the position. Gingrich initiated a feedback loop of negative news stories about Speaker Jim Wright in mid-1987 and persuaded Common Cause to call for an investigation into Wright's background, the first domino to fall in a chain of events that eventually compelled his resignation. Then, as GOP whip, Gingrich gradually put pressure on Bob Michel to step down as minority leader. Although he had already grown weary of serving in the leadership, Michel was made keenly aware after the 1992 elections that Gingrich would almost certainly run against him, increasing the costs of remaining in his post beyond what he was willing to pay. Gingrich had already tarnished Michel's reputation by implicitly deriding him as an ideological moderate who did not do enough to help the House GOP seize power.[12] These three changes in leadership had profound consequences. The retirements of Rhodes and Michel removed two high-ranked Gingrich skeptics from the chamber, Wright's departure improved the Georgian's stature nationally and within the Conference, and the exodus of Michel created a vacancy in the party's top post that would be filled by Gingrich himself.

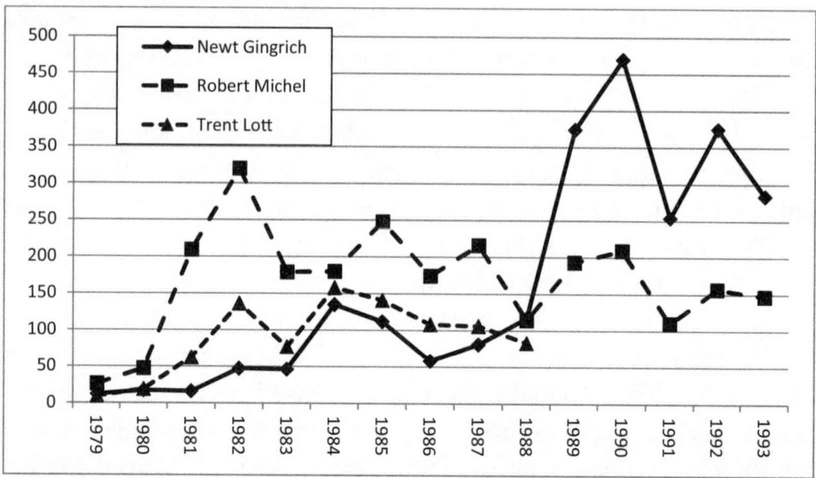

Figure 7.1. Number of Mentions of Gingrich in Major Newspapers vs. House Republican Leaders, 1979–1993. *Source*: ProQuest search in the *New York Times, Washington Post,* and *Wall Street Journal.*

Third, Gingrich contributed to several major institutional changes in the House and, as Speaker, substantial legislative successes in Congress. The creation of the COS could be considered one institutional innovation that owed its existence to Gingrich. Revisions to the Republican Conference's rules throughout the 1980s and early 1990s, though often instigated by others, mirrored changes that Gingrich had advocated for in order to empower party leaders and halt intraparty defections. The most dramatic institutional developments, however, occurred in his first term as Speaker, where for the first time he had the capacity to dramatically restructure the chamber itself. Committee staff was thinned dramatically, committees were merged or disbanded altogether, funds for legislative service organizations were cut off, and benefits and services that had helped incumbents remain in power were eliminated. Coupled with the major legislative initiatives that passed in the first one hundred days of the new Republican House, these developments made the early Gingrich speakership one of the most consequential in the history of Congress. Over the longer term, Gingrich's moves hastened the decline of congressional committees and their capacity to conduct rigorous oversight and develop intelligent policy, diminished the importance of seniority, constrained the ability of rank and file members to

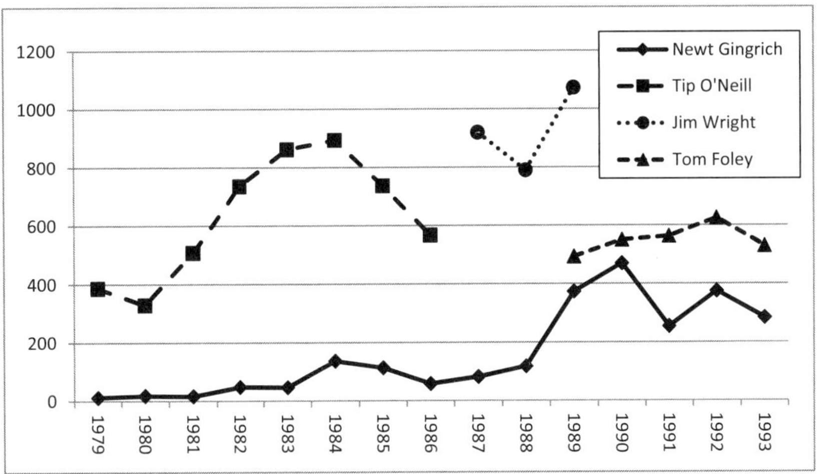

Figure 7.2. Number of Mentions of Gingrich in Major Newspapers vs. House Democratic Leaders, 1979–1993. *Source*: See figure 7.1.

legislate, and arguably weakened Congress as an institution. Indeed, as of this writing, the number of House committee staff has yet to return to its pre-1995 levels, and reformers bemoan how the elimination of the Office of Technology Assessment under Gingrich has prevented the chamber from making well-informed, science-based decisions despite facing such major policy issues as Internet privacy, global warming, and a viral pandemic.[13] It was an ironic outcome for a Speaker who had dreamed of making the House of Representatives the center of American governance.

Finally, Gingrich helped pull the House Republican Party in a direction that was more amenable to his own strategic outlook. Measuring and identifying lawmakers' attitudes toward political strategy is a difficult task at best, but several proxy measures do exist. Take, for instance, the proportion of House Republicans who were members of Gingrich's COS in each Congress. The COS was founded by Gingrich and several other GOP lawmakers to inject greater public partisan activism into the Conference, and the organization became an invaluable caucus for House conservatives who sought to embarrass Democrats and increase party unity. (Its membership was also kept private, so Republicans did not join for mere position-taking purposes.) Figure 7.3 illustrates the percentage of Republican leaders and rank and file members who were in the group from its founding in 1983

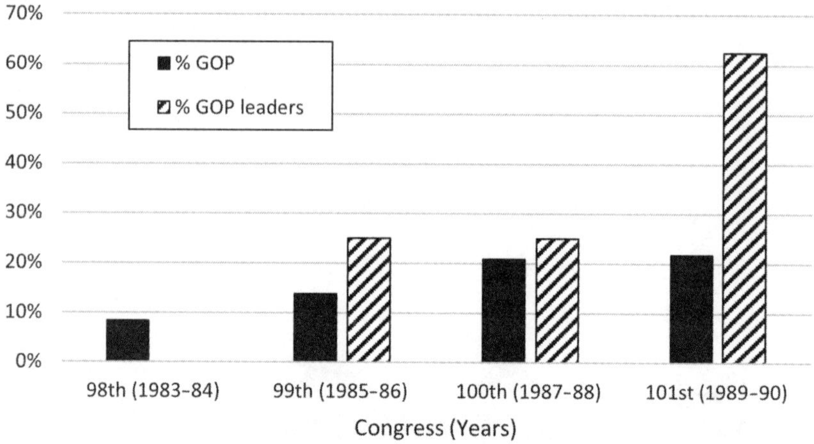

Figure 7.3. Percentage of House GOP/GOP Leaders Affiliated with COS, 1983–1990. *Source*: COS membership lists, NLG and RW.

through 1990. The proportion of the party in COS nearly tripled during that period, making it big enough to serve as a beneficial bloc of activists for Gingrich, but also indicative of an expanding acceptance of his view of proper party behavior. Its members also successfully ran for formal party leadership positions, where they could carry out COS tactics with greater ease.[14]

Another measure of this growing embrace of Gingrich's approach to politics is how many Republicans shared his belief in the political benefits of expanding the scope of party conflict. Some of that expansion manifested itself in the GOP's use of floor speeches to critique the other party. This development predated the COS, fueled by the introduction of televised floor sessions in 1979,[15] but it continued to grow in the 1980s and early 1990s. A textual analysis of congressional speeches revealed that rhetoric in Congress became more polarized starting in 1993, when Gingrich had enough allies in the Conference to implement an aggressive and confrontational line of attack against Democrats.[16] In addition, Gingrich not only encouraged partisan floor talk but also invited criticisms of the ethics of the governing party specifically. As figure 7.4 shows, the percentage of the Conference and of its leaders who joined Gingrich in voting for proposals (and, in one case, cosigning a letter) to highlight the unethical behavior of

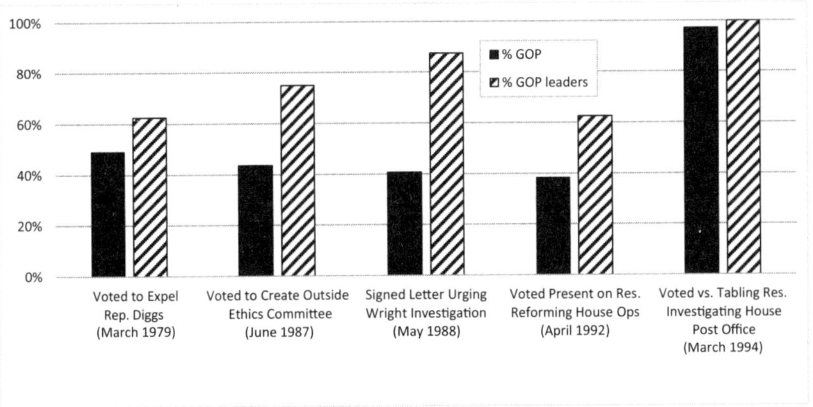

Figure 7.4. Percentage of House GOP/GOP Leaders Supporting Ethics Investigations, Reforms, or Punishments.

Democrats grew over time, and by mid-1994 the Conference had taken a nearly unanimous position in favor of condemning the Democratic Party's ethics. One could argue that the decision of House Republicans to pursue impeachment against President Clinton in 1998, which was supported on the floor by nearly every member of the Conference, was the logical culmination of this strategy, though the advocates of impeachment insisted they were motivated by legal, not political, considerations.[17]

Another important Gingrich-backed strategy adopted by the Conference was partisan team play. More than just party members voting as a bloc on bills and amendments, team play involves unity in the use of, and support for, procedural motions, an intolerance of public intraparty dissent, and coordinated messaging that extols one's own political party over the other. Efforts at greater party harmony were hardly a Gingrich innovation; for instance, House Republicans tried pressuring their party to stand together more often on key floor votes in the 1960s.[18] But during Gingrich's time in Congress, and often with his urging or that of his followers, House Republicans increasingly emphasized that party unity was essential. Gingrich and other COS members complained that the Conference lacked enforcement mechanisms to keep the party together, and as previously noted, the GOP gradually adopted rules that discouraged or prohibited leaders and committee ranking members from taking positions distinct from the Conference. The COS also identified allies within committees who could serve as conservative watchdogs, and after 1994, Gingrich and his leadership team demanded loyalty from committee chairs and tried to resolve intraparty disagreements in private to project unity and protect the party's reputation. Gingrich was, to a great extent, the progenitor of the kind of party discipline and unity in Congress that had been advocated by "party responsibility" scholars in the mid-twentieth century.[19]

Gingrich did much to motivate his party to accept these strategic ideas and norms of behavior. His periodic party retreats helped "build up a policy agenda" and "build consensus" within the Conference, one former GOP aide recalled.[20] His persuasive skills also explain why some members of Congress like Steve Gunderson chose to follow Gingrich despite differences in temperament or ideology. Gingrich took particular care to frame each election in a way that might convince his congressional brethren to heed his advice. Lawmakers hold as an article of faith that elections convey a message, and just as presidents and political parties create narratives that explain defeat at the polls and direct a course of action to win the next election, Gingrich pointed to each failed election as additional proof that the party needed to follow his political strategy. No spin was needed for the blockbuster 1994 elections, which persuaded both Democrats and Republicans that nationalizing elections, differentiating the two parties, and prioritizing partisan communication were necessary to winning control of Congress and should therefore take precedence over bipartisan legislating.[21]

Gingrich's electioneering was an important part of the adoption process too. When he started identifying, recruiting, and funding victorious Republican candidates for the House in the late 1980s, he was also constructing a coalition of like-minded lawmakers in the Conference who were grateful for his assistance. "If you were a younger member coming in[to the House] for the first time," said one former GOP leader, "you could spend the rest of your career in the minority with people sitting around being passive," or join the side that "has a vision of being competitive. . . . We were winning probably two-thirds of the freshmen."[22] Though it is difficult to know whether the people he urged to run for the House would have done so even without his cajoling, Gingrich's outreach to candidates is correlated with their subsequent behavior in Congress. Studies have found that Republicans who received tapes from GOPAC were more likely to vote with Gingrich as Speaker, and those who received contributions from him voted more conservatively and were more likely to participate in floor speeches.[23] The replacement of more senior leaders with COS members signaled to the rank and file that confrontation and team play would be rewarded, and those members progressively incorporated Gingrich's outlook into the development of party strategy.[24]

Gingrich's ceaseless struggle to mold the strategic thinking of the House Republican Party is more than a lesson in the power of party entrepreneurship. His career also underscores how the embrace of partisan confrontation, party differentiation, and team play in Congress was a *strategic choice embraced by the House Republican Party over time.* No single election or event transformed the GOP Conference. Instead, bit by bit, Congress by Congress, it went from being a party that practiced partisan opposition in moderation and was open to cooperation when doing so might generate legislative wins, to being one that opposed Democrats on a wide scope of issues and operated with considerable unity. Taken together, these changes constituted a party that, as Dick Armey had hoped, was turning itself into a potential, or incipient, cartel—specifically, a procedural cartel that could more effectively control the House's legislative agenda when it became a majority party.[25]

Gingrich's approach to party tactics and strategy continued in Congress well past his tenure there. In the 104th Congress, Democrats took a page from Gingrich's own playbook by repeatedly questioning his ethics and protesting the more radical elements of the GOP's agenda. In the early 2000s, Minority Leader Nancy Pelosi (D-CA) and other Democratic leaders pressed their party to act as a unit and deny majority party Republicans the votes they needed to restructure Social Security or pass other major legislation, and Democrats offered their own version of a Contract with America before every House election.[26] When this strategy appeared to pay off in 2006, Republicans returned the favor by uniformly opposing the Affordable Care Act, forcing Democrats to perform a series of legislative somersaults to enact it, and the GOP started proposing campaign-year, Contract-like documents as well. As one former Obama White House aide saw it, "Republicans hoped to take back Washington by obstructing Obama and then calling him out for breaking his promises to bring back bipartisan cooperation." Republicans regained the House majority in 2010.[27]

Other contemporary features of congressional politics also echo

Gingrich's strategy and tactics. Lawmakers continue to use special-order speeches to repeat partisan messages, just as the COS did in the 1980s. In 1987, Gingrich had proposed to his COS colleagues that Republicans use government shutdowns to force Democrats to slash nonmilitary spending,[28] and shutdowns were not only tried in the 104th Congress but continued to be used against future Democratic presidents. The team play ethos has become pervasive in the House: though there is more cross-party agreement in Congress than many people realize, partisans often vote together on proposals even if there are no ideological reasons to do so, and party leaders are loath to violate the so-called "Hastert Rule," a norm that requires leaders to never permit votes on legislation opposed by a majority of their own party. Fifteen years after Gingrich left Congress, Democratic Minority Whip Steny Hoyer (MD) explained that his objective as whip was to create a "psychology of consensus" in his party, meaning "I [want] people to get up in the morning and think, 'I want to be with the team.'"[29]

One important counterargument to the thesis that Gingrich drove this change in GOP strategy is that external factors—most notably the growing competitive strength of the Republican Party—created the necessary incentives for the team-play mindset to take hold.[30] As the preceding chapters make clear, though, for most of Gingrich's time in the minority party, Michel and many congressional Republicans, plus most election observers, thought a House majority was little more than a pipe dream. As a consequence, they held firm to the (not unreasonable) idea that cooperating with Democrats in the legislative process, or at least offering constructive alternatives to the majority party's agenda, was indispensable to their political and policy success. ("You've gotta get votes from the other side to make anything go," Michel told a reporter after leaving Congress.)[31] Even when Republicans did well enough in elections to suggest that control of the House was within their grasp, as in 1980 (and, to a lesser extent, after the GOP's more modest seat gains in 1984), many party members remained unconvinced that differentiating the two parties was a good strategy. They were skeptical not only because they didn't believe they needed it—their party could still influence policy so long as they controlled the Senate, the White House, or both—but also because it was not (yet) widely assumed that such a method was the best way to win elections. As late as 1991, some influential Republicans were still expressing doubt that they would ever be the majority party, and even Gingrich himself concurred at one point with Michel, Edwards, Jerry Lewis, and party moderates who all insisted that the nationalization approach to electioneering was hurting the GOP, not helping it. So while all minority parties face the contradictory goals of opposing the majority party and participating in the governing process, and the promise of a competitive political environment encourages minority parties to emphasize partisan differentiation and communication over legislating, only in stages did the House Republican Conference come to share that view—in large part because of Gingrich's unflagging entrepreneurialism.[32] The counterfactual argument of Richard Fenno that Congress would have become more partisan and conflictual even absent Gingrich discounts the efforts of the Georgian to gradually assemble a critical mass of congressional Republicans who believed in nationalizing elections, position-taking, aggressive partisan combat, and greater team play, the strategies that eventually seemed to yield the results he promised.[33]

This is not to say that Gingrich succeeded in his endeavors all by himself. His victories relied heavily on the assistance of political players and organizations who reinforced his conflictual view of politics and encouraged others to follow his lead. They included Paul Weyrich, Dick Armey, the other founding members of the COS, conservative media outlets and celebrity commentators like Rush Limbaugh, freshmen lawmakers (who were often recruited by Gingrich or GOPAC), Republicans who were already in Congress when Gingrich first arrived and agreed with Gingrich's strategy, and new GOP-leaning lobbying groups and think tanks such as Americans for Tax Reform.[34] Moreover, Gingrich's successes were hardly foreordained, and luck and events beyond his control played an important role. He narrowly survived multiple competitive races for his congressional seat; the death, departure, or retirement of key leaders like Trent Lott and Silvio Conte opened the door for him and his acolytes to take their places; he came just two votes shy of being defeated for whip in 1989; and Gingrich would not have run for whip in the first place had John Tower, George H. W. Bush's first choice for Defense Secretary, not been rejected by the Senate.

One should especially not understate how House Democrats inadvertently strengthened Gingrich and boosted his cause. While in the majority, their steady winnowing away of procedural rights and legislative opportunities for the minority party, coupled with moments of serious abuse of chamber rules, encouraged desperate and frustrated Republicans to adopt more aggressive partisan tactics and cooperate less with Democrats over time.[35] For instance, when the Democratic Party in the mid-1970s started passing chamber rules at the start of each Congress that stacked the procedural deck in their favor, unanimous Republican opposition to House rules became standard practice.[36] Or take another minor but equally telling example: the seemingly routine approval of the daily journal of the House. Prior to the months-long kerfuffle over the 1985 contested election in Indiana between Democrat Frank McCloskey and Republican Richard McIntyre, few Republicans voted against approving the journal. Starting that year, however, the percentage of the minority party that opposed the journal shot up from 15 percent to 77 percent, and it never again dropped below a majority of the Conference. What had started as a symbolic means of protesting a contested election became a new norm of partisan behavior. As one former Republican lawmaker recalled, people who blame Gingrich for greater party conflict in Congress "seem to forget the election in Indiana that was stolen from us."[37] Faced with more and more evidence that cooperation with Democrats would not bear fruit, Republicans who had found Gingrich's aggressive tactics distasteful changed their tune or left the House altogether, replaced by newer legislators more personally aligned with Gingrich's highly partisan approach to politics.[38] When Democrats won unified control of government in 1992, their decision to craft major bills like health care reform entirely within their own ranks gave Republicans even less incentive to cooperate. Whether these Democratic maneuvers were justified by the provocative and dilatory tactics used by Republicans, they served as yet another resource for Gingrich—just as, in a military conflict, one's success often hinges upon whether the reaction by an opponent increases one's strategic advantages.[39]

In short, Gingrich deserves significant credit for bolstering his own media profile, pushing out several party leaders, steering major bills and procedural reforms through the House, and popularizing a conflict-oriented party strategy in the Conference. What about his strategic objectives beyond the chamber, like nationalizing congressional elections, differentiating the parties, or hurting the reputation of Congress? Despite Gingrich's many efforts to achieve these goals, there is little evidence that he did very much to bring them about. Take, for example, the public's view of

Congress. The institution was not especially popular during the 1980s and early 1990s, and research suggests that greater partisanship in congressional voting—something that Gingrich wanted, and that did increase in the 1980s and early 1990s—contributes to the declining approval of Congress (as does lawmaker misconduct, such as the House banking scandal, which Gingrich's Gang of Seven allies publicized). Yet other factors outside Gingrich's sphere of influence also shape congressional approval, such as views of the economy, presidential approval ratings, and whether the governing party pursues an agenda that strays from the preferences of the public.[40]

Or consider the nationalization of elections, a phenomenon that some have attributed to Gingrich.[41] The relative contribution of nation-wide factors to vote choice started to rise in the mid-1960s, well before Gingrich was in Congress. Voter loyalty to same-party candidates in contested House races, and the correlation between congressional and presidential voting, began increasing in the mid-1980s, when Gingrich was still a rising backbencher with little ability to raise money for the party, determine the Conference's communication strategy, or recruit candidates.[42] Though Gingrich long proclaimed that Republicans running for Congress must use identical partisan language to help nationalize elections, one study found that GOP challengers in 1994 often used varying rhetoric and campaign themes, suggesting that a nationalized message was only selectively implemented by Republican candidates.[43]

Closely related to voter nationalization is voter polarization, in which self-identified partisans draw clearer boundaries with the opposite party on questions of policy and move further away ideologically from partisan opponents. This too emerged independently of Gingrich.[44] As shown in figure 7.5, the percentage of self-identified conservatives in the American populace grew only slightly, if at all, during Gingrich's first eighteen years in Congress. Other studies have shown that policy preferences and party identification started to coincide—i.e., Democrats becoming more liberal, and Republicans more conservative—in the mid-1970s, when Gingrich was not yet in Congress.[45] Similarly, surveys asking for Americans' perceived differences over time between the two major political parties showed a slow but steady rise in the percentage who saw some differences, and a commensurate decline in those perceiving no difference at all, but this trend began when Gingrich had only just founded the COS and did not yet enjoy

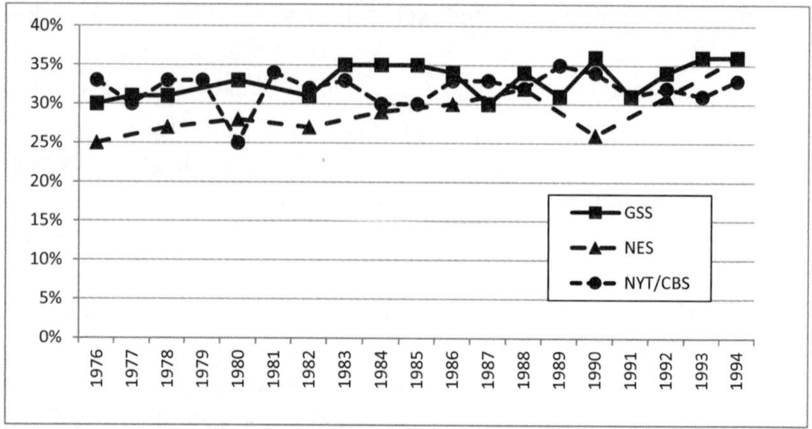

Figure 7.5. Percentage of Self-Identified Conservatives in the United States, 1976–1994. *Source*: General Social Surveys (annual), National Election Surveys (biennial), and *New York Times*/CBS News surveys, taken in April (1978), May (1982, 1987, and 1989), July (1977 and 1988), or June (all other years).

the national profile of other leaders (see figure 7.6). One study found that citizens' views of their opposing political party followed a negative trend beginning in the late 1970s and early 1980s, before Gingrich's rise to power, and another revealed that those with negative attitudes toward the opposition had become increasingly loyal to their own party starting in the early 1980s.[46] Political scientist James Campbell documents this trend starting even earlier, citing the 1994 elections as the eighth and final stage of a long-term, piecemeal process of party realignment that began in 1958, and he argues that political actors like Gingrich were at best "middle men" who encouraged polarization but did not start it.[47] And even though Gingrich had long used partisan rhetoric in interviews and public speeches, intending to polarize the public, research has shown that, while messaging by politicians and party leaders might change how voters discuss political matters, it has little if any effect on their underlying opinions.[48] There is far stronger evidence that voter polarization and/or shifts in voting for the Republican Party were due to larger social and political forces, including population changes in the South, adjustments in the GOP platform that appealed to Democratic-voting conservatives,[49] income inequality,[50] polarizing racial

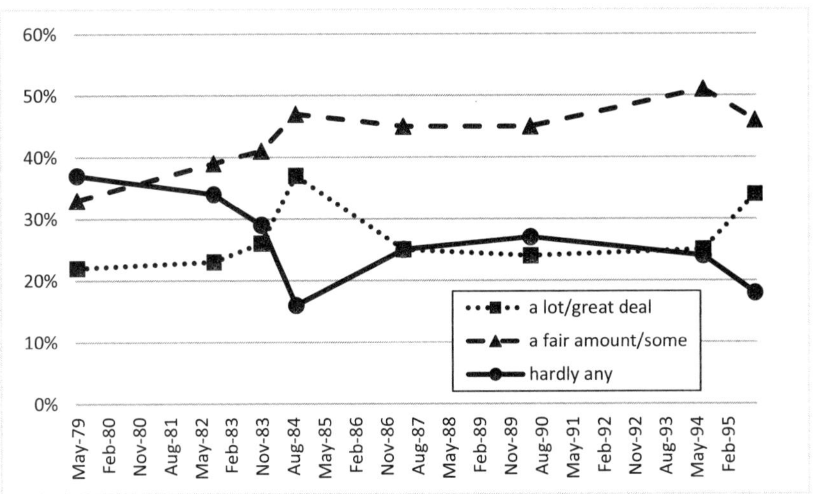

Figure 7.6. Public Perception of Differences between the Democratic and Republican Parties, 1979–1995. *Source*: ABC News, *Washington Post*, and Public Policy Polling.

and religious attitudes,[51] the growth of ideologically driven interest groups and media outlets,[52] and reactions to an expanding national policy agenda.[53]

As a result, even though Gingrich gladly accepted praise from his fellow Republicans for the 1994 GOP takeover of Congress, it is doubtful that his years of toil in the minority were solely responsible for bringing it about.[54] To be sure, he did a great deal in the twenty-four months leading up to the 1994 election that helped his party. Gingrich raised a considerable amount of campaign funds for the GOP, and his successful, albeit indirect, blockade of Clinton's health care bill may have dampened the popularity of the Democratic Party. In addition, as political scientists Jamie Carson and Gary Jacobson have argued, Gingrich's party gained control of the House in part by recruiting strong candidates in GOP-amenable districts and "by persuading voters to blame a unified Democratic regime for government's failures," both tactics that were touted by Gingrich.[55] But by 1994, voters did not need much additional persuasion from members of Congress to cast their ballots for the GOP, given the aforementioned trends in political nationalization, voter polarization, and voting patterns in key regions such as the South. Even in the short run, Gingrich's attempts to create a

Republican House took advantage of circumstances he had little to do with. Bill Clinton's election created the necessary condition for Republicans to hold Democrats culpable for voter unhappiness and thereby lose districts that were already friendly territory for Republican challengers. Surveys taken during the 103rd Congress registered growing dissatisfaction with Clinton and congressional Democrats well before campaign season was underway, and certainly before the release of the Contract with America, a document that few Americans were familiar with and that even fewer indicated would be crucial to determining their vote choice.[56] Furthermore, while House Republicans benefited from Gingrich's recruitment of strong candidates and his campaign fundraising for the 1994 elections, the Georgian was aided by many others. One of Gingrich's most important allies was Bill Paxon, whose masterful leadership of the NRCC—following the pattern set by former DCCC Chair Tony Coelho (D-CA) in the 1980s—yielded a huge increase in financial contributions from incumbents that could then be spent to elect more Republicans to Congress. Tellingly, Gingrich himself occasionally admitted that lawmakers could not do much to win control of Congress. In 1992, for instance, he confessed that most of what the GOP needed to do to become a majority was "beyond his colleagues' reach," and he acknowledged that his party was the beneficiary of partisan shifts in the South starting in the mid-twentieth century.[57]

Even within Congress, several changes ascribed to Gingrich cannot be readily traced to him. Some, for instance, have accused Gingrich of imposing a three-day workweek in the House, which kept lawmakers from socializing across party lines, but the so-called "Tuesday-Thursday Club" had a long pedigree, and in the 104th Congress especially, the House had more lengthy workweeks than had been seen in years.[58] Also, while Gingrich wanted lawmakers to vote more along party lines to differentiate the two parties, and he did encourage the Conference to pursue obstruction for its own sake during the first two years of Bill Clinton's presidency, it is debatable whether he had much to do with congressional polarization writ large. On the one hand, more polarized voting by Republicans happened "across-the-board" in the party during the early 1990s, "as intended by Gingrich and his associates,"[59] and the level of partisan voting in the 104th Congress was higher than had been recorded in decades.[60] Political scientist Sean Theriault also identified a connection between the growth of voting polarization in the US Senate and the election of Republican senators who had served with Gingrich in the House.[61] On the other hand, greater party alignment in voting began many years prior to Gingrich's arrival in Washington, DC, and scholars have found little evidence that party leaders like Gingrich can do much to increase congressional polarization overall.[62] Other studies have shown that factors outside of Gingrich's control explain growing House polarization in the 1980s and 1990s, such as systemic disincentives for moderates and cooperative-minded individuals to run for office,[63] demographic changes in districts and states,[64] parties fighting each other for votes in an increasingly competitive electoral environment,[65] and citizen activists pressing their representatives into following stronger partisan behavior.[66] In short, though Gingrich may have been a critical avatar of polarizing political behavior inside Congress, the origins of voting polarization are far too complex to trace to just a single person, even someone with as much renown and entrepreneurial energy as Newt Gingrich.

Other Party Entrepreneurs in Congress

Gingrich is far from the only member of Congress to have acted entrepreneurially on behalf of their party. A cursory look at recent congressional history suggests several other legislators who, at least at first glance, fit the definition of a party entrepreneur.[67] A number of them have served in formal leadership positions; and while one might argue that all party leaders are expected to help out their party, some went beyond the basic job description of their post and tried novel tactics and strategies to achieve their party's collective goals. For instance, in the late 1970s, Senate Minority Leader Howard Baker (R-TN) used his party's traditional weekly lunch meetings to develop party strategy, and he tasked groups of senators to come up with policy proposals that would favorably contrast the GOP with the Carter White House.[68] Speaker Tip O'Neill expanded his media profile following the 1980 elections with the objective of protecting the Democratic Party's brand and winning political and policy battles against President Ronald Reagan.[69] Tony Coelho turned the sleepy Democratic Congressional Campaign Committee into a money-generating machine by requiring incumbents to raise more funds for the committee, thus helping Democrats maintain their majority status by making cash infusions into the campaigns of vulnerable candidates. Coelho also came up with a way to monetize meetings with Speaker O'Neill by offering exclusive time with the Speaker to generous donors. Bill Paxon followed Coelho's lead when he took over the NRCC in 1992, making it an electoral powerhouse for the Republican Conference in part by working with Gingrich to connect the committee assignment process with the amount of money donated by lawmakers to the organization.

More intriguing are members of Congress who acted entrepreneurially despite not being party leaders. As a second-term Texas congressman, Lyndon Johnson tapped into his connections with the oil industry in Texas and began distributing campaign contributions to fellow Democrats in 1940, a potentially difficult election year for his party.[70] Richard Nixon, who had encouraged Gingrich to create what became the COS, was himself a charter member of the Chowder and Marching Club, a loosely organized group of House Republicans formed in 1949 to share information and mentor junior lawmakers in the party.[71] Phil Burton (D-CA) was both a masterful legislative entrepreneur—crafting landmark liberal legislation on issues ranging from Social Security to parkland—and a savvy party entrepreneur, raising and distributing money for Democratic challengers in 1974 and, after the 1980 census, single-handedly redrawing the boundaries of California's congressional districts to effectively deny reelection to several Republicans.[72] Another California House Democrat, Henry Waxman, pioneered the creation of leadership political action committees (LPACs), which are created and managed by rank and file lawmakers in order to raise and distribute money to fellow partisans, thereby aiding the party as a whole. In 2008, Senator Jim DeMint (R-SC) formed his own LPAC, the Senate Conservative Fund, which spent sizable amounts not only to defeat incumbent Democrats but also to get conservatives elected to his chamber, echoing Gingrich's own longtime objective of building a conservative Republican majority in Congress.[73]

These examples, along with the story of Gingrich's congressional career, suggest a few commonalities about party entrepreneurship in Congress. First, it is often tied to personal ambition. Lyndon Johnson hoped to cultivate the loyalty of fellow Democrats as a means of climbing the steps of power in Congress, which he eventually did (albeit by running for the Senate). Burton, a transparently ambitious congressman, wanted other

Democrats to be indebted to him so he could ask for their support in future leadership elections. Waxman used LPACs to win over colleagues in anticipation of a run for a party or committee leadership post, and he was eventually elected chairman of the House Energy and Commerce Committee.[74] And Gingrich, himself desirous of more influence, built up a base of political support within the Conference and cultivated a reputation for successfully taking on Democrats—both useful in his climb up the leadership ladder.

Second, party entrepreneurs do not necessarily benefit from empirical proof of their success, but rather from lawmakers' *belief* that the entrepreneurial ventures have worked or will work in the future. As we have argued, the evidence that Gingrich's party-oriented entrepreneurialism created a Republican majority in 1994 is inconclusive at best; what really mattered was the confidence of the GOP rank and file that his efforts were more likely to succeed than those of the party's old guard. Similarly, the year that LBJ began distributing campaign checks to fellow Democrats proved to be a good one for Democrats nationally, not just in the House, but what benefited Johnson was the perception that his checks had helped his party withstand strong electoral challenges.

Finally, party entrepreneurship in Congress often leaves an enduring legacy in the form of new rules, tactics, and norms of political behavior. Burton demonstrated the electoral advantages of crafting congressional district lines with great precision, something both parties adopted with relish and enhanced with sophisticated computer technology. Waxman's LPACs are now ubiquitous in Congress, as is the expectation that party leaders must follow O'Neill's example by appearing frequently in the news media to protect and improve the image of their party. And as already mentioned, what today's congressional parties do in the name of winning or keeping power in the House is the heritage of Gingrich's entrepreneurialism.

After Congress

Though Gingrich was forced to resign from Congress following the 1998 election results, a man with his ambition, rhetorical gifts, and strong sense of self could never vanish entirely from the political stage. Following the well-worn path of other former lawmakers, he started his own consulting firm, offered advice to politicians and corporate clients, and periodically advised House Republicans on how to win elections.[75] Unlike most erstwhile lawmakers, though, he maintained a very public profile, writing various fiction and nonfiction books, appearing frequently as an expert guest on cable news shows, and writing provocative editorials on subjects ranging from health care reform and mismanagement at the US State Department to the bailout of automobile manufacturers in 2008.[76]

Gingrich also continued to pursue his political ambitions. He threw his hat in the ring for the 2012 Republican nomination for president, and he did relatively well for a candidate who had not held public office in over a decade. He performed respectably in the Iowa Republican caucuses, won the South Carolina primary, and came in second in the Florida primary. He also demonstrated his pugnacious rhetorical style and enduring futurist vision, promising at one point to establish an American moon colony during his presidency.[77] Weak fundraising and poor showings in subsequent primaries led him to quit the race. Nonetheless, he remained in or near various political circles, and when real estate mogul and reality television star Donald Trump decided to run for president, the former Speaker astutely developed strong ties with Trump, offering advice to the neophyte candidate on how to manage a presidential campaign, endorsing his candidacy early on, and marketing himself as an erudite interpreter of his election and presidency (and writing one of the very first books about Trump). Gingrich's wife, Callista, would later be appointed by President Trump to serve as ambassador to Vatican City.[78]

Indeed, some have argued that Trump's presidential campaign and subsequent presidency were the natural consequence of Gingrich's "smashmouth" approach to politics: demonizing the opposite party, using aggressive rhetoric, refusing to apologize for past behavior, and engaging in dramatic confrontations with opponents to garner more news coverage.[79] Trump was willing to accuse his foes of wrongdoing with little or no evidence, just as Gingrich had done (such as against Speaker Jim Wright), and his public rhetoric could be as nasty and personal as the Gingrich-like phrases recommended by GOPAC in 1990, with words like "corrupt," "evil," "crooked," and "scum." Trump even issued an election-year "contract" promising several actions within his first one hundred days in office.[80] For his part, Gingrich expressed an affinity with the president's distrust of "elites" who, he argued, unfairly maligned his disruptive style of leadership, and he encouraged Trump to attack the media just as he himself had been fond of doing. Gingrich even defended Trump's quixotic effort to reverse his 2020 election loss by returning to his old mantra of Democratic corruption and recalling his insistence in 1985 that Democratic wins that year were not legitimate. "I will not accept Joe Biden as president," Gingrich wrote, mimicking Trump's refusal to do the same. "He was really Donald Trump in an early form," one former Republican lawmaker told us.[81]

Gingrich may share some blame for the controversial Trump presidency, but Trumpian politics depart in important ways from the vision laid out by Gingrich when he was in Congress. As a congressman, Gingrich was no libertarian; he had recognized the existence of social problems like poverty, environmental damage, and subpar education, and though he was not an active legislator, he advocated for creative conservative policy solutions to such problems.[82] By contrast, today's GOP features a strong libertarian wing that is arguably defined more by its emotional appeals than its policy proposals and by what it opposes rather than what it supports.[83] Furthermore, the election of Trump threatened to identify the Republican Party with protectionism, racial intolerance, and xenophobia, positions that were quite different from those held by Congressman Gingrich, who generally supported free trade, hoped to persuade African American voters to join the GOP, and was even part of a faction of House Republicans who crossed President Reagan by endorsing sanctions on the apartheid regime of South Africa.

As of this writing, Gingrich continues to pursue an active career in writing, consulting, politics, and media commentary. But it was during his time in the House of Representatives—not just as Speaker, but as a formal and informal leader in the minority wilderness—that he made a name for himself as a relentless and history-making party entrepreneur.

NOTES

Abbreviations of Archival Collections

GVJ Guy A. Vander Jagt Congressional Papers, Special Collections & University Archives, Grand Valley State University, Allendale, Michigan.

ME Mickey Edwards Collection, Carl Albert Congressional Research and Studies Center, University of Oklahoma, Norman, Oklahoma.

NLG Newt Gingrich Papers, Special Collections, University of West Georgia, Carrollton, Georgia.

RAG Richard A. Gephardt Collection, Missouri History Museum, St. Louis, Missouri.

RHM Robert H. Michel Collection, Dirksen Congressional Center, Pekin, Illinois.

RKA Richard K. Armey Collection, Carl Albert Congressional Research and Studies Center, University of Oklahoma, Norman, Oklahoma.

RP Ron Peters Collection, Carl Albert Congressional Research and Studies Center, University of Oklahoma, Norman, Oklahoma.

RW Robert Walker Papers, Archives & Special Collections, Millersville University, Millersville, Pennsylvania.

WAR William A. Rusher Papers, Library of Congress, Washington, DC.

WJC Clinton Digital Library, William J. Clinton Presidential Library & Museum, Little Rock, Arkansas.

USC US Capitol Historical Society Oral History Interviews, Library of Congress, Washington, DC.

Preface

1. Gingrich himself has been far more skeptical of political scientists than of historians. See, e.g., Ronald M. Peters Jr., "Newt Gingrich versus Political Science: A Study in Cause and Effect," working paper.

Chapter 1. Newt Gingrich, Party Entrepreneur

1. *Congressional Record*, May 14, 1984, 12042, and May 15, 1984, 12198–12202; www.c-span.org/video/?93662-1/speakers-words-ordered (14:20–44:41); Tip O'Neill (with William Novak), *Man of the House: The Life and Political Memoirs of Speaker Tip O'Neill* (New York: Random House, 1987), 424–425.

2. Ronald M. Peters Jr., *The American Speakership: The Office in Historical Perspective*, 2nd ed. (Baltimore: Johns Hopkins University Press, 1997), 299; Frank Gregorsky, "The Basics of Newt Gingrich," April–September 1983, 1, Box 230, Folder: The Basics of Newt Gingrich/Frank Gregorsky, NLG; interview with former Republican leader, July 20, 2020.

3. Richard F. Fenno Jr., *Learning to Govern: An Institutional View of the 104th Congress* (Washington, DC: Brookings Institution Press, 1997), 17; see also Nelson W. Polsby, *How Congress Evolves: Social Bases of Institutional Change* (New York: Oxford University Press, 2004), 132. Frances Lee makes the case that, rather than length of time in the minority, electoral competitiveness between the congressional parties drives party strategy. When that competitiveness increased after 1980, she argues, it created a "political logic" for more confrontational strategies, though Republicans debated for some time whether to adopt those strategies. Frances E. Lee, *Insecure Majorities: Congress and the Perpetual Campaign* (Chicago: University of Chicago Press, 2016), 74.

4. Barbara Sinclair, "Transformational Leader or Faithful Agent?: Principal-Agent Theory and House Majority Party Leadership," *Legislative Studies Quarterly* 24, no. 3 (1999): 421–449.

5. Joseph Cooper and David W. Brady, "Institutional Context and Leadership Style: The House from Cannon to Rayburn," *American Political Science Review* 75, no. 2 (1981): 411–425; Gary W. Cox and Mathew D. McCubbins, *Legislative Leviathan: Party Government in the House* (Berkeley: University of California Press, 1993); David W. Rohde, *Parties and Leaders in the Postreform House* (Chicago: University of Chicago Press, 1991); Steven S. Smith, *Party Influence in Congress* (New York: Cambridge University Press, 2007).

6. Ronald M. Peters Jr. and Craig A. Williams, "The Demise of Newt Gingrich as a Transformational Leader: Does Organizational Leadership Theory Apply to Legislative Leaders?," *Organizational Dynamics* 30, no. 3 (2002): 257–268, 261, 266.

7. John J. Pitney Jr., "Understanding Newt Gingrich," prepared for delivery at the American Political Science Association annual meeting, San Francisco (1996), 2; see also William F. Connelly Jr., *James Madison Rules America: The Constitutional Origins of Congressional Partisanship* (Lanham, MD: Rowman & Littlefield, 2010), 86–100. Gingrich himself admitted in an interview that "I'm not a natural leader [because] I'm too intellectual, I'm too abstract, I think too much," and former aide Gregorsky wrote that "Newt has no philosophy, and certainly no 'ideology.' What he has is a way of being, a way of thinking." Connie Bruck, "The Politics of Perception," *New Yorker* (October 9, 1995), 50; Gregorsky, "The Basics of Newt Gingrich," 16.

8. Ronald Brownstein, *The Second Civil War: How Extreme Partisanship Has Paralyzed Washington and Polarized America* (New York: Penguin, 2007), 123; Tom Davis, Martin Frost, and Richard E. Cohen, *The Partisan Divide: Congress in Crisis* (Campbell, CA: Premiere, 2014), 265; Thomas E. Mann and Norman J. Ornstein, *The Broken Branch: How Congress Is Failing America and How to Get It Back on Track*

(New York: Oxford University, 2006), 103; Ronald M. Peters Jr. and Cindy Simon Rosenthal, *Nancy Pelosi and the New American Politics* (New York: Oxford University Press, 2010), 238; Peters and Williams, "The Demise of Newt Gingrich"; Pitney, "Understanding Newt Gingrich," 22–23.

9. John M. Barry, *The Ambition and the Power* (New York: Viking, 1989), 165–166, 365; Eleanor Clift and Tom Brazaitis, *War without Bloodshed: The Art of Politics* (New York: Scribner, 1996), 218; Matthew N. Green, *Underdog Politics: The Minority Party in the U.S. House of Representatives* (New Haven: Yale University Press, 2015); Jonathan Mark Morstein, "Gingrich's Challenge: The Power of Escalation to Force Change in Institutions" (PhD diss., University of Maryland, College Park, 1998); Julian E. Zelizer, *Burning Down the House: Newt Gingrich, the Fall of a Speaker, and the Rise of the New Republican Party* (New York: Penguin, 2020), 304–306.

10. Dan Balz and Ronald Brownstein, *Storming the Gates: Protest Politics and the Republican Revival* (Boston: Little, Brown, 1996), 39; Brownstein, *The Second Civil War*, 138; Bruck, "The Politics of Perception," 58, 62; J. Dennis Hastert, *Speaker: Lessons from Forty Years in Coaching and Politics* (Washington, DC: Regnery, 2004), 121, 147–148; Haynes Johnson and David S. Broder, *The System: The American Way of Politics at the Breaking Point* (Boston: Little, Brown, 1996), 545; Zelizer, *Burning Down the House*, 13–14. Some facets of Gingrich's leadership also suggest similarities to two leadership types identified by James MacGregor Burns, "opinion leadership" and "intellectual leadership." James MacGregor Burns, *Leadership* (New York: Harper & Row, 1978), chap. 6. They also fit under the broader category of theories that identify the role of individual personality and style in shaping lawmaker and leader behavior. See, e.g., William Bernhard and Tracy Sulkin, *Legislative Style* (Chicago: University of Chicago Press, 2018); and Hubert Bruce Fuller, *The Speakers of the House* (Boston: Little, Brown, 1909).

11. Randall Strahan, *Leading Representatives: The Agency of Leaders in the Politics of the U.S. House* (Baltimore: Johns Hopkins University Press, 2007), 39; Randall Strahan and Daniel J. Palazzolo, "The Gingrich Effect," *Political Science Quarterly* 119, no. 1:89–114.

12. Matthew N. Green, *The Speaker of the House: A Study of Leadership* (New Haven: Yale University Press, 2010), 123–124.

13. Rohde, *Parties and Leaders*, 38; Arturo Vega and Ronald M. Peters Jr., "Principal-Agent Theories of Party Leadership under Preference Heterogeneity: The Case of Simpson-Mazzoli," *Congress & the Presidency* 23, no. 1 (1996): 15–32.

14. Bruce Miroff, "Entrepreneurship and Leadership," *Studies in American Political Development* 17, no. 2 (October 2003): 205. For more on the definition and impact of political entrepreneurship, see Morris P. Fiorina and Kenneth A. Shepsle, "Formal Theories of Leadership: Agents, Agenda Setters, and Entrepreneurs," from *Leadership in Politics: New Perspectives in Political Science*, ed. Bryan D. Jones (Lawrence: University Press of Kansas, 1989); Norman Frohlich, Joe A. Oppenheimer, and Oran R. Young, *Political Leadership and Collective Goods* (Princeton: Princeton

University Press, 1971); Terry M. Moe, *The Organization of Interests: Incentives and the Internal Dynamics of Political Interest Groups* (Chicago: University of Chicago Press, 1980); and Adam Sheingate, "Political Entrepreneurship, Institutional Change, and American Political Development," *Studies in American Political Development* 17, no. 2 (October 2003): 185–203.

15. R. Douglas Arnold, *The Logic of Congressional Action* (New Haven: Yale University Press, 1990), chap. 5; Glenn R. Parker, *Institutional Change, Discretion, and the Making of Modern Congress: An Economic Interpretation* (Ann Arbor: University of Michigan Press, 1992), 33; Eric Schickler, *Disjointed Pluralism: Institutional Innovation and the Development of the U.S. Congress* (Princeton: Princeton University Press, 2001), 14–15; Wendy J. Schiller, "Senators as Political Entrepreneurs: Using Bill Sponsorship to Shape Legislative Agendas," *American Journal of Political Science* 39, no. 1 (1995): 186–203; Gregory Wawro, *Legislative Entrepreneurship in the U.S. House of Representatives* (Ann Arbor: University of Michigan Press, 2000), 2.

16. James M. Curry and Frances E. Lee, *The Limits of Party: Congress and Lawmaking in a Polarized Era* (Chicago: University of Chicago Press, 2020).

17. Cox and McCubbins, *Legislative Leviathan*, 109–122; David R. Mayhew, *Congress: The Electoral Connection* (New Haven: Yale University Press, 1974).

18. Richard F. Fenno Jr., *Congressmen in Committees* (Boston: Little, Brown, 1973), 1.

19. Matthew N. Green and Douglas B. Harris, *Choosing the Leader: Leadership Elections in the U.S. House of Representatives* (New Haven: Yale University Press, 2019).

20. Avinash B. Dixit and Barry J. Nalebuff, *Thinking Strategically: The Competitive Edge in Business, Politics, and Everyday Life* (New York: Norton, 1991); Peter C. Ordeshook, *Game Theory and Political Theory: An Introduction* (New York: Cambridge University Press, 1986). For examples of congressional scholarship that do consider strategy, see Gregory Koger and Matthew J. Lebo, *Strategic Party Government: Why Winning Trumps Ideology* (Chicago: University of Chicago Press, 2017); and Lee, *Insecure Majorities*, 8.

21. Carl von Clausewitz, *On War*, trans. by Michael Howard and Peter Paret (New York: Oxford University Press, 2007 [1832]), bk. 1, chap. 1.

22. William F. Connelly Jr. and John J. Pitney Jr., *Congress' Permanent Minority?: Republicans in the U.S. House* (Lanham, MD: Rowman & Littlefield, 1994), 103–104; John J. Pitney Jr., *The Art of Political Warfare* (Norman: University of Oklahoma Press, 2001); Barbara Sinclair, *Party Wars: Polarization and the Politics of National Policy Making* (Norman: University of Oklahoma Press, 2006); Sean M. Theriault, *The Gingrich Senators: The Roots of Partisan Warfare in Congress* (New York: Oxford University Press, 2013), 12; James I. Wallner, *On Parliamentary War: Partisan Conflict and Procedural Change in the U.S. Senate* (Ann Arbor: University of Michigan Press, 2017).

23. For other military definitions of strategy, see Clausewitz, *On War*, bk. 2,

chap. 1; and B. H. Liddell Hart, *Strategy*, 2nd rev. ed. (New York: Meridian, 1991 [1967]), 335.

24. Arthur F. Lykke Jr., "Defining Military Strategy = E + W + M," *Military Review* 69, no. 5 (May 1989): 6.

25. Green, *The Speaker of the House*, 123–124; Dale Russakoff and Dan Balz, "Mr. Speaker: The Rise of Newt Gingrich," *Washington Post*, December 19, 1994, A19.

26. Barry, *The Ambition and the Power*, 365; Bruck, "The Politics of Perception," 58; Clift and Brazaitis, *War without Bloodshed*, 220; Hastert, *Speaker*, 118; Wawro, *Legislative Entrepreneurship*, 136–137; see also chapters 5 and 6. A Congress technically ends in January of an odd-numbered year, but we list the end of each Congress as its second (even-numbered) year to ease interpretation.

27. Craig Volden and Alan E. Wiseman, *Legislative Effectiveness in the United States Congress: The Lawmakers* (New York: Cambridge University Press, 2014).

28. Fenno, *Learning to Govern*, 31–32; Peters, *The American Speakership*, 302; Schickler, *Disjointed Pluralism*, 242–246.

29. For an early reference to Gingrich as a party entrepreneur, see Bruck, "The Politics of Perception," 61. In addition, William Bernhard and Tracy Sulkin categorize Gingrich's style after 1994 as an "ambitious entrepreneur" and, prior to the 1994 elections, as a "party builder." Bernhard and Sulkin, *Legislative Style*, 49, 112.

30. Bruck, "The Politics of Perception," 50; Clift and Brazaitis, *War without Bloodshed*, 207; Pitney, "Understanding Newt Gingrich," 16–19; Pitney, *The Art of Political Warfare*, 65; Gail Sheehy, "The Inner Quest of Newt Gingrich," *Vanity Fair*, September 1995; Benjamin Sheffner, "Gingrich: 'Politics Is War without Blood,'" *Roll Call*, May 29, 1995. Gingrich was also inspired by the business guru Peter Drucker and his book *The Effective Executive*.

31. Interview with Vin Weber, from "The Long March of Newt Gingrich," *Frontline* (1996), www.pbs.org/wgbh/pages/frontline/newt/newtintwshtml/weber2.html; David Rogers, "Assault from the Right," *Wall Street Journal*, May 23, 1984, 62; interview with former Republican member of Congress, May 8, 2019.

32. Interview with former Republican leadership aide, April 11, 2019.

33. Barry, *The Ambition and the Power*, 363; Pitney, "Understanding Newt Gingrich," 17; Susan F. Rasky, "From Political Guerilla to Republican Folk Hero," *New York Times*, June 15, 1988, A24.

34. "Cooking up a Republican Majority for the 1980's," 1, Box 465, Folder: unlabeled, NLG.

35. Lawrence Freedman, *Strategy: A History* (New York: Oxford University Press, 2013), xii.

36. Gregorsky, "The Basics of Newt Gingrich," 16, 45.

37. For examples of Gingrich's early memos, see "COS Activists' Manual," Box 459, Folder 31, NLG; Newt Gingrich and Marianne Gingrich, "Key Steps in Developing a Survivable United States," and "Creating a Republican Legislative Agenda for a Conservative Opportunity Society," Box 34, Folder 7, WAR. In this respect, Gingrich

was almost Marxist in his belief that a revolution could be brought about by raising citizens' consciousness about flaws in the political and social status quo. Freeman, *Strategy*, 259–260.

38. Interview with Dennis Hastert, User Clip: Gingrich Coup Attempt, C-SPAN, August 4, 2004, www.c-span.org/video/?c4383050/user-clip-gingrich-coup-attempt &start=1187 (3:35–3:45); interview with former leadership aide, October 17, 2019; interview with former Republican leadership aide, April 11, 2019.

39. Balz and Brownstein, *Storming the Gates*, 144; Ezra Klein, "Newt Gingrich's Big, Bad Ideas," *Washington Post*, January 24, 2012. The joke may have originated as a prank by NRCC staff using actual filing cabinets. Russakoff and Balz, "Mr. Speaker," A19.

40. Major Garrett, "Gingrich: Managerial Disaster?," *Atlantic*, December 9, 2011.

41. Gregorsky, "The Basics of Newt Gingrich," 1, 14.

42. Fenno, *Learning to Govern*, 15; Mel Steely, *The Gentleman from Georgia: The Biography of Newt Gingrich* (Macon, GA: Mercer University Press, 2000), 117.

43. Gingrich speech to Georgia College Republicans, June 24, 1978, reprinted in *West Georgia News*, from Pat Schroeder material, Subgroup: Speechwriting, Series: Michael Waldman, Folder: GOP [Clippings] [1], WJC; interview with Frank Gregorksy, from "The Long March of Newt Gingrich," *Frontline* (1996), www.pbs .org/wgbh/pages/frontline/newt/newtintwshtml/gregorsky.html.

44. Balz and Brownstein, *Storming the Gates*, 35–36; Steven V. Roberts, "House G.O.P. Freshmen Are Speaking Up on Party Issues," *New York Times*, October 29, 1979, A16. See also Zachary C. Smith, "From the Well of the House: Remaking the House Republican Party, 1978–1994" (PhD diss., Boston University, 2012), 70; and interview in 1996 with Vander Jagt, from "The Long March of Newt Gingrich, *Frontline*, www.pbs.org/wgbh/pages/frontline/newt/newtintwshtml/vanderjagt1.html.

45. Dennis Farney, "Power Bloc: 'New Right' Adherents In Congress Now Play Mainly Defensive Role," *Wall Street Journal*, September 16, 1980, emphasis added; House Counsel newsletter, June 12, 1980, 2, Leadership, Box 2, Folder: 96th Leadership Contests, 1980(1), RHM; "Cooking up a Republican Majority for the 1980's," 2, Box 465, Folder: unlabeled, NLG.

46. Interview with Charlie Rose, July 6, 1995, https://charlierose.com/videos/23715 (38:48—39:20).

47. Barry, *The Ambition and the Power*, 364; Bruck, "The Politics of Perception," 56; Pitney, "Understanding Newt Gingrich," 2–13, quote p. 20; Steely, *The Gentleman from Georgia*, 117; Sheryl Gay Stolberg, "For Gingrich in Power, Pragmatism, not Purity," *New York Times*, December 20, 2011. Gingrich liked to say that when he was first elected to Congress, his goals were not only a Republican majority but also the defeat of the Soviet empire and an end to the welfare state.

48. Reid Spearman, "A Dialogue on COS: Figuring Out What We're Doing," May 11, 1983, Part One ("Vision"), 4, Box 463, NLG.

49. Newt Gingrich and Marianne Gingrich, "Key Steps in Developing a

Survivable United States," 15–16, Box 34, Folder 7, WAR. See also Newt Gingrich, *Lessons Learned the Hard Way: A Personal Report* (New York: HarperCollins, 1998), 16.

50. Clift and Brazaitis, *War without Bloodshed*, 239; Interview with Charlie Rose, July 6, 1995 (7:02–7:47), https://charlierose.com/videos/23715; and interview with Bill Kristol, November 21, 2014, pt. 1, https://conversationswithbillkristol.org/transcript/newt-gingrich-transcript/.

51. Bruck, "The Politics of Perception," 60; Julia Ioffe, "The Millennial's Guide to Newt Gingrich," *Politico*, July 14, 2016; Jerry Markon, "Gingrich Archives Show His Public Praise, Private Criticism," *Washington Post*, February 19, 2012; Stolberg, "For Gingrich in Power." One of Gingrich's former students at West Georgia University recounted to the authors that Gingrich had told him he planned not only to be elected to Congress as a Republican, but also to become Speaker of the House.

52. Interview with former leadership aide, October 17, 2019.

53. Bruck, "The Politics of Perception," 60.

54. His presidential aspirations may well have predated his speakership. Former Gingrich aide Chip Kahn commented in 1985 that while Gingrich knew better than to admit an interest in the presidency, "he will be whatever he can be, as high as he can go." David Osborne, "Newt Gingrich: Shining Knight of the Post-Reagan Right," *Mother Jones* (November 1984): 17, from Pat Schroeder material, Subgroup: Speechwriting, Series: Michael Waldman, Folder: GOP [Clippings] [1], WJC.

55. Austin Ranney, *The Doctrine of Responsible Party Government: Its Origins and Present State* (Urbana: University of Illinois Press, 1954); American Political Science Association, "Toward a More Responsible Two-Party System: A Report of the Committee on Political Parties," *American Political Science Review* 44, no. 3 (1950). See also Sam Rosenfeld, *The Polarizers: Postwar Architects of Our Partisan Era* (Chicago: University of Chicago Press, 2018), 4–5; and John Kenneth White, "E. E. Schattschneider and the Responsible Party Model," *PS: Political Science & Politics* 25, no. 2 (1992): 167–171.

56. Jonathan Morstein argues that Gingrich's objective was to "artificially induce a sense of political crisis and generat[e] . . . voter anger" that would induce a political realignment. Morstein, "Gingrich's Challenge," 721.

57. Mann and Ornstein, *The Broken Branch*, 65; memo to Fellow Republicans, March 18, 1982, 1, Box 456, Folder 12, NLG.

58. Green, *Underdog Politics*, 20.

59. John A. Farrell, *Tip O'Neill and the Democratic Century* (Boston: Little, Brown, 2001), 627; Lawrence R. Jacobs and Robert Y. Shapiro, *Politicians Don't Pander: Political Manipulation and the Loss of Democratic Responsiveness* (Chicago: University of Chicago Press, 2000); Katherine Q. Seelye, "Gingrich First Mastered the Media and Then Rose to Be King of the Hill," *New York Times*, December 14, 1994, A1.

60. It may seem contradictory that a party entrepreneur would subvert his own party's leaders. But the temptation to do so is not uncommon for would-be

entrepreneurs in Congress insofar as their behavior may be, as with legislative entrepreneurs, "often counter to the designs of party leaders." Parker, *Institutional Change*, 34.

61. See, e.g., Fenno, *Learning to Govern*, 14–16, and Lee, *Insecure Majorities*, 104. Fenno describes confrontation as Gingrich's "instrumental" goal (p. 15), but we break that instrumental goal into its component parts (tarnishing the House's reputation, distinguishing the two parties, etc.).

62. On a party's productivity brand, see Matthew N. Green and William Deatherage, "When Reputation Trumps Policy: Party Productivity Brand and the 2017 Tax Cut and Jobs Act," *Forum* 16, no. 3 (2018): 419–440.

63. Interview with former Republican leader, July 22, 2020.

64. Barry, *The Ambition and the Power*, 162; Myra MacPherson, "Newt Gingrich, Point Man in a House Divided," *Washington Post*, June 12, 1989, C8; Robert P. Hey, "Gingrich Win Hints at More-Partisan House," *Christian Science Monitor*, March 24, 1989, 2, from Box 81, Folder 19, ME.

65. Markon, "Gingrich Archives Show."

66. Zelizer, *Burning Down the House*, 207; "Principles for Creating a Republican Majority in the House," 4–5, Box 456, Folder 11, NLG.

67. Stolberg, "For Gingrich in Power."

68. Bruck, "The Politics of Perception," 58; Paul Gigot, "Newtron Newt Could Become GOP's Coelho," *Wall Street Journal*, March 17, 1989, A14.

Chapter 2. Entrepreneurial Outsider (1979–1984)

1. Richard L. Lyons, "House Schorr Probe Is Over," *Washington Post*, September 23, 1976, A1; Mel Steely, *The Gentleman from Georgia: The Biography of Newt Gingrich* (Macon, GA: Mercer University Press, 2000), 61, 76.

2. Gingrich speech to Georgia College Republicans, June 24, 1978, reprinted in *West Georgia News*, from Pat Schroeder material, Subgroup: Speechwriting, Series: Michael Waldman, Box 4, Folder: GOP [Clippings] [1], WJC.

3. "Characteristics of the 96th Congress," *CQ Almanac 1979*, 35th ed. (Washington, DC: Congressional Quarterly, 1980), 33–45. This included Ron Paul (R-TX), who had actually served a partial term in 1976.

4. Jerry Markon, "Gingrich Archives Show His Public Praise, Private Criticism," *Washington Post*, February 19, 2012.

5. Interview with Mickey Edwards, July 14, 2020.

6. Dan Balz and Ronald Brownstein, *Storming the Gates: Protest Politics and the Republican Revival* (Boston: Little, Brown, 1996), 35–36; "GOP Freshmen: Aiming at a Majority," *Congressional Quarterly Weekly Report*, July 7, 1979, 1340; Zachary C. Smith, "From the Well of the House: Remaking the House Republican Party, 1978–1994" (PhD diss., Boston University, 2012), 39.

7. Interview with former leadership aide, October 17, 2019.

8. "House Defeats Attempt to Expel Rep. Diggs," *Wall Street Journal*, March 2, 1979, 6; Craig Winneker and Glenn R. Simpson, "Newt's Freshman Year," *Roll Call*, April 17, 1995, 22. The vote on the motion to refer H. Res. 142 to committee was cast on March 1, 1979. Gingrich continued to press the matter privately. For instance, in February 1980 he urged his freshmen class colleagues to "move on Diggs; he has shown his arrogance and contempt for integrity." Minutes, Republican Freshmen Class Meeting, February 12, 1980, 2, Box 139, Folder: Republican Freshmen Class, NLG.

9. Alan Ehrenhalt, "Those Militant GOP Freshmen," *Conservative Digest*, May 1979, Box 139, Folder: Republican Freshmen Class, NLG; "GOP Freshmen."

10. Winneker and Simpson, "Newt's Freshman Year," 22–23.

11. Julian E. Zelizer, *Burning Down the House: Newt Gingrich, the Fall of a Speaker, and the Rise of the New Republican Party* (New York: Penguin, 2020), 7.

12. Newt Gingrich, Letter to the Editor, *Wall Street Journal*, December 10, 1979, 25; "Applying O.D. to the U.S. Congress—House of Representatives" memo, O.D. Resources Inc., and letter from John Rhodes to C. W. Bill Young, September 26, 1979, from "Building a Republican Team in the House," O.D. Resources, Inc., 58, Box 40, Folder: Project Majority, NLG. Gingrich was not the only advocate of a positive alternative agenda for the Republican Party. Former presidential aide David Gergen warned shortly after the 1978 elections that the GOP desperately needed "to develop and articulate a coherent body of ideas for the future, their own positive vision of what America should be." David Gergen, "Wanted: A GOP Program," *Washington Post*, November 19, 1978, C8.

13. John J. Pitney Jr., "The Conservative Opportunity Society," prepared for delivery at the American Political Science Association annual meeting, San Francisco (1988), 5; Smith, "From the Well of the House," 41–42; draft minutes, Meeting of the Republican Freshmen Class, January 17 and March 6, 1979, Box 139, Folder: Republican Freshman Class, NLG.

14. Mary Russell, "Today's Vote on GOP Leadership Post Seen as Test of Freshmen's Influence," *Washington Post*, June 20, 1979, A3; memo to Gingrich from Roger France, August 16, 1979, and Preliminary Staff Directory, Budget of Hope Project, Box 294, Folder: Opposition to Democrats, NLG.

15. "Media Plan/Budget of Hope," June 26, 1979, Box 294, Folder: Tax Cut Information, NLG; memo to Brock, Vander Jagt, Stockmeyer, Killough, Mongoven, Smith, and Warnick from Gingrich, July 24, 1979, Box 294, Folder: Opposition to Democrats, NLG; memo from Ed Bethune to Members of Freshman Class, August 1, 1979, Box 294, Folder: Budget of Hope Project, NLG; and "On Cutting Taxes and Cutting Spending," September 6, 1979, Box 294, Folder: Tax Cuts, NLG.

16. Report on the Project Majority Task Force and the Budget of Hope Project, September 24, 1979, 3, Box 287, Folder: Strategy Papers (4-6-80), NLG; "Binding Budget Levels," *CQ Almanac 1979*, 35th ed. (Washington, DC: Congressional Quarterly, 1980), 175–182; Pitney, "The Conservative Opportunity Society," 5.

17. Rowland Evans and Robert Novak, "Out-Hoovering Carter," *Washington Post*, March 10, 1980, A27; letter to Dave Hoppe, October 5, 1979, Box 295, Folder: Strategy Group, NLG; Association Briefing on H. Con. Res. 314, April 17, 1980, Box 139, Folder: Budget, NLG; draft letter, May 1, 1980, memo to "Newt et al.," April 30, 1980, and Dear Colleague letter, April 28, 1980, Box 140, Folder: Budget, NLG; and Latta/Giaimo Lobbying Report Forms, Box 137, Folder: National Attention, NLG. Gingrich was also involved at least secondarily with another initiative that shone a spotlight on Democratic refusals to cut taxes. See memo to GOP members and staff participants in Demo Tax Increase Day, March 24, 1980, Box 140, Folder: Miscellaneous, NLG.

18. Memo from Gingrich to Republican Freshman Class Members, January 31, 1980, 1, Box 139, Folder: Republican Freshman Class, NLG.

19. "Applying O.D. to the U.S. Congress—House of Representatives," O.D. Resources, Inc., 3, Box 40, Folder: Project Majority, NLG.

20. Letter from John Rhodes to C. W. Bill Young, September 26, 1979, from "Building a Republican Team in the House," O.D. Resources, Inc., Box 40, Folder: Project Majority, NLG; and J. Killough, "Discussion Piece: Coordinated Marketing Program for 1980," July 19, 1979, Box 139, Folder: Budget of Hope Masters, NLG.

21. Eleanor Clift and Tom Brazaitis, *War without Bloodshed: The Art of Politics* (New York: Scribner, 1996), 220–224; "The Need for a Strategic Republican Program," Box 140, Folder: Miscellaneous, NLG; and "Agenda, Long-Range Planning Taskforce of the NRCC," Box 2158B, Folder: Majority Task Force Meeting, May 23, 1979, NLG.

22. Remark by former Republican staffer, annual meeting of the Association of Centers for the Study of Congress, Washington, DC, May 10, 2019; interview with former GOP leader, July 22, 2020; memo from Frank Gregorsky and David Warnick, February 25, 1980, Box 287, Folder: Candidate feedback, NLG; and "Economic Handbook for Republican House Challengers," October 1980, Box 289, Folder: Economic Handbook, NLG.

23. Steven V. Roberts, "Votes Influenced by Use of Records," *New York Times*, December 14, 1981, A25.

24. Clift and Brazaitis, *War without Bloodshed*, 224–225; Frank Gregorsky, ed., *Elephants in the Room: A History of the House Republican Future* (Exacting Times, 2016), 83; Pitney, "The Conservative Opportunity Society," 9; "The Need for a Strategic Republican Program," Box 140, Folder: Miscellaneous, NLG. It is unclear whether Jack Kemp (R-NY), a corporate executive, or Gingrich himself first came up with the idea for a public pledge. See, e.g., Pitney, "The Conservative Opportunity Society," 8; Steely, *The Gentleman from Georgia*, 127. Much later, Gingrich claimed that the event had helped Republicans win control of the Senate. Gingrich interview with Bill Kristol, November 21, 2014, pt. 5, https://conversationswithbillkristol.org/transcript/newt-gingrich-transcript/.

25. Clift and Brazaitis, *War without Bloodshed*, 224–225; Matthew N. Green,

Underdog Politics: The Minority Party in the U.S. House of Representatives (New Haven: Yale University Press, 2015), 60. What little press coverage the gathering received was not positive. David Broder, one of the few journalists to write about Governing Team Day, described it as a "phony media event." David S. Broder, "Capitol Steps Theatrical," *Washington Post*, September 10, 1980, A19.

26. Ehrenhart, "Those Militant GOP Freshmen"; Mary Russell, "Bob Bauman, Modern House Watchdog," *Washington Post*, May 14, 1979, A3.

27. Myra MacPherson, "Newt Gingrich, Point Man In a House Divided," *Washington Post*, June 12, 1989, C8.

28. John J. Rhodes with Dean Smith, *I Was There* (Salt Lake City, UT: Northwest, 1995), 234–235. The poll may have been conducted by the Atlanta consulting firm mentioned previously, which sharply criticized Rhodes for "lacking in initiative [and] aggressiveness," and being "unimaginative in his planning of 'Republican team' efforts." "Project Majority: Building a Republican Team," O.D. Resources, Inc., 1–8, and "Project Majority: Building a Republican Team/Interview Data Analysis," O.D. Resources, Inc., November 5, 1979, 20, Box 40, Folder: Project Majority, NLG.

29. Ehrenhalt, "Those Militant GOP Freshmen"; Smith, "From the Well of the House," 46; Report on the Project Majority Task Force and the Budget of Hope Project, September 24, 1979, 4, Box 287, Folder: Strategy Papers (4–6-80), NLG.

30. Ronald Brownstein, *The Second Civil War: How Extreme Partisanship Has Paralyzed Washington and Polarized America* (New York: Penguin, 2007), 138. It is also worth considering whether Gingrich's criticism of GOP leaders served his own ambitions for power by fueling a narrative that Rhodes and other leaders were not serving the party well and that he, by implication, would serve it better.

31. Irwin B. Arieff, "House Freshmen Republicans Seek Role as Power Brokers," *Congressional Quarterly Weekly Report*, July 7, 1979, 1339; Michael Barone, "Who Is This Newt Gingrich?," *Washington Post*, August 26, 1984, 78; Ehrenhalt, "Those Militant GOP Freshmen"; Report on the Project Majority Task Force and the Budget of Hope Project, September 24, 1979, 5, Box 287, Folder: Strategy Papers (4–6-80), NLG.

32. Dennis Farney, "John Rhodes Takes His Leave of the House," *Wall Street Journal*, December 23, 1982, 8; Rhodes and Smith, *I Was There*, 234; Smith, "From the Well of the House," 57, 61. Like-minded freshmen in the 96th Congress included class president Ed Bethune (R-AR), Richard Cheney (R-WY), James Courter (R-NJ), Ken Kramer (R-CO), Dan Lungren (R-CA), Gerald Solomon (R-NY), and Bill Thomas (R-CA). See, e.g., Pitney, "The Conservative Opportunity Society," 3–4; Steven V. Roberts, "House G.O.P. Freshmen Are Speaking Up on Party Issues," *New York Times*, October 29, 1979, A16; David W. Rohde, *Parties and Leaders in the Postreform House* (Chicago: University of Chicago Press, 1991), 122; minutes, Republican Freshmen Class Meeting, February 12, 1980, draft minutes, Meeting of the Republican Freshmen Class, March 6, 1979, and memo to Freshmen Class Members from Ken Kramer Re: FY 1981 Budget, April 2, 1980, Box 139, Folder:

Republican Freshman Class, NLG; letter from Bethune to Robert Michel, April 6, 1981, Box 458, Folder 22, NLG. Freshman class president Ed Bethune was a particular irritant to Rhodes, especially when Bethune declared that the freshmen represented "Day One of the new Republican Party." Gregorsky, *Elephants in the Room*, 33. The class may have been among the first to benefit from funding and training by outside conservative interest groups, such as the Committee for the Survival of a Free Congress, possibly steering them in a more confrontational direction. Ehrenhalt, "Those Militant GOP Freshmen."

33. See, e.g., Art Pine, "Remarks from Hill Show Budget Plan Not Out of the Woods," *Washington Post*, March 22, 1980, A5.

34. Arieff, "House Freshmen Republicans Seek Role as Power Brokers," 1341; Scott R. Meinke, *Leadership Organizations in the House of Representatives: Party Participation and Partisan Politics* (Ann Arbor: University of Michigan Press, 2016), 123; see also John A. Lawrence, *The Class of '74: Congress after Watergate and the Roots of Partisanship* (Baltimore: Johns Hopkins University Press, 2018), 186–187. Another senior Republican, Bill Frenzel of Minnesota, served as a "full-time coach" to Gingrich in 1980 on fiscal and budgetary policy and strategy. Memo from Frank to David, February 8, 1980, Box 294, Folder: Budget Information, NLG.

35. Brownstein, *The Second Civil War*, 140; Connie Bruck, "The Politics of Perception," *New Yorker*, October 9, 1995, 55; Clift and Brazaitis, *War without Bloodshed*, 226; Lee Edwards, *The Conservative Revolution: The Movement That Remade America* (New York: Free Press, 1999), 277; Rowland Evans and Robert Novak, "Fiasco in Room EF100," *Washington Post*, September 3, 1980, A19. Between 1979 and 1982, six columns by Evans and Novak mentioned Gingrich, four of them positively and none of them negatively; between 1983 and 1986, the number of mentions grew to twenty-four, six of them positive in tone and the others neutral. An Evans staffer named John Fund would later serve as editor for the Conservative Opportunity Society newsletter. Weekly Highlights, 9/22/83–9/26/83, Box 462, Folder: 63, NLG.

36. Clift and Brazaitis, *War without Bloodshed*, 225–226.

37. The class included several moderate-minded lawmakers, including Bill Clinger (R-PA), Doug Bereuter (R-NE), Jerry Lewis (R-CA), and Olympia Snowe (R-ME).

38. Clift and Brazaitis, *War without Bloodshed*, 221–222; Matthew N. Green and Douglas B. Harris, *Choosing the Leader: Leadership Elections in the U.S. House of Representatives* (New Haven: Yale University Press, 2019), 178–187.

39. Frances E. Lee, *Insecure Majorities: Congress and the Perpetual Campaign* (Chicago: University of Chicago Press, 2016), 34–35, 38–39, 84, 91.

40. Alan Ehrenhalt, "Conservatives in House Begin Effort to Develop Majority Coalition," *Washington Star*, November 13, 1979, A5; John A. Farrell, *Tip O'Neill and the Democratic Century* (Boston: Little, Brown, 2001), 631; Charles O. Jones, "Joseph G. Cannon and Howard W. Smith: An Essay on the Limits of Leadership in the House of Representatives," *Journal of Politics* 30, no. 3 (1968): 617–646; "The Dirty

Thirty" memo and list of committees, Chairmen Democrats, and Chairmen in Conservative Coalition, Box 288, Folder: Dump O'Neill Project, NLG; interview with former Republican leader, July 22, 2020. The plan had been germinating since at least November 1979, when Gingrich and Weyrich sponsored a meeting of Republicans to discuss the possibility of a conservative coalition controlling the House after 1980. Two months later, Dan Crane (R-IL) privately reported that several Democrats unhappy with O'Neill wondered if Republicans might vote for another Democrat to be Speaker. Memo from Gingrich to Republican Freshman Class Members, January 31, 1980, 2, Box 139, Folder: Republican Freshman Class, NLG. Gingrich saw it as a win-win effort, because if O'Neill were still elected, it would "destroy [the] perception that [the] House is really with us [i.e., controlled by Republicans] and set up anti-Reagan Democrats for defeat in 1982." Draft Outline for Newt's Presentation, December 1, 1980, Box 288, Folder: Dump O'Neill Project, NLG.

41. Lee, *Insecure Majorities*, 102. Vote choice in leadership elections, it should be noted, is often dictated by considerations other than a candidate's leadership style. For example, several of the more conservative or confrontation-oriented members of the House, including John Ashbrook, Richard Cheney, and John Rousselot supported Michel. Green and Harris, *Choosing the Leader*, 85–98.

42. Interview with former leadership aide, October 17, 2019.

43. Clift and Brazaitis, *War without Bloodshed*, 227; Lee, *Insecure Majorities*, 35–36. Interestingly, in a letter Gingrich wrote to his Republican colleagues urging them to join his effort to depose O'Neill, he acknowledged that historical patterns indicated Republicans would lose seats in 1982. Dear Republican Colleague letter, December 3, 1980, Box 288, Folder: Dump O'Neill Project, NLG.

44. Julian E. Zelizer, *On Capitol Hill: The Struggle to Reform Congress and Its Consequences, 1948–2000* (New York: Cambridge University Press, 2004), 213.

45. Steely, *The Gentleman from Georgia*, 139; letter to Newt Gingrich from Michel and Lott, March 25, 1981, Leadership, Box 4, Folder: 97th. Republican Task Forces, RHM.

46. Frank Gregorsky, "The Basics of Newt Gingrich," April–September 1983, 17, Box 230, Folder: The Basics of Newt Gingrich/Frank Gregorsky, NLG; see also "A Republican Agenda for a Conservative Opportunity Society," Box 459, Folder 33, NLG. Gingrich may have been inspired by Paul Weyrich, who suggested at a retreat that Republicans run on an alternative conservative agenda; see note 52.

47. Matthew N. Green and Douglas B. Harris, "Michel as Minority Leader," from *Robert H. Michel: Leading the Republican House Minority*, ed. Frank H. Mackaman and Sean Q Kelly (Lawrence: University Press of Kansas, 2019), 100–101; memo to Tidewater Conference from Newt Gingrich Re: A Republican Strategy for the 1983–85 Budgets, March 12, 1982, 2, Box 456, Folder 12, NLG.

48. Dennis Farney, "Republicans Reflect on What They've Wrought," *Wall Street Journal*, August 6, 1981, 22. Gingrich had also advertised the 1980 Governing Team Day as a way to create a quasi-parliamentary, Republican-led government.

Pitney, "The Conservative Opportunity Society," 8. Two years before, Gingrich had observed in an interview that "one of my goals is to make the House the co-equal of the White House." "GOP Freshmen: Aiming at a Majority," *Congressional Quarterly Weekly Report*, July 7, 1979, 1340.

49. Steely, *The Gentleman from Georgia*, 128.

50. Letter from Newt Gingrich to James Baker, February 25, 1982, Box 34, Folder 7, WAR. Reflecting Gingrich's view of the ideal use of television, the letter also offered some unsolicited advice, such as limiting the number of one's messages to three, which could in turn be used by congressional candidates. In the same letter, for which he later apologized, Gingrich portrayed himself as the spokesperson for Republican freshmen, complaining that Baker's meeting with them was received very poorly. "Reagan Aide Gets an Apology," *New York Times*, March 7, 1982, 25.

51. Dear Fellow Republican letter, March 18, 1982, 2 & 12–13, Box 456, Folder 12, NLG.

52. Steely, *The Gentleman from Georgia*, 141–142; Newt and Marianne Gingrich, "Key Steps in Developing a Survivable United States," Box 34, File 7, WAR. In typical Gingrich-ese, the manual explained that winning elections was but one of four "zones" of importance; to win elections durably, the party also needed to influence "iron triangles," "paradigms," and "world views." The phrase "conservative opportunity society" may have been inspired by the Ripon Society, a moderate Republican group that Gingrich was affiliated with in his early political career; further refined during a retreat that was organized by Paul Weyrich; and poll-tested by GOP pollster Robert Teeter. Clift and Brazaitis, *War without Bloodshed*, 227; John J. Pitney Jr., "Understanding Newt Gingrich," prepared for delivery at the American Political Science Association annual meeting, San Francisco, 1996, 9; Sheryl Gay Stolberg, "For Gingrich in Power, Pragmatism, Not Purity," *New York Times*, December 20, 2011.

53. Markon, "Gingrich Archives Show."

54. Matthew S. Mendez, "Leading Gently on Taxes," in Mackaman and Kelly, *Robert H. Michel*, 144–148; Steely, *The Gentleman from Georgia*, 140; *Congressional Record*, Extensions of Remarks, May 6, 1981, 8753.

55. David S. Broder, "Conservative 'Yellow Jackets' Buzz Michel," *Washington Post*, May 28, 1982, A4.

56. Thomas B. Edsall, "Tax Bill Is Double-Edged Sword for Both of the Political Parties," *Washington Post*, August 22, 1982, A11; Dennis Farney, Leonard M. Apcar, and Rich Jaroslovsky, "Playing Hardball: How Reaganites Push Reluctant Republicans to Back Tax-Rise Bill," *Wall Street Journal*, August 18, 1982, 1; Newt Gingrich, "The Tax Bill Is a Turkey," *Washington Post*, August 8, 1982, C8; Howell Raines, "Leadership Image Risked," *New York Times*, August 17, 1982, A1; "Reagan Tax Plea Joined by O'Neill," *New York Times*, August 19, 1982, A1; Steven V. Roberts, "Tax Rise Opposition Increases," *New York Times*, August 6, 1982, D1. The partisan breakdown of the vote was 123–118 Democrats, 103–89 Republicans. More than half

of GOP freshmen and sophomores voted against the measure, and 55 percent of all Republicans who opposed it were serving in their first or second term. Afterward, Gingrich and the Reagan White House reportedly tried to repair the rift, though Gingrich had earned an enduring reputation as a "disgruntled conservative." Albert R. Hunt, "Reagan Is Planning Some Peace Offerings to GOP Dissenters, but on His Own Terms," *Wall Street Journal*, August 27, 1982, 3.

57. William F. Connelly Jr. and John J. Pitney Jr., *Congress' Permanent Minority?: Republicans in the U.S. House* (Lanham, MD: Rowman & Littlefield, 1994), 75–77; Rohde, *Parties and Leaders*, 152–153; Trent Lott, *Herding Cats: A Life in Politics* (New York: HarperCollins, 2005), 84–88.

58. Steven V. Roberts, "The G.O.P.: A Party In Search of Itself," *New York Times Magazine*, March 6, 1983, 80; Steven V. Roberts, "One Conservative Faults Two Parties," *New York Times*, August 11, 1983, A18.

59. Lee, *Insecure Majorities*, 94. Though the GOP Conference met more often after 1980, they may have done so to keep the party unified on key votes they could win or to coordinate legislative strategy with the Reagan White House, rather than to emphasize collective messaging. "Aid Bill Gives President Broader Authority," *CQ Almanac 1981*, 37th ed. (Washington, DC: Congressional Quarterly, 1982); Thomas B. Edsall, "Reagan Goes to the Hill on Tax Bill," *Washington Post*, July 25, 1981, A1; Richard Forgette, "Party Caucuses and Coordination: Assessing Caucus Activity and Party Effects," *Legislative Studies Quarterly* 29, no. 3 (2004): 407–430; Lee, *Insecure Majorities*, 91–92.

60. Dear Republican Colleague letter, undated, Leadership, Box 4, Folder "97th Dear Colleague 10/82"; and memo for Bob from Mike Re: The Gingrich Memorandum, May 5, 1982, Press Series, Box 1, Folder: Memoranda, 1981–88(1), RHM.

61. Connelly and Pitney, *Congress' Permanent Minority?*, 116; Lee, *Insecure Majorities*, 94.

62. Steven V. Roberts, "Democrats Regain Control in House," *New York Times*, November 4, 1982, A19; Reid Spearman, "A Dialogue on COS: Figuring Out What We're Doing," Part One (Vision), May 11, 1983, 1, Box 463, NLG.

63. Balz and Brownstein, *Storming the Gates*, 118; Ruth Bloch Rubin, *Building the Bloc: Intraparty Organization in the U.S. Congress* (New York: Cambridge University Press, 2017), 277–278; Steely, *The Gentleman from Georgia*, 164; interview with former GOP leader, July 22, 2020.

64. Eric Schickler, *Disjointed Pluralism: Institutional Innovation and the Development of the U.S. Congress* (Princeton: Princeton University Press, 2001), 243–244. All but one of its original members were in their third term or less, and the largest percentage (53 percent) were sophomores. COS's "up-front" leadership included Bob Walker, Vin Weber, Connie Mack, and Gingrich; other initial members were Judd Gregg (NH), Dan Lungren (CA), Duncan Hunter (CA), Dan Coats (IN), and Barbara Vucanovich (NV). A memo from the Gingrich Papers also lists Jerry Lewis (CA), Mark Siljander (MI), Bob McEwen (OH), Toby Roth (WI), Bobbi Fiedler (CA),

Larry Craig (ID), and Hank Brown (CO) as members, but excludes Gregg. Brownstein, *The Second Civil War*, 139–140; Jonathan Mark Morstein, "Gingrich's Challenge: The Power of Escalation to Force Change in Institutions" (PhD diss., University of Maryland, College Park, 1998), 294; Steely, *The Gentleman from Georgia*, 167; COS Group, Box 456, Folder 10A, NLG. Walker traces the origins of COS to Gingrich's Project Majority Task Force and the election of Reagan. Steely, *The Gentleman from Georgia*, 166.

65. Balz and Brownstein, *Storming the Gates*, 119; interview with former Republican member of Congress, May 8, 2019.

66. Peter Bachrach and Morton S. Baratz, "Two Faces of Power," *American Political Science Review* 56 (December 1962): 947–952; Clift and Brazaitis, *War without Bloodshed*, 230; E. E. Schattschneider, *The Semisovereign People: A Realist's View of Democracy* (New York: Holt, Rinehart and Winston, 1960); "Principles for Creating a Republican Majority in the House," 2–3, Box 456, Folder 11, NLG.

67. Lawrence Freedman, *Strategy: A History* (New York: Oxford University Press, 2013), 209; memo to Gingrich, Weber et al. from Bill Lee, February 17, 1984, 2, Box 457, Folder 15, NLG.

68. Newt Gingrich, "Conservative Opportunity Society Brings Old-Time Hope," *Atlanta Constitution*, April 25, 1983; Newt Gingrich memo, May 9, 1983, 3–4, Box 9A, Folder: COS-1983 (1), RW; memo from Janis to Gingrich and Weber, March 1, 1984, Box 456, Folder 10A, NLG. According to Gingrich aide Frank Gregorsky, Gingrich hoped to get members of his party in both chambers to adopt the COS's agenda in the fall of 1983. Frank Gregorsky, "The Basics of Newt Gingrich," April-September 1983, 15, Box 230, Folder: The Basics of Newt Gingrich/Frank Gregorsky, NLG.

69. Schickler, *Disjointed Pluralism*, 243; Reid Spearman, "A Dialogue on COS: Figuring Out What We're Doing," Part One (Vision), 5, May 11, 1983, Box 463, NLG.

70. Balz and Brownstein, *Storming the Gates*, 119, 120; interview with former Republican member of Congress, May 8, 2019; interview with former Republican leadership aide, April 11, 2019.

71. Markon, "Gingrich Archives Show."

72. Balz and Brownstein, *Storming the Gates*, 119–120; Brownstein, *The Second Civil War*, 141; Steven S. Smith, *Call to Order: Floor Politics in the House and Senate* (Washington, DC: Brookings Institution, 1989), 67; Reid Spearman, "A Dialogue on COS: Figuring Out What We're Doing," Part Two (Management), May 11, 1983, 4, Box 463, Folder 22, NLG; memo to COS members from Hank Brown Re: Budget Compliance, June 28, 1983, Box 458, Folder 22, NLG.

73. Diane Granat, "Televised Partisan Skirmishes Erupt in House," *Congressional Quarterly Weekly Report*, February 11, 1984, 246; T. R. Reid, "House Democrats Set to Huddle, Call TV Signals," *Washington Post*, May 9, 1984, A2.

74. "Democrats Make Changes in House Rules," *CQ Almanac 1983*, 39th ed. (Washington, DC: CQ Press, 1984); Granat, "Televised Partisan Skirmishes"; David Rogers, "Assault from the Right," *Wall Street Journal*, May 23, 1984, 62; Vin Weber,

"Tyranny of the Majority," from *A House of Ill Repute*, ed. Dan Renberg (Princeton: Princeton University Press, 1987). The majority party's shenanigans had been bothering the GOP even before the 98th Congress had convened. For instance, Democrats brought the Equal Rights Amendment to the House floor in November 1982 with little advance warning and without the opportunity for Republicans to amend it. Richard E. Cohen, "Frustrated House Republicans Seek More Aggressive Strategy for 1984 and Beyond," *National Journal*, March 3, 1984, 413, Box 460, Folder: 39, NLG; Weber, "Tyranny of the Majority," 62.

75. Green and Harris, "Michel as Minority Leader," 105–106; Zelizer, *On Capitol Hill*, 214.

76. Interview with former Republican leadership aide, April 11, 2019; interview with former Republican leadership aide, October 17, 2019; John M. Barry, *The Ambition and the Power* (New York: Viking, 1989), 164; Cohen, "Frustrated House Republicans," 416; Granat, "Televised Partisan Skirmishes"; Lott, *Herding Cats*, 93–94; Nicol C. Rae, *The Decline and Fall of the Liberal Republicans* (New York: Oxford University Press, 1989), 185; T. R. Reid, "'Minority Objector' Conscientiously Flays Foes with House Rules," *Washington Post*, March 21, 1984; Robert V. Remini, *The House: The History of the House of Representatives* (New York: Harper Perennial, 2007), 463; Steely, *The Gentleman from Georgia*, 167; memo to COS Wednesday Team, May 18, 1983, Box 9A, Folder: COS-1983 (1), RW; "COS Activities Overview," Box 459, Folder 30, NLG. Gingrich called Lott "our chief sponsor" and the "godfather" of COS. Newt Gingrich, *Lessons Learned the Hard Way: A Personal Report* (New York: HarperCollins, 1998), 170; Steely, *The Gentleman from Georgia*, 166.

77. Bruck, "The Politics of Perception," 58; Cohen, "Frustrated House Republicans," 413–414; Granat, "Televised Partisan Skirmishes"; Farrell, *Tip O'Neill*, 627; memo to COS members from Dan Coats Re: January 21, 1984 meeting, Box 9A, Folder: COS-1984(1), RW; memo to Bob from Mike Re: The Gingrich Memorandum, May 5, 1982, Press Series, Box 1, Folder: Memoranda, 1981–88(1), RHM; interview with Newt Gingrich, C-SPAN, August 21, 1984; interview with former Republican leadership aide, April 11, 2019.

78. Steven V. Roberts, "Congressman Asks Expulsion of Two," *New York Times*, July 19, 1983, A22; Roberts, "One Conservative Faults Two Parties"; Steely, *The Gentleman from Georgia*, 150; letter from Newt Gingrich to Robert Michel, June 8, 1983, Box 458, Folder 22, NLG; letter from Trent Lott to Newt Gingrich, August 31, 1983, Box 456, Folder 12, NLG.

79. Steely, *The Gentleman from Georgia*, 168; Dear Republican Colleague letter, June 8, 1983, Box 458, Folder 22, NLG.

80. Memo to Gingrich, Weber et al. from Bill Lee, February 17, 1984, 1–2, Box 457, Folder 15, NLG; see also Balz and Brownstein, *Storming the Gates*, 119.

81. Roberts, "One Conservative Faults Two Parties." Examples of careful scheduling of floor speeches can be found in Newt Gingrich's papers. See, e.g., "Special Order Schedule as of 5/16/84" and May and June 1984 calendars, Box 456, Folder

6, NLG. The group also met on some Saturdays to hear special guests invited by Gingrich, such as Alvin Toffler. Noah Weiss, "The Republican Revolution?: The Transformation and Maturation of the House Republican Party, 1980–1995" (Senior Honors Thesis, Department of History, University of Pennsylvania, April 2009), 22.

82. Pitney, "The Conservative Opportunity Society," 12–13; "House OKs, Senate Rejects Nuclear Freeze," *Congressional Quarterly 1983*, 205–213.

83. See, e.g., "A Vision of Our Time and Future Place," Box 9A, Folder: COS-1983 (2); draft memo from Judd Gregg Re: Outline of Organization, April 11, 1983; and minutes of COS Wednesday meetings, April 13, 27, May 4 and 11, 1983, Box 9A, Folder: COS-1983(1), RW.

84. See, e.g., letter from Joe Fisher to Janis Kerrigan, May 13, 1983, Box 459, Folder 34, NLG.

85. Cohen, "Frustrated House Republicans"; interview with former Republican member of Congress, May 8, 2019. A group of fifty-five lawmakers had agreed to attend one or more days of the three-day conference. "Agenda for the Baltimore Conference"; Dear Republican Colleague letter, August 3, 1983; Memo to Leslie Russell from Norm Lent, Box 462, Folder 65, NLG.

86. Diane Granat, "Junior House Republicans Seeking 'Zzazip,'" *Congressional Quarterly Weekly Report*, November 5, 1983, 2343.

87. Memo to Gingrich from Eddie Mahe Jr. Re: Finishing of Thursday's Meeting, October 21, 1983, Box 465, Folder: unlabeled, NLG.

88. Balz and Brownstein, *Storming the Gates*, 120; "Successful 1984 Strategy" memo, COS Planning Meeting, November 18, 1983, Box 459, Folder 30, NLG.

89. See, e.g., Green, *Underdog Politics*, 84–85; memo from Ed Bethune to members of freshmen class, August 1, 1979, Box 139, Folder: Republican Freshman Class, NLG; Dear Republican Colleague letter, May 3, 1980, Box 140, Folder: Budget, NLG; and Dear Republican Colleague letter, September 28, 1983, Leadership, Box 6, Folder: 98th, Dear C. 9.28.83, RHM.

90. Granat, "Televised Partisan Skirmishes"; "Successful Start of Session," Box 459, Folder 30, NLG; "Activities for Implementing our Charter" and "Proposed Floor Action Plan (First Week)," Box 464, Folder 75, NLG; interview with former Republican congressman, May 8, 2019.

91. "House Floor Strategy for Republicans," 3, Box 459, Folder 30, NLG.

92. Memo to Gingrich and Weber from Mahe, "Initial Thoughts on Integrated Legislative/Campaign Plan for 1984," 2, 5, and 6, and memos to COS Group from Janis Kerrigan-Roberts, December 9 and 20, 1983, Box 459, Folder 30, NLG.

93. Proposal for Restructuring COS, 3, 5, Box 9A, Folder: COS-1984 (1), RW.

94. The first two issues were among several suggested by Eddie Mahe Jr. in his memo from 1983. They also had the advantage of wide popularity: one survey from April 1984 found that 67 percent of respondents favored a constitutional amendment to allow school prayer, while another from June 1983 reported 71 percent

supporting a balanced budget constitutional amendment. Harris poll, April 4–8, 1984 (USHARRIS.051484.R1) and Gallup poll, June 10–13, 1983 (USGALLUP.071083.R2).

95. *Congressional Record,* January 23, 1984, 83–95, quote p. 91.

96. *Congressional Record,* January 24, 1984, 248–249; Granat, "Televised Partisan Skirmishes"; Barbara Sinclair, *Party Wars: Polarization and the Politics of National Policy Making* (Norman: University of Oklahoma Press, 2006), 114. The NRCC press releases were not coincidental. Notes from one meeting (likely of the COS) recorded that Gregg would "coordinate floor action w/NRCC" and "sell leadership" on their tactics. Handwritten notes, 3, Box 459, folder 30, NLG.

97. See, e.g., 1984 *Congressional Record,* January 31, 1062; February 1, 1188; February 2, 1411; February 6, 1892–93; March 1, 3995; March 6, 4616–17; "Unanimous Consent Requests—Check List," March 8, 1984, Box 464, Folder: Floor, NLG.

98. Gingrich and his allies also tried to force committees to report conservative legislation directly to the floor via the House's little-used Calendar Wednesday, without much success. Granat, "Televised Partisan Skirmishes."

99. See, e.g., Dear Colleague letter from Duncan Hunter, March 1, 1984, Box 464, Folder 75, NLG; COS Agenda, May 9, 1984, Box 456, Folder 6; undated meeting notes, 4 ("Action Items"), Box 456, Folder 6, NLG; memo to Vin Weber, Newt Gingrich, and Connie Mack from Janis, April 11, 1984, Box 466, Folder: unlabeled, NLG; memo to COS from Barbara Vucanovich Re: Crime Town Meeting Project, April 3, 1984, Box 466, Folder: unlabeled, NLG; and "COS Meeting, Back Home Articulation Proposal" by Barbara Vucanovich, January 21, 1984, Box 9A, Folder: COS-1984 (1), RW.

100. "Key Premise," 1, Box 457, Folder 15, NLG.

101. Clift and Brazaitis, *War without Bloodshed,* 229; "Conservatives Attack Letter by Democrats," *Washington Post,* April 25, 1984, A6; letter to Commandante Daniel Ortega, March 20, 1984, Box 460, Folder 44, NLG. COS members read portions of a lengthy paper by Republican Study Committee staffer and former Gingrich aide Frank Gregorsky, which blamed several Democrats for being excessively sympathetic to communist regimes and which had originally been written in response to Democratic lawmakers voting to curtail Contra funding in 1983. Rogers, "Assault from the Right"; Frank Gregorsky, "What's the Matter with Democratic Foreign Policy," May 7, 1984, Box: Staff Series, Billy Pitts Files, Private Bills 94–1, Folder: Staff. Pitts. Republican Study Committee 1984, RM. Gingrich, Walker, and Weber had written a letter to Democrats warning them that they would be named on the floor, but it was sent with less than twenty-four hours' notice, and some lawmakers complained they never received it. Dear Colleague letter, May 8, 1984, Box 460, Folder 44, NLG.

102. *Congressional Record,* May 10, 1984, 11894; Reid, "House Democrats Set to Huddle"; T. R. Reid, "O'Neill Pans Republicans," *Washington Post,* May 12, 1984, A1. The day may have been chosen deliberately, when the NRCC was having its annual

dinner, so not many Republicans would be in the House to take notice. Interview with former Republican member of Congress, May 8, 2019.

103. Reid, "O'Neill Pans Republicans"; Steely, *The Gentleman from Georgia*, 171; letter from Bob Michel to Tip O'Neill, May 11, 1984, 2, Box 458, Folder 26, NLG; *Congressional Record*, May 14, 1984, 12042–43. O'Neill was especially upset that one of his close friends, Eddie Boland (D-MA), was among those named during the COS special order. Gingrich later claimed that he expected Boland to respond on the floor, not O'Neill, though he should not have been surprised: O'Neill had gotten in trouble at least twice before for verbally attacking other lawmakers. Mark Green, *Who Runs Congress?*, 3rd ed. (New York: Viking, 1979), 211; Remini, *The House*, 464.

104. Farrell, *Tip O'Neill*, 632–636; see also chapter 1. The debate that day remained heated, and O'Neill lost his patience on several occasions, helping give the COS more attention and signaling that their tactics had struck a nerve.

105. Barry, *The Ambition and the Power*, 166; Brownstein, *Storming the Gates*, 142; Farrell, *Tip O'Neill*, 635; Howard Fineman, "For the Son of C-Span, Exposure = Power," *Newsweek*, April 3, 1989, 22.

106. Barry, *The Ambition and the Power*, 158; Rowland Evans and Robert Novak, "Rep. Gingrich Isn't Guilty," *Washington Post*, May 23, 1984, A21. Michel nonetheless expressed unhappiness at a Conference meeting with O'Neill's behavior. "Republicans Assail O'Neill," *New York Times*, May 18, 1984, A15.

107. Barry, *The Ambition and the Power*, 166; Farrell, *Tip O'Neill*, 2001, 635; Morstein, "Gingrich's Challenge." By September 1984, Lott was advocating a more aggressive and less deferential approach to Democrats in the House. Rogers, "House's Frustrated Minority," *Wall Street Journal*, September 5, 1984, 60.

108. Smith, *Call to Order*, 66–67; "Mack Projects for Week of May 21," Box 456, Folder 6, NLG; memo to COS from Daniel E. Lungren, May 29, 1984, Box 692, Folder: May Files, NLG.

109. See, e.g., "Honor Roll Signatures as of June 29, 1984," Box 461, Folder 48B, NLG; sign-up sheets for special orders in May, Box 466, Folder: Special Orders, 1 Min., NLG; Dear Republican Colleague letter from Connie Mack, May 21, 1984, Box 456, Folder 6, NLG; "Mack Projects for Week of May 21," Box 464, Folder: Floor, NLG; "Candidate School" agenda, Box 692, Folder: May Files, NLG; memo to Vin Weber from Don Eberly, June 4, 1984, Box 456, Folder 6, NLG; letter to Newt Gingrich from Vin Weber, June 6, 1984; memo to COS members from Vin Weber, July 31, 1984, and memo to PW, CRCM from JE, October 17, 1984, Box 456, Folder 10A, NLG.

110. Farrell, *Tip O'Neill*, 636; "Selected Grenadian Material Released by State, Defense," *Washington Post*, October 5, 1984, A30.

111. David S. Broder and Lou Cannon, "Both Wings of GOP Hope to Spice Up a Bland Party Platform," *Washington Post*, July 25, 1984, A3; Greg McDonald, "Newt Gingrich Is Current Superman of GOP Convention," *Atlanta Constitution*, August 22, 1984; Bill Peterson, "Conservatives Control GOP '84 Platform," *Washington Post*,

August 17, 1984, A1; Steven V. Roberts, "Platform Is Seen as Map of Future," *New York Times*, August 19, 1984, 33; Steely, *The Gentleman from Georgia*, 176; "Weekly Highlights 2/16/84," Box 462, Folder 63, NLG; memo from Eddie Mahe Jr. to Newt Gingrich and Vin Weber, November 30, 1983, Box 1078, Folder: Correspondence—Eddie Mahe Jr., NLG.

112. Balz and Brownstein, *Storming the Gates*, 128–129; Steven V. Roberts, "Tax Plank Battle on G.O.P. Platform Appears Settled," *New York Times*, August 15, 1984, A1; letter from Vin Weber, Newt Gingrich, and Bob Walker to Trent Lott, July 24, 1984, Box 458, Folder 24, NLG; interview with former Republican leader, July 22, 2020. The original sentence had read, "we therefore oppose any attempt to increase taxes which would harm the recovery and reverse the trend toward restoring control of the economy to individual Americans." Republican Party Platform, August 20, 1984, 4, Box 39, Box 39, Folder: Campaign and Politics. Republican National Convention. 1984. Platform (1), RHM. The COS later took credit for this revision, but several other Republicans, most notably Kemp and Lott, had also called for a firmer pledge against tax increases, and conservative Senator Jesse Helms (R-NC) played a central role in crafting the language of the platform. Broder and Cannon, "Both Wings of GOP"; Peterson, "Conservatives Control GOP '84 Platform"; "Conservative Opportunity Society with Republicans at Federal Hall," March 1987, 2, Box 8, Folder: RHM General, RHM.

113. See, e.g., Barone, "Who Is This Newt Gingrich?"; David Karol, *Party Position Change in American Politics: Coalition Management* (New York: Cambridge University Press, 2009), 167–175; McDonald, "Newt Gingrich Is the Current Superman"; Peterson, "Conservatives Control GOP '84 Platform"; memo to Gingrich and Weber from Ladonna Lee and Eddie Mahe Jr., July 30, 1984; COS Agenda, August 8, 1984, and Dear Republican Colleague letter from Gingrich, August 10, 1984, Box 458, Folder 24, NLG; interview with former Republican leader, July 22, 2020. The White House resisted a COS idea to sponsor a COS-centered televised event at the convention. Memo to Newt Gingrich and Vin Weber from Eddie Mahe, April 3, 1984; handwritten note from Weber to Gingrich; letter from James Baker and Michael Deaver to Weber and Gingrich, April 18, 1984, Box 458, Folder 24, NLG. Gingrich may have been inspired by former Rep. Bob Wilson (R-CA), who tried to make the lengthy Democratic control of Congress a theme of the 1976 Republican convention. Letter from Bill Frenzel to Gingrich, February 21, 1980, Box 140, Folder: Miscellaneous, NLG.

114. Two aspiring first-time Republican candidates who came to COS events at the convention, and later became key members of the GOP leadership under Gingrich, were Texans Dick Armey and Tom DeLay. Interview with former Republican member of Congress, May 8, 2019.

115. Memo to Gingrich and Weber from Ladonna Y. Lee and Eddie Mahe Jr., July 30, 1984, Box 458, Folder 24, NLG; undated memo from Janis to Newt Re: Dallas, 2–3, Box 458, Folder 24, NLG.

116. Robert W. Merry, "Caution or Boldness?: Reagan's Campaign Quandary," *Wall Street Journal*, August 27, 1984, 34; Steven V. Roberts, "Draft by G.O.P. Leaves Opening for a Tax Hike," *New York Times*, August 14, 1984, A1; Steely, *The Gentleman from Georgia*, 178.

117. Barone, "Who Is This Newt Gingrich?"; Cohen, "Frustrated House Republicans," 414; Dennis Farney, "Policy Debate within GOP to Heat Up Whether or Not Reagan Seeks Reelection," *Wall Street Journal*, January 27, 1984, 58; Newt Gingrich, "'A Grand Compromise Would Smother a Peaceful Revolution,'" *Washington Post*, November 11, 1984, D8; Richard Reeves, "The Republicans," *New York Times Magazine*, September 9, 1984, 56; Thomas F. Schaller, *The Stronghold: How Republicans Captured Congress but Surrendered the White House* (New Haven: Yale University Press, 2015), 45.

118. Daniel Stid, "Transformational Leadership in Congress?," prepared for delivery at the American Political Science Association annual meeting, San Francisco (1996), 3; "Invitations Pending," Box 464, Folder 80, NLG; memo to Joe Gaylord from Bob McAdam, September 1, 1983, Box 466, Folder: Communication, NLG; note from Scott McMurray to Newt Gingrich, Box 456, Folder 10B, NLG.

119. See "Principles for Creating a Republican Majority in the House," Box 456, Folder 11, NLG; "On Protecting Republican Congressional Incumbents," June 14, 1983, Box 456, Folder 12, NLG.

120. Sandra Evans Teeley, "House Censures Crane and Studds," *Washington Post*, July 21, 1983, A1. Interestingly, passage of the crime bill was the result of cooperation between Michel, who had instigated the maneuver, and COS member Dan Lungren, who had put it into play with a procedural motion and who had later suggested that the COS's year-long campaign to try bringing conservative proposals to the House floor made some Democrats eager to defect on the motion to recommit. Smith, "From the Well of the House," 98n68; Mary Thornton, "Waggling on Crime Bill, Democrats Load GOP Campaign Cannon," *Washington Post*, October 1, 1984, A3.

121. Cohen, "Frustrated House Republicans"; "Principles for Creating a Republican Majority in the House," 1, Box 456, Folder 11, NLG.

122. Suzanne Garment, "What to Watch for When the Votes Start Marching In," *Wall Street Journal*, November 2, 1984, 28; Gary C. Jacobson, "It's Nothing Personal: The Decline of the Incumbency Advantage in US House Elections," *Journal of Politics* 77, no. 3 (2015): 863; Hedrick Smith, *The Power Game: How Washington Works* (New York: Random House, 1988), 663.

123. James A. Stimson, *Public Opinion in America: Moods, Cycles, and Swings.* (Boulder, CO: Westview, 1991); James A. Stimson, Michael B. Mackuen, and Robert S. Erikson, "Dynamic Representation," *American Political Science Review* 89, no. 3 (1995): 543–565.

124. Rae, *The Decline and Fall of the Liberal Republicans*, 185.

125. Jacobson, "It's Nothing Personal," figs. 4 and 5, 864–865; Lee, *Insecure*

Majorities, 24, fig. 2.3; Hedrick Smith, "Republicans See Opportunity," *New York Times*, February 4, 1985, A1; Smith, *The Power Game*, 664.

126. "Congress and the Public," Gallup, https://news.gallup.com/poll/1600/congress-public.aspx.

127. "House Party Committees, 98th Congress," *CQ Almanac 1983*, 39th ed. (Washington, DC: Congressional Quarterly, 1984).

128. Memo to Vin Weber from Newt Gingrich Re: "For Discussion, 1984 Election: What is Left to be Done?," Box 456, Folder 10A, NLG.

129. Interview with former Republican member of Congress, May 8, 2019. See also Diane Granat, "Splits in Style, Substance: Deep Divisions Loom Behind House GOP's Apparent Unity," *Congressional Quarterly Weekly Report*, March 23, 1985, 535.

Chapter 3. Ascendant Party Warrior (1985–1989)

1. Eleanor Clift and Tom Brazaitis, *War without Bloodshed: The Art of Politics* (New York: Scribner, 1996), 231, 235; David Osborne, "Newt Gingrich: Shining Knight of the Post-Reagan Right," *Mother Jones* (November 1984), from Pat Schroeder material, Subgroup: Speechwriting, Series: Michael Waldman, Folder: GOP [Clippings] [1], WJC; Lois Romano, "Newt Gingrich, Maverick on the Hill," *Washington Post*, January 3, 1985, B1.

2. Romano, "Newt Gingrich," B3; "Key Strategic Objectives of COS," March 27, 1985, Box 9B, Folder: COS 1985, RW.

3. Gingrich asked to step down as RSC treasurer in late 1985. Letter to Thomas J. Bliley from Newt Gingrich, November 21, 1985, Box 1071, Folder: Congressional Politics—Rep. Study Committee Stuff 1986, NLG.

4. Romano, "Newt Gingrich," B3.

5. Dear Republican Colleague from Newt Gingrich, December 4, 1984, Box 456, Folder 10B, NLG; "Framing the 1986 Election and Explaining the 1984 Election," memo to COS members from Newt Gingrich, November 5, 1984, Box Staff Series, Billy Pitts Files, Private Bills 94–1, Folder: Republican Committee on Committees, 1974–85 (2), RHM.

6. James F. Clarity and Warren Weaver Jr., "Washington Talk Briefing," *New York Times*, February 2, 1985, 5; Nicholas Lemann, "Conservative Opportunity Society," *Atlantic* (May 1985), 33–34, Box 9B, Folder: COS 1985, RW.

7. Daniel J. Balz, "Frustrations Embitter House GOP," *Washington Post*, April 29, 1985, A4; Connie Bruck, "The Politics of Perception," *New Yorker*, October 9, 1995, 56; Romano, "Newt Gingrich." One news report argued that Gingrich's hubris grew after his 1982 reelection. Dale Russakoff and Dan Balz, "Mr. Speaker: The Rise of Newt Gingrich," *Washington Post*, December 19, 1994, A19.

8. Interview with former Republican House member, July 30, 2020.

9. Mickey Edwards, "A Revolution? Now? Against What?," *Washington Post*, December 2, 1984, D8; C. Lawrence Evans and Walter J. Oleszek, *Congress under*

Fire: Reform Politics and the Republican Majority (Boston: Houghton Mifflin, 1997), 30; Diane Granat, "Splits in Style, Substance: Deep Divisions Loom behind House GOP's Apparent Unity," *Congressional Quarterly Weekly Report,* March 23, 1985, 535. See also Daniel J. Balz, "GOP Official Critical of '84 Strategy," *Washington Post,* November 16, 1984, A16; and David W. Rohde, *Parties and Leaders in the Postreform House* (Chicago: University of Chicago Press, 1991), 130.

10. Letter to Robert Michel, June 29, 1984, Box Campaigns and Politics 39, Folder: C & P. Republican National Convention. 1984(1), RHM.

11. Rowland Evans and Robert Novak, "The Michel/Gingrich Split," *Washington Post,* March 11, 1985, A15. Multiple COS members claimed they were denied beneficial committee assignments as punishment for being in the group, but a comparison of committee assignments from the 98th to the 99th Congresses shows that, of sixteen identified COS members, seven saw no change in committee assignment, and another eight were given an additional assignment, promoted to a more prestigious committee, or both. Only one, Larry Craig of Idaho, lost an assignment, to the relatively minor Select Committee on Aging. Clift and Brazaitis, *War without Bloodshed,* 231.

12. David S. Broder, "The Other Republicans," *Washington Post,* April 7, 1985, F7; Granat, "Splits in Style, Substance"; Robert G. Kaiser, "How Bad Will '85 Be?," *Washington Post,* December 9, 1984, C1; memo to COS members from Mark Siljander, March 27, 1985, Box 9B, Folder: COS 1985, RW.

13. Romano, "Newt Gingrich," B1; Edward Walsh, "GOP House 'Guerillas' Soften Their Tactics," *Washington Post,* September 30, 1985, A10. Gingrich's media appearances did decline in 1985; see chapter 7.

14. Walsh, "GOP House 'Guerillas'"; memo to Richard Norman, Bruce Eberle and Associates from Bob Weed, October 28, 1984, Box 464, Folder: 78, NLG; "Proposal for Restructuring COS," Box 9A, Folder: COS-1984(1), RW; Conservative Opportunity Society Political Action Committee certification of incorporation, Commonwealth of Virginia, November 23, 1984, Box 9B, Folder: COS PAC 1985, RW. The COS, under the leadership of Duncan Hunter, may have lost some focus and assertiveness during this period. Zachary C. Smith, "From the Well of the House: Remaking the House Republican Party, 1978–1994" (PhD diss., Boston University, 2012), 181–182.

15. Clift and Brazaitis, *War without Bloodshed,* 236; Steve Gunderson and Rob Morris (with Bruce Bawer), *House and Home* (New York: Dutton, 1996), 97. Interestingly, Gunderson was one of the Republicans who had signed the letter warning Michel against supporting COS-sponsored activities at the Democrats' 1984 convention.

16. Dewar, "Republicans Wage Civil War"; "'Grambo Commandos' Organize," *Congressional Quarterly Weekly Report,* January 18, 1986, 107; Janet Hook, "House GOP: Plight of a Permanent Minority," *Congressional Quarterly Weekly Report,* June 21, 1986, 1393; "COS Weekly Members," Box 9B, Folder: COS 1985 and Box 9B,

Folder: RSW—Chair of COS 1987–88(1), RW. Two GOP leaders, Republican Policy Chair Dick Cheney and Minority Whip Trent Lott, are listed as COS members, but Lott claimed he was more an observer of the group than an active participant. Trent Lott, *Herding Cats: A Life in Politics* (New York: HarperCollins, 2005), 93–94. The retirements of more accommodationist-minded Republicans like Barber Conable (R-NY), who left in 1984, may have also weakened the ranks of those who opposed Gingrich. David Rogers, "House's Frustrated Minority," *Wall Street Journal*, September 5, 1984, 60.

17. Letter to Mickey Edwards from Paul Weyrich, November 21, 1984, Box 459, Folder 29, NLG.

18. Stanley Bach and Steven S. Smith, *Managing Uncertainty in the House of Representatives: Adaption and Innovation in Special Rules* (Washington, DC: Brookings Institution Press, 1988); Alan Ehrenhalt, "Media, Power Shifts Dominate O'Neill's House," *Congressional Quarterly Weekly Report*, September 13, 1986, 2131; Ryan Grim, "Haunted by the Reagan Era," *Washington Post*, July 5, 2019; Hook, "House GOP"; Rogers, "House's Frustrated Minority"; Rohde, *Parties and Leaders*, 99–104; Donald R. Wolfensberger, "Open vs. Restrictive Rules in the House, 94th–113rd Congresses," Bipartisan Policy Center, https://bipartisanpolicy.org/wp-content/uploads/2019/03/houserules.pdf.

19. "The Camera in the House," *Washington Post*, November 26, 1984, A14; Steven V. Roberts, "Democrats Give Up on Limiting G.O.P. on House Speeches for TV," *New York Times*, December 6, 1984, B18. Republicans had also lost hope of having greater influence after Speaker O'Neill successfully quashed multiple efforts within his party in the early 1980s to replace him with a conservative Democrat or even a Republican. John A. Farrell, *Tip O'Neill and the Democratic Century* (Boston: Little, Brown, 2001), 650–652. In addition, Republicans complained that they were given an unfair percentage of committee seats in the 99th Congress (1985–86). One journalist claimed this had happened in 1983 as well, but the gap between the proportion of committee seats and House seats for Republicans actually declined between the 97th Congress (1981–82) and 98th Congress (1983–1984), though it did grow substantially in 1981. Jonathan Fuerbringer, "A House Divided by Political Rancor," *New York Times*, March 16, 1988, A22; Rogers, "House's Frustrated Minority."

20. "House Battles Over Contested Indiana Seat," *CQ Almanac 1985*, 41st ed. (Washington, DC: Congressional Quarterly, 1986); Nicholas Lemann, "Conservative Opportunity Society," 32; "Parties Bicker On House Seat," *Washington Post*, January 30, 1985, A6; memo to PW, CRCM from JE, October 17, 1984, Box 456, Folder 10A, NLG.

21. Mel Steely, *The Gentleman from Georgia: The Biography of Newt Gingrich* (Macon, GA: Mercer University Press, 2000), 181; Evans and Novak, "The Michel/Gingrich Split"; *Congressional Record*, April 2, 1985, H1725-H1735; memo to Larry Coughlin, February 26, 1985, memo to Jack Hiler and Ed Goas, March 25, 1985,

and letters to Dan Lungren and Robert Michel from Newt Gingrich, April 3, 1985, Box 472, Folder: Memos, Etc., NLG; McIntyre Meeting notes, February 19, 1985, two undated memos, and "McIntyre Project," Box 464, Folder: 84, NLG; memo to Bob Walker from Newt Gingrich, "Proposed Freshmen Class Projects," February 21, 1985, Box 9B McIntyre, Folder: McIntyre IN#8, RW.

22. Fred Barnes, "Raging Representatives," *New Republic,* June 3, 1985, 8.

23. Daniel J. Balz and Margaret Shapiro, "House in Disarray over Indiana Seat," *Washington Post,* April 26, 1985, A1; William F. Connelly Jr. and John J. Pitney Jr., *Congress' Permanent Minority?: Republicans in the U.S. House* (Lanham, MD: Rowman & Littlefield, 1994), 79–81; "House Battles over Contested Indiana Seat"; Andy Plattner, "Partisan Ill-Will Remains High," *Congressional Quarterly Weekly Report,* May 4, 1985, 821; "Leadership Recommendations for House Republican Conference" and Dear Republican Colleague letter, April 29, 1985, Box 471, Folder: Republican Leadership, NLG.

24. Peter Bragdon, "House Again Refuses to Seat McIntyre," *Congressional Quarterly Weekly Report,* February 9, 1985, 282; "House Battles over Contested Indiana Seat"; Smith, "From the Well of the House," 176; "McIntyre Media Strategy" and "Proposed Freshmen Class Projects," Box Staff. Pitts (7), Folder: McIntyre (3), RHM; Dear Republican Colleague letter from Bob Michel, April 29, 1985, Box Leadership (9), Folder: 99th. Joint Letters 4/29/85, RHM.

25. Steely, *The Gentleman from Georgia,* 182–183; "The McIntyre Opportunity," March 1985, Box Staff. Pitts (7), Folder: McIntyre (3), RHM. For instance, Martin at one point urged Michel to host a special-order period in which Republicans would apologize to the residents of the 8th District for Democrats' behavior, a Gingrich-like idea that she admitted "wasn't mine." Letter from Lynn Martin to Robert Michel, February 7, 1985, Box Staff. Pitts (8), Folder: Correspondence (1), RHM.

26. Granat, "Splits in Style, Substance"; memo from Bill Frenzel, April 19, 1985, Box 471, Folder: Republican Leadership, NLG. Frenzel was deeply involved in the election battle from the beginning. See, e.g., memo from Bill Frenzel, January 4, 1985, Box Staff. Pitts (8), Folder: McIntyre Correspondence (1), RHM. Another lawmaker, freshman COS member Joe Barton (R-TX), encouraged other Republicans to fight for the seat, and he mounted personal protests in front of Speaker Wright's district office and at a subcommittee hearing being held in the state. Jeff Cirillo, "How Joe Barton Struck Out," *Roll Call,* August 27, 2018; memo to Members of the Republican Conference from Joe Barton, February 26, 1985, Box RHM Staff, Pitts (8), Folder: McIntyre Papers, RHM. See also Barnes, "Raging Representatives," 10.

27. Barnes, "Raging Representatives," 9; Evans and Robert Novak, "The Michel/Gingrich Split"; Granat, "Splits in Style, Substance"; Steely, *The Gentleman from Georgia,* 181; Steve V. Roberts, "Forging Alliances to Get Minority's Plans Passed," *New York Times,* May 13, 1985, A14.

28. Connelly and Pitney, *Congress' Permanent Minority?,* 80; Margaret Shapiro, "The Toll of Turmoil," *Washington Post,* July 13, 1985, A5.

29. Stephen Engelberg, "G.O.P. Plans a Showdown Today on Disputed Indiana House Seat," *New York Times*, April 30, 1985, A21.

30. Those two proposals were supported by 68 percent and 75 percent, respectively, of Republicans in attendance at the Conference meeting. Far more (over 95 percent) approved proposals to hold one-minute and special-order speeches, ask the public to call for a new election, and move to vacate the seat. Memo from Mike Johnson, April 25, 1985, Box Staff. Pitts (8), Folder: McIntyre Correspondence (2), RHM.

31. Alan Ehrenhalt, "House Democrats Help Breed GOP Rebels," *Congressional Quarterly Weekly Report*, March 9, 1985, 471.

32. Interview with former Republican leader, July 22, 2020.

33. Thomas E. Mann and Norman J. Ornstein, *The Broken Branch: How Congress Is Failing America and How to Get It Back on Track* (New York: Oxford University, 2006), 68; Shapiro, "The Toll of Turmoil."

34. Jeffrey H. Birnbaum and Alan S. Murray, *Showdown at Gucci Gulch: Lawmakers, Lobbyists, and the Unlikely Triumph of Tax Reform* (New York: Vintage, 1988), 155–165; David S. Broder, "The Right Signals," *Washington Post*, September 2, 1986, A1; Margaret Shapiro, "House GOP Revolt Was Fed by Years Of Feeling Ignored," *Washington Post*, December 15, 1985, A1; Anne Swardson and Lou Cannon, "GOP Warned of Backlash if Tax Bill Dies," *Washington Post*, December 10, 1985. COS founder Vin Weber had sent a letter to the White House in October signed by thirty-eight Republicans opposing the House bill for being too liberal. Margaret Shapiro, "Reagan Urged to Withdraw Tax Plan," *Washington Post*, November 2, 1985, A5.

35. Anne Swardson and Dale Russakoff, "Reagan Sets New Appeal on Tax Bill," *Washington Post*, December 14, 1985, A1.

36. Birnbaum and Murray, *Showdown at Gucci Gulch*, 168–175; Broder, "The Right Signals"; Rowland Evans and Robert Novak, "Kemp's Transition . . . ," *Washington Post*, December 20, 1985, A23.

37. Gingrich's long-term goal of winning the House may also help explain another of his noteworthy acts in the 99th Congress: public advocacy for sanctions against the apartheid regime in South Africa. Though Reagan and some conservative groups opposed the sanctions, Gingrich and other COS members saw sanctions as a way for the GOP to reach nonwhite voters. Pauline Baker, "The Sanctions Vote: A G.O.P. Milestone," *New York Times*, August 26, 1986, A17; Francis X. Clines, "A Fledgling Protest Movement Gathers Steam," *New York Times*, August 5, 1985, B4.

38. Robin Toner, "Lessons on Being a Good Candidate," *New York Times*, August 26, 1986, A14; "NRCC Vice Chairmen," Box Leadership #9, Folder: Leadership, 99th, Republican Congressional Committee, RHM.

39. David S. Broder, "Revolution, Stage 2," *Washington Post*, July 28, 1985, B7; Newt Gingrich, "Helping Lead America through an Era of Change: A Message to Republican Candidates about the 1986 Campaign," July 25, 1986, 7 & 37, Box 9B, Folder: COS 1986, RW.

40. Steely, *The Gentleman from Georgia*, 185–186.

41. David Beers, "The Cases against Gingrich," *Mother Jones*, September 1, 1989; Howard Kurtz and Charles R. Babcock, "Two 'Nonpolitical' Foundations Push Grenada Rallies," *Washington Post*, October 4, 1984, A1.

42. Dan Balz and Ronald Brownstein, *Storming the Gates: Protest Politics and the Republican Revival* (Boston, MA: Little, Brown, 1996), 145; Bruck, "The Politics of Perception," 61; Steely, *The Gentleman from Georgia*, 186–87.

43. Bruck, "The Politics of Perception," 60–61; Newt Gingrich Memo, May 9, 1983, 4–5, Box 9A, Folder: COS-1983 (1), RW.

44. Steely, *The Gentleman from Georgia*, 183.

45. Barnes, "Raging Representatives," 9; Connelly and Pitney, *Congress' Permanent Minority?*, 49–50; Timothy E. Cook, "The Electoral Connection in the 99th Congress," *PS: Political Science & Politics* 19, no. 1 (Winter 1986): 16–22. In the early 1980s, Republicans had considered changing their rules to require GOP bill managers to hew to party policy positions. "House Republican Party Positions," Box Staff Series. Billy Pitts Files (10), Folder: Republican Conference, 1982–84(2), RHM.

46. Linda Douglass interview with Tom DeLay, pt. 1, February 10, 2015, John Brademas Center for the Study of Congress, www.nyu.edu/content/dam/nyu/brademasCenter/documents/Research/transcript_delay.pdf.

47. "A Conversation with Newt Gingrich," C-SPAN video archives, December 10, 1986, www.c-span.org/video/?150870-1/conversation-newt-gingrich (00:00–01:04); John M. Barry, "The Man of the House," *New York Times Magazine*, November 23, 1986, 56; Rowland Evans and Robert Novak, "Kemp in the Dentist's Chair," *Washington Post*, October 17, 1986, A23; Fuerbringer, "A House Divided by Political Rancor"; Steely, *The Gentleman from Georgia*, 187.

48. At one time or another during the 99th Congress, the COS's newest members included future GOP whip Tom DeLay (R-TX) and future Speaker Dennis Hastert (R-IL). "COS Members," Box 1063, Folder: COS Action Team, NLG; memo from Tracy Updegraff to Connie Thumma, March 13, 1987, Box 9B, Folder: RSW—Chair of COS 1987–88 (1), RW; and "Walker Becomes Chairman of COS," COS News Release, Box 8, Folder: RHM General, RHM.

49. Susan Rasky, "From Political Guerilla to Republican Folk Hero," *New York Times*, June 15, 1988, A24; Dear COS Letter from Robert Walker and Newt Gingrich, April 16, 1987, and letter from Robert Walker, January 30, 1987, 2, Box 9B, Folder: RSW—Chair of COS 1987–88 (1), RW; memo to Connie Mack from Newt Gingrich, June 3, 1987, Box 1078, Folder: Correspondence—Connie Mack, NLG; memo from Tracy Updegraff to Bob Walker and Newt Gingrich, April 15, 1988, 1, Box 9B, Folder: RSW—Chair of COS 1987–88 (2), RW; "Promises for the week ending April 1, 1988," Box 1063, Folder: S.G. Memos to Newt, NLG; memo to COS Members from Tracy Updegraff, May 14, 1987, Box 58, Folder: 18, RKA.

50. "COS Executive Committee," January 29, 1987; memo from Tracy Updegraff to Connie Thumma, March 13, 1987; memo from Tracy Updegraff to COS-92

Policy Review, September 23, 1988, Box 9B COS Chair 1987–88, Folder: RSW—Chair of COS 1987–88 (1), RW; and minutes, COS Wednesday Morning Meeting, September 30, 1987, Box 9B COS Chair 1987–88, Folder: RSW—Chair of COS 1987–88 (2), RW. Gunderson was a member of the COS Executive Committee principally as a representative of the '92 Group. memo to RSW from CT, August 3, 1987, Box 9B COS Chair 1987–88, Folder: RSW—Chair of COS 1987–88 (1), RW.

51. "The Conservative Action Team Model" by the Honorable Robert Walker; "Conservative Action Team"; and minutes, COS Executive Committee Meeting, June 2, 1987, Box 1063, Folder: COS Action Team, NLG. One document suggests that the COS could count on multiple members from committees, as well as an individual from each entering class since 1979, to serve on a "House Conservative Leadership Team." House Conservative Leadership Team roster, Box 9B, Folder: RSW—Chair of COS 1987–88 (1), RW. The Republican Study Committee was also an important partner, coordinating, for instance, the activity of the Conservative Action Team.

52. COS Executive Committee Meeting, June 24, 1987, 2, Box 9B, Folder: RSW—Chair of COS 1987–88 (2), RW. Despite this potential for cooperation, conflict continued between Edwards and the Research Committee, on one hand, and Gingrich and the COS, on the other. Tempers flared in February 1988 when Edwards allegedly excluded conservative groups, including the Republican Study Committee, from strategizing over a Contra aid bill. Confidential memo to Bob Walker and Newt Gingrich from Tracy Updegraff, February 10, 1988, Box 9B, Folder: RSW—Chair of COS 1987–88 (2), RW.

53. See, e.g., Michael Schrage, "Tariffs Seen as Way to Cut Deficits," *Washington Post*, January 10, 1987, C2; Helen Dewar and Edward Walsh, "Lawmakers Say President Must Take Blame and Reassert Control," *Washington Post*, February 27, 1987, A17.

54. COS Morning Meeting, April 1, 1987, and COS Wednesday Morning Meeting, April 29, 1987, 2, Box 9B, Folder: RSW—Chair of COS 1987–88 (2), RW. See also Balz and Brownstein, *Storming the Gates*, 134.

55. "Briefing," *New York Times*, August 26, 1987, A16; Paul Gigot, "Guerilla Gingrich Lights a Fire under the GOP," *Wall Street Journal*, August 19, 1988; minutes, COS Executive Committee Meeting, June 2, 1987, Box 9B, Folder: RSW—Chair of COS 1987–88 (2), RW.

56. Jacqueline Calmes, "Lingering Ethics Controversy Surrounds . . . Six Democratic Members of the House," *Congressional Quarterly Weekly Report*, April 4, 1987, 594; Dody Tsiantar, "A Dozen Public Officials May Be Indicted in Wedtech Case," *Washington Post*, February 5, 1987, A3.

57. John M. Barry, *The Ambition and the Power* (New York: Viking, 1989), 214; Clift and Brazaitis, *War without Bloodshed*, 236; Steven V. Roberts, "Counterattacking G.O.P. Sees a Campaign Issue," *New York Times*, June 9, 1988, B12. Another motive may have been to cloud positive coverage of the Democratic National Convention

in 1988, which Wright would be chairing. Roberts, "Counteracting G.O.P. Sees a Campaign Issue." Gingrich may have also been following the advice of Paul Weyrich to return to exposing corruption, his trademark theme. Bruck, "The Politics of Perception," 59.

58. Minutes, COS Wednesday Morning Meeting, September 16, 1987, Box 9B, Folder: RSW—chair of COS 1987–88 (2), RW. Nelson Polsby argues that the ethics attacks against Democrats were, like the anti-Communist crusade of Sen. Joseph McCarthy in the 1950s, strategic efforts of a minority party desperate to regain power. Nelson W. Polsby, *How Congress Evolves: Social Bases of Institutional Change* (New York: Oxford University Press, 2004), 130–132.

59. Jacqueline Calmes, "Committee Remains Silent on Boner Case," *Congressional Quarterly Weekly Report,* August 8, 1987, 1809; Howard Kurtz, "Probe Clears Rep. St Germain," *Washington Post,* April 16, 1987, 18; "3 GOP Lawmakers to Urge Review of St Germain Probe," *Washington Post,* July 28, 1987, A7; letters to Julian Dixon from Newt Gingrich, April 23 and April 30, 1987, Box 663, Folder: St Germain Case/Newt Letters 1987, NLG.

60. The amendment was rejected, 77 to 297. Jacqueline Calmes, "Ethics Challenge Rebuffed: House Votes $1.4 Billion for Housekeeping," *Congressional Quarterly Weekly Report,* July 4, 1987; Julie Johnson, "Pennsylvanian's Case Seen as Big Test for Ethics Unit," *New York Times,* December 10, 1987; Tom Kenworthy, "House Rejects 'Corruption' Inquiry," *Washington Post,* June 30, 1987; Smith, "From the Well of the House," 191, 211; minutes, COS Executive Committee Meeting, March 10, 1987, Box 9B COS Chair 1987–88, Folder: RSW—Chair of COS 1987–88 (2), RW.

61. Roger H. Davidson, "The New Centralization on Capitol Hill," *Review of Politics* 50, no. 3 (1988): 345–364; Janet Hook, "House Leadership Elections: Wright Era Begins," *Congressional Quarterly Weekly Report,* December 13, 1986, 3067; Janet Hook, "Speaker Jim Wright Takes Charge in the House," *Congressional Quarterly Weekly Report,* July 11, 1987, 1483; Mary McGrory, "On Resenting Wright," *Washington Post,* May 26, 1988, A2; Steven V. Roberts, "The Foreign Policy Tussle," *New York Times Magazine,* January 24, 1988, 26; Jim Wright, "Challenges That Speakers Face," from *Inside the House: Former Members Reveal How Congress Really Works,* ed. Lou Frey Jr. and Michael T. Hayes (Lanham, MD: University Press of America, 2001), 123.

62. Bach and Smith, *Managing Uncertainty in the House of Representatives,* 122–123; Janet Hook, "GOP Chafes under Restrictive House Rules," *Congressional Quarterly Weekly Report,* October 10, 1987, 2449; Rohde, *Parties and Leaders,* 132–133; Barbara Sinclair, *Party Wars: Polarization and the Politics of National Policy Making* (Norman: University of Oklahoma Press, 2006), 152–153.

63. Lawrence Freeman, *Strategy: A History* (New York: Oxford University Press, 2013), 91.

64. Barry, *The Ambition and the Power*, 530–536; J. Brooks Flippen, *Speaker Jim Wright: Power, Scandal, and the Birth of Modern Politics* (Austin: University of Texas Press, 2018), 374–375; Kenworthy, "House Rejects 'Corruption' Inquiry"; minutes, COS Wednesday Morning Meeting, July 1, 1987, Box 9B, Folder: RSW—Chair of COS 1987–88 (2), RW.

65. Barry, *The Ambition and the Power*, 391–392, 585; Flippen, *Speaker Jim Wright*, 333–334.

66. Calmes, "Ethics Challenge Rebuffed"; minutes, COS Executive Committee Meeting, March 24, 1987, and minutes, COS Wednesday Morning Meeting, May 13, 1987, Box 9B, Folder: RSW—Chair of COS 1987–88 (2), RW; Conservative Opportunity Society, "1987—Laying the Groundwork," 3, Box 157B, Folder COS 1987(1), RW. Gingrich and Walker pushed back against reports that they were unhappy with the lack of support from Michel on the amendment. Letter to the Editor of *Roll Call* from Walker and Gingrich, July 8, 1987, Box 9B, Folder: RSW—Chair of COS 1987–88 (1), RW.

67. Smith, "From the Well of the House," 209, 213–14; Steely, *The Gentleman from Georgia*, 189–190; minutes, COS Wednesday Morning Meeting, September 9, 1987, 1, Box 9B, Folder: RSW—chair of COS 1987–88 (2), RW.

68. Barry, *The Ambition and the Power*, 397–413, 457–474; Connelly and Pitney, *Congress' Permanent Minority?*, 82–83; *Congressional Record*, October 29, 1987, 30238. Gingrich had sharply criticized Wright on the floor immediately after the failure of the first rule, a tactical mistake that rallied Democrats to Wright's defense and perhaps kept Democrats united long enough to pass the second rule. Barry, *The Ambition and the Power*, 459–460; Jonathan Fuerbringer, "Tax Rise Is Passed by House," *New York Times*, October 30, 1987, D6.

69. Barry, *The Ambition and the Power*, 472; minutes, COS Executive Committee Meeting, November 3, 1987, 2, Box 9B, Folder: RSW—chair of COS 1987–88 (2), RW.

70. Barry, *The Ambition and the Power*, 472, 482; Connelly and Pitney, *Congress' Permanent Minority?*, 83.

71. Barry, *The Ambition and the Power*, 480–482.

72. Barry, 368–369, 390, 531; Flippen, *Speaker Jim Wright*, 374; John E. Yang, "Gingrich's Fiery Fight to Prove Wright Is Wrong Has GOP House Colleagues Scurrying for Cover," *Wall Street Journal*, May 20, 1988, 52; Julian E. Zelizer, *Burning Down the House: Newt Gingrich, the Fall of a Speaker, and the Rise of the New Republican Party* (New York: Penguin, 2020), 121.

73. Gingrich sent the article to Michel, highlighting his quote and scrawling a note below it: "*What* is your ethics agenda? I am deeply disappointed. I have taken the risks. I thought you could at least have been positive." Article from *Fort Worth Star-Telegram* with notations by Newt Gingrich, December 20, 1987, Box 12, Folder: Republican Party—House (3), Series Staff—Kehl, RHM.

74. Barry, *The Ambition and the Power*, 607; Tom Kenworthy, "Democrats Seek Probe of Rep. Gingrich's PAC," *Washington Post*, February 13, 1988, A15. Democrats claimed that Gingrich's political action committee, Conservatives for Hope and Opportunity, had broken federal law by failing to disclose contributions from corporations and by falsely promising to give funds directly to Republican candidates. The group ceased raising money and the Federal Election Commission eventually dropped its investigation. "Fund Raising Is Halted by Conservative Group," *New York Times*, February 11, 1988, A31; Beers, "The Cases against Gingrich"; Don Phillips, "FEC Dismisses Complaint against Gingrich," *Washington Post*, May 25, 1988, A3.

75. Minutes, COS Wednesday Morning Meeting, February 17, 1988, 2, Box 9B, Folder: RSW—chair of COS 1987–88 (2), RW.

76. Barry, *The Ambition and the Power*, 602–603; interview with Bob Livingston by Frank Gregorsky, February 27, 2009, www.exactingeditor.com/BobLivingston.pdf.

77. Barry, *The Ambition and the Power*, 592–593; John Felton with Janet Hook, "House Defeat Clouds Outlook for Contra Aid," *Congressional Quarterly Weekly Report*, March 5, 1988, 555; Eric Pianin, "House GOP's Frustrations Intensify," *Washington Post*, December 21, 1987, A11.

78. Douglas B. Harris, "Anticipating the Revolution: Michel and Republican Congressional Reform Efforts," from *Robert H. Michel: Leading the Republican House Minority*, ed. Frank H. Mackaman and Sean Q Kelly (Lawrence: University Press of Kansas, 2019), 196; Rohde, *Parties and Leaders*, 134–135.

79. For examples of conflicts between committee Republicans, who sometimes worked with Democrats to pass legislation even under restrictive rules, and conservative rank and file members who often did not, see Frances E. Lee, *Insecure Majorities: Congress and the Perpetual Campaign* (Chicago: University of Chicago Press, 2016), 99–100, and Rohde, *Parties and Leaders*, 133–134.

80. Minutes, COS Wednesday Morning Meeting, July 1, 1987, Box 9B, Folder: RSW—chair of COS 1987–88 (2), RW. Republicans on the Appropriations and Rules Committees were an especial irritant to Gingrich and the COS, particularly after GOP appropriators pushed back against junior Republicans on the House floor in late June 1987. Lee, *Insecure Majorities*, 78, 96–99; Elizabeth Wehr, "GOP Rank-and-File vs. Appropriators: Loyalty Test: Party First, Committee Second?," *Congressional Quarterly Weekly Report*, August 1, 1987, 1720. At the same COS meeting on July 1, 1987, Dan Lungren (R-CA) wryly noted that plenty of loyal Republicans were readily available to take the place of Appropriations members who felt obliged to cooperate with Democrats. During a COS Executive Committee meeting three months before, Gingrich suggested that Jimmy Quillen (R-TN) be kicked off the Rules Committee for voting too often with Democrats. Minutes, COS Executive Committee Meeting, April 8, 1987, Box 9B, Folder RSW-Chair of COS 1987–88(1), RW.

81. John Felton, "Contra-Aid Denial Shifts Burden to Democrats," *Congressional*

Quarterly Weekly Report, February 6, 1988, 235; minutes, COS Wednesday Morning Meeting, February 3, 1988, Box 9B, Folder: RSW—chair of COS 1987–88 (2), RW. The Conference did consider demoting ranking committee members who worked with the majority party on major spending bills. Fuerbringer, "A House Divided by Political Rancor."

82. Pianin, "House GOP's Frustrations Intensify," A1, A11. Lott's view was echoed by political scientist Norman Ornstein, who told one reporter at the end of 1987 that Republicans "have few realistic prospects of gaining a majority." George Lardner Jr., "Charges of Favoritism, Tests of Credibility at House Ethics Panel," *Washington Post*, December 15, 1987, A21.

83. Connelly and Pitney, *Congress' Permanent Minority?*, 83; Fuerbringer, "A House Divided by Political Power."

84. Barry, *The Ambition and the Power*, 534–535; Flippen, *Speaker Jim Wright*, 374–375.

85. Barry, *The Ambition and the Power*, 604–606, 611–613, 617–618; Barry, "The House of Jim Wright," *Politico*, May 7, 2015; Zelizer, *Burning Down the House*, 129–130.

86. Barry, *The Ambition and the Power*, 367–368, 618–619; Tom Kenworthy, "In Response to Group's Call for Ethics Probe, Wright Defends His Record," *Washington Post*, May 20, 1988, A13.

87. Smith, "From the Well of the House," 215–216; letter to Julian Dixon, May 26, 1988, Box 673, Folder: Ethics Handout, NLG.

88. Janet Hook, "Ethics Panel to Open Broad Inquiry on Wright," *Congressional Quarterly Weekly Report*, June 11, 1988, 1570; Zelizer, *Burning Down the House*, 152–153.

89. Tom Kenworthy, "Outside Probe of Wright Gains Reagan's Support," *Washington Post*, June 16, 1988, A4; Zelizer, *Burning Down the House*, 138, 147.

90. Rasky, "From Political Guerilla to Republican Folk Hero."

91. Flippen, *Speaker Jim Wright*, 377.

92. Dear Republican Colleague letter, September 2, 1988, Box 664, Folder: Dear Colleague: 17 members, NLG.

93. "The House Republican Obligation to Focus on Ethics and Election Reform," September 6, 1988, 3, Box 1063, Folder: Strategy Papers, Fall 1988, NLG.

94. Smith, "From the Well of the House," 217.

95. Steely, *The Gentleman from Georgia*, 195; "Shaping the Congress of Tomorrow, Working Paper," June 1988, Box 1063, Folder: 1988 Political, NLG.

96. Minutes, COS Executive Committee Meeting, April 22, 1987, Box 9B, Folder: RSW—chair of COS 1987–88 (2), RW; "Promises for the week ending April 1, 1988," 2, Box 1063, Folder: S.G. Memos to Newt, NLG.

97. Stephen Engelberg and Katharine Q. Seelye, "Gingrich: Man in Spotlight and Organization in Shadow," *New York Times*, December 18, 1994, 1.

98. Steely, *The Gentleman from Georgia*, 186–187; minutes, COS Executive

Committee Meeting, April 22, 1987, Box 9B, Folder: RSW—chair of COS 1987–88 (2), RW.

99. "Three Republican Themes for the 1988 Campaign," September 20, 1988, Box 1063, Folder: Strategy Papers, Fall 1988, NLG. The use of audio recordings to inspire potential or sitting lawmakers was not an entirely new tactic. For instance, COS member Vin Weber (R-MN) would listen to recordings of Jack Kemp (R-NY) for inspiration while on the campaign trail. Interview with former Republican leadership aide, April 11, 2019.

100. Bruck, "The Politics of Perception," 62; "Achieving Majority Status in the House/Developing Outside Interest," March 16, 1988, Box 1063, Folder: 1988 Political, NLG.

101. "Briefing," *New York Times*, August 11, 1987, A16; "The Jack Kemp for President National Steering Committee," 16, and letter to Jack Kemp from Newt Gingrich, September 24, 1987, Box 1070, Folder: Presidential Politics-Jack Kemp, Presidential Candidate, NLG.

102. Letter to Vice President George Bush from Robert Walker, March 25, 1987, Box 9B, Folder: RSW—chair of COS 1987–88 (1), RW; minutes, COS Executive Committee Meeting, June 2, 1987, 2, Box 1063, Folder: COS Action Items, NLG.

103. Memo to COS Members from Tracy Updegraff, August 31, 1988, Box 9B, Folder: RSW—chair of COS 1987–88 (1), RW.

104. E. J. Dionne, "Emotional Address," *New York Times*, August 16, 1988, A22; Gigot, "Guerilla Gingrich Lights a Fire under the GOP"; Steely, *The Gentleman from Georgia*, 195–196; "Bush Campaign—Conservative Movement/Decision Framework," 6, Box 1069, Folder: Projects-Bush Campaign, NLG.

105. "A Republican 'Menu' of Legislative Reforms," July 27, 1988, Box 9B, Folder: RSW—Chair of COS 1987–88 (1), RW; minutes, COS Wednesday Morning Meeting, July 13, 1988, Box 9B, Folder: RSW—Chair of COS 1987–88 (2), RW.

106. Mike Mills, "Close Race to Lead Republican Conference," *Congressional Quarterly Weekly Report*, December 10, 1988, 3474; Rohde, *Parties and Leaders*, 137.

107. Barry, *The Ambition and the Power*, 667; Connelly and Pitney, *Congress' Permanent Minority?*, 54–55; Tom Kenworthy, "House GOP Signals It's in a Fighting Mood," *Washington Post*, December 26, 1988, A1. The selection of Dick Cheney as Conference Chair and Jerry Lewis as Policy Chair in mid-1987 may have also contributed to a more proactive and unified approach to minority party leadership. Barry, *The Ambition and the Power*, 363. Another COS member, Barbara Vucanovich (R-NV), became chair of the Republican Study Committee in 1988. "Leadership Positions in the New Congress," *Associated Press*, January 4, 1989.

108. Interview with former leadership aide, October 17, 2019.

109. Matthew N. Green and Douglas B. Harris, "The Minority Party Leadership of Bob Michel," in *Robert H. Michel: Leading the Republican House Minority*, ed. Frank H. Mackaman and Sean Q Kelly (Lawrence: University Press of Kansas, 2019), 102, 104.

110. Minutes, COS Wednesday Morning Meeting, December 9, 1987, 2, Box 9B, Folder: RSW—Chair of COS 1987–88 (2), RW.

111. Gigot, "Guerilla Gingrich Lights a Fire under the GOP"; Hedrick Smith, *The Power Game: How Washington Works* (New York: Random House, 1988), 16, 448.

112. December 1988 easel sheets, A-8, Box 2629, NLG; memo to COS Members from Tracy Updegraff, March 2, 1989, Box 157B, Folder: COS 3, RW.

113. Memo to Bob from Jack, July 12, 1984, Box 9A, Folder: COS—1984(2), RW; minutes, COS Executive Committee Meeting, June 2, 1987, 3, Box 1063, Folder: COS Action Items, NLG; minutes, COS Wednesday Morning Meeting, February 17, 1988, 3, Box 9B, Folder: RSW—Chair of COS 1987–88 (2), RW.

114. Barnes, "Raging Representatives," 9; "100th Congress Marks End of the Reagan Era," *CQ Almanac* 1988, 44th ed. (Washington, DC: Congressional Quarterly, 1989).

115. It was, of all people, the conservative activist and Gingrich mentor Paul Weyrich who would help sink the Tower nomination by claiming to have witnessed the senator's illicit behavior. Philip Shenon, "Brett Kavanaugh Isn't Robert Bork. He's John Tower," *Politico Magazine*, October 2, 2018.

116. Major Garrett, "Gingrich: Managerial Disaster?," *Atlantic*, December 9, 2011, www.theatlantic.com/politics/archive/2011/12/gingrich-managerial-disaster/249746/.

117. Memo to COS Members from Tracy Updegraff Re: COS Project Update, March 10, 1989, Box 157B, Folder: COS(3), RW.

118. Gingrich interview with Bill Kristol, November 21, 2014, pt. 1, https://conversationswithbillkristol.org/transcript/newt-gingrich-transcript/.

119. Douglas L. Koopman, *Hostile Takeover: The House Republican Party, 1980–1995* (Lanham, MD: Rowman & Littlefield, 1996), 13–14; Zelizer, *Burning Down the House*, 184–185. For a fuller analysis of the race and the reasons for Gingrich's victory, see Matthew N. Green and Douglas B. Harris, *Choosing the Leader: Leadership Elections in the U.S. House of Representatives* (New Haven: Yale University Press, 2019), 79–85.

120. Interview with former Republican leadership aide, April 11, 2019.

121. Steve Gunderson and Rob Morris with Bruce Bawer, *House and Home* (New York: Dutton, 1996), 100.

122. Interview with former Republican House member, July 30, 2020.

123. Evans and Oleszek, *Congress under Fire*, 33; Green and Harris, *Choosing the Leader*, 85; Koopman, *Hostile Takeover*, 18; Smith, "From the Well of the House," 222–223; Robin Toner, "Tired of Cooling Their Heels, the Republicans Turn Up the Heat," *New York Times*, January 16, 1989, A13. Gingrich would later give credit to C-SPAN for helping elevate his public profile enough to be a strong candidate for whip. Stephen Frantzich and John Sullivan, *The C-SPAN Revolution* (Norman: University of Oklahoma Press, 1996), 274–275. Gingrich claimed that

one Republican, William Broomfield, switched from Michel to Gingrich after being mistreated by the Democratic chairman of his committee, because, he said, "Newt is the only guy who will stand up to these people." Gingrich interview with Bill Kristol, November 21, 2014, pt. 1, https://conversationswithbillkristol.org/transcript/newt-gingrich-transcript/.

124. Thomas Edsall, "The Great Divider," *Washington Post*, March 23, 1989.

125. Newt Gingrich, "The Gingrich Manifesto," *Washington Post*, April 9, 1989, B1; Janet Hook, "Gingrich's Selection as Whip Reflects GOP Discontent," *Congressional Quarterly Weekly Report*, March 25, 1989, 625.

126. Jim Wright, *Worth It All: My War for Peace* (Washington, DC: Potomac, 1993), 231; Zelizer, *Burning Down the House*, 176–179, 202–203.

127. Barry, *The Ambition and the Power*, 716–719; Flippen, *Speaker Jim Wright*, 383–384. Before the Ethics Committee announced its verdict, Gingrich had drafted a GOP resolution demanding the committee reveal all of its evidence against Wright; John Myers (R-IN), ranking member of the committee and a secret advocate for investigating the Speaker, assured his colleagues that it would not be necessary. Barry, *The Ambition and the Power*, 630, 676.

128. Richard E. Cohen, "Full Speed Ahead," *National Journal*, January 30, 1988, 240; Matthew N. Green, *The Speaker of the House: A Study of Leadership* (New Haven: Yale University Press, 2010), 118–121; Tom Kenworthy, "The Speaker's Cloudy Future," *Washington Post*, October 19, 1988, A1; Polsby, *How Congress Evolves*, 133–134; Roberts, "The Foreign Policy Tussle," 31.

129. Barry, *The Ambition and the Power*, 718, 723–728, 742–743, 752; Barry, "The House of Jim Wright"; Flippen, *Speaker Jim Wright*, 384–385; Zelizer, *Burning Down the House*, 239–240, 262–266.

130. Balz and Brownstein, *Storming the Gates*, 126; Don Phillips, "Republicans Bridle at Wright Speech," *Washington Post*, June 2, 1989, A7.

131. Time/CNN/Yankelovich Clancy Shulman Poll, March 2, 1989 [USYANKCS.89MAR2.R10USYANKCS.89MAR2.R10]; *Washington Post* Poll, April 19–23, 1989 [USWASHP.89917E.R01].

132. Matthew N. Green, *Underdog Politics: The Minority Party in the U.S. House of Representatives* (New Haven: Yale University Press, 2015), 73; Time/CNN/Yankelovich Clancy Shulman Poll, May 4, 1989 [USYANKCS.89MAY.R09], [USYANKCS.89MAY.R12].

Chapter 4. Entrepreneurial Insider (1989–1994)

1. Peter J. Boyle, "Good Newt, Bad Newt," *Vanity Fair*, July 1989, from "The Long March of Newt Gingrich," *Frontline* (1996), www.pbs.org/wgbh/pages/frontline/newt/boyernewt1.html; Tom Kenworthy, "Gingrich Faces New Ethics Charges," *Washington Post*, October 26, 1989, A13; Tom Kenworthy, "House Ethics Panel to Drop Investigation of Rep. Gingrich," *Washington Post*, March 8, 1990, A6; Myra

MacPherson, "Newt Gingrich, Point Man in a House Divided," *Washington Post*, June 12, 1989, C8; Mel Steely, *The Gentleman from Georgia: The Biography of Newt Gingrich* (Macon, GA: Mercer University Press, 2000), 202, 205–207; memo from Mel and Steve to Newt Re: Ethics Investigation, May 28, 1989, Box 1890, Folder: Odds and Ends, Newt and Pres. Bush—1991, NLG.

2. MacPherson, "Newt Gingrich, Point Man in a House Divided"; personal recollections, 38, Box Personal (2), Folder: Personal. Member Notes, RHM.

3. Eleanor Clift and Tom Brazaitis, *War without Bloodshed: The Art of Politics* (New York: Scribner, 1996), 242, 246; Interview with former Republican member of Congress, May 8, 2019.

4. Janet Hook, "Gingrich Finds Rhetoric Must Toe Party Line," *Congressional Quarterly Weekly Report*, July 22, 1989; Eric Pianin, "Michel Enjoys a Political Revival of Sorts," *Washington Post*, November 29, 1991, A22.

5. Gingrich did send personal thank-you notes to Michel. See, e.g., handwritten letter from Newt to Bob Michel, May 2, 1989, Box Leadership (13), Folder: Leadership. 101st. Leadership Meeting Notes (1), RHM.

6. John M. Barry, *The Ambition and the Power* (New York: Viking, 1989), 744; Josh Getlin, "Gingrich, Right's Bad Boy, Target of Angry Democrats," *Los Angeles Times*, June 11, 1989.

7. Kim Mattingly, "Michel Says House Is 'Den of Inequity,'" *Roll Call*, April 2, 1990; Walter J. Oleszek, *Congressional Procedure and the Policy Process*, 7th ed. (Washington, DC: CQ Press, 2007), table 4–3, 129; David W. Rohde, *Parties and Leaders in the Postreform House* (Chicago: University of Chicago Press, 1991), 187–188.

8. Tom Kenworthy, "Gingrich to Seek Tougher Penalty for Frank," *Washington Post*, July 25, 1990, A12; Don Phillips, "Rep. Gingrich Appears Transformed by the Crack of the Whip," *Washington Post*, August 7, 1989, A1; Rohde, *Parties and Leaders*, 188; Maralee Schwartz and David Maraniss, "Gingrich: No More Mr. Nice Guy," *Washington Post*, March 30, 1990, A16A; Richard Wolf, "Newt Gingrich Has Softer Style," *USA Today*, March 27, 1990, 4A, from Box 160B, Folder: Newt Gingrich, RW.

9. Interview with Newt Gingrich, *The Ripon Forum* (25:2), May 1989, https://riponsociety.org/article/a-conversation-with-new-gingrich/.

10. Major Garrett, "Gingrich: Managerial Disaster?," *Atlantic*, December 9, 2011, www.theatlantic.com/politics/archive/2011/12/gingrich-managerial-disaster/249746/; Steve Gunderson and Rob Morris with Bruce Bawer, *House and Home* (New York: Dutton, 1996), 107; Steely, *The Gentleman from Georgia*, 213; memo to Members of the Strategy Whip Organization from Gingrich and Gunderson, May 26, 1989, and letter to Rep. Ben Garrido Blaz, July 7, 1989, Box 64, Folder 1, RKA; "Staying Ahead of the Curve," Box 1063, Folder: Whip Organization, NLG.

11. C. Lawrence Evans, *The Whips: Building Party Coalitions in Congress* (Ann Arbor: University of Michigan Press, 2018); Scott R. Meinke, *Leadership Organizations in the House of Representatives: Party Participation and Partisan Politics* (Ann

Arbor: University of Michigan Press, 2016), 101–102, 128–129, 172; Strategy Whip Organization Meeting Agenda, November 7, 1989, Box 2683, Folder: Strategy Whip Team Meetings '89, NLG.

12. Steely, *The Gentleman from Georgia*, 213; interview with former Republican member of Congress, May 8, 2019. House Democrats, recognizing the potential value of partisan messaging, formed their own communication arm called the Democratic Message Board. Matthew N. Green, *Underdog Politics: The Minority Party in the U.S. House of Representatives* (New Haven: Yale University Press, 2015), 77.

13. Gunderson and Morris, *House and Home*, 108; Steely, *The Gentleman from Georgia*, 214; Strategy Whip Organization Planning Paper and Meeting Agenda, January 24, 1990, Box 2683 Folder: Strategy Whip Team Meetings 1990 (2), NLG.

14. See, for example, various whip counts and questions in Box 2690, Folder: Whip Check Information, NLG; Strategy Whip Organization agenda, June 6, 1990, 3, Box 2683, Folder: Strategy Whip Meetings '90(1) and (2), NLG; and Meinke, *Leadership Organizations in the House of Representatives*, 128–129.

15. These included Joe Barton (R-TX), Porter Goss (R-FL), Fred Grandy (R-IA), Susan Molinari (R-NY), and Fred Upton (R-MI). Strategy Whip Organization Meeting, July 18, 1989, 2, Box 2683, Folder: Strategy Whip Team Meetings '89, NLG; and Invitees to Weekly Strategy Whip Meeting, attendance for October 16, 1990, Box 2683, Folder: Strategy Whip Team Meetings '90, NLG.

16. Clift and Brazaitis, *War without Bloodshed*, 243–244; Steely, *The Gentleman from Georgia*, 192–193; Rowland Evans and Robert Novak, "Et tu, Newt?," *Washington Post*, November 20, 1989, A15.

17. Albert R. Hunt, "Now Bush Needs a Mandate Campaign," *Wall Street Journal*, November 11, 1988, A14; Zachary C. Smith, "From the Well of the House: Remaking the House Republican Party, 1978–1994" (PhD diss., Boston University, 2012), 240–241; Steely, *The Gentleman from Georgia*, 238–240.

18. Steely, *The Gentleman from Georgia*, 240; memo to Mickey Edwards from Christopher Cox, March 24, 1989, Box 43, Folder 37, ME; memo to COS Members from Tracy Updegraff, May 19, 1989, 4, Box 1074, Folder: Polls and Surveys—COS, NLG; "Macro-Campaign Planning for a Reform Republican Majority," 2, Box 1063, Folder: COS/92 Working Group Papers—11/88, NLG.

19. Dan Balz and Ronald Brownstein, *Storming the Gates: Protest Politics and the Republican Revival* (Boston: Little, Brown, 1996), 178; Tom Kenworthy, "Gingrich Says Bush Must Choose between a Reform and a 'Second Eisenhower' Era," *Washington Post*, November 28, 1990, A10; Don Phillips and Ann Devroy, "Gingrich Wanted Rollins Fired in GOP Strategy Feud," *Washington Post*, November 30, 1989, A4. Some of Gingrich's ideas may have been adopted by the White House, such as the concept of "wedge issues." Phillips, "Rep. Gingrich Appears Transformed," A7.

20. Gloria Borger, "The Making of a Rebellion," *U.S. News & World Report*, October 15, 1990, 38; "Budget Adopted after Long Battle," *CQ Almanac* 1990, 46th ed. (Washington, DC: Congressional Quarterly, 1991); Steely, *The Gentleman from*

Georgia, 222–223; John E. Yang, "Rep. Gingrich 'Prepared' to Back Increase in Taxes," *Washington Post*, July 20, 1990, A6.

21. Richard L. Burke, "Shouts of Revolt Rise Up in Congressional Ranks," *New York Times*, October 1, 1990, B8; David Rogers and Michel McQueen, "Bush Campaigns for the Passage of Budget Pact," *Wall Street Journal*, October 2, 1990, A3.

22. Richard L. Berke, "Gingrich, in Duel with White House, Stays True to His Role as an Outsider," *New York Times*, October 5, 1990, A25; Rogers and McQueen, "Bush Campaigns for the Passage of Budget Pact."

23. "Budget Adopted after Long Battle," *CQ Almanac 1990*, 46th ed. (Washington, DC: Congressional Quarterly, 1991); George Hager, "Defiant House Rebukes Leaders," *Congressional Quarterly Weekly Report*, October 6, 1990, 3183; Steven Mufson and John E. Yang, "Emotional Pleas Failed to Halt House Revolt," *Washington Post*, October 6, 1990, A8; David E. Rosenbaum, "Congress Is Pushed," *New York Times*, October 6, 1990, 1; draft letter from Robert Dole and Robert H. Michel, October 4, 1990, Box Leadership #13, Folder: Leadership. 101st. Joint Letters. 10/4/90: Budget Resolution, RHM; Dear Republican Colleague letter from Robert H. Michel, October 3, 1990, Box Leadership #13, Folder: Dear Republican Colleague Notebook, 1990(4), RHM.

24. Berke, "Gingrich, in Duel with White House"; Steely, *The Gentleman from Georgia*, 225; Janet Hook, "Gingrich Weathers a Rough First Term but His Biggest Challenges Lie Ahead," *Congressional Quarterly Weekly Report*, December 1, 1990, 3998; Bob Woodward, "Debut of a Power Player," *Washington Post*, December 25, 2011. There had been early hints that Gingrich would oppose the agreement if it included tax increases. Thomas B. Edsall, "Gingrich Bars Tax Rise to Obtain Budget Deal," *Washington Post*, August 23, 1990, A16; Steely, *The Gentleman from Georgia*, 226.

25. "Budget Adopted after Long Battle"; Lee Edwards, *The Conservative Revolution: The Movement That Remade America* (New York: Free Press, 1999), 285–286; Michel McQueen, "Sununu's Old Abrasive Self, Submerged since Joining White House, Returns in Budget Talks," *Wall Street Journal*, October 8, 1990, A14; Mufson and Yang, "Emotional Pleas Failed to Halt House Revolt"; Smith, "From the Well of the House," 262.

26. Balz and Brownstein, *Storming the Gates*, 136–137; "Honor Thy Pledge," *Wall Street Journal*, October 2, 1990, A26; letter to Mickey Edwards from Dick Armey, March 20, 1989, Box 43, Folder 37, ME; memo from Teresa Sewell, April 3, 1990, Box 81B, Folder: COS 90, RW. Gingrich himself admitted in a private interview in March 1990 that "the conservative wing of the Republican party will not support a tax increase under any circumstances." Transcript of interview with House Minority Whip Newt Gingrich by Frank van der Linden, 11, March 15, 1990, USC.

27. Berke, "Gingrich, in Duel with White House"; David S. Broder, "Loyalty, Ideology, Ambition—and Newt Gingrich," *Washington Post*, October 7, 1990, D7; E. J. Dionne, "Gingrich Calls for Darman to Resign," *Washington Post*, November 29,

1990, A20; Gwen Ifill, "Gingrich Escalates Criticism of Bush's Domestic Policy," *Washington Post*, December 1, 1990, A2; Woodward, "Debut of a Power Player."

28. Borger, "The Making of a Rebellion."

29. Clift and Brazaitis, *War without Bloodshed*, 246; COS Membership List (1989), Box 2353, Folder: COS '89, NLG; "Republican Conference, December 3, 1990, First Item of Business on Monday," letter to Jerry Lewis from Dana Rohrabacher, November 29, 1990, and draft Republican Conference Resolution, Box 15, Folder: 102nd Republican Conference Resolutions(1), Box 15, Folder: 102nd Republican Conference Resolutions (1), Series: Leadership, RHM.

30. Memo to Bob Walker from John Walker RE: COS Strategy Meeting Agenda, 2, Box 81B, Folder: COS 92, RW; COS Wednesday Morning Meeting, February 21, 1990, and COS Strategy Session Agenda, Box 1074, Folder: Polls and Surveys—COS, NLG; memo to COS Members from Jon Kyl RE: 24 February Planning Session, March 1, 1989, Box 81, Folder 19, ME; letter to John Blowers from Robert Walker, October 23, 1991, Box 9B, Folder: COS 1989–96, RW. COS members appointed by Gingrich to serve as deputy or strategy whips included, in addition to Walker, Dick Armey, Harry Bartlett (R-TX), John Buechner (R-MO), Larry Craig (R-ID), and Jon Kyl. "Staying Ahead of the Curve," 9, Box 1063, Folder: Whip Organization, NLG.

31. "GOPAC in the 1990s," November 1, 1989, from *In the Matter of Rep. Newt Gingrich*, Report of the Select Committee on Ethics, January 17, 1997, H. Rept. 105–1, pt. 2, 144–149.

32. "Driving Realignment from the Presidency down to the Precincts," February 10–11, 1989, Agenda and Participants List, and Specific Items for Discussion and Decision, Box 1063, Folder: Realignment Meeting February 10 & 11, NLG. Gingrich subsequently shared his "proposed vision" with COS. Memo to COS Members from Tracy Updegraff, March 2, 1989, Box 157B, Folder: COS Folder (3), RW.

33. Katherine Q. Seelye, "Birth of a Vision: Files Show How Gingrich Laid a Grand G.O.P. Plan," *New York Times*, December 3, 1995, 26; memo to Gingrich from Bo Callaway, August 13, 1990, 2, from Select Committee on Ethics, *In the Matter of Rep. Newt Gingrich*, pt. 4, 307–308; Steely, *The Gentleman from Georgia*, 217–219.

34. Donald Lambro, "Gingrich Reaching Out to Tap the Grass Roots," *Washington Times*, January 26, 1990, F3; Paul Taylor, "GOP-Backed Teleconference Stresses Community-Based Solutions," *Washington Post*, May 20, 1990, A24; "American Opportunities Workshops: New Solutions for the 1990s," Strategy Whip Organization Agenda, February 6, 1990, Box 2683, Folder: Strategy Whip Team Meetings '90 [2], NLG; "American Opportunities Workshop: Rewriting Grassroots Political Movements," from Select Committee on Ethics, *In the Matter of Rep. Newt Gingrich*, part 2, 161; "GOPAC Focus Groups: Analysis," July 10, 1990, from Select Committee on Ethics, *In the Matter of Rep. Newt Gingrich*, pt. 3, 242–270. Gingrich asked freshmen to help recruit other lawmakers to participate in the *American Opportunities Workshop*. Memo to Kay et al. from Bo, January 20, 1990, from Select Committee on Ethics, *In the Matter of Rep. Newt Gingrich*, part 2, 190; memo to Bo Callaway from

Jeff Eisenach, February 8, 1990, from Select Committee on Ethics, *In the Matter of Rep. Newt Gingrich*, pt. 3, 293–294.

35. It featured the "nine-dot problem," in which nine dots arranged in a three-by-three array must be connected with only four straight lines. "The America That Can Be," December 1, 1989, Box 2629, Folder: Newt Originals, NLG.

36. Daniel J. Balz and Serge F. Kovaleski, "Gingrich Divided GOP, Conquered the Agenda," *Washington Post*, December 21, 1994, A19; "GOPAC: An Overview," 2, from Select Committee on Ethics, *In the Matter of Rep. Newt Gingrich*, pt. 2, 142; interview with former Republican congressman, May 8, 2019; interview with former Republican congressman, July 20, 2020.

37. Michael Oreskes, "For G.O.P. Arsenal, 133 Words to Fire," *New York Times*, September 9, 1990; David Pace, "Ford Resigns as Honorary Chairman of PAC Headed by Gingrich," *Associated Press*, November 20, 1990; "Dear Friend" letter and "Language: A Key Mechanism of Control," Box 917, Folder 3, RAG.

38. "Gingrich Presidential Bid Plotted by GOPAC Officials Back in 1990," *Roll Call*, December 4, 1995.

39. Toni Locy and Ruth Marcus, "Timing Is Key in FEC Suit against GOPAC," *Washington Post*, December 3, 1995; Ruth Marcus and Toni Locy, "FEC Says GOPAC Aided Gingrich Race despite Law," *Washington Post*, November 30, 1995; Oreskes, "For G.O.P. Arsenal"; Select Committee on Ethics, *In the Matter of Rep. Newt Gingrich*, pt. 1, 4–5; David Willman, "Major GOPAC Donors Got Special Access, Files Show," *Los Angeles Times*, December 17, 1995.

40. Kitty Dumas, "Democrats Drive Voter Bill, but Big Potholes Remain," *Congressional Quarterly Weekly Report*, February 10, 1990, 411. One such activist, Morton Blackwell, balked at contributing to the *American Opportunities Workshop* because Gingrich supported a Democratic bill to ease voter registration. Memorandum for Bo Callaway, February 8, 1990, from *In the Matter of Rep. Newt Gingrich*, pt. 3, 294.

41. Glenn R. Simpson, "As One-Minutes Grow More Coordinated, a Great Tradition May Be Self-Destructing," *Roll Call*, May 7, 1990; Douglas B. Harris, "Partisan Framing in Legislative Debates," from *Winning with Words: The Origins and Impact of Political Framing*, ed. Brian F. Schaffner and Patrick J. Sellers (New York: Routledge, 2009); memo to House Republican Leadership from Mickey Edwards, June 27, 1989, Box 81 Folder 19, ME.

42. Phillips and Devroy, "Gingrich Wanted Rollins Fired"; letter to Newt Gingrich from Mickey Edwards, February 8, 1989, Box 44, Folder 1; Mickey Edwards, "Achieving a Republican Majority in the U.S. House of Representatives," December 8, 1989, 5–6, Box 81, Folder 1, ME.

43. Laura Parker, "Close Contest Brings Gingrich's Attention Back Home," *Washington Post*, November 11, 1990, A12; Steely, *The Gentleman from Georgia*, 207–210.

44. John Yang, "House GOP Challengers Fall Short," *Washington Post*, December 4, 1990, A15. Gingrich reportedly helped NRCC Chair Guy Vander Jagt fight

off a challenge for his post from White House–backed candidate Don Sundquist (R-TN). E-mail to authors from former Republican aide, May 17, 2019; interview with Bob Livingston by Frank Gregorsky, February 27, 2009, www.exactingeditor.com/BobLivingston.pdf.

45. Geoffrey Kabaservice, *Rule and Ruin: The Downfall of Moderation and the Destruction of the Republican Party, from Eisenhower to the Tea Party* (New York: Oxford University Press, 2012), 371.

46. Richard Bradee, "GOP Campaign Group Blasted by Gingrich," *Milwaukee Sentinel*, December 4, 1990; Select Committee on Ethics, *In the Matter of Rep. Newt Gingrich*, 142; Federal Election Committee data. Santorum later said he was an avid listener of Gingrich's GOPAC tapes. Connie Bruck, "The Politics of Perception," *New Yorker*, October 9, 1995, 62; William Corkery, "Newt Gingrich and GOPAC: Training the Farm Team that Helped Win the Republican Revolution of 1994," (BA honors thesis, College of William and Mary, 2011), 28. Gingrich gave over $40,000 from his political action committee to GOP candidates in the 1990 election cycle.

47. Jacqueline Calmes, "In an About-Face, Gingrich Becomes an Apostle of Grass-Roots Politics, Averting Clashes in GOP," *Wall Street Journal*, March 27, 1991, A16; memorandum to House Republican Leadership from Mickey Edwards Re: Becoming a Majority in the House of Representatives, February 21, 1991, 1–2, 6, Box 81, Folder 14, ME; "Proposed Agenda for Leadership Breakfast, Draft Copy," February 7, 1991, Box 81B, Folder: COS 91, RW.

48. Guy Gugliotta, "Check-Bouncing 'Is Over,' Foley Says," *Washington Post*, September 26, 1991, A21; Tom Kenworthy, "Guess Who Bounced 8,331 Checks in 1 Year," *Washington Post*, September 20, 1991, A25; Walter Pincus, "Bouncing Checks at Capitol's Bank," *Washington Post*, February 8, 1990, A23.

49. C. Lawrence Evans and Walter J. Oleszek, *Congress under Fire: Reform Politics and the Republican Majority* (Boston: Houghton Mifflin, 1997), 34; Gugliotta, "Check-Bouncing 'Is Over'"; Guy Gugliotta, "5 Freshman Republicans Urge Foley to Release Names of Check Bouncers," *Washington Post*, September 27, 1991, A27; Smith, "From the Well of the House," 289–291, 303; one-minute speech by Jim Nussle, October 1, 1991, www.c-span.org/video/?c4368856/rep-nussle-wears-paper-bag-head.

50. Guy Gugliotta, "House Votes to Shut, Audit Bank," *Washington Post*, October 4, 1991, A1; Clifford Krauss, "Bank Overdrafts Split Republicans," *New York Times*, March 11, 1992, A17; Clifford Krauss, "Foley, in Defeat, Agrees to Naming of Check Abuses," *New York Times*, March 13, 1992, A1; Smith, "From the Well of the House," 291–292, 296, 302, 304.

51. Adam Clymer, "House Revolutionary," *New York Times Magazine*, August 23, 1992, 40; Evans and Oleszek, *Congress under Fire*, 34; Guy Gugliotta, "Taking Account of the Bank," *Washington Post*, October 7, 1991, A19; Clifford Krauss, "Gingrich Takes No Prisoners in House's Sea of Gentility," *New York Times*, March 17,

1992; Shira Toeplitz, "Santorum and Gingrich Share Complicated Past," *Roll Call*, January 26, 2012.

52. Clifford Krauss, "G.O.P. Success in House Splits Party Leadership," *New York Times*, March 20, 1992, A17. During the March debate over whether to reveal the names of lawmakers who had overdrawn checks, Michel's defense of his colleagues earned him a standing ovation, but they hissed at Gingrich when he was yielded time on the floor. Krauss, "Bank Overdrafts"; Smith, "From the Well of the House," 303; www.c-span.org/video/?24899-1/house-session, (2:53:50–2:54:10) and (4:26:40–4:26:50).

53. Clymer, "House Revolutionary," 47; Gugliotta, "Taking Account of the Bank"; Krauss, "Committee Names All Who Withdrew at the House Bank," *New York Times*, April 17, 1992, A1; Krauss, "Committee Names All"; Krauss, "G.O.P. Success."

54. Adam Clymer, "Congressmen Said to Be Dining on the House," *New York Times*, October 31, 1991, A16; "Post Office Probe Hints at Larger Scandal," *CQ Almanac 1992*, 48th ed. (Washington, DC: Congressional Quarterly, 1993), 47–51; Smith, "From the Well of the House," 290, 293.

55. *Congressional Record*, February 5, 1992, 1505, and March 12, 1992, 5549–5550; www.c-span.org/video/?24899-1/house-session (4:35:45–4:36:00).

56. A probe into the House Post Office also revealed that the Postmaster was leaking GOP-only letters to Democrats. William F. Connelly Jr. and John J. Pitney Jr., *Congress' Permanent Minority?: Republicans in the U.S. House* (Lanham, MD: Rowman & Littlefield, 1994), 88.

57. "Clinton's Win Spurs Rapid Organization," *CQ Almanac 1992*, 48th ed. (Washington, DC: Congressional Quarterly, 1993); Clymer, "House Revolutionary"; Beth Donovan, "Busy Democrats Skirt Fights to Get House in Order," *Congressional Quarterly Weekly Report*, December 12, 1992, 3777; Oleszek, *Congressional Procedure and the Policy Process*, table 4–3, 129. During debate over creation of the new administrative officer, Republicans offered an alternative proposal that would have revised chamber rules to give the minority more procedural rights. When it failed, Michel attempted to orchestrate a walkout from the floor. "The House: Approval of Administrator Creates More Rancor," *Congressional Quarterly Weekly Report*, April 11, 1992, 929.

58. See, e.g., various memoranda in Box 2683, Folder: Strategy Dinner Meetings, NLG.

59. "Unemployment Benefits Extended," *CQ Almanac 1991*, 47th ed. (Washington, DC: Congressional Quarterly, 1992), 301–310; agenda, COS Meeting, February 20, 1991 and memo to Jim Bunning from Newt Gingrich, February 20, 1991, Box 9B, Folder: COS 91, RW; letter to John Blowers from Robert Walker, October 23, 1991, Box 9B, Folder: COS 1989–96, RW.

60. "Confrontational Politics," COS Agenda, March 6, 1991; "Term Limitation

or Bold Reform: The Legislative Branch Crisis of 1991," 2, and Agendas, COS Meeting, October 16 and 23, 1991, Box 81B, Folder: COS 91, RW.

61. For instance, in May 1992 Gingrich criticized the Democratic Party's push for more funding to help urban areas on the grounds that "their basic approach is hopeless and self-destructive." "Cities Seek Help from Congress," *CQ Almanac 1992*, 48th ed. (Washington, DC: Congressional Quarterly, 1993).

62. *Congressional Record*, January 30, 1992, 915–916; "The Vision of a Republican Congress," from "The Republican Congress: A Manifesto for Change," Box Leadership #15, Folder: Leadership. 102nd. "The Republican Congress: A Manifesto for Change" (1), RHM.

63. Adam Clymer, "A G.O.P. Leader Aims at 'Welfare State' Values," *New York Times*, January 5, 1992, 19; "The Vision of a Republican Congress," from "The Republican Congress: A Manifesto for Change," 6, Box Leadership #15, Folder: Leadership. 102nd. "The Republican Congress: A Manifesto for Change" (1), RHM; "The Necessary Revolution: What Americans Must Do to Create Jobs, Prosperity and Security," December 3, 1991, Box 151, Folder: Newt Gingrich 1992, RW; "Launching the Necessary Revolution to Replace the Welfare State: An Initial Report," February 2, 1992, 2–3, Box 2629, Folder: Newt Originals, NLG.

64. Adam Clymer, "G.O.P. Announces a Welfare Policy," *New York Times*, April 29, 1992, D23; Clymer, "House Revolutionary."

65. E. J. Dionne Jr., "Conservatives Find Reason to Cheer Bush," *Washington Post*, January 31, 1991, A9; Gwen Ifill, "Conservatives Mute Criticism of Bush Domestic Policy," *Washington Post*, February 9, 1991, A4; Gary Lee, "Partisan Cross-Fire over Gulf Votes Escalates on Capitol Hill," *Washington Post*, March 11, 1991, A15.

66. Krauss, "G.O.P. Success in House"; Lucy Howard and Ned Zeman, "Bush: Blocking Newt?," *Newsweek*, March 25, 1991, 5.

67. Clift and Brazaitis, *War without Bloodshed*, 247; Rowland Evans and Robert Novak, "Gingrich: Unwelcome Messenger," *Washington Post*, June 12, 1992; Katharine Q. Seelye, "Birth of a Vision"; Steely, *The Gentleman from Georgia*, 238–241. See, for example, memo to President George Bush from Newt Gingrich, "Leadership in the Cultural Civil War," May 19, 1992, Box 151, Folder: Newt Gingrich 1992, RW.

68. Krauss, "G.O.P. Success in House"; Pianin, "Michel Enjoys."

69. Clymer, "House Revolutionary"; Linda Feldmann, "Taking Back the House," *Christian Science Monitor*, March 26, 1992, 6; Sharyn Wizda, "Gingrich-Chaired Group Plans to Return House to the GOP," *States News Service*, February 14, 1992; letter from Jeffrey Eisenach to Randolph Richardson, February 27, 1992, Select Committee on Ethics, *In the Matter of Rep. Newt Gingrich*, pt. 4, 362; "Process for a Successful America," Box 81B, Folder: COS 91, RW.

70. Nicole Asmussen Mathew and Mathew Kunz, "Recruiting, Grooming, and Reaping the Rewards: The Case of GOPAC in the 1992 Congressional Elections," *Congress & the Presidency* 44, no. 1 (2017): 77–101; Connelly and Pitney, *Congress' Permanent Minority?*, 35; Robert H. Durr, John B. Gilmour, and Christina

Wolbrecht, "Explaining Congressional Approval," *American Journal of Political Science* 41, no. 1 (January 1997): 175–207; Gallup, "Congress and the Public," https://news.gallup.com/poll/1600/congress-public.aspx; *Times Mirror* survey, March 26–29, 1992 [USPSRA.040392.R047]; *Los Angeles Times* survey, March 27–29, 1992 [USLAT.275A.R66].

71. Stephen Engelberg and Katharine Q. Seelye, "Gingrich: Man in Spotlight and Organization in Shadow," *New York Times*, December 18, 1994, 32.

72. Jeffrey H. Birnbaum, "GOP Political Action Group Draws Criticism over Slim Disbursement of Funds to Candidates," *Wall Street Journal*, June 10, 1992, A16; letter from Jeffrey Eisenach and Randolph Richardson, February 27, 1992, Select Committee on Ethics, *In the Matter of Rep. Newt Gingrich*, pt. 4, 326.

73. Linda Feldmann, "Keeping the House: Democrats Grip Seats," *Christian Science Monitor*, March 27, 1992, 2; Rohde, *Parties and Leaders*, 181; Seelye, "Birth of a Vision"; Donald R. Wolfensberger, *Congress and the People: Deliberative Democracy on Trial* (Baltimore: Johns Hopkins University Press, 2000), 149.

74. Sunil Ahuja, Staci L. Beavers, Cynthia Berreau, Anthony Dodson, Patrick Hourigan, Steven Showalter, Jeff Walz, and John R. Hibbing, "Modern Congressional Election Theory Meets the 1992 House Elections," *Political Research Quarterly* 47, no. 4 (December 1994): 909–921; Michael A. Dimock and Gary C. Jacobson, "Checks and Choices: The House Bank Scandal's Impact on Voters in 1992," *Journal of Politics* 57, no. 4 (November 1995): 1143–1159; Gary C. Jacobson and Michael A. Dimock, "Checking Out: The Effects of Bank Overdrafts on the 1992 House Elections," *American Journal of Political Science* 38, no. 3 (August 1994): 601–624. The scandal may have hurt Republicans more than Democrats. Harold D. Clarke, Frank B. Feigert, Barry J. Seldon, and Marianne C. Stewart, "More Time with My Money: Leaving the House and Going Home in 1992 and 1994," *Political Research Quarterly* 52, no. 1 (March 1999): 67–85. For a contrary view of the significance of the banking scandal on retirements, see Sean M. Theriault, "Moving up or Moving out: Career Ceilings and Congressional Retirement," *Legislative Studies Quarterly* 23, no. 3 (August 1998): 419–433.

75. Associated Press, "Oklahoma Congressman Is Loser in Race Tainted by Bank Scandal," *New York Times*, August 27, 1992, A20.

76. Steely, *The Gentleman from Georgia*, 230–237. GOPAC may have helped by paying the state GOP for computer equipment needed to draw districts favorable to Gingrich and other Georgia Republicans. Bruck, "The Politics of Perception," 64.

77. Balz and Brownstein, *Storming the Gates*, 209–240; Nelson W. Polsby, *How Congress Evolves: Social Bases of Institutional Change* (New York: Oxford University Press, 2004).

78. "Conte Died after Surgery," *CQ Almanac 1991*, 47th ed. (Washington, DC: Congressional Quarterly, 1992).

79. Douglas L. Koopman, *Hostile Takeover: The House Republican Party, 1980–1995* (Lanham, MD: Rowman & Littlefield, 1996), 51; "1993 GOPAC Political

Program, Status Report," April 26, 1993, from Select Committee on Ethics, *In the Matter of Rep. Newt Gingrich*, pt. 2, 153.

80. Jill Zuckman, "Most House Chairmen Hold On," *Congressional Quarterly Weekly Report*, December 12, 1992, 3785.

81. Jack Anderson and Michael Binstein, "Newt Gone Nuclear," *Washington Post*, April 19, 1992, C7; Balz and Brownstein, *Storming the Gates*, 148; Connelly and Pitney, *Congress' Permanent Minority?*, 57; Phil Duncan, "House GOP: No More Mr. Nice Guy?," *Congressional Quarterly Weekly Report*, February 9, 1991; Frank H. Mackaman, "Michel Calls It Quits," from *Robert H. Michel: Leading the Republican House Minority*, ed. Frank H. Mackaman and Sean Q Kelly (Lawrence: University Press of Kansas, 2019), 336; Barbara Sinclair, *Party Wars: Polarization and the Politics of National Policy Making* (Norman: University of Oklahoma Press, 2006), 120.

82. Adam Clymer, "Many Offer to Help New Lawmakers Get Acquainted with Capital's Mores," *New York Times*, November 8, 1992, 29; David Rogers, "Armey of Texas Ousts California's Lewis as Chairman of House GOP Caucus," *Wall Street Journal*, December 8, 1992, A6; A. B. Stoddard, "Livingston Takes Page from Newt Playbook," *The Hill*, March 25, 1998.

83. Clift and Brazaitis, *War without Bloodshed*, 248–249; Phil Kuntz, "Soon to Lose White House Clout, Republicans Rethink Strategy," *Congressional Quarterly Weekly Report*, November 14, 1992, 3624; Steely, *The Gentleman from Georgia*, 247.

84. Connelly and Pitney, *Congress' Permanent Minority?*, 23, 57; Holly Idelson, "PARTY UNITY: Signs Point to Greater Loyalty on Both Sides of the Aisle," *Congressional Quarterly Weekly Report*, December 19, 1992, 3849; Sinclair, *Party Wars*, 122; Smith, "From the Well of the House," 320. One political scientist estimated that Republicans who were "enterprisers" (a group that included Gingrich) and "moralists" (highly conservative lawmakers) had grown to encompass over a third of the Conference combined in the 103rd Congress. Koopman, *Hostile Takeover*, 91–105. For more on the effect of cohort on legislative voting behavior, see Jordan M. Ragusa, "Partisan Cohorts, Polarization, and the Gingrich Senators," *American Politics Research* 44, no. 2 (2015): 296–325.

85. Balz and Brownstein, *Storming the Gates*, 148–149.

86. Connelly and Pitney, *Congress' Permanent Minority?*, 26; House Republican Conference Directory, 103rd Congress, Box 56, Folder 22, RKA.

87. Resolution of the House Republican Conference offered by Mr. Gingrich, Box Staff Series, Folder: Legislative. Karen Buttaro Files. Opening Day of the 103rd. Organizational Conference (1992–93), RHM.

88. Republican Whip Organization roster, House Republican Conference Directory, 103rd Congress, Box 56, Folder 22, RKA; Whip Office Plan for 1994, Box 2604, Folder: Strategy and Planning—Dec. 97, NLG. The whip office plan also urged Gingrich to "be punctual," use "less lecturing [and] more listening," and "allow expression of warm/smiling/softer side."

89. Steve Kornacki, "Why Fred Upton Is Actually the Perfect Pick for John

Boehner and the GOP," *Salon*, August 10, 2011, www.salon.com/2011/08/10/fred_upton/; Mackaman, "Michel Calls It Quits," 336.

90. Balz and Brownstein, *Storming the Gates*, 37, 47–48; Juliet Eilperin and Jim VandeHei, "'Contract' High to Coup Low: How It Fell Apart," *Roll Call*, October 6, 1997, 1; Kuntz, "Soon to Lose White House Clout"; memo to House GOP Press Secretaries from Ed Gillespie Re: Rapid Response Team, January 26, 1993, Box 57, Folder 17, DA; interview with former Republican leader, July 20, 2020. For more on Armey, see Balz and Brownstein, *Storming the Gates*, 148–150.

91. "How to Flip the House: The 1994 Republican Revolution," podcast, *Washington Post*, June 26, 2018, www.washingtonpost.com/podcasts/can-he-do-that/1994-the-midterm-election-that-broke-bipartisanship/.

92. Balz and Brownstein, *Storming the Gates*, 167–171; Kathleen Hall Jamieson and Joseph N. Cappella, *Echo Chamber: Rush Limbaugh and the Conservative Media Establishment* (New York: Oxford University Press, 2010); Brian Rosenwald, *Talk Radio's America: How an Industry Took over a Political Party That Took over the United States* (Cambridge, MA: Harvard University Press, 2019).

93. Balz and Brownstein, *Storming the Gates*, 84; Clift and Brazaitis, *War without Bloodshed*, 249; Steven M. Gillon, *The Pact: Bill Clinton, Newt Gingrich, and the Rivalry That Defined a Generation* (New York: Oxford University Press, 2008), 109, quote p. 110.

94. Connelly and Pitney, *Congress' Permanent Minority?*, 88–89.

95. Newt Gingrich, *Lessons Learned the Hard Way: A Personal Report* (New York: HarperCollins, 1998), 30–31.

96. Memo to COS members from John Boehner Re: Response to Clinton Economic Plan, February 19, 1993, Box 157B, Folder: Spotlight—COS & Walker Folder 1, RW.

97. Connelly and Pitney, *Congress' Permanent Minority?*, 89; George Hager, "RESCISSION: Arm-Twisting Yields House Win for Spending-Control Bill," *Congressional Quarterly Weekly Report*, May 1, 1993, 1069. For more on tightening agenda control in the 103rd Congress and the early signs of Democratic disunity that may have prompted it, see Wolfensberger, *Congress and the People*, 155–56.

98. Karen Foerstel, "Republicans Unveil Strategy to Combat Restrictive Rules," *Roll Call*, April 22, 1993; letter to President Clinton from Michel, Gingrich, and Armey, March 16, 1993, Box 56, Folder 5, DA; letter to Tom Foley from Michel, Gingrich, Armey, and Hyde, March 19, 1993, Box General (17), Folder: Joint Letters, L/Msc 1993, RHM; House Democracy Project Action Plan, Republican Leadership Task Force on Deliberative Democracy in the House, April 20, 1993, Box: Legislative Series. Special Subjects 6, Folder: 103rd. Reform. Deliberative Democracy Task Force, RHM.

99. Evans, *The Whips*, 220–225; Matthew N. Green, *The Speaker of the House: A Study of Leadership* (New Haven: Yale University Press, 2010), 134–135; Steely, *The Gentleman from Georgia*, 256–257; "Coordinated Response to Reconciliation Vote,

Republican Leadership Alert!," House Republican Conference, Box 57, Folder 11, RKA; Letter to Roy Willis, May 19, 1993, Box 56, Folder 4, RKA.

100. Thomas E. Mann and Norman J. Ornstein, *The Broken Branch: How Congress Is Failing America and How to Get It Back on Track* (New York: Oxford University Press, 2006), 92.

101. Steely, *The Gentleman from Georgia*, 265.

102. David S. Cloud, "NAFTA Boosters Win in Court But Lose with Gephardt," *Congressional Quarterly Weekly Report*, September 25, 1993, 2532; Frederick W. Mayer, *Interpreting NAFTA: The Science and Art of Political Analysis* (New York: Columbia University Press, 1998), 277.

103. John R. MacArthur, *The Selling of "Free Trade": NAFTA, Washington, and the Subversion of American Democracy* (Berkeley: University of California Press, 2001), 167–168; Mayer, *Interpreting NAFTA*, 276, 290. See also various NAFTA documents in Shelly White Files, Box Staff Series. Shelly White, RHM.

104. Matthew N. Green and Douglas B. Harris, "Michel as Minority Leader: Minority Party Strategies and Tactics in the Postreform House," in Mackaman and Kelly, *Robert H. Michel*; letter to Dennis Hastert from Robert Michel, February 3, 1993, Box 56, Folder 4, RKA; House Republican Conference Directory, 103rd Congress, Box 56, Folder 22, RKA.

105. Janet Hook, "House GOP Prepares for Leadership Shuffle," *Congressional Quarterly Weekly Report*, May 16, 1987, 959.

106. Burdett A. Loomis, "Bob Michel in the Land of Giants: Relationship Politics in the 1980s," in Mackaman and Kelly, *Robert H. Michel*, 47; Mackaman, "Bob Michel Calls It Quits"; letter from Bob Michel to Newt Gingrich, November 12, 1998, Box Post-Congressional Correspondence 1998, Folder: Post-Cong. Subjects, Gingrich, Newt, RHM.

107. Jeanne Ponessa, "Fate of Select Panels in Doubt after House Rejects One," *Congressional Quarterly Weekly Report*, January 30, 1993, 207; "House Republicans Manage to Win One despite Themselves," *Washington Times*, February 7, 1993, from Box 55, Folder 23, RKA; Mackaman, "Michel Calls It Quits," 341–342.

108. Bruck, "The Politics of Perception," 66; "House Republicans Manage to Win One"; Juliet Eilperin and Jim VandeHei, "GOP Intrigue Is Old Hat to This Ex-Michel Aide," *Roll Call*, July 24, 1997; Janet Hook, "House GOP Hones a Sharper Edge as Michel Turns In His Sword," *Congressional Quarterly Weekly Report*, October 9, 1993, 2714; Ray LaHood with Frank H. Mackaman, *Seeking Bipartisanship: My Life in Politics* (Amherst, NY: Cambria, 2015), 18; Mackaman, "Michel Calls It Quits," 336. Gingrich admitted behind the scenes that he was at least prepared to run against Michel. Charles Fenyvesi, "Succession Scramble," *U.S. News & World Report*, October 4, 1993, 32; Steely, *The Gentleman from Georgia*, 265.

109. Connelly and Pitney, *Congress' Permanent Minority?*, 58–59; Janet Hook, "Gingrich Apparently Locks Up Race for Minority Leader," *Congressional Quarterly Weekly Report*, October 16, 1993; Susan Molinari with Elinor Burkett, *Representative*

Mom: Balancing Budgets, Bill and Baby in the U.S. Congress (New York: Doubleday, 1998), 111; Stoddard, "Livingston Takes Page from Newt Playbook"; Mackaman, "Michel Calls It Quits," 344–345; statement of Newt Gingrich, October 7, 1993, Box General (17), Folder: Joint Letters, L/Msc 1993, RHM. Michel expressed some bitterness about Gingrich's eagerness to replace him. In a none-too-subtle reference to the Georgia congressman, he later recalled that in his congressional career, "I didn't have to claw my way up the [leadership] ladder and stomp over people." Mackaman, "Michel Calls It Quits," 346.

110. Quoted in Thomas F. Schaller, *The Stronghold: How Republicans Captured Congress but Surrendered the White House* (New Haven: Yale University Press, 2015), 84.

111. Balz and Brownstein, *Storming the Gates,* 150–151; Clift and Brazaitis, *War without Bloodshed,* 250; Congress of Tomorrow, Salisbury State University, January 27, 1994, 3–4, Frank Luntz, "From Minority to Majority: A Strategy for the Republican House Leadership," January 27, 1994, 36, Planning and Learning Team Memo from Jerry Climer, April 19, 1994, and memo from Newt, January 29, 1994, Box 2629, Folder: Planning/Strategy Memos, NLG.

112. *Catalyst* 1, no. 1 (Spring 1994); and "Dear Friend" letter, April 1994, Box 57, Folder 11, DA.

113. Haynes Johnson and David S. Broder, *The System: The American Way of Politics at the Breaking Point* (Boston: Little, Brown, 1997), 187; letter to Bill Clinton, October 1, 1993, Box 16, Folder: Leadership. 103rd. Joint Letters. 10/1/93: Health Care Reform, RHM.

114. Clift and Brazaitis, *War without Bloodshed,* 252–253; Gillon, *The Pact,* 116–117; Johnson and Broder, *The System,* 11, 270, 275, 301–304, 547; Smith, "From the Well of the House," 352–353.

115. Johnson and Broder, *The System,* 327–28; House Republican Conference Directory, 103rd Congress, 6, Box 56, Folder 22, DA. Gingrich was, however, given a subcommittee chairmanship within the party's task force. "Republican Leaders' Task Force on Health, Subgroup Membership," Box 112B, Folder: Task Force on Health 1993, RW.

116. Johnson and Broder, *The System,* 270–272, 275–276, 364–365, 547; Smith, "From the Well of the House," 348, 350–351, 360; letter to Ira Magaziner from Dick Armey, October 13, 1993, Box 56, Folder 5, RKA.

117. Balz and Brownstein, *Storming the Gates,* 249–253; Johnson and Broder, *The System,* 233–234; Smith, "From the Well of the House," 351–52.

118. David S. Broder, "Gingrich Takes 'No-Compromise' Stand on Health Care Plan," *Washington Post,* December 15, 1993, A11; Johnson and Broder, *The System,* 426, 466; Cathie Jo Martin, "Inviting Business to the Party: The Corporate Response to Social Policy," in *The Social Divide: Political Parties and the Future of Activist Government,* ed. Margaret Weir (Washington, DC: Brookings Institution Press, 1998), 253; Smith, "From the Well of the House," 359–60; Steely, *The Gentleman*

from Georgia, 258; letter to Robert Andrews from Michel, Gingrich, and Armey, February 18, 1994, and Dear COS Member letter from John Boehner, February 28, 1994, Box 9B, Folder COS 1989–96, RW.

119. Balz and Brownstein, *Storming the Gates*, 196; Clift and Brazaitis, *War without Bloodshed*, 254–255; Johnson and Broder, *The System*, 485–486; Steely, *The Gentleman from Georgia*, 263. Sen. Majority Leader George Mitchell (D-ME) claimed that he abandoned health care reform in his chamber when Gingrich threatened to kill the General Agreement on Tariffs and Trade if he did not. George Hager, "The Gingrich Ascendancy," *Congressional Quarterly Weekly Report*, October 8, 1994, 2848.

120. Kenneth J. Cooper and Kevin Merida, "House Democrats Say Fate in Midterm Races Is Tied to Clinton Agenda," *Washington Post*, January 29, 1994, A10; David E. Rosenbaum, "A Republican Who Sees Himself as a Revolutionary on the Verge of Victory," *New York Times*, July 24, 1994, 22.

121. Balz and Brownstein, *Storming the Gates*, 46; Hager, "The Gingrich Ascendancy"; "Lobbying Disclosure Bill Dies," *CQ Almanac 1994*, 50th ed. (Washington, DC: Congressional Quarterly, 1995), 36–42; Ronald G. Shaiko, "Lobby Reform: Curing the Mischiefs of Factions?," in *Remaking Congress: Change and Stability in the 1990s*, ed. James A. Thurber and Roger H. Davidson (Washington, DC: CQ Press, 1995); Steely, *The Gentleman from Georgia*, 267. When a modified crime bill passed with Republican votes, donations to the RNC declined. Balz and Brownstein, *Storming the Gates*, 195.

122. GOPAC Report to Shareholders, April 26, 1993, Select Committee on Ethics, *In the Matter of Rep. Newt Gingrich*, pt. 2, 150.

123. Bruck, "The Politics of Perception," 67; Jeanne Cummings, "Donors' Names Kept Secret," *Atlanta Journal and Constitution*, August 19, 1994; Engelberg and Seelye, "Gingrich: Man in Spotlight and Organization in Shadow," 32; "Gingrich's Contributors Include Who's Who of Wealthy, Powerful," *Chicago Tribune*, August 21, 1994, from Subgroup: Speechwriting, Series: Michael Waldman, Folder: To Read: Gingrich and Lobbyists, WJC.

124. Balz and Brownstein, *Storming the Gates*, 48–49; James Gimpel, *Legislating the Revolution: The Contract with America in Its First 100 Days* (Boston: Allyn and Bacon, 1996), 9–11; Katharine Q. Seelye, "With Fiery Words, Gingrich Builds His Kingdom," *New York Times*, October 27, 1994; Glenn R. Simpson, "Republicans Step Up Pressure on PACs as November Gains Look More Certain," *Roll Call*, October 6, 1994; Steely, *The Gentleman from Georgia*, 267–268; interview with former Republican leader, July 20, 2020.

125. Cooper and Merida, "House Democrats Say Fate in Midterm Races Is Tied to Clinton Agenda"; Steely, *The Gentleman from Georgia*, 273.

126. Balz and Brownstein, *Storming the Gates*, 22–26; Johnson and Broder, *The System*, 463; Ronald G. Shafer, "Washington Wire," *Wall Street Journal*, July 15, 1994; Steely, *The Gentleman from Georgia*, 273. In June 1994, Gingrich told a breakfast

audience that the GOP would win between fifteen and sixty-five House seats and between three and seven Senate seats. Memo from Donna Ledder, Jack Pope and Kerry Perkins to the News Media, June 21, 1994, Box 2142, Folder: Newt's Floor Speeches Health Care, NLG.

127. Interview with former Republican leadership aide, April 11, 2019.

128. Alison Mitchell, "Gingrich's Views on Slayings Draw Fire," *New York Times*, November 23, 1995; Claire Hopson Procopio, "A Brave Newt World?: Republican Campaign Strategies in the 1994 Congressional Elections" (PhD diss., Indiana University, 1999), 36–40; Cover of *Time*, November 7, 1994.

129. Newt's Easel Sheets, 2, December 18, 1992, Select Committee on Ethics, *In the Matter of Rep. Newt Gingrich*, pt. 4, 400 and part 9, 415. See also Daniel J. Balz and Charles Babcock, "Mr. Speaker: The Rise of Newt Gingrich: Gingrich, Allies Made Waves and Impression; Conservative Rebels Harassed the House," *Washington Post*, December 20, 1994; Gillon, *The Pact*, 126; Planning Assumptions for 1994, Box 2604, Folder: Strategy and Planning—Dec. '97, NLG; A Centrist Revolution for 1994–2000, Box 2629, Folder: Newt Originals, NLG; *Congressional Record*, January 25, 1993, 1107–1114.

130. Engelberg and Seelye, "Gingrich: Man in Spotlight and Organization in Shadow"; Steely, *The Gentleman from Georgia*, 250–253.

131. Charles Babcock, "PAC Ties to Gingrich Class Questioned," *Washington Post*, September 9, 1993, A1; Engelberg and Seelye, "Gingrich: Man in Spotlight and Organization in Shadow"; Steely, *The Gentleman from Georgia*, 248, 250–253; Select Committee on Ethics, *In the Matter of Rep. Newt Gingrich*, pt. 1, 4–5, 45–46.

132. Green, *Underdog Politics*, 60; David Mayhew, *America's Congress: Actions in the Public Sphere, James Madison through Newt Gingrich* (New Haven: Yale University Press, 2002), 236–238; Steely, *The Gentleman from Georgia*, 109. See also chapters 2 and 3.

133. John B. Bader, *Taking the Initiative: Leadership Agendas in Congress and the "Contract with America"* (Washington, DC: Georgetown University Press, 1996); Balz and Brownstein, *Storming the Gates*, 37; Bruck, "The Politics of Perception," 69.

134. Steely, *The Gentleman from Georgia*, 255; House Republican Focus for 1994, 2, Box 2629, Folder: Planning/Strategy Memos, NLG.

135. Renewing American Civilization, October 15, 1993, Box 2629, Folder: Newt Originals, NLG; House Republican Focus for 1994, 2, Box 2629, Folder: Planning/Strategy Memos, NLG; Whip Office Plan for 1994, 3, Box 2604, Folder: Strategy and Planning—Dec. 97, NLG.

136. The choice of one hundred days echoed the bold start of President Franklin Delano Roosevelt's first administration, and Gingrich later claimed it kept Republicans from making time-consuming compromises with Democrats in the 104th Congress. Gingrich initially proposed twenty items to be enacted in just ninety days, but revised the plan following complaints that it was too unrealistic. Balz and Brownstein, *Storming the Gates*, 38–39; Donna Cassata, "Swift Progress of 'Contract'

Inspires Awe and Concern," *Congressional Quarterly Weekly Report*, April 1, 1995, 910; Lou Dubose and Jan Reid, *The Hammer: Tom DeLay, God, Money, and the Rise of the Republican Congress* (New York: Public Affairs, 2004), 89–90; House Republican Focus for 1994, 2, Box 2629, Folder: Planning/Strategy Memos, NLG.

137. Daniel Stid, "Transformational Leadership in Congress?," prepared for delivery at the Annual Meeting of the American Political Science Association, San Francisco (1996), 6.

138. Interview with Betsy Wright Hawkings, Chief of Staff, Rep. Chris Shays, April 18, 2016, 35–36, Oral History Transcripts, Office of the Historian, US House of Representatives, https://history.house.gov/Oral-History/Transcripts/Index/.

139. Balz and Brownstein, *Storming the Gates*, 40–42; Steely, *The Gentleman from Georgia*, 268; Stid, "Transformational Leadership in Congress?," 6–7.

140. Bruck, "The Politics of Perception," 69–70; Steely, *The Gentleman from Georgia*, 268; memo for John Boehner et al. from Jerry Climer, April 19, 1994, Box 2629, NLG.

141. Clift and Brazaitis, *War without Bloodshed*, 251; interview with former Republican leadership aide, April 11, 2019; letter to Newt (Gingrich) from Frank (Luntz), 2, undated, Box 2608, Folder: Memos From Your Binder and Bag for Your Review, NLG.

142. Bader, *Taking the Initiative*, 172–173; Balz and Brownstein, *Storming the Gates*, 39–40, 42, 199; Trent Lott, *Herding Cats: A Life in Politics* (New York: HarperCollins, 2005), 127; Reid Wilson, "Consequential GOP Class of 1994 All but Disappears," *The Hill*, September 24, 2019.

143. Katherine Q. Seelye, "Voters Disgusted with Politicians as Election Nears," *New York Times*, November 3, 1994, A1.

144. Balz and Brownstein, *Storming the Gates*, 51–52; "Excerpts From Clinton's News Conference on His Programs," *New York Times*, October 8, 1994, A15; memo to Democratic Members from Gephardt Re: Message For the Fall Campaign: Making Our Case, October 12, 1994, 5–6, Series 7, Subseries 30 (O'Brien), Box 847, Folder 12, RAG.

145. Balz and Brownstein, *Storming the Gates*, 52; Steely, *The Gentleman from Georgia*, 274; "Contract with America Red Book," September 1994, Box 1977, NLG; memo to Interested Parties, October 24, 1994, Box 56, Folder 6, RKA.

146. Daniel J. Balz, "Vote '94: Democrats Agree They'll Lose Seats—Worry Is, How Many?," *Washington Post*, September 8, 1994, A1; Bill Clinton, *My Life* (New York: Knopf, 2004), 631; E. J. Dionne, "The Not-So-Inevitable GOP Landslide," *Washington Post*, October 4, 1994, A7; Gingrich Attack Pack—Update, Series 7, Subseries 35 (Staff Files), Box 918, Folder 6, RAG; memo to Democratic Members from Gephardt Re: Message For the Fall Campaign: Making Our Case, October 12, 1994, 2, Series 7, Subseries 30 (O'Brien), Box 847, Folder 12, RAG; memo to Michael Waldman from Dan Collins, October 6, 1994, Subgroup: Speechwriting, Series: Michael Waldman, Folder: To Read: Gingrich and Lobbyists, WJC.

147. David Broder, "GOP Poised to Grab Control of Senate," *Washington Post*, November 6, 1994, A1; Charles O. Jones, *Clinton and Congress, 1993–1996: Risk, Restoration, and Reelection* (Norman: University of Oklahoma Press, 1999), 96. The *Washington Post* surveyed fourteen pollsters, correspondents, and election experts in late 1994; only three predicted a GOP House, and all three underestimated the number of seats Republicans would win. David S. Broder, "Naked Punditry," *Washington Post*, November 6, 1994, C1.

148. LaHood, *Seeking Bipartisanship*, 16; Linda Douglass interview with Tom DeLay, pt. 1, John Brademas Center, New York University, July 19, 2006, www.nyu.edu/content/dam/nyu/brademasCenter/documents/Research/transcript_delay.pdf.

149. Johnson and Broder, *The System*, 552; William Safire, "No Nyah-Nyah," *New York Times*, October 10, 1994, A35; *Time*, November 21, 1994; "Republicans Sweep Both Houses," *National Journal's Congress Daily*, November 9, 1994; Richard Sammon, "Republican Takeover Brings Sea Change to Capitol," *Congressional Monitor*, November 10, 1994, 3.

150. Mann and Ornstein, *The Broken Branch*, 97.

151. Former Rep. Barney Frank (D-MA) makes this same point in his autobiography. Barney Frank, *Frank: A Life in Politics from the Great Society to Same-Sex Marriage* (New York: Farrar, Straus and Giroux, 2015), 177.

152. Gerald F. Seib and Dennis Farney, "GOP Conservatives, after 8 Years in Ascendancy, Brood over Lost Opportunities, Illusory Victories," *Wall Street Journal*, August 17, 1988, 44.

Chapter 5. Promise and Pitfalls (1995–1996)

1. Dan Balz and Ronald Brownstein, *Storming the Gates* (Boston: Little, Brown, 1996), 114–116.

2. Elizabeth Drew, *Showdown: The Struggle between the Gingrich Congress and the Clinton White House* (New York: Simon & Schuster, 1996), 26.

3. Herbert F. Weisberg and Samuel C. Patterson, "Theatre in the Round: Congress in Action," in *Great Theatre: The American Congress in the 1990s*, ed. Herbert F. Weisberg and Samuel C. Patterson (New York: Cambridge University Press, 1998), 9.

4. Newt Gingrich, *Lessons Learned the Hard Way: A Personal Report* (New York: HarperCollins, 1998), 37; see also Randall Strahan, *Leading Representatives: The Agency of Leaders in the Politics of the U.S. House* (Baltimore: Johns Hopkins University Press, 2007), 142.

5. Samuel C. Patterson and David C. Kimball, "Unsympathetic Audience: Citizens' Evaluations of Congress," in Weisberg and Patterson, *Great Theatre*, 80.

6. Former Vice Chair of the Republican Conference Susan Molinari (R-NY) writes in her memoir that Gingrich's "vision of our regaining the majority, a possibility most people never took seriously, was like a magnet." See Susan Molinari

with Elinor Burkett, *Representative Mom: Balancing Budgets, Bill, and Baby in the U.S. Congress* (New York: Doubleday, 1998), 173. Senator Lindsey Graham (R-SC), who had served with Gingrich in the House earlier in his career, was quoted in 2011 as saying that Gingrich could both "bring us together and alienate the hell out of us." Sheryl Gay Stolberg, "For Gingrich in Power, Pragmatism, Not Purity," *New York Times*, December 20, 2011.

7. James A. Thurber, "Remaking Congress after the Electoral Earthquake of 1994," in *Remaking Congress: Change and Stability in the 1990s*, ed. James A. Thurber and Roger H. Davidson (Washington, DC: CQ Press, 1995), 5; Balz and Brownstein, *Storming the Gates*, 148; Eleanor Clift and Tom Brazaitis, *War without Bloodshed: The Art of Politics* (New York: Scribner, 1996), 262; Katharine Q. Seelye, "Birth of a Vision: Files Show How Gingrich Laid a Grand G.O.P. Plan" *New York Times*, December 3, 1995; Daniel Stid, "Transformational Leadership in Congress?," prepared for delivery at the Annual Meeting of the American Political Science Association, San Francisco (1996), 4.

8. John H. Aldrich and David W. Rohde, "The Transition to Republican Rule in the House: Implications for Theories of Congressional Politics," *Political Science Quarterly* 112, no. 4 (1997–1998): 541–567; Strahan, *Leading Representatives*, 151; John E. Owens, "The Return of Party Government in the U.S. House of Representatives: Central Leadership-Committee Relations in the 104th Congress," *British Journal of Political Science* 27, no. 2 (April 1997): 263–264; Randall Strahan and Daniel J. Palazzolo, "The Gingrich Effect," *Political Science Quarterly* 19, no. 1 (Spring 2004): 101; Mel Steely, *The Gentleman from Georgia: The Biography of Newt Gingrich* (Macon, GA: Mercer University Press, 2000), 282. Interestingly, Republicans more distant ideologically from Gingrich were more likely to quit the chamber. Kristin Kanthak, "The Hidden Effects of Rules Not Broken: Career Paths, Institutional Rules and Anticipatory Exit in Legislatures," *British Journal of Political Science* 41, no. 4 (October 2011): 841–857.

9. Owens, "The Return of Party Government," 263; Gingrich compared the job of Speaker to being a head coach and admitted it is "much harder work than I thought [it would be]" in an interview with Charlie Rose. Interview with Charlie Rose on July 6, 1995, https://charlierose.com/videos/23715.

10. Timothy J. Burger, "The Inner Circles: His Closest Advisers," *Roll Call*, January 23, 1995; Steely, *The Gentleman from Georgia*, 297.

11. Stephen Engelberg and Katharine Q. Seelye, "Gingrich: Man in Spotlight and Organization in Shadow," *New York Times*, December 18, 1994, 1; Ronald M. Peters Jr., "The Republican Speakership," prepared for delivery at the 1996 American Political Science Association Annual Meeting, from Box 164A, 1996 Misc. Files, Folder: Republican Leadership 1996 (Republican Strategic Plan for '96), RW.

12. "New House Speaker Envisions Cooperation, Cuts, Hard Work." *CQ Weekly*, November 12, 1994, 3296.

13. "House GOP Freshmen Orientation: Leadership for America's 21st Century," November 30, 1994, Box 1976, Folder: GOP Freshman Orientation Handout, NLG. According to the handout, those "five great truths" were: (1) society must adapt to the "information revolution," which Gingrich saw as "the third great wave of change in human history," following previous waves of "agriculture" and "industry," (2) American children will have to distinguish themselves professionally in a "world market," (3) the "welfare state has failed," (4) citizens feel estranged from their government, and (5) "an opportunity society" will reinvest power in individuals, informal groups, and the private sector ahead of government.

14. Connie Bruck, "The Politics of Perception," *New Yorker*, October 9, 1995, 62; 69; Gingrich address to the Washington Research Symposium, November 11, 1994, reprinted in *CQ Weekly Report*, November 12, 1994.

15. Peters, "The Republican Speakership," 8; "Language of the New Majority Communication Check List," Box 2601, Folder: Strategy and Planning 1996, NLG.

16. Bill Clinton, *My Life* (New York: Knopf, 2004), 629, 632. Rep. Harold Volkmer (D-MO) observed in an interview, "This was the first time I was ever in the minority—it wasn't any fun." He viewed his role in Congress as trying to pass laws to aid his constituents, "it wasn't to stymie stuff—it was to do things." Interview with Harold Volkmer, December 11, 2008.

17. Matthew N. Green, *Underdog Politics: The Minority Party in the U.S. House of Representatives* (New Haven: Yale University Press, 2015), 26.

18. Drew, *Showdown*, 46–47; Gingrich, *Lessons Learned*, 36.

19. Speech to the Cosmetic, Toiletry, and Fragrance Association, New York City, November 30, 1994, Box Speeches and Trips Series 1956–1994. Folder: Speech and Trips 1994 Nov 30, RHM. Special thanks to Frank Mackaman of the Dirksen Congressional Center for providing this reference.

20. Peter Applebome, "Gingrich Gives Up $4 Million Advance on His Book Deal," *New York Times*, December 31, 1994; Samuel C. Patterson and Herbert F. Weisberg, "'The Play's the Thing': Congress and the Future," in Weisberg and Patterson, *Great Theatre*, 279; David Streitfeld and Charles R. Babcock, "Gingrich $4.5 Million Book Deal Draws Fire," *Washington Post*, December 23, 1994.

21. See, e.g., Kenneth J. Cooper, "House Back to Normal: Fractious: Fight Over Criticism of Speaker Ends GOP Honeymoon," *Washington Post*, January 19, 1995; Tim Curran, "Book Deal Sparks Nasty Floor Brawl," *Roll Call*, January 19, 1995; Tim Curran, "Gingrich Deal Goes to Ethics," *Roll Call*, January 26, 1995.

22. Drew, *Showdown*, 14; Richard F. Fenno Jr., *Learning to Govern: An Institutional View of the 104th Congress* (Washington, DC: Brookings Institution Press, 1997); Tim Groseclose and David C. King, "Little Theatre: Committees in Congress," in Weisberg and Patterson, *Great Theatre*, 145. Gingrich's concern for language was also reflected in a letter from May 30, 1995, by famed economist Milton Friedman to Dick Armey, which asked, "Why have the Republicans fallen for the

Democratic rhetoric?" and instead encouraged "stressing the gains to the bulk from taking away privileges for the few." Box 46, Folder 10, Series 12, RKA.

23. Clinton, *My Life*, 621–22; Gingrich, *Lessons Learned*, 10, 55; Haynes Johnson and David S. Broder, *The System: The American Way of Politics at the Breaking Point* (Boston: Little, Brown, 1996), 564–65; Gingrich address to the Washington Research Symposium, November 11, 1994, reprinted in *CQ Weekly Report*, November 12, 1994, 3295; Dear Republican Colleague letter from Newt Gingrich, June 8, 1983, 2, Box 458, Folder 22, NLG.

24. Steely, *The Gentleman from Georgia*, 294. For more on the importance of party size, see Steven S. Smith, *Party Influence in Congress* (New York: Cambridge University Press, 2007).

25. Johnson and Broder, *The System*, 565. According to one study, "almost 55 percent of House freshmen were under 45 years of age, and only about 53 percent declared to have previously held an elected office, versus 70 percent of returning incumbents." Quote from Norman J. Ornstein and Amy L. Schenkenberg, "The 1995 Congress: The First Hundred Days and Beyond," *Political Science Quarterly* 110, no. 2 (1995): 188.

26. Lou Dubose and Jan Reid, *The Hammer: Tom DeLay, God, Money, and the Rise of the Republican Congress* (New York, NY: PublicAffairs, 2004), 65, 88; Matthew N. Green and Douglas B. Harris, *Choosing the Leader: Leadership Elections in the U.S. House of Representatives* (New Haven: Yale University Press, 2019); Linda Killian, *The Freshmen: What Happened to the Republican Revolution?* (Boulder, CO: Westview, 1998), 27, 71; Thomas E. Mann and Norman J. Ornstein, *The Broken Branch: How Congress Is Failing America and How to Get It Back on Track* (New York: Oxford University, 2006), 104–105.

27. Quoted in Steven M. Gillon, *The Pact: Bill Clinton, Newt Gingrich, and the Rivalry That Defined a Generation* (New York: Oxford University Press, 2008), 143.

28. Gingrich, *Lessons Learned*, 103, 111; Steely, *The Gentleman from Georgia*, 277, 284, 286; Karen Tumulty, "Gingrich: At Long Last, Power" *Los Angeles Times*, October 3, 1994; "Newt: Seven Things to Remember about the New Republican Speaker," DNC Research (Draft), December 1, 1994, Box: Communications, Don Baer, Folder: Gingrich '94 Midterms, WJC; interview with former Republican leader, July 22, 2020.

29. C. Lawrence Evans and Walter J. Oleszek, *Congress under Fire: Reform Politics and the Republican Majority* (Boston: Houghton Mifflin, 1997), 1–2, 84; Nicol C. Rae, *Conservative Reformers: The Republican Freshmen and the Lessons of the 104th Congress* (Armonk, NY: M. E. Sharpe, 1998), 68. For a full list and discussion of the institutional reforms instituted by the new Republican Congress, see Roger H. Davidson, "Building a Republican Regime on Capitol Hill," in the December 1995 issue of *Extension of Remarks*, Lawrence C. Dodd, ed., from Gingrich File, 1994–1995, RP; Roger H. Davidson, "Congressional Committees in the New Reform Era: From

Combat to the Contract," in Thurber and Davidson, *Remaking Congress*, 28–52; and Evans and Oleszek, *Congress under Fire*.

30. There is an abundance of scholarship on this subject. See, e.g., Evans and Oleszek, *Congress under Fire*; Mann and Ornstein, *The Broken Branch*; David W. Rohde, *Parties and Leaders in the Postreform House* (Chicago: University of Chicago Press, 1991); Eric Schickler, *Disjointed Pluralism: Institutional Innovation and the Development of the U.S. Congress* (Princeton: Princeton University Press, 2001); and Barbara Sinclair, *Party Wars: Polarization and the Politics of National Policy Making* (Norman: University of Oklahoma Press, 2006).

31. David S. Cloud, "Audit Uncovers Financial Chaos in Chamber's Record-Keeping," *CQ Weekly Report*, July 22, 1995, 2140; Evans and Oleszek, *Congress under Fire*, 107–8; Ruth Bloch Rubin, *Building the Bloc: Intraparty Organization in the U.S. Congress* (New York: Cambridge University Press, 2017), 278–279; Jathan Sadowski, "The Much-Needed and Sane Congressional Office That Gingrich Killed Off and We Need Back," *Atlantic*, October 26, 2012; see also Peters, "The Republican Speakership," 8.

32. Evans and Oleszek, *Congress under Fire*, 84, 91–101, 107; Owens, "The Return of Party Government," 247–272; Peters, "The Republican Speakership," 7; Rae, *Conservative Reformers*, 68–69; Strahan, *Leading Representatives*, 151; Donald R. Wolfensberger, *Congress & the People: Deliberative Democracy on Trial* (Baltimore: Johns Hopkins University Press, 2000), 181.

33. Evans and Oleszek, *Congress under Fire*, 90–91; Scott R. Meinke, *Leadership Organizations in the House of Representatives: Party Participation and Partisan Politics* (Ann Arbor: University of Michigan Press, 2016), 106; Rae, *Conservative Reformers*, 70; Sinclair, *Party Wars*, 124–125; Strahan, *Leading Representatives*, 150; Dear Colleague letter, November 21, 1994, Box 2597, Folder: Transition for 104th, NLG.

34. John H. Aldrich and David W. Rohde, "Conditional Party Government Revisited: Majority Party Leadership and the Committee System in the 104th Congress," *Extension of Remarks*, December 1995, Carl Albert Center, from Gingrich Series, RP; Timothy J. Burger, "New Plan: Govern by Task Force," *Roll Call*, January 23, 1995; Evans and Oleszek, *Congress under Fire*, 88–89; Guy Gugliotta, "Democrats Protest as Republicans Shrink Hill Committees," *Washington Post*, December 10, 1994; Paul S. Herrnson, "Directing 535 Leading Men and Leading Ladies," in Weisberg and Patterson, *Great Theatre*, 117; Deborah Kalb, "The Official Gingrich Task Force List," *Hill*, March 29, 1995; Killian, *The Freshmen*, 11–12; Norman J. Ornstein, "Is Speaker Gingrich Plotting to Overthrow the Committee System?," *Roll Call*, November 9, 1995, from Gingrich File, 1994–1995, RP; Sinclair, *Party Wars*, 125–126; Strahan, *Leading Representatives*, 149–150.

35. See generally Douglas B. Harris, "The Rise of the Public Speakership," *Political Science Quarterly* 113, no. 2 (Summer 1998): 193–212.

36. Harris, "The Rise of the Public Speakership," 202. Gingrich, a fan of

conservative radio, even provided some conservative "radio talk show hosts [with] space in the Capitol for the first time ever." See Norman J. Ornstein and Amy L. Schenkenberg, "Congress Bashing: External Pressures for Reform and the Future of the Institution," in Thurber and Davidson, *Remaking Congress*, 125; Bruck, "The Politics of Perception," 70; Stephen Frantzich and John Sullivan, *The C-SPAN Revolution* (Norman: University of Oklahoma Press, 1996), 339–340; "Lessons of the 1980 Reagan Campaign," Box 2601, Folder: Strategy and Planning 1996, NLG.

37. "As Elections Loom, GOP Ardor Gives Way to Pragmatism," *CQ Almanac* 1996, 52nd ed. (Washington, DC: Congressional Quarterly, 1997), 1-3–1-14; Frantzich and Sullivan, *The C-SPAN Revolution*, 339–340; Harris, "The Rise of the Public Speakership," 209; Herrnson, "Directing 535 Leading Men and Leading Ladies," 129.

38. "104th Congress Ushers in New Era of GOP Rule," *CQ Almanac* 1995, 51st ed. (Washington, DC: Congressional Quarterly, 1996), 1-3–1-15; "Congress Brought under Labor Laws," *CQ Almanac* 1995, 51st ed. (Washington, DC: Congressional Quarterly, 1996), 1-31–1-35.

39. See our discussion in chapter 4 of Frank Luntz and items to be included in the Contract.

40. "GOP's 'Contract with America,'" *CQ Almanac* 1994, 50th ed. (Washington, DC: Congressional Quarterly, 1995), 22–26; Norman J. Ornstein, "Next Hundred Days: Handicapping How the GOP's Ambitious Agenda Will Fare," *Roll Call*, January 9, 1995.

41. Herbert F. Weisberg and Samuel C. Patterson, "Theatre in the Round: Congress in Action," in Weisberg and Patterson, *Great Theatre*, 15. One Republican member later referred to this period of intense work as the "one hundred day death march." Interview from July 20, 2020.

42. Owens, "The Return of Party Government," 259.

43. "GOP's 'Contract with America,'" *CQ Almanac* 1994, 50th ed. (Washington, DC: Congressional Quarterly, 1995), 22–26. For more on the content of the Contract, see Ed Gillespie and Bob Schellhas, eds., *Contract with America: The Bold Plan by Rep. Newt Gingrich, Rep. Dick Armey and the House Republicans to Change the Nation* (New York: Times Books, 1994), 9–11.

44. "104th Congress Ushers in New Era of GOP Rule," *CQ Almanac* 1995, 51st ed. (Washington, DC: Congressional Quarterly, 1996), 1-3–1-15; "Budget Amendment Sinks in Senate," *CQ Almanac*, 51st ed. (Washington, DC: Congressional Quarterly, 1996), 2-34–2-40; Matthew N. Green, *The Speaker of the House: A Study of Leadership* (New Haven: Yale University Press, 2010), 150–152; Killian, *The Freshmen*, 30; "Few Lawmakers Grieve as Supreme Court Justices Give Line-Item Veto the Ax," *CQ Almanac* 1998, 54th ed. (Washington, DC: Congressional Quarterly, 1999), 6-17–6-23.

45. Marcia Gelbart, "Contract Watch," *Hill*, February 15, 1995; Sinclair, *Party*

Wars, 128; Strahan, *Leading Representatives*, 153. To mark a successful vote on a Contract item, Gingrich would punch a hole through a laminated card listing the promises of the Contract. Interview with Republican staffer, March 14, 2003.

46. Johnson and Broder, *The System*, 567–69; Molinari and Burkett, *Representative Mom*, 181; letter to Dick Armey from Frank Wolf, February 23, 1995, Box 55, Folder 7, DA.

47. Stid, "Transformational Leadership in Congress?," 7–8. To Charles O. Jones, the Republicans' ability to successfully fulfill their promise on the Contract items within one hundred days also "had the effect of crystallizing and focusing accountability, shifting it from the White House to Capitol Hill." Charles O. Jones, *Clinton & Congress, 1993–1996: Risk, Restoration and Reelection* (Norman: University of Oklahoma Press, 1999), 95.

48. "Term Limits Amendment Falls Short," *CQ Almanac* 1995, 51st ed. (Washington, DC: Congressional Quarterly, 1996), 1-35–1-38; Killian, *The Freshmen*, 48.

49. Green, *The Speaker of the House*, 152–154; Strahan, *Leading Representatives*, 161–163.

50. R. W. Apple Jr., "Tax-Cutters and the '96 Election," *New York Times*, April 7, 1995; "House Gets Early Start on Tax Bill," *CQ Almanac* 1995, 51st ed. (Washington, DC: Congressional Quarterly, 1996), 2-71–2-73; David R. Mayhew, "The Contract: Newt's Mandate?," *Roll Call*, January 9, 1995.

51. Susan Molinari later observed that "it was a time to celebrate, but no one had the energy. We were relieved to be done . . . but we could do nothing more than go home and sleep." See Molinari and Burkett, *Representative Mom*, 185; Francis X. Clines, "At Capitol Rally, G.O.P. Lawmakers Applaud Themselves and Their Work," *New York Times*, April 8, 1995.

52. Katharine Q. Seelye, "Speaker, Celebrating 100 Days, Pledges to 'Remake Government,'" *New York Times*, April 8, 1995.

53. Rae, *Conservative Reformers*, 81.

54. PL 104–132; "Anti-Terrorism Provisions," *CQ Almanac* 1996, 52nd ed. (Washington, DC: Congressional Quarterly, 1997), 5-24–5-25.

55. "Taxpayer Relief Act of 1997," 105th Congress (1997–1998). PL 105–34; and the "Small Business Job Protection Act of 1996," PL 104–188. 104th Congress (1995–1996), www.govinfo.gov/app/details/PLAW-104publ188.

56. "Foreign Adoption and Child Pornography Bills Clear Congress," *CQ Almanac* 1995, 51st ed. (Washington, DC: Congressional Quarterly, 1996), 6-29–6-33; PL 104–71.

57. "The Health Insurance Portability and Accountability Act of 1996," PL 104–191. 104th Congress (1995–1996); "Social Security Recipients Get Earnings Limit Increase," *CQ Almanac* 1996, 52nd ed. (Washington, DC: Congressional Quarterly, 1997), 6–26; PL 104–121, "Contract with America Advancement Act of 1996," 104th Congress (1995–1996), www.congress.gov/bill/104th-congress/house-bill/3136.

58. PL 105–34, August 5, 1997.

59. "Law Restricts Unfunded Mandates," *CQ Almanac* 1995, 51st ed. (Washington, DC: Congressional Quarterly, 1996), 3-15–3-20. The law was PL 104–4.

60. "Republicans Narrow Focus of Deregulatory Agenda," *CQ Almanac* 1996, 52nd ed. (Washington, DC: Congressional Quarterly, 1997), 3-3–3-6. The law was PL 104–13.

61. "Bill Curbs Shareholder Lawsuits," *CQ Almanac* 1995, 51st ed. (Washington, DC: Congressional Quarterly, 1996), 2-90–2-92. The law was PL 104–67.

62. Killian, *The Freshmen*, 239; Steely, *The Gentleman from Georgia*, 305; Bob Woodward, *The Choice* (New York: Simon & Schuster, 1996), 200, 248, 283, 330.

63. Gillon, *The Pact*· 141; Jones, *Clinton & Congress, 1993–1996*, 154; Norman J. Ornstein, "Of Budget Politics, the Truman Years, Clinton & Gingrich," *Roll Call*, June 26, 1995, Clinton and Gingrich folder, RP; Karen Tumulty, "Man with a Vision," *Time*, January 9, 1995, Gingrich Series, RP; Woodward, *The Choice*, 48.

64. Reid Wilson, "Consequential GOP Class of 1994 All but Disappears," *The Hill*, September 24, 2019; C-SPAN, Clip of Presidential News Conference dated April 18, 1995, www.c-span.org/video/?c4451444/clinton-president-relevant.

65. "Bosnian War Sparks Conflict at Home," *CQ Almanac* 1995, 51st ed. (Washington, DC: Congressional Quarterly, 1996), 10-10–10-15; Ryan C. Hendrickson, "War Powers, Bosnia and the 104th Congress," *Political Science Quarterly* 113, no. 2 (Summer 1998): 253.

66. Strahan, *Leading Representatives*, 154. A Republican strategist lamented later that the Contract was "a focused document, but who remembers what the Republicans did afterwards? [They had] no agenda, no theme," highlighting how the absence of a unifying agenda led to trouble for Gingrich following the Contract's passage. Interview with GOP strategist, June 6, 2003.

67. Nancy Gibbs and Karen Tumulty, "Newt Gingrich; Master of the House," *Time*, December 25, 1995.

68. Gingrich, *Lessons Learned*, 6; Annie Tin, "Lawmakers Raced through Opening Days," *Congressional Monitor*, April 17, 1995.

69. "Clinton Leads Mexico Bailout Effort," *CQ Almanac* 1995, 51st ed. (Washington, DC: Congressional Quarterly, 1996), 10-16–10-17.

70. David Maraniss and Michael Weisskopf, *"Tell Newt to Shut Up!"* (New York: Simon & Schuster, 1996), 85, 88–89, 91–97.

71. Jerry Gray, "Freshmen Challenge G.O.P. Elders," *New York Times*, October 21, 1995; David Hosansky, "Panel Rejects Farm Overhaul in a Rebuke to Leadership," *CQ Weekly*, September 23, 1995, 2875; Killian, *The Freshmen*, 152, 157–159, 243; "Lawmakers Enact Lobbying Reforms," *CQ Almanac* 1995, 51st ed. (Washington, DC: Congressional Quarterly, 1996), 1-38–1-41.

72. Strahan, *Leading Representatives*, 169–170.

73. Killian, *The Freshmen*, 103; David Maraniss and Michael Weisskopf, "Coaxing House GOP Factions to Toe the Budget Line," *Washington Post*, May 26, 1995;

Strahan, *Leading Representatives*, 170–171; House Republican Conference Talking Points, May 17, 1995, Box 2238, Folder: "Budget," NLG.

74. Balz and Brownstein, *Storming the Gates*, 157; Gillon, *The Pact*, 151; Guy Gugliotta, "Farm Bill Handed Off," *Washington Post*, September 28, 1995; Johnson and Broder, *The System*, 578–579; Mann and Ornstein, *The Broken Branch*, 109; "No Winners in Budget Showdown," *CQ Almanac* 1995, 51st ed. (Washington, DC: Congressional Quarterly, 1996), 2-44–2-63; Eric Pianin and Guy Gugliotta, "Farm, Tax Cut Plans Leave GOP Shy of Budget Votes; Party Leaders Try to Defuse Resistance," *Washington Post*, October 25, 1995; John E. Yang and Eric Pianin, "House Approves Bill to Balance Budget," *Washington Post*, October 27, 1995; memo to Republican Leaders from Haley Barbour, Republican National Committee, September 5, 1995, Box 2058, Folder: Sept. 18–24 1995, NLG.

75. Clinton, *My Life*, 682.

76. Gingrich candidly explained to Charlie Rose that the House GOP strategy was to force the president to either agree to the Republican balanced budget plan or veto the appropriations bill and accept the government shutdown. Interview with Charlie Rose on July 6, 1995, https://charlierose.com/videos/23715; Gillon, *The Pact*, 148; Steely, *The Gentleman from Georgia*, 307; Strahan, *Leading Representatives*, 171–172.

77. Killian, *The Freshmen*, 104.

78. Gillon, *The Pact*, 115–116, 151–158; Johnson and Broder, *The System*, 585; Killian, *The Freshmen*, 147, 169–170; Woodward, *The Choice*, 316–317.

79. Ann Devroy and John E. Yang, "No Progress In Budget Negotiations," *Washington Post*, November 12, 1995; Gillon, *The Pact*, 159–160; Killian, *The Freshmen*, 188; "Government Shuts Down Twice Due to Lack of Funding," *CQ Almanac* 1995, 51st ed. (Washington, DC: Congressional Quarterly, 1996), 11-3–11-6; Woodward, *The Choice*, 319–322.

80. Clinton, *My Life*, 683; Gingrich, *Lessons Learned*, 44–45; Lars-Erik Nelson, "Gingrich Shows Pique & Volleys Crisis Reveals Newt Depths of Pettiness," *New York Daily News*, November 16, 1995; Steely, *The Gentleman from Georgia*, 310–311.

81. John F. Harris and John E. Yang, "As Speaker Backpedals, Democrats Pile On," *Washington Post*, November 17, 1995; Alexander Nazaryan, "Newt Gingrich, Crybaby: The Famous Daily News Cover Explained," *New York Daily News*, January 6, 2012, www.nydailynews.com/blogs/pageviews/newt-gingrich-crybaby-famous-daily-news-cover-explained-blog-entry-1.1637386; Elaine S. Povich, "Gingrich Relishes His Love-Hate Relationship with Hill Press Corps," *Roll Call*, April 22, 1996; Elizabeth Shogren, "The Budget Impasse: Democrats Take Gingrich to Task," *Los Angeles Times*, November 17, 1995; Woodward, *The Choice*, 323–324. One Republican leader observed that the "crybaby" incident "probably broke the magic" of Gingrich among his fellow Republicans, who were less satisfied with Gingrich's leadership after that point. Interview with former Republican leader, May 8, 2019.

82. For instance, in a CBS News poll from November 19, 1995, 51 percent blamed Republicans for the shutdown and 28 percent held Clinton more accountable for it. See David E. Rosenbaum, "Battle over the Budget: The Overview; as Standoff Ends, Clinton Is Seeking the High Ground," *New York Times*, November 21, 1995.

83. "Government Shuts Down Twice," *CQ Almanac* 1995; Green, *Underdog Politics*, 104–105; Killian, *The Freshmen*, 193; Woodward, *The Choice*, 326–327.

84. William Branigin and David Segal, "Lacking Passports, Travelers Frozen in Place," *Washington Post*, January 4, 1996; Clinton, *My Life*, 682; Richard L. Berke, "Clinton's Ratings over 50% in Poll as G.O.P. Declines," *New York Times*, December 14, 1995; Gillon, *The Pact*, 166; "Government Shuts Down Twice," *CQ Almanac* 1995; Message from the President of the United States, Veto of H.R. 2491, House Document 104–141, December 6, 1995; Rae, *Conservative Reformers*, 118, 119, 127; Steely, *The Gentleman from Georgia*, 308; Weisberg and Patterson, "Theatre in the Round," 16; Woodward, *The Choice*, 328; John E. Yang, "House, Senate Adopt GOP Spending Plan," *Washington Post*, November 18, 1995.

85. Clinton, *My Life*, 682; "Government Shuts Down Twice," *CQ Almanac* 1995; Gregorsky, *Elephants in the Room*, 130–131; Frank Gregorsky interview with Bob Livingston, February 27, 2009, exactingeditor.com/BobLivingston.pdf; David Maraniss, "As House Plan Flops, GOP Shifts the Blame for Federal Shutdown," *Washington Post*, December 31, 1995; Eric Pianin and Ann Devroy, "House Republicans Derail Budget Talks," *Washington Post*, December 21, 1995. Tom DeLay said in an interview that Dole had entered into an agreement with Clinton that both surprised House Republicans and squandered the chance to defeat the president. Tom DeLay interview with Linda Douglass, July 19, 2006, pt. 1, www.youtube.com/watch?v=t3dnQ6D_4e4&list=PLSfSYqO9OfaEjtajTAA_WlfpIJ1QjA7Ti.

86. Elizabeth Drew, *Whatever It Takes: The Real Struggle for Political Power in America* (New York: Viking, 1997), 44; "Government Shuts Down Twice," *CQ Almanac* 1995; Killian, *The Freshmen*, 256; "No Winners in Budget Showdown," *CQ Almanac* 1995, 51st ed. (Washington, DC: Congressional Quarterly, 1996), 2-44–2-63; Eric Pianin, "House Republicans Derail Budget Talks," *Washington Post*, December 21, 1995; Eric Pianin and John F. Harris, "Clinton Signs Measures to Halt Shutdown," *Washington Post*, January 6, 1996; Ronald M. Peters Jr., *The American Speakership: The Office in Historical Perspective*, 2nd ed. (Baltimore: Johns Hopkins University Press, 1997), 308–309; Strahan, *Leading Representatives*, 173; Woodward, *The Choice*, 341.

87. Gillon, *The Pact*, 171.

88. "Man of the Year," *Time*, December 25, 1995; Drew, *Whatever It Takes*, 45; Gillon, *The Pact*, 171; Woodward, *The Choice*, 273. Charles O. Jones points out that Gingrich's approval and disapproval numbers were roughly equal near the beginning of 1995, but his disapproval number "was twice that of the approval number"

during the federal budget negotiations that concluded the year. Jones, *Clinton & Congress*, 162.

89. Killian, *The Freshmen*, 260; Jackie Koszczuk, "Gingrich's Woes May Damage Rank and File, GOP Agenda," *CQ Weekly*, December 9, 1995, 3705.

90. Herrnson, "Directing 535 Leading Men and Leading Ladies," 120.

91. See, e.g., Hook, "Speaker Jim Wright Takes Charge in the House."

92. "House Republican National Strategic Plan for 1996," Box 2426, Folder: Strategic Plan for House, 1996; "House Republican National Strategic Plan for 1996" and "Strategy for Fall 1996," Box 2433, Folder: Strategy and Planning 1996, NLG. On a document filed in Gingrich's archives at the University of West Georgia, Mel Steely, a longtime Gingrich confidante and historian, quoted Gingrich as being interested in running for president in 2000 if Dole failed to defeat Clinton in 1996. Jerry Markon, "Gingrich Archives Show His Public Praise, Private Criticism of Reagan," *Washington Post*, February 19, 2012.

93. "As Elections Loom, GOP Ardor Gives Way to Pragmatism," *CQ Almanac* 1996, 52nd ed. (Washington, DC: Congressional Quarterly, 1997), 1-3–1-14; Drew, *Whatever It Takes*, 58–59; Killian, *The Freshmen*, 291; Steely, *The Gentleman from Georgia*, 315.

94. Strahan, *Leading Representatives*, 158; "Welfare Bill Clears under Veto Threat," *CQ Almanac* 1995, 51st ed. (Washington, DC: Congressional Quarterly, 1996), 7-35–7-52; "Strategy for Fall 1996," Box 2433, Folder: Strategy and Planning 1996, NLG.

95. Balz and Brownstein, *Storming the Gates*, 283–288; Strahan, *Leading Representatives*, 158–159; Jennifer Senior, "GOP Women Echo Democratic Concerns about Welfare Reform Proposals," *The Hill*, January 25, 1995; R. Kent Weaver, *Ending Welfare as We Know It* (Washington, DC: Brookings Institution Press, 2000).

96. Strahan, *Leading Representatives*, 160; "Welfare Bill Clears under Veto Threat," *CQ Almanac* 1995, 51st ed., 7-35–7-52. "After 60 Years, Most Control Sent to States," *CQ Almanac* 1996, 52nd ed. (Washington, DC: Congressional Quarterly, 1997), 6-3–6-24. See Vetoes by President William J. Clinton, United States Senate, www.senate.gov/legislative/vetoes/ClintonWJ.htm.

97. Alison Mitchell, "Gingrich's Views on Slayings Draw Fire," *New York Times*, November 23, 1995; "Strategy for Fall 1996," Box 2433, Folder: Strategy and Planning 1996, NLG.

98. Drew, *Whatever It Takes*, 58, 98, 99–100, 131, 169, 181; Green, *The Speaker of the House*, 136–138; Strahan, *Leading Representatives*, 160; "After 60 Years, Most Control Sent to States," *CQ Almanac* 1996, 52nd ed., 6-3–6-24.

99. C. Lawrence Evans and Walter J. Oleszek, "The Strategic Context of Congressional Party Leadership," *Congress & the Presidency* 26, no. 1 (Spring 1999): 4, 9; "Praise, Protest Greet Telecom Bill," *CQ Almanac* 1996, 52nd ed. (Washington, DC: Congressional Quarterly, 1997), 3-43–3-47.

100. "Congress Clears Wage Increase with Tax Breaks for Business," *CQ*

Almanac 1996, 52nd ed. (Washington, DC: Congressional Quarterly, 1997), 7-3–7-9; Gillon, *The Pact*, 177.

101. "Clinton Signs Cuba Sanctions Bill," *CQ Almanac* 1996, 52nd ed. (Washington, DC: Congressional Quarterly, 1997), 9-6–9-8.

102. "President Signs Anti-Terrorism Bill," *CQ Almanac* 1996, 52nd ed. (Washington, DC: Congressional Quarterly, 1997), 5-18–5-26.

103. Lawmakers Debate Flat Tax for D.C., Taxpayer Bill of Rights," *CQ Almanac* 1996, 52nd ed. (Washington, DC: Congressional Quarterly, 1997), 2-41–2-42.

104. "Pesticide Rewrite Draws Wide Support," *CQ Almanac* 1996, 52nd ed. (Washington, DC: Congressional Quarterly, 1997), 3-27–3-34; "Drinking Water Act Wins Broad Support," *CQ Almanac* 1996, 52nd ed. (Washington, DC: Congressional Quarterly, 1997), 4-4–4-12.

105. "Bill Makes Health Insurance 'Portable,'" *CQ Almanac* 1996, 52nd ed. (Washington, DC: Congressional Quarterly, 1997), 6-28–6-39.

106. "New Law Discourages Gay Marriages," *CQ Almanac* 1996, 52nd ed. (Washington, DC: Congressional Quarterly, 1997), 5-26–5-29.

107. David Maraniss and Michael Weisskopf, "Speaker and His Directors Make the Cash Flow Right," *Washington Post*, November 27, 1995; Peters, *The American Speakership*, 305; Steely, *The Gentleman from Georgia*, 304.

108. See, e.g., Drew, *Whatever It Takes*, 66, 96, 103, 141, 220; Peters, *The American Speakership*, 310.

109. Drew, *Whatever It Takes*, 158.

110. See, e.g., Killian, *The Freshmen*, 291; Maraniss and Weisskopf, "Speaker and His Directors."

111. Drew, *Whatever It Takes*, 116.

112. Drew, 169; Gingrich, *Lessons Learned*, 12; Woodward, *The Choice*, 406.

113. Balz and Brownstein, *Storming the Gates*, 352; Drew, *Whatever It Takes*, 95–97, 215; "GOP Retains House Majority," *CQ Almanac* 1996, 52nd ed. (Washington, DC: Congressional Quarterly, 1997), 11-23–11-27; "1996 Adjournment Packet," House Republican Conference, September 26, 1996.

114. Balz and Brownstein, *Storming the Gates*, 256; Timothy Conlan, *From New Federalism to Devolution: Twenty-Five Years of Intergovernmental Reform* (Washington, DC: Brookings Institution Press, 1998), 243, 254–256; Charles O. Jones, *The Presidency in a Separated System*, 2nd ed. (Washington, DC: Brookings Institution Press, 2005), 217.

115. See, for example, Herrnson, "Directing 535 Leading Men and Leading Ladies," 128.

116. "104th Congress Ushers in New Era of GOP Rule," *CQ Almanac*, 51st ed. (Washington, DC: Congressional Quarterly, 1996), 1-3–1-15; "Promises Made, Promises Kept. Transition of House Operations," Dear Colleague letter from Bill Thomas, June 14, 1995 (on file with the authors).

117. Gregorsky, *Elephants in the Room*, 123; Herrnson, "Directing 535 Leading

Men and Leading Ladies," 128. "Memo from Pete Hoekstra to Newt Re: The Future," December 4, 1996, Box 2551, Folder: Planning Documents (2 of 2), NLG.

118. Susan Molinari observes in her memoir that Gingrich is "incredibly smart and pragmatic, [and] he is at his best when he is building a team. He is at his worst and most self-destructive when he swells with his own sense of invulnerability and moves to the front and center." Molinari and Burkett, *Representative Mom*, 224.

119. Drew, *Whatever It Takes*, 261; Gingrich, *Lessons Learned*, 3; Killian, *The Freshmen*, 360; letter to Gingrich from Armey, February 9, 1996, Box 62, Folder 2, RKA.

Chapter 6. A Failing Speakership (1997–1998)

1. Mel Steely, *The Gentleman from Georgia: The Biography of Newt Gingrich* (Macon, GA: Mercer University Press, 2000), 329–330; Linda Killian, *The Freshmen: What Happened to the Republican Revolution?* (Boulder, CO: Westview, 1998), 421; "Largent Urges Gingrich to Give Up Speaker Post," *Associated Press*, November 11, 1996.

2. "Gingrich Priority Phone List," November 5, 1996, and "Speaker's Race Calls 11/18," Box 2551, Folder: Speaker's Vote 1997, NLG.

3. Newt Gingrich, *Lessons Learned the Hard Way: A Personal Report* (New York: HarperCollins, 1998), 117; Killian, *The Freshmen*, 421.

4. Gingrich, *Lessons Learned the Hard Way*, 119–122; John E. Yang, "Speaker Gingrich Admits House Ethics Violation," *Washington Post*, December 22, 1996, 1.

5. The conversation had been taped by two private citizens who picked up the call on their police scanner, and it eventually made its way to the *New York Times*, which revealed it just days after the Speaker vote. See Adam Clymer, "Gingrich is Heard Urging Tactics in Ethics Case," *New York Times*, January 10, 1997, A1, and Rick Bragg, "2 Floridians Talk of How They Taped Gingrich," *New York Times*, January 14, 1997, A1.

6. Steely, *The Gentleman from Georgia*, 337; "A Joint Statement from House Republican Leaders," December 21, 1996, Box 2629, Folder: Newt Investigation Information, NLG; see also call lists, "Talking Points for Member Calls," and Dear Republican Colleague letter from John Boehner, December 21, 1996, Box 2629, Folder: Newt Investigation Information, NLG; Gingrich, *Lessons Learned the Hard Way*, 123–124.

7. Gingrich, *Lessons Learned the Hard Way*, 124–125; letter to Tom DeLay from Porter Goss and Steve Schiff, December 31, 1996, Box 2551, Folder: Speaker's Vote 1997, NLG.

8. They included Ann Northrup (R-KY) and Roger Wicker (R-MS). Gingrich call sheet, December 31, 1996, Box 2551, Folder: Speaker's Vote 1997, NLG.

9. Gingrich call sheets, December 31, 1996 and January 2 and 3, 1997, Box 2551, Folder: Speaker's Vote 1997, NLG.

10. John E. Yang, "4 More Break Ranks," *Washington Post*, January 7, 1997, A1.

11. Adam Clymer, "Gingrich Makes Appeal to Party," *New York Times*, January 7, 1997, A1; Ian Fisher, "Critic of Gingrich Is Warmly Praised at Home," *New York Times*, December 31, 1996, B5. Forbes later left the GOP for the Democratic Party, complaining that the party had been taken over by "extremists." He became the first Republican in Congress to switch parties in almost twenty-five years. See James Dao, "House Republican Defects to Democrats," *New York Times*, July 18, 1999, 1.

12. Gingrich, *Lessons Learned the Hard Way*, 125; Katharine Q. Seelye, "Nine Uncomfortable Davids, and Goliath Still Alive," *New York Times*, January 8, 1997, B9; Dear Colleague letter, January 3, 1997, Box 2551, Folder: Speaker's Vote 1997, NLG; Dear Republican Colleague letter from Tom DeLay, January 2, 1997, Box 2629, Folder: Newt Investigation Information, NLG.

13. Gingrich, *Lessons Learned the Hard Way*, 126; Killian, *The Freshmen*, 422.

14. Adam Clymer, "Gingrich Strains to Retain His Hold on the House," *New York Times*, January 3, 1997, A1. An undated memo in the Gingrich Papers suggests that twenty-three Republicans were undecided about whether to vote for Gingrich, plus one definite no (Forbes). Undated list of Republican members, Box 2629, Folder: Newt Investigation Information, NLG. By denying Gingrich the speakership, these twenty Republicans would not necessarily have handed the Speaker's gavel to Gephardt. Since the Speaker must be elected by an absolute majority of all votes cast, the result would have likely resulted in no winning candidate, thus forcing future rounds of voting.

15. Major Garrett, "Gingrich: Managerial Disaster?," *Atlantic*, December 9, 2011.

16. Adam Clymer, "9 Defect in Vote," *New York Times*, January 8, 1997, A1; Seelye, "9 Uncomfortable Davids"; John E. Yang, "House Leader Offers Thanks, Apologies in Close Call for GOP," *Washington Post*, January 8, 1997, A1. The nine defectors were Leach, Wolf, Forbes, Morella, Tom Campbell (R-CA), John Hostettler (R-IN), Scott Klug (R-WI), Linda Smith (R-WA), and Mark Neumann (R-WI).

17. Killian, *The Freshmen*, 423.

18. Blaine Harden, "The Gingrich Ethics Case: A Solemn Day," *Washington Post*, January 18, 1997, A14; John E. Yang, "House Reprimands, Penalizes Speaker," *Washington Post*, January 22, 1997, A1; John E. Yang and Helen Dewar, "Ethics Panel Supports Reprimand of Gingrich, $300,000 Sanction for House Rules Violations" *Washington Post*, January 18, 1997, A1.

19. Francis X. Clines, "The Scene: A Not-So-Tidy Lesson in American History, Courtesy of the House," *New York Times*, January 22, 1997, A18; Harden, "The Gingrich Ethics Case."

20. Gingrich, *Lessons Learned the Hard Way*, 129; Hanna Rosin, "The Madness of Speaker Newt," *New Republic*, March 17, 1997; Steely, *The Gentleman from Georgia*, 342.

21. Dan Balz, "Speaker Faces Smaller Role," *Washington Post*, December 23, 1996, A1; Elizabeth Drew, *Whatever It Takes: The Real Struggle for Political Power in America* (New York: Viking, 1997), 261.

22. Francis X. Clines, "Gingrich, Role as House Leader Intact, Offers Clinton an Olive Branch," *New York Times*, November 7, 1996, A1.

23. Killian, *The Freshmen*, 423.

24. Peter King, "Why I Oppose Newt," *Weekly Standard* 2, no. 28 (March 31, 1997): 22; Steely, *The Gentleman from Georgia*, 343.

25. Adam Clymer, "G.O.P. Intensifies Bid for Inquiries Over Fund-Raising," *New York Times*, March 5, 1997, A1; Seth Faison, "Gingrich Warns China That U.S. Would Step in to Defend Taiwan," *New York Times*, March 31, 1997, A1; Katharine Q. Seelye, "Gingrich Continues to Reach Out to G.O.P. Conservatives," *New York Times*, April 11, 1997, A1; John E. Yang, "Once Again, Speaker Hikes Up His Profile in the House," *Washington Post*, April 12, 1997, A4.

26. Dan Balz, "Speaker Faces Smaller Role; Others Likely to Assume Dominance over GOP Agenda," *Washington Post*, December 23, 1996, A1.

27. Gingrich, *Lessons Learned*, 79; Kevin Sack, "Gingrich Attacks Press as Out of Touch," *New York Times*, April 23, 1997, D21; memo to staff from Newt, March 1997, Box 2608, Folder: Memos from Newt—March 97, NLG.

28. Steely, *The Gentleman from Georgia*, 345; Dear Republican Colleague letter, November 20, 1996, Box 2551, Folder: Planning Documents (2 of 2), NLG.

29. Jackie Koszczuk, "A Full Circle," Players, Politics and Turf of the 105th Congress, *Congressional Quarterly*, March 22, 1997, 10.

30. Memo to Sue Myrick from Nancy Johnson, "Overcoming Division and Divisiveness within Conference," Box 2551, Folder: Member Releases, NLG.

31. Killian, *The Freshmen*, 425–426; Ruth Bloch Rubin, *Building the Bloc: Intraparty Organization in the U.S. Congress* (New York: Cambridge University Press, 2017), 280.

32. Juliet Eilperin and Jim VandeHei, "Speaker May Return to a Smaller Leadership," *Roll Call*, June 16, 1997; Steely, *The Gentleman from Georgia*, 342–343. Tom Coburn (R-OK), who joined the House as part of the "Republican Revolution" and later served in the Senate, wrote in his book *Breach of Trust* that "Gingrich talked a lot about the importance of listening, but he was often not interested in discussing our ideas." Quoted in Sheryl Gay Stolberg, "For Gingrich in Power, Pragmatism, Not Purity," *New York Times*, December 21, 2011, A1.

33. Rosin, "The Madness of Speaker Newt"; letter to Newt from Frank (Luntz), undated, Box 2608, Folder: Memos from Your Binder and Bag for Your Review, NLG.

34. David E. Rosenbaum, "Gingrich on a Slippery Surface with a Firm Base," *New York Times*, March 25, 1997, A22.

35. Email from Krister Holladay, March 18, 1997, Box 2052, Folder: Taxes, NLG.

36. Jennifer Bradley, "GOP Rebel Says Leadership Rebuff Was Coordinated," *Roll Call*, March 27, 1997; Killian, *The Freshmen*, 429; Jackie Koszczuk, "LEADERSHIP," *CQ Weekly*, March 22, 1997, 679–681; Rosenbaum, "Gingrich on a Slippery Surface."

37. Timothy J. Barnett, *Legislative Learning: The 104th Republican Freshmen in the House* (New York, NY: Routledge, 1999), 11–12; Killian, *The Freshmen*, 426; Rosenbaum, "Gingrich on a Slippery Surface." Those eleven defectors were Steve Chabot (R-OH), Tom Coburn (R-OK), Lindsey Graham (R-SC), Peter Hoekstra (R-MI), Bob Inglis (R-SC), Steve Largent (R-OK), Mark Neumann (R-WI), Matt Salmon (R-AZ), Mark Sanford (R-SC), Joe Scarborough (R-FL), and Mark Souder (R-IN). See Donna Cassata and Rebecca Carr, "Woodshed Session Works Both Ways," *CQ Weekly*, March 22, 1997, 681.

38. Donna Cassata and Rebecca Carr, "Woodshed Session Works Both Ways," *CQ Weekly*, March 22, 1997, 681; Sandy Hume, "Defiance of Leaders Carries No Penalty," *The Hill*, April 9, 1997; Killian, *The Freshmen*, 426–427; Jackie Koszczuk, "Gingrich's Friends Turn to Foes as Frustration Builds," *CQ Weekly*, March 22, 1997, 679–681; Koszczuk, "LEADERSHIP."

39. Guy Gugliotta, "'Liar,' 'Liar,' 'Liar' Sets the House Afire," *Washington Post*, April 18, 1997, A14; Koszczuk, "LEADERSHIP"; Seelye, "Gingrich Continues to Reach Out."

40. King, "Why I Oppose Newt."

41. Koszczuk, "LEADERSHIP"; Rosenbaum, "Gingrich on a Slippery Surface."

42. "GOP Backs Down on Disaster Aid Bill," *CQ Almanac* 1997, 53rd ed. (Washington, DC: Congressional Quarterly, 1998), 9-84–9-90; Helen Dewar and John F. Harris, "President Vetoes Flood Relief Bill: Amendments on Shutdowns, Census Sampling Unresolved," *Washington Post*, June 10, 1997, A1; Killian, *The Freshmen*, 427; Andrew Taylor, "Appropriations: Clinton Signs 'Clean' Disaster Aid after Flailing GOP Yields to Veto," *CQ Weekly*, June 14, 1997.

43. "Tone, Tenor of First Session Seemed Like Old Times," *CQ Almanac* 1997, 53rd ed. (Washington, DC: Congressional Quarterly, 1998), 1-3–1-11; "GOP Backs Down on Disaster Aid Bill," *CQ Almanac* 1997, 53rd ed. (Washington, DC: Congressional Quarterly, 1998), 9-84–9-90; Andrew Taylor, "House Passes Emergency Spending, But 'Automatic CR' Invites Veto," *Congressional Quarterly Weekly Report*, May 17, 1997.

44. Juliet Eilperin and Jim VandeHei, "'Contract' High to Coup Low: How It Fell Apart," *Roll Call*, October 6, 1997; Gingrich, *Lessons Learned*, 141, 143–144, 146–147; "GOP Backs Down on Disaster Aid Bill," *CQ Almanac* 1997, 53rd ed. (Washington, DC: Congressional Quarterly, 1998), 9-84–9-90.

45. Barnett, *Legislative Learning*, 16–17; Jennifer Bradley and Jim VandeHei, "Leaders Vote against Gingrich," *Roll Call*, June 16, 1997; Gingrich, *Lessons Learned*, 147, 150–151; Killian, *The Freshmen*, 427–428.

46. Barnett, *Legislative Learning*, 18; Killian, *The Freshmen*, 428–430. By one estimate, some forty Republicans had attended one or more meetings of the "Gang of Eleven" rebels, expressing a diversity of complaints about the Speaker, though not necessarily advocating for his ouster. They included Helen Chenoweth (R-ID), John

Doolittle (R-CA), Mike Forbes (R-NY), Van Hilleary (R-TN), Sam Johnson (R-TX), David McIntosh (R-IN), Sue Myrick (R-NC), and Richard Pombo (R-CA). Jim VandeHei, "Inside the Republican Conference," *Roll Call*, September 15, 1997. If most Republicans opted to keep Gingrich in power, the scheme would only have worked had Democrats also voted for the motion to vacate the chair. It is unclear whether any Democrats were prepared to do so.

47. John Boehner, *On the House: A Washington Memoir* (New York: St. Martin's, 2021), 76; Juliet Eilperin and Jim VandeHei, "Some Wounds Never Heal," *Roll Call*, October 2, 1997; Gingrich, *Lessons Learned*, 151–152; Sandy Hume, "Gingrich Foils Coup by Deputies," *The Hill*, July 16, 1997; Jackie Koszczuk, "Gingrich under Fire as Discord Simmers from Rank to Top," *CQ Weekly*, June 21, 1997, 1415.

48. "GOP Rebels Downplay Confrontation with Leadership," *National Journal's CongressDaily/A.M.*, June 18, 1997; Hume, "Gingrich Foils Coup"; Jackie Koszczuk, "The Gingrich Coup, Hour by Hour," *Congressional Quarterly Weekly Report*, July 19, 1997, 1673.

49. Barnett, *Legislative Learning*, 20; Gingrich, *Lessons Learned*, 155–56; Hume, "Gingrich Foils Coup"; Koszczuk, "The Gingrich Coup"; Rosin, "The Madness of Speaker Newt"; Steely, *The Gentleman from Georgia*, 350.

50. Ceci Connolly, David S. Broder, and Dan Balz, "GOP's House Divided," *Washington Post*, July 28, 1997, A1; Killian, *The Freshmen*, 430–431; Hume, "Gingrich Foils Coup."

51. Barnett, *Legislative Learning*, 21; Sandy Hume, "House GOP Rebels Meet on Newt's Fate," *The Hill*, June 18, 1997; Koszczuk, "Gingrich under Fire."

52. Letter to Gingrich from Armey, July 22, 1997, Box 2527, Folder: Armey, Richard, NLG.

53. Jackie Koszczuk, "Coup Attempt Throws GOP Off Legislative Track," *Congressional Quarterly Weekly Report*, July 19, 1997, 1671–72; Jackie Koszczuk, "Party Stalwarts Will Determine Gingrich's Long-Term Survival," *Congressional Quarterly Weekly Report*, July 26, 1997; Eilperin and VandeHei, "'Contract' High to Coup Low."

54. Killian, *The Freshmen*, 431; Koszczuk, "The Gingrich Coup."

55. Barnett, *Legislative Learning*, 22; Connolly, Broder, and Balz, "GOP's House Divided"; letter from Bill Paxon to Newt Gingrich, July 17, 1997, Box 2518, Folder: Paxon, Bill, NLG. Paxon would later retire from the House after an abortive attempt to run against Armey for majority leader in early 1998, a move opposed by Gingrich, who did not trust Paxon to be his second in command. Thomas Galvin, "Five Reasons Why Paxon Quit," *National Journal's Cloakroom*, February 26, 1998.

56. Killian, *The Freshmen*, 431; Koszczuk, "Coup Attempt Throws GOP Off Legislative Track"; Koszczuk, "Gingrich under Fire."

57. Juliet Eilperin and Jim VandeHei, "GOP Intrigue Is Old Hat to This Ex-Michel Aide," *Roll Call*, July 24, 1997; handwritten leadership notes, July 22, 1997,

Box 2551, Folder: 105th Leadership, NLG. Those warning against the follow-up party meeting included Boehner, DeLay, Mike Crapo (R-ID), David McIntosh (R-IN), and John Thune (R-SD).

58. Jerry Gray, "Gingrich Calls for Healing at Revival-Style Meeting of House G.O.P.," *New York Times*, July 24, 1997, B8; Killian, *The Freshmen*, 432; Kevin Sack, "Gingrich Reminds Rebels He's 'Head Coach,'" *New York Times*, July 22, 1997, A1; Jim VandeHei, "Yesterday's Rebels Say They're Angry No More," *Roll Call*, July 28, 1997; John E. Yang, "House Republicans Close Ranks," *Washington Post*, July 24, 1997, A1.

59. Koszczuk, "Party Stalwarts."

60. John E. Yang, "Session Changes Gingrich," *Washington Post*, November 15, 1997, A1; Lindsay Sobel and Albert Eisele, "DeLay Says Coup Helped Gingrich by Prompting Change in Leadership Style," *The Hill*, March 11, 1998.

61. Newt Gingrich and Ward Connerly, "Face the Failure of Racial Preferences," *New York Times*, June 15, 1997, E15; John E. Yang, "Gingrich Tests New Fund-Raising Model," *Washington Post*, June 8, 1997, A8.

62. Koszczuk, "Gingrich under Fire"; David Hosansky and Alissa J. Rubin, "Shuster's Steamroller Stopped—for Now," *CQ Weekly Report*, May 24, 1997, 1183; Eric Pianin and John E. Yang, "Gephardt Denounces Balanced Budget Plan," *Washington Post*, May 21, 1997; Eilperin and VandeHei, "'Contract' High to Coup Low."

63. Adam Clymer, "Passage Is Likely," *New York Times*, July 29, 1997, A1; Daniel J. Palazzolo, *Done Deal?: The Politics of the 1997 Budget Agreement* (Washington, DC: CQ, 1999); "Reconciliation Package: An Overview," *CQ Almanac* 1997, 53rd ed. (Washington, DC: Congressional Quarterly, 1998), 2-27–2-30.

64. Lee Edwards, *The Conservative Revolution: The Movement That Remade America* (New York: Free Press, 1999), 314; "Gingrich Weakened by Ethics Case," *CQ Almanac* 1997, 53rd ed. (Washington, DC: Congressional Quarterly, 1998), 1-11–1-15; "Pact Aims to Erase Deficit by 2002," *CQ Almanac* 1997, 53rd ed. (Washington, DC: Congressional Quarterly, 1998), 2-18–2-23; Katharine Q. Seelye, "Gingrich Draws Fire from the Right," *New York Times*, October 25, 1998, 24; VandeHei, "Inside the Republican Conference."

65. "Transportation Law Benefits Those Who Held the Purse Strings," *CQ Almanac* 1998, 54th ed. (Washington, DC: Congressional Quarterly, 1998), 24-3–24-27.

66. "Clinton Signs into Law IRS Overhaul Bill That 'Respects Taxpayers,'" *CQ Almanac* 1998, 54th ed. (Washington, DC: Congressional Quarterly, 1999), 21-3–21-9; David Hosansky, "TAXES: Resounding Votes for a Tax Cut May Amount to Little This Year," *CQ Magazine*, June 20, 1998, 1682.

67. "Congress Clears Legislation to Consolidate More Than 60 Job Training Programs," *CQ Almanac* 1998, 54th ed. (Washington, DC: Congressional Quarterly, 1999), 10-3–10-4.

68. "Congress Takes Steps to Shield Children from Internet Porn, Predators,"

CQ Almanac 1998, 54th ed. (Washington, DC: Congressional Quarterly, 1999), 22-10–22-13.

69. Victoria A. Grzelak, "Mickey Mouse & Sonny Bono Go to Court: The Copyright Term Extension Act and Its Effect on Current and Future Rights," *John Marshall Review of Intellectual Property Law* 2, no. 1 (Fall 2002): 101; "Lawmakers Update Nations' Copyright Law for the Digital Age," *CQ Almanac* 1998, 54th ed. (Washington, DC: Congressional Quarterly, 1999), 22-3–22-9; "Public Laws, 105th Congress, 2nd Session," *CQ Almanac* 1998, 54th ed., E-1–E-19.

70. Gingrich, *Lessons Learned the Hard Way*, 171; Peters and Williams, "The Demise of Newt Gingrich," 263.

71. A. B. Stoddard, "Livingston Takes Page from Newt Playbook," *The Hill*, March 25, 1998; Steely, *The Gentleman from Georgia*, 367.

72. Jackie Koszczuk, "On the Hill and at Home, GOP Is Torn by Internal Strife," *Congressional Quarterly Weekly Report*, April 4, 1998.

73. William F. Connelly Jr. and John J. Pitney, "The House GOP's Civil War: A Political Science Perspective," *PS: Political Science and Politics* 30, no. 4 (December 1997): 701; Steely, *The Gentleman from Georgia*, 378–379.

74. Juliet Eilperin and Jim VandeHei, "House GOP Leadership's Fractured Present Pits Gingrich-Armey Alliance against DeLay-Paxon," *Roll Call*, October 9, 1997; Eliza Newlin Carney and Richard E. Cohen, "Newt's Kitchen Cabinet," *National Journal*, August 2, 1997.

75. *Clinton v. Jones*, 520 U.S. 681 (1997); Karen O'Connor and John R. Hermann, "The Courts: The Perils of Paula," in *The Clinton Scandal and the Future of American Government*, ed. Mark J. Rozell and Clyde Wilcox (Washington, DC: Georgetown University Press, 2000), 46, 48–51; Nicol C. Rae and Colton C. Campbell, *Impeaching Clinton: Partisan Strife on Capitol Hill* (Lawrence: University Press of Kansas, 2004), 2.

76. Peter Baker and Susan Schmidt, "Tripp Gave Affidavit to Lawyers for Jones," *Washington Post*, February 6, 1998, A27; O'Connor and Hermann, "The Courts," 53–54; Rae and Campbell, *Impeaching Clinton*, 2–3.

77. "Explosive Starr Report Outlines Case for Impeachment," *CNN*, September 11, 1998, www.cnn.com/ALLPOLITICS/stories/1998/09/11/starr.report/; O'Connor and Hermann, "The Courts," 55; Rae and Campbell, *Impeaching Clinton*, 3.

78. Rae and Campbell, *Impeaching Clinton*, 53; Steely, *The Gentleman from Georgia*, 380.

79. Peter Baker, *The Breach: Inside the Impeachment and Trial of William Jefferson Clinton* (New York: Scribner, 2000), 145; Dan Balz and Juliet Eilperin, "Gingrich Attacks Energize the GOP but Worry It, Too," *Washington Post*, May 10, 1998, A1; Dale Russakoff and Dan Balz, "After Political Victory, a Personal Revolution," *Washington Post*, December 19, 1994, A1; Thomas F. Schaller, *The Stronghold: How Republicans Captured Congress but Surrendered the White House* (New Haven: Yale University

Press, 2015), 146–147; Steely, *The Gentleman from Georgia*, 365, 375, 379–380; Jim VandeHei, "Gingrich Promises to Focus on Taxes, Not Impeachment," *Roll Call*, July 16, 1998. Dennis Hastert later claimed that Gingrich and Tom DeLay were the biggest advocates of impeachment behind the scenes. J. Dennis Hastert, *President George W. Bush Oral History Project*, Miller Center, University of Virginia, May 16, 2014, https://millercenter.org/the-presidency/presidential-oral-histories/j-dennis-hastert-oral-history. In an interview, Tom DeLay hinted that someone in "Republican leadership" had "a personal thing" that made them reluctant to push for impeachment, a possible reference to Gingrich's affair with House staffer (and later wife) Callista Bisek. Tom DeLay, interview by Linda Douglass, *Reflections with Rep. Tom DeLay—Part 2*, YouTube video, July 19, 2006, www.youtube.com/watch?v=unHs4yXQrZY&list=PLSfSYqO9OfaEjtajTAA_WlfpIJ1QjA7Ti&index=2.

80. Letter to Gingrich from Bob Barr, April 22, 1998, Box 2690, Folder: Impeachment Petitions Against Clinton, NLG. Phil Burton (IN), chairman of the House Government Reform and Oversight Committee, was another frequent and polarizing critic of the president. See, e.g., Balz and Eilperin, "Gingrich Attacks Energize the GOP."

81. Baker, *The Breach*, 145; Rae and Campbell, *Impeaching Clinton*, 98–99. In a time of emerging cable news and the Internet, Gingrich understood that the future would feature increasingly nationalized elections, yet still believed that his regional approach to the Clinton-Lewinsky ads would somehow fly under the nation's collective radar.

82. Paul S. Herrnson, "The Money Maze: Financing Congressional Elections," in *Congress Reconsidered*, 7th ed., ed. Lawrence C. Dodd and Bruce I. Oppenheimer (Washington, DC: CQ Press, 2001), 114–115; Peters and Williams, "The Demise of Newt Gingrich," 262; Steely, *The Gentleman from Georgia*, 360, 382–384; Seelye, "Gingrich Draws Fire from the Right"; Leslie Wayne, "Gingrich, Politically Weakened, Remains Top G.O.P. Fund-Raiser," *New York Times*, March 23, 1997, 1.

83. Guy Gugliotta and Juliet Eilperin, "Gingrich Steps Down as Speaker in Face of House GOP Rebellion," *Washington Post*, November 7, 1998, A1.

84. Steely, *The Gentleman from Georgia*, 390; Alison Mitchell and Eric Schmitt, "Regrouping Hinted," *New York Times*, November 5, 1998, A1; Katharine Q. Seelye and Melinda Henneberger, "Gingrich Is under Siege in Struggle for Speaker's Job," *New York Times*, November 6, 1998, A1.

85. One study found that the Speaker's poor public approval cut the GOP's share of the vote in House elections by 1.4 percent, a small but not insignificant amount for highly competitive races. Benjamin Highton, "Bill Clinton, Newt Gingrich, and the 1998 House Elections," *Public Opinion Quarterly* 66, no. 1 (March 2002): 15.

86. Edwards, *The Conservative Revolution*, 318; Lawrence C. Dodd and Bruce I. Oppenheimer, "A House Divided: The Struggle for Partisan Control, 1994–2000," in *Congress Reconsidered*, 7th ed., ed. Lawrence C. Dodd and Bruce I.

Oppenheimer (Washington, DC: CQ Press, 2001), 31; and C. Lawrence Evans, "Committees, Leaders, and Message Politics," in Dodd and Bruce I. Oppenheimer, *Congress Reconsidered*, 241–242. For more on the factors influencing the 1998 elections, see Highton, "Bill Clinton, Newt Gingrich, and the 1998 House Elections," 1–17; and Walter Shapiro, "1998 Was a *Seinfeld* Election—Not an Impeachment Referendum," *New Republic*, June 6, 2019, https://newrepublic.com/article/154085/1998-election-not-referendum-clinton-impeachment.

87. "1998 Plan for Speaker's Office—Draft," Box 2426, Folder: Strategies, ELC & Leadership, NLG.

88. Alison Mitchell, "The Fall of Gingrich, an Irony in an Odd Year," *New York Times*, November 7, 1998, A1; Katharine Q. Seelye, "Gingrich Is Admitting His Vision Is Blurred," *New York Times*, November 5, 1998, B1.

89. Baker, *The Breach*, 156; Seelye and Henneberger, "Gingrich Is under Siege"; Jake Tapper, "Gingrich Admits to Affair during Clinton Impeachment," *ABC News*, March 12, 2007, https://abcnews.go.com/Politics/story?id=2937633&page=1. Gingrich would later marry Bisek.

90. Alan Fram, "Livingston Will Challenge Gingrich," *Associated Press*, November 6, 1998; Gugliotta and Eilperin, "Gingrich Steps Down"; Mitchell, "The Fall of Gingrich"; Steely, *The Gentleman from Georgia*, 390.

91. Mitchell, "The Fall of Gingrich"; Katharine Q. Seelye, "A Scramble Begins," *New York Times*, November 7, 1998, A1; Steely, *The Gentleman from Georgia*, 391–392.

Conclusion

1. Interview with former Republican leader, July 22, 2020.

2. David S. Broder, "Gingrich's Legacy," *Washington Post*, November 8, 1998, A21.

3. Guy Gugliotta and Juliet Eilperin, "Gingrich Steps Down in Face of Rebellion," *Washington Post*, November 7, 1998, A1.

4. Interview with former Republican leader, July 20, 2020.

5. Gingrich interview with Bill Kristol, November 21, 2014, pt. 1, https://conversationswithbillkristol.org/transcript/newt-gingrich-transcript/.

6. Matthew N. Green, *The Speaker of the House: A Study of Leadership* (New Haven: Yale University Press, 2010); Ronald M. Peters Jr. and Craig A. Williams, "The Demise of Newt Gingrich as a Transformational Leader: Does Organizational Leadership Theory Apply to Legislative Leaders?," *Organizational Dynamics* 30, no. 3 (2002): 266.

7. Newt Gingrich, *Lessons Learned the Hard Way: A Personal Report* (New York: HarperCollins, 1998), 141–143, 151, 169.

8. McKay Coppins, "The Man Who Broke Politics," *Atlantic*, November 2018; Michelle Cottle, "Newt Broke Politics—Now He Wants Back In," *Atlantic*, July 14, 2016; Steve Kornacki, *The Red and the Blue: The 1990s and the Birth of Political Tribalism* (New York: Ecco, 2018), 6; Alex Seitz-Wald, "How Newt Gingrich Crippled

Congress," *Nation*, January 30, 2012; David M. Shribman, "The Congressional Whirlwind That Was Newt Gingrich," *Boston Globe*, July 2, 2020; Julian E. Zelizer, *Burning Down the House: Newt Gingrich, the Fall of a Speaker, and the Rise of the New Republican Party* (New York: Penguin, 2020), 292, 297.

9. See e.g. Isaiah Berlin, *The Hedgehog and the Fox*, 2nd ed. (Princeton: Princeton University Press, 2013 [1951]).

10. Catherine E. Rudder, "The Politics of Taxing and Spending in Congress: Ideas, Strategy, and Policy," in *Congress Reconsidered*, 8th ed., ed. Lawrence C. Dodd and Bruce I. Oppenheimer (Washington, DC: CQ Press, 2005), 327–328.

11. Thirty-eight percent (fifty-one) of the stories from 1984 appeared in May or August, and they were almost entirely about the fight with O'Neill or the Republican Party platform and convention. To test whether the growth in the number of stories about Gingrich stems from his increased quotability in the press, rather than his actual accomplishments, we compared them with the number of pages in the *Congressional Quarterly Almanac* (a subscription-only journal read largely by insiders) that mentioned Gingrich. The correlation from 1979 to 1990 is 0.96, suggesting Gingrich's media coverage reflects his actual behavior in Congress.

12. Had Lott remained as whip, it is exceedingly unlikely he would have criticized Michel as aggressively as Gingrich did. Daniel J. Balz and Serge F. Kovaleski, "Gingrich Divided GOP, Conquered the Agenda," *Washington Post*, December 21, 1994, A19.

13. See, e.g., David S. Broder, "Analysis: Gingrich's Legacy: Permanent Change; a Partisan Edge; Georgian Reshaped House, Speakership; Exit Costs Clinton His Favorite Foe," *Washington Post*, November 8, 1998; Andrew J. Clarke, "Congressional Capacity and the Abolition of Legislative Service Organizations," *Journal of Public Policy* 40, no. 2 (June 2020): 214–235; Juliet Eilperin, "House GOP's Impact," *Washington Post*, January 4, 2000, A4; Paul Glastris and Haley Sweetland Edwards, "The Big Lobotomy," *Washington Monthly*, June/July/August 2014; "Modernizing Congressional Capacity," Report of APSA Presidential Task Force Subcommittee on Congressional Capacity, September 2019, 4–5, 9, www.legbranch.org/app/uploads/2019/09/APSA-memo-capacity-subcommittee-report-09-2019.pdf; *Vital Statistics on Congress* (2019), Brookings Institution, table 5–1, www.brookings.edu/multi-chapter-report/vital-statistics-on-congress/; Craig Volden and Alan E. Wiseman, "Congress Is Back in Town. Here's Why Lawmakers Will Struggle to Get Much Done," *The Monkey Cage (Washington Post)*, September 12, 2019, https://beta.washingtonpost.com/politics/2019/09/12/congress-is-back-town-heres-why-lawmakers-will -struggle-get-much-done/.

14. We could not locate COS membership lists for the years following 1990, but nearly every GOP leader from that year forward had been a member of the group at some point. Some leaders, such as Mickey Edwards, may have joined to keep tabs on the group, not because they shared its strategic vision.

15. Ronald Garay, *Congressional Television: A Legislative History* (Westport, CT: Greenwood, 1984), 140–141; Matthew N. Green, *Underdog Politics: The Minority Party in the U.S. House of Representatives* (New Haven: Yale University Press, 2015), 84–85.

16. Jacob Jensen, Ethan Kaplan, Suresh Naidu, and Laurence Wilse-Samson, "Political Polarization and the Dynamics of Political Language: Evidence from 130 Years of Partisan Speech," Brookings Papers on Economic Activity (Fall 2012).

17. Nicol C. Rae and Colton C. Campbell, *Impeaching Clinton: Partisan Strife on Capitol Hill* (Lawrence: University Press of Kansas, 2004). Political scientists Benjamin Ginsberg and Martin Shefter described this use of aggressive ethics-related tactics as RIP—"revelation, investigation, and prosecution"—and they cited as examples the ethics accusations against Senator John Tower, Speaker Jim Wright, Tony Coelho, and Newt Gingrich. Benjamin Ginsberg and Martin Shefter, *Politics by Other Means: Politicians, Prosecutors, and the Press from Watergate to Whitewater*, 3rd ed. (New York: Norton, 2002), 26, 29–30.

18. Frances E. Lee, *Beyond Ideology: Politics, Principles, and Partisanship in the U.S. Senate* (Chicago: University of Chicago Press, 2009), 3; Nelson W. Polsby, *How Congress Evolves: Social Bases of Institutional Change* (New York: Oxford University Press, 2004), 129.

19. See chapter 1.

20. Interview with former GOP aide, July 6, 2020.

21. Julia Azari, *Delivering the People's Message: The Changing Politics of the Presidential Mandate* (Ithaca: Cornell University Press, 2014); Seth Masket, *Learning from Loss: The Democrats, 2016–2020* (New York: Cambridge University Press, 2020); David R. Mayhew, *Congress: The Electoral Connection* (New Haven: Yale University Press, 1974), 71; Sam Rosenfeld, *The Polarizers: Postwar Architects of Our Partisan Era* (Chicago: University of Chicago Press, 2017), 271.

22. Interview with former Republican leader, July 22, 2020.

23. Nicole Asmussen Mathew and Mathew Kunz, "Recruiting, Grooming, and Reaping the Rewards: The Case of GOPAC in the 1992 Congressional Elections," *Congress & the Presidency* 44, vol. 1 (2017): 77–101; Sean M. Theriault, *The Gingrich Senators: The Roots of Partisan Warfare in Congress* (New York: Oxford University Press, 2013), 29–30.

24. Geoffrey Kabaservice, *Rule and Ruin: The Downfall of Moderation and the Destruction of the Republican Party, from Eisenhower to the Tea Party* (New York: Oxford University Press, 2012), 375.

25. William F. Connelly Jr. and John J. Pitney Jr., *Congress' Permanent Minority?: Republicans in the U.S. House* (Lanham, MD: Rowman & Littlefield, 1994); Gary W. Cox and Mathew D. McCubbins, *Setting the Agenda: Responsible Party Government in the U.S. House of Representatives* (New York: Cambridge University Press, 2005); Kabaservice, *Rule and Ruin*, 375; see also chapter 3. Gingrich often described these

changes as cultural as much as rational or strategic. Dan Balz and Ronald Brownstein, *Storming the Gates: Protest Politics and the Republican Revival* (Boston: Little, Brown, 1996), 145.

26. Juliet Eilperin, *Fight Club Politics: How Partisanship Is Poisoning the U.S. House of Representatives* (Lanham, MD: Rowman & Littlefield, 2007), 63–66, 68–69 74–75; Green, *Underdog Politics*, 63–64; Donald R. Wolfensberger, *Changing Cultures in Congress: From Fair Play to Power Play* (New York: Columbia University Press, 2018), 26–27.

27. John Cannan, "A Legislative History of the Affordable Care Act: How Legislative Procedure Shapes Legislative History," *Law Library Journal* 105, no. 2 (2013): 131–173. For more on how Gingrich influenced subsequent party leaders, see Douglas B. Harris, "The Rise of the Public Speakership," *Political Science Quarterly* 113, no. 2 (1998): 193–212; Ronald M. Peters Jr. and Cindy Simon Rosenthal, *Nancy Pelosi and the New American Politics* (New York: Oxford University Press, 2010), 60.

28. COS Wednesday Morning Meeting Minutes, May 6, 1987, Box 9B COS Chair 1987–88, Folder: RSW—Chair of COS 1987–88 (2), RW.

29. Matthew N. Green and Briana Bee, "Keeping the Team Together: Examining Party Discipline and Dissent in the U.S. Congress," in *Party and Procedure in the United States Congress*, ed. Jacob R. Straus and Matthew Glassman, 2nd ed. (Lanham, MD: Rowman & Littlefield, 2016), 53; Lee, *Beyond Ideology*; James M. Curry and Frances E. Lee, *The Limits of Party: Congress and Lawmaking in a Polarized Era* (Chicago: University of Chicago Press, 2020).

30. Frances E. Lee, *Insecure Majorities: Congress and the Perpetual Campaign* (Chicago: University of Chicago Press, 2016).

31. Quoted in Polsby, *How Congress Evolves*, 126.

32. Lee, *Insecure Majorities*, 35–36, 108–110.

33. Richard F. Fenno Jr., *Learning to Govern: An Institutional View of the 104th Congress* (Washington, DC: Brookings Institution Press, 1997), 17.

34. See, e.g., Balz and Brownstein, *Storming the Gates*; Lee Edwards, *The Conservative Revolution: The Movement that Remade America* (New York: Free Press, 1999); John A. Lawrence, *The Class of '74: Congress after Watergate and the Roots of Partisanship* (Baltimore: Johns Hopkins University Press, 2018), 186–187, 280–281; "From Minority to Majority: A Strategy for the Republican House Leadership," 36, January 27, 1994, Box 2629, NLG. GOP consultant Lee Atwater, who was famous for his "smashmouth" political tactics, was another important advocate for a confrontational approach to politics. Atwater was a Gingrich contemporary who also loved military history. Lawrence Freedman, *Strategy: A History* (New York: Oxford University Press, 2013), 444–448.

35. Connelly and Pitney, *Congress' Permanent Minority?*, 7–8; Lee, *Insecure Majorities*, 106–108; David W. Rohde, *Parties and Leaders in the Postreform House* (Chicago: University of Chicago Press, 1991), 128–129.

36. Eric Schickler and Andrew Rich, "Controlling the Floor: Parties as Procedural Coalitions in the House," *American Journal of Political Science* 41, no. 4 (1997): 1340–1375, 1345–1349.

37. Interview with a former Republican member of Congress, May 8, 2019.

38. See, e.g., Sean Theriault, "Moving Up or Moving Out: Career Ceilings and Congressional Retirement," *Legislative Studies Quarterly* 23, no. 3 (August 1998): 419–433, 422. However, a review of the stated reasons lawmakers left the House in the 1980s and 1990s found that fewer than 5 percent explicitly cited partisanship. Matthew N. Green, "Polarization and Procedural Partisan Discord in the U.S. House of Representatives," presented at the American Political Science Annual Meeting, Washington, DC, 2005.

39. Lawrence Freeman, *Strategy: A History* (New York: Oxford University Press, 2013), 21.

40. Mark D. Ramirez, "The Dynamics of Partisan Conflict on Congressional Approval," *American Journal of Political Science* 53, no. 3 (July 2009): 681–694; Mark D. Ramirez, "The Policy Origins of Congressional Approval," *Journal of Politics* 75, no. 1 (December 2012): 198–209.

41. Kabaservice, *Rule and Ruin*, 376; Mel Steely, *The Gentleman from Georgia: The Biography of Newt Gingrich* (Macon, GA: Mercer University Press, 2000), 186–187.

42. Alan I. Abramowitz and Steven Webster, "The Rise of Negative Partisanship and the Nationalization of U.S. Elections in the 21st Century," *Electoral Studies* 41 (2016): 12–22; David W. Brady, Robert D'Onofrio, and Morris P. Fiorina, "The Nationalization of Electoral Forces Revisited," in *Continuity and Change in House Elections* (Stanford: Stanford University Press, 2000); Morris P. Fiorina, "The (Re) Nationalization of Congressional Elections," essay series no. 7, Hoover Institution, Stanford University, 2016; Gary C. Jacobson and Jamie L. Carson, *The Politics of Congressional Elections*, 9th ed. (Lanham, MD: Rowman & Littlefield, 2016), 151. For more on the complex origins of political nationalization in the United States, see Daniel J. Hopkins, *The Increasingly United States: How and Why American Political Behavior Nationalized* (Chicago: University of Chicago Press, 2018).

43. Claire Hopson Procopio, "A Brave Newt World?: Republican Campaign Strategies in the 1994 Congressional Elections" (PhD diss., Indiana University, 1999), chap. 6.

44. Gingrich has often been blamed for polarizing the country's politics, or worse. For instance, in a review of Sam Rosenfeld's book *The Polarizers*, Norman Ornstein wrote that Gingrich "sharply moved our politics from polarization to tribalism." Norman J. Ornstein, "Divided We Stand," *Democracy Journal*, Fall 2018.

45. Jacobson and Carson, *The Politics of Congressional Elections*, 153.

46. Abramowitz and Webster, "The Rise of Negative Partisanship," 16, fig. 4; Shanto Iyengar, Gaurav Sood, and Yphtach Lelkes, "Affect, Not Ideology: A Social

Identity Perspective on Polarization," *Public Opinion Quarterly* 76, no. 3 (2012): 405–431, 412–413.

47. James E. Campbell, *Polarized: Making Sense of a Divided America* (Princeton: Princeton University Press, 2016), 152, 156–166. Steven Levitsky and Daniel Ziblatt, *How Democracies Die* (New York: Crown, 2018), 149. Some have challenged the claim that American voters have become more polarized. Nolan McCarty, *Polarization: What Everyone Needs to Know* (New York: Oxford University Press, 2019), 50–55.

48. George C. Edwards III, *On Deaf Ears: The Limits of the Bully Pulpit* (New Haven: Yale University Press, 2006); Daniel J. Hopkins, "The Exaggerated Life of Death Panels?: The Limited but Real Influence of Elite Rhetoric in the 2009–2010 Health Care Debate," *Political Behavior* 40 (2018): 681–709.

49. Earl Black and Merle Black, *The Rise of Southern Republicans* (Cambridge, MA: Belknap Press, 2003); David Lublin, *The Republican South: Democratization and Partisan Change* (Princeton: Princeton University Press, 2004); Angie Maxwell and Todd Shields, *The Long Southern Strategy: How Chasing White Voters in the South Changed American Politics* (New York: Oxford University Press, 2019); Seth C. McKee, *Republican Ascendancy in Southern U.S. House Elections* (Boulder, CO: Westview, 2010); Polsby, *How Congress Evolves*, 94.

50. Nolan McCarty, Keith T. Poole, and Howard Rosenthal, *Polarized America: The Dance of Ideology and Unequal Riches* (Cambridge, MA: MIT Press, 2006).

51. Edward G. Carmines and James A. Stimson, *Issue Evolution: Race and the Transformation of American Politics* (Princeton: Princeton University Press, 1989); Geoffrey Layman, *The Great Divide: Religious and Cultural Conflict in American Party Politics* (New York: Columbia University Press, 2001).

52. Ronald Brownstein, *The Second Civil War: How Extreme Partisanship Has Paralyzed Washington and Polarized America* (New York: Penguin, 2007); Barbara Sinclair, *Party Wars: Polarization and the Politics of National Policy Making* (Norman: University of Oklahoma Press, 2006).

53. Bryan D. Jones, Sean Theriault, and Michelle Whyman, *The Great Broadening: How the Vast Expansion of the Policymaking Agenda Transformed American Politics* (Chicago: University of Chicago Press, 2019).

54. See, e.g., Jonathan Mark Morstein, "Gingrich's Challenge: The Power of Escalation to Force Change in Institutions" (PhD diss., University of Maryland, College Park, 1998); Zachary C. Smith, "From the Well of the House: Remaking the House Republican Party, 1978–1994" (PhD diss., Boston University, 2012), 10; Steely, *The Gentleman from Georgia*, 187.

55. Jacobson and Carson, *The Politics of Congressional Elections*, 207.

56. Gary C. Jacobson, "Reversal of Fortune: The Transformation of U.S. House Elections in the 1990s," in Brady, D'Onofrio, and Fiorina, *Continuity and Change in House Elections*; Linda Killian, *The Freshmen: What Happened to the Republican Revolution?* (Boulder, CO: Westview, 1998), 6.

57. Connelly and Pitney, *Congress' Permanent Minority?*, 156; Polsby, *How Congress Evolves*, 97–100.

58. Eilperin, *Fight Club Politics*, 32; Timothy Nokken and Brian R. Sala, "Institutional Evolution and the Rise of the Tuesday-Thursday Club in the House of Representatives," in *Party, Process, and Political Change in Congress*, ed. David W. Brady and Mathew D. McCubbins (Stanford: Stanford University Press, 2002).

59. Jason M. Roberts and Steven S. Smith, "Procedural Contexts, Party Strategy, and Conditional Party Voting in the U.S. House of Representatives, 1971–2000," *American Journal of Political Science* 47, no. 2 (2003): 305–317, 315.

60. "Party Line Vote Rate Soars," *CQ Almanac 1995*, 51st ed. (Washington, DC: Congressional Quarterly Press, 1996), C-8.

61. David W. Rohde and Sean M. Theriault, "The Gingrich Senators and Party Polarization in the U.S. Senate," *Journal of Politics* 73, no. 4 (August 2011): 1011–1024; Sean M. Theriault, *The Gingrich Senators: The Roots of Partisan Warfare in Congress* (New York: Oxford University Press, 2013).

62. Jeremy F. Duff and David W. Rohde, "Rules to Live By: Agenda Control and the Partisan Use of Special Rules in the House," *Congress & The Presidency* 39, no. 1 (2012): 28–50; Richard Fleisher and Jon R. Bond, "The Shrinking Middle in the US Congress," *British Journal of Political Science* 34, no. 3 (July 2004): 429–451; McCarty, *Polarization*, 81–84; Roberts and Smith, "Procedural Contexts."

63. Andrew B. Hall, *Who Wants to Run?: How the Devaluing of Political Office Drives Polarization* (Chicago: University of Chicago Press, 2019); Adam Ramey, Jonathan D. Klingler, and Gary E. Hollibaugh Jr., *More Than a Feeling: Personality, Polarization, and the Transformation of the US Congress* (Chicago: University of Chicago Press, 2017).

64. Jeffrey M. Stonecash, Mark D. Brewer, and Mack D. Mariani, *Diverging Parties: Social Change, Realignment, and Party Polarization* (Boulder, CO: Westview, 2003).

65. Gregory Koger and Matthew J. Lebo, *Strategic Party Government: Why Winning Trumps Ideology* (Chicago: University of Chicago Press, 2017), 139–153.

66. Seth Masket, *No Middle Ground: How Informal Party Organizations Control Nominations and Polarize Legislatures* (Ann Arbor: University of Michigan Press, 2011).

67. Though we have limited our discussion to the US Congress, other examples of party entrepreneurs can be found elsewhere. Former Alabama House Speaker Mike Hubbard (R) rose to power in large part by successfully engineering his party's takeover of the state house in 2010. Another example is the British Prime Minister Benjamin Disraeli—who, probably not coincidentally, served as a major role model for Gingrich. Ronald M. Peters Jr., "Newt Gingrich versus Political Science: A Study in Cause and Effect," working paper, 11–13; "Why The GOP Is Winning The Statehouse War," *Fresh Air*, National Public Radio, January 15, 2014.

68. Lee, *Insecure Majorities*, 78–79.

69. John A. Farrell, *Tip O'Neill and the Democratic Century* (Boston: Little, Brown, 2001).

70. Robert A. Caro, *The Path to Power* (New York: Knopf, 1982), 609–652.

71. Marjorie Hunter, "G.O.P. Success Recipe Often Includes Chowder," *New York Times*, March 15, 1982, A14.

72. John Jacobs, *A Rage for Justice: The Passion and Politics of Phillip Burton* (Berkeley: University of California Press, 1995), 252–253, chap. 18.

73. Alan K. Ota, "Jim DeMint's Mission: To Strike the Big Tent," *Congressional Quarterly Weekly Report*, January 18, 2010, 163.

74. See Marian Currinder, *Money in the House: Campaign Funds and Congressional Party Politics* (Boulder, CO: Westview, 2009), 24–26; Matthew N. Green and Douglas B. Harris, *Choosing the Leader: Leadership Elections in the U.S. House of Representatives* (New Haven: Yale University Press, 2019), 201; Laurence Leamer, *Playing for Keeps in Washington* (New York: Dial, 1977), 356.

75. Matt Bai, "Newt. Again," *New York Times Magazine*, March 1, 2009. In 2018, for instance, he suggested that the party use the murder of a young woman by an undocumented worker to win votes. Nicole Goodkind, "Trump Ally Newt Gingrich: 'If Mollie Tibbetts Is a Household Name by October, Democrats Will Be in Deep Trouble,'" *Newsweek*, August 23, 2018, www.newsweek.com/mollie-tibbetts-murder-iowa-manafort-cohen-midterms-immigration-1088637.

76. Newt Gingrich, "Rogue State Department," *Foreign Policy* (June 2003); "Gingrich on Why Bailout Plan Is 'Just Wrong,'" *National Public Radio*, September 22, 2008, www.npr.org/templates/story/story.php?storyId=94900671.

77. Julia Ioffe, "The Millennial's Guide to Newt Gingrich," *Politico*, July 14, 2016; Thomas F. Schaller, *The Stronghold: How Republicans Captured Congress but Surrendered the White House* (New Haven: Yale University Press, 2015), 222–223.

78. Coppins, "The Man Who Broke Politics."

79. Ioffe, "The Millennial's Guide to Newt Gingrich"; Zelizer, *Burning Down the House*, 304–305.

80. See, for example, Peter Baker, "Trump Hails Acquittal and Lashes Out at His 'Evil' and 'Corrupt' Opponents," *New York Times*, February 6, 2020; Kevin Liptak, "Trump's 100-Day Score Card," April 24, 2017, CNN, www.cnn.com/2017/04/24/politics/donald-trump-100-day-scorecard/index.html.

81. Nick Corasaniti, Jim Rutenberg, and Kathleen Gray, "Threats and Tensions Rise as Trump and Allies Attack Elections Process," *New York Times*, November 18, 2020; Robert Costa, "Media Is a Target, Too, Gingrich Underscores," *Washington Post*, July 8, 2016; Newt Gingrich, "Why I Will Not Accept Joe Biden as President," *Washington Times*, December 21, 2020, www.washingtontimes.com/news/2020/dec/21/why-i-will-not-accept-joe-biden-as-president/; interview with former Republican House member, July 30, 2020. After Trump lost reelection, he consulted Gingrich about developing a Contract with America–like policy document

that Republicans could run on in the 2022 midterm elections. Meridith McGraw, "Trump Is Starting to Put Together His Own Contract with America. And He's Teaming Up with Newt," *Politico*, May 25, 2021.

82. See, e.g., Gerald F. Seib and Dennis Farney, "GOP Conservatives, after 8 Years in Ascendancy, Brood over Lost Opportunities, Illusory Victories," *Wall Street Journal*, August 17, 1988, 44.

83. See, e.g., John Kenneth White, *What Happened to the Republican Party?: And What It Means for American Presidential Politics* (New York: Routledge, 2016), 92–95.

BIBLIOGRAPHIC ESSAY

A great deal has been written about Newt Gingrich, and a major challenge with composing a comprehensive and objective biography of the man is how to successfully navigate that voluminous material. Three excellent books about Gingrich and his time in Congress served as invaluable guides as we began our research. The first, *The Gentleman from Georgia* by history professor and former Gingrich aide Mel Steely, offers a thorough and accessible insider's view of Gingrich's career. The second, *Storming the Gates* by journalists Dan Balz and Ronald Brownstein, covers some of Gingrich's early activities in Congress, which are seldom examined in much depth, and combines sharp journalistic attention to detail with an understanding of the larger social and political forces that helped propel Gingrich and his party to power in 1994. Finally, *Congress' Permanent Minority?* by William F. Connelly Jr. and John J. Pitney Jr. remains one of the best scholarly works about the psychology of House Republicans in the 1980s and early 1990s as they struggled with seemingly unending life in the minority.

Other overviews of Gingrich's career, personality, and strategic objectives that we found especially helpful during the early stages of writing this book include Connie Bruck's *New Yorker* essay "The Politics of Perception" (1995); Eleanor Clift and Tom Brazaitis's chapter about Gingrich in their book *War without Bloodshed* (1996); Douglas L. Koopman's book *Hostile Takeover* (1996); John J. Pitney Jr.'s conference paper "Understanding Newt Gingrich" (1996), which provides a probing examination of Gingrich's thinking; and Zachary C. Smith's excellent dissertation "From the Well of the House: Remaking the Republican Party, 1978–1994" (2012).

In addition to these accounts, we consulted over 150 books, dissertations, journal articles, and press reports about Newt Gingrich and other members of the US House of Representatives who served between the

1970s and the 1990s. We also gathered primary documents from nearly a dozen archival collections to understand some of Gingrich's behind-the-scenes entrepreneurial endeavors. Notably, these collections included the Newt Gingrich Papers at the University of West Georgia, a rich lode of material including internal office memos, strategic plans, letters from Gingrich to his colleagues, minutes of Conservative Opportunity Society (COS) meetings, and the names of lawmakers working with Gingrich and the COS on various initiatives to create a Republican majority in the House. Finally, we conducted interviews with several former members of Congress and congressional staff who shared fresh insider accounts and unique perspectives of Gingrich.

Certain sources were especially useful for individual chapters. In chapter 2, Clift and Brazaitis's *War without Bloodshed* provided informative tidbits about Gingrich's early years in Congress, particularly the first meetings of the Project Majority Task Force. We also drew from John A. Farrell's *Tip O'Neill and the Democratic Century*, one of the best books about the House of Representatives during the latter half of the twentieth century. Archival materials from the Newt Gingrich Papers were indispensable for uncovering Gingrich's activities during his first two terms in the House. Among other things, the collection contains a remarkable memo written by longtime aide Frank Gregorsky titled "The Basics of Newt Gingrich," which offers an astute analysis of Gingrich's leadership style and worldview. We are also grateful to former congressman Mickey Edwards for bringing to our attention the important role of Robert Novak and Rowland Evans in boosting Gingrich's public profile via their regular *Washington Post* columns.

On Gingrich's "Budget of Hope" initiative—one of his first uses of legislation to differentiate Republicans and Democrats—we drew from excellent reporting by the journal *Congressional Quarterly*, articles by journalist Alan Ehrenhalt, and documents from the Gingrich Papers. Those papers included never before disclosed details of Gingrich's one-man campaign to build a cross-party coalition that would replace O'Neill as Speaker with a more conservative Democrat. His largely forgotten but critical participation in the successful maneuver to rewrite the Republican Party platform in 1984 is documented by news accounts, particularly stories by Steven V. Roberts of the *New York Times*, and we also benefited from insights offered by a former GOP staffer who spoke to us anonymously.

Regarding the organization and floor tactics of the COS, we drew from archival texts, journalistic sources, the *Congressional Record*, and C-SPAN footage. Diane Granat's writings in *Congressional Quarterly* offer perhaps the most accurate and penetrating reviews of what the COS was doing, why it was doing it, and how leaders of both parties perceived the group. Among other works, Richard E. Cohen's *National Journal* article "Frustrated House Republicans Seek More Aggressive Strategy for 1984 and Beyond," published in 1984, has an incisive description of the internal dynamics of the GOP Conference in the spring of that year.

Several books provided helpful scholarly insights into Congress and Gingrich during the period covered in chapter 3, perhaps most notably *Parties and Leaders in the Postreform House* by political scientist David W. Rohde. Lois Romano's profile of Gingrich in the *Washington Post* on January 3, 1985, adeptly captures Gingrich's grandiose vision, his unbounded confidence, and the resentment he engendered among many Republicans in the House. We relied principally on news reports and archival material from several collections, especially the Robert Michel Papers, for our account of the infamous contested Indiana election in 1985 that converted more House Republicans to Gingrich's views about party strategy. *Showdown at Gucci Gulch* by Jeffrey H. Birnbaum and Alan S. Murray is an excellent account of how tax reform narrowly passed the 99th Congress.

John M. Barry's *The Ambition and the Power* is arguably the most comprehensive book about Speaker Jim Wright's resignation and the ways that Gingrich helped bring it about. We also drew upon two more recent studies that shed additional light on Gingrich's role in the fall of Wright, Julian E. Zelizer's *Burning Down the House* and J. Brooks Flippen's *Speaker Jim Wright*. The Robert Walker Papers contain valuable minutes of Conservative Opportunity Society meetings during this period that document Gingrich's intense ethics campaign against Wright and other Democrats, resistance to that campaign from within the COS, and Republican disgruntlement with both the Democratic majority and defections within the GOP that hurt the party on key floor votes.

Our account of Gingrich's crucial victory in the tight race for whip in 1989 is drawn from several sources. *Choosing the Leader* by Matthew N. Green and Douglas B. Harris includes a chapter on the race and an analysis of the final vote. We also found additional insights from an interview that Newt Gingrich gave to Bill Kristol in 2014, and from interviews we conducted with former lawmakers and an erstwhile GOP aide who served on the same committee as Gingrich's opponent, Ed Madigan.

For chapter 4, we benefited greatly from C. Lawrence Evans's *The*

Whips and Scott R. Meinke's *Leadership Organizations in the House of Representatives* and their analyses of how Gingrich restructured the House whip system. The Gingrich Papers contain useful memos explaining the revitalized whip organization and what Gingrich hoped to accomplish with it. Balz and Brownstein also offer numerous insights into Gingrich's career after he was elected whip in 1989, including his fateful clash with President George H. W. Bush on tax policy. We drew extensively from the Robert Walker Papers for details about the COS's endeavors and Gingrich's participation in them during the late 1980s. The Gingrich Papers contain some insightful material on GOPAC, but the House's ethics report on Gingrich from 1997 remains the most complete source of data on the organization's electioneering activities. The Mickey Edwards Papers were invaluable for understanding the strategic vision of Congressman Edwards, and though Edwards was one of Gingrich's most prominent skeptics, his vision was shared by many other Republicans at the time. Journalistic accounts of the House bank scandal were highly beneficial in tracing the chronology of the scandal and the role played by the Gang of Seven.

Multiple books and journalistic accounts provided the basis for our discussion of the 103rd Congress, the House Democrats' last as a majority party until 2007. Though published over two decades ago, Haynes Johnson and David S. Broder's *The System* is still the single best study of Bill Clinton's failed health care plan and Gingrich's role in bringing about that failure. Steven M. Gillon's *The Pact* has some intriguing insights into the relationship between Gingrich and Clinton and the former man's perception of the latter. The Bill Clinton Papers include some valuable memos and documents, including material on the White House's efforts to tarnish Gingrich's reputation in the run-up to the 1994 midterm elections. John R. MacArthur's *The Selling of Free Trade* and Frederick W. Mayer's *Interpreting NAFTA* have useful details on both the campaign to pass NAFTA and Gingrich's contribution to that campaign. Several chapters from Frank H. Mackaman and Sean Q Kelly's edited volume *Robert H. Michel* contain key insights into Michel's final years as minority leader.

In addition to archival material, there are several good accounts of the crafting and advertising of the Contract with America that we drew on for this chapter. We gained considerable knowledge from Daniel Stid's conference paper "Transformational Leadership in Congress?" (1996) and are grateful to the author for sharing it with us. On the events of election night, including press accounts of the historic Republican win, one of the authors drew from his own collection of newspaper articles and from his remembrances of working on Capitol Hill at the time.

In chapters 5 and 6, which are about Gingrich's speakership, many of the sources that we cite cover similar events, and several of the same sources are consulted regularly throughout both chapters. As with elsewhere in the book, we found a few book-length studies by journalists to be extremely valuable. Among these, we relied on Balz and Brownstein's *Storming the Gates*, as noted earlier, along with Linda Killian's *The Freshmen* and Elizabeth Drew's *Showdown*. We also looked at contemporary accounts of Gingrich's speakership as documented by the *Congressional Quarterly Almanac* and *Congressional Quarterly Weekly Report*, as well as by journalists at the *New York Times*, the *Washington Post*, the *Los Angeles Times*, the *New York Daily News*, and *Roll Call*, among others.

Ronald M. Peters Jr. pointed us toward "The Republican Speakership," an excellent conference paper about Gingrich that he wrote for the 1996 meeting of the American Political Science Association. Other scholars also contributed useful work that focused on this time period. Particularly helpful for chapters 5 and 6 were Steely's *The Gentleman from Georgia*; Randall Strahan's *Leading Representatives*; C. Lawrence Evans and Walter J. Oleszek's *Congress under Fire*; Nicol C. Rae's *Conservative Reformers*; Charles O. Jones's *Clinton & Congress, 1993–1996*; and Matthew N. Green's *The Speaker of the House*. We relied as well on chapters from a pair of terrific edited volumes: Herbert F. Weisberg and Samuel C. Patterson's *Great Theatre* and James A. Thurber and Roger H. Davidson's *Remaking Congress*.

Gingrich and Clinton wrote memoirs in which they offered their impressions of events that occurred during the Gingrich speakership. Observations from Gingrich's *Lessons Learned the Hard Way* and Clinton's *My Life* were incorporated into these two chapters. For a sense of what life was like for Republican legislators during the first hundred days of the 104th Congress, we relied on other firsthand accounts as well, including *Representative Mom* by former Rep. Susan Molinari (with Elinor Burkett), who served with Gingrich and then in the GOP leadership in the late 1990s. The Gingrich Papers included valuable handwritten notes of Gingrich's conversations with fellow Republicans as he tried to shore up support for his election as Speaker in 1996, and insider information on the failed coup attempt against him in 1997.

INDEX

Note: page numbers followed by *f* and *t* refer to figures and tables respectively. Those followed by n refer to notes, with note number.